Y0-BZB-343

American Stories

Volume I: To 1877

American Stories

Living American History

Jason Ripper

M.E.Sharpe
Armonk, New York
London, England

Copyright © 2008 by M.E. Sharpe, Inc.

All rights reserved. No part of this book may be reproduced in any form
without written permission from the publisher, M.E. Sharpe, Inc.,
80 Business Park Drive, Armonk, New York 10504.

Library of Congress Cataloging-in-Publication Data

Ripper, Jason, 1970–
American stories : living American history / Jason Ripper.
   v. cm.
Includes bibliographical references and index.
Contents: v. 1. To 1877 — v. 2. From 1865.
ISBN 978-0-7656-1918-1 (v. 1 : pbk. : alk. paper)
ISBN 978-0-7656-1920-4 (v. 2 : pbk. : alk. paper)
1. United States—History—Study and teaching. 2. United States—Biography.
3. Education—United States—Biographical methods. 4. United States—Biography—Study
and teaching. I. Title.

E175.8.R57 2008
973.07—dc22   2007037356

Printed in the United States of America

The paper used in this publication meets the minimum requirements of
American National Standard for Information Sciences
Permanence of Paper for Printed Library Materials,
ANSI Z 39.48-1984.

BM (p) 10   9   8   7   6   5   4   3   2

Book # _____

Property of

EOPS Lending Library

EOPS/CARE Office (707) 468-3113

Mendocino College

Contents

Preface and Acknowledgments

This book tells the history of America through the stories of its inhabitants. As you turn the pages, a noisy jumble of people will be found bartering for land, saving each other's souls, selling each other's bodies, chopping down trees, writing love letters, dreaming up revolutions, and moving, always moving. There are Pequot fighters, Powhatan diplomats, Puritan "goodwives," English adventurers, African-American slaves, British-American servants, violin-playing scientists, male preachers, female missionaries, gold miners, story tellers, historical giants, and historical shrimps. Each chapter features at least one (but usually two or three) prominent biographies, which travel the historical continuum from the persecuted Massachusetts midwife Anne Hutchinson to the philosophical Pennsylvania tinkerer Benjamin Franklin to the independent South Carolina planter Elizabeth Lucas Pinckney to the visionary Shawnee statesman Tecumseh.

The details of people's lives are connected to their surroundings and to the larger Atlantic world. So while this is the interwoven story of humans' ambitions, frailties, and triumphs, it is also the interlocked history of cultural fusion, social chaos, and political development. The English brought honey bees to North America, learned the word "raccoon" from Algonquian-speaking Native Americans, and together they created a trade economy based on mutual distrust and a desire for the finer things in life: deer skins, bear meat, iron skillets, black-powder muskets, honey, and raccoon-skin hats. Benjamin Franklin's contributions to the formulation of the U.S. Constitution may have derived, in part, from his fascination with Iroquois governance, but before he could help shape the Constitution, he went off to represent the United States in France—where he wore a fur cap, playing up the country bumpkin image French courtiers had of American frontiersman (which Franklin certainly was not). Congress formed the U.S. Navy to fight Muslim pirates from the north coast of Africa, and President Andrew Jackson—who did as much as any one white man could to steal Native people's land—raised a Native American youth, Lyncoya, as an adopted son. And during the Civil War, the best-known female spy from the Confederacy, Rose O'Neale Greenhow, took a book tour of Europe and made so much money advertising the Southern cause that she literally drowned from the weight of it while trying to get back to America. This book tells a story of America through the eyes, ears, noses, and emotions of the people who lived the days and years that make it all history.

Years ago my father and I had a conversation about artists, about whether a writer, or painter, or musician can be part of a family and write, or paint, or make music fully and without reservation. I said that surely a person could be committed to both, could create great literature or compose an epic symphony and share the duties and responsibilities at the heart of family. He did not think so. He was more right than I knew.

My wife, Diane, did not write a single word of this book, but she helped me write it all the same. While I sat hunched over my bone-white iBook day and night, she fed our children every meal they ate, cleaned up every spill, read them stories about talking worms and hungry bears, and tucked them into bed after each long day. Diane encouraged me to take on this project, and she unfailingly did everything she could to give me the space to research and write. Thank you, Diane.

My mother has more college degrees than she knows what to do with, so I tricked her into reading the entire manuscript two or three times over. She corrected my spelling, gently nudged me back into line when my sarcasm got the better of me, and cradled the phone to her ear at least once a day while I rattled on about the Constitutional Convention or about *Star Trek* as a perfect metaphor for peace. Thank you, mother, for donating one more year of your life to me.

At the base of my brain are the conversations I have had with my father since I was very young. He has always treated me like a son and a friend. We have talked about writing, about the way words fit together or do not, about the power of love—to borrow a line from one of his poems, "Love is the power to resist ruin." I did not resist as many cups of coffee as I should have, and if I had really been thinking, I would have resisted a degree in history in favor of a cushy career in law or banking. But I have always enjoyed people's stories, and that is with what I wanted to fill this book. If love is the power to resist ruin, I think that stories told lovingly may have the same effect.

So I dedicate this book to my children, Phineas and June, in the hopes that you who read this book take the better parts of the past with you into the future—a future I hope you and my children will share together in harmony.

This is starting to feel like the Academy Awards. Next I would like to thank my editor, Steve Drummond, who believed in the ideas I had and helped usher them through the many desks, hands, and meetings necessary for me, an abstract dreamer with a paperwork disability, to write a book. Nicole Cirino at M.E. Sharpe has been upbeat, full of answers, and enjoyable to work with.

Thank you, Steve and Nicole. Henrietta Toth, project editor at Sharpe, ensured the "project" would become a book. Laurie Lieb, the copyeditor, checked my spelling, facts, syntax, style, and logic; finding all of it in distress, she thankfully came to the rescue.

Three colleagues from Everett Community College donated summertime hours to the cause and reviewed a few chapters at the last minute. Thank you Dr. Tom Gaskin for your good-natured corrections of the chapter on Andrew Jackson; and thank you Sharon Stultz and Ross Angeledes for pointing out the simplicities, errors, and strengths you found in my writing.

Second to last, a caffeinated thank you to the owners, Diana and Luke, and to the barristas at Caffe Adagio in Bellingham. The lattes, turkey sandwiches, and kind smiles were a welcome part of my days and kept my head above the proverbial water.

Finally, my thanks to the people who wrote the diaries, letters, newspaper stories, and books that made up the best part of the research. I spent a whole afternoon in the library reading Sally Wister's diary. She was a sixteen-year-old Quaker girl from Philadelphia whose family escaped to their country home when the British occupied the city during 1777. Most days during her temporary exile, Sally wrote to her friend Deborah, and I sat there, face inches away from the diary, sucked back in time 250 years. The room around me disappeared, and I could hear the clatter of horse hooves as Continental officers arrived at Sally's house to request rooms and food. I saw her coyly flirting and teasing, and then running up to her room to laugh about the fun and mischief she was making. As she said to Deborah, "I have a thousand things to tell thee. I shall give thee so droll an account of my adventure that thee will smile."

Whatever Deborah's response may have been I smiled all afternoon long—especially when I read about a prank some of the officers played. Sally had purchased a life-size painted wooden model of a British soldier that, she said, made "a martial appearance." As the Wister family and the officers chatted merrily in the evening, some servants snuck outside and placed the British grenadier by the front door. Then a "Negro" servant apprised the group that someone outside wanted to have a word. The officers—all but one named Tilly in on the prank—got up from the table to see who was at the door. Tilly looked outside, saw the British soldier, and "darted like lightning out the front door, through the yard, bolted o'er the fence. Swamps, fences, thorn-hedges, and plough'd fields no way impeded his retreat. He was soon out of hearing." Sally and company roared with laughter. Tilly ran over the snow and into the forest before realizing he had been set up. When he got back, everybody laughed at him for half an hour and then went to bed.

That is history to me. I hope to have transferred to you the laughter and pain I read in the letters and journals. If this book works, you will care about the Sally Wisters, Zora Neale Hurstons, and Elvis Presleys as much as I did.

Prologue

Native Americans and Europeans Up to 1600

Tenochtitlán, in What Is Now Central Mexico: Circa 1500

In the midst of Lake Texcoco, the lake sitting in the middle of a conquered empire of 5 million subjects or more, three causeways led into the streets of Tenochtitlán. This was lord Moctezuma's royal city of nearly 300,000 people where order radiated out from the central temple pyramid. More than 200 years earlier, Moctezuma's ancestors had traveled down from the north and allied themselves with locals, serving as warriors, gradually adopting the vestigial Toltec culture, and finally becoming the masters. Moctezuma was Mexica (me-shee-ka), but he and his people were also known as the Aztecs. The male children studied poetry, learned their history (or did not), and trained for war. Early in the morning, markets filled with merchants and shoppers: traders hawked exotic feathers and precious stones in exchange for the region's currency: cacao beans (chocolate). In noblemen's houses, servants made drinks of frothy cacao, the liquid poured from such a height that it foamed in the waiting cup. Sometimes cacao was mixed with chili or honey; but however it was made, "when an ordinary amount is drunk, it gladdens one, refreshes one, consoles one, invigorates one."[1] Priests plotted the movements of sun and moon; artists carved the likenesses of gods into stone destined for new temples. Watching this swarm and march of human busyness was the supreme god Huitzilopochtli, the sun god governing the age of the Fifth Sun. This world would end just as the previous four had. The Mexicas could preside over the earthly realm until then, sating themselves and appeasing the gods' needs, which sometimes involved donations of blood. Taxes in maize and human bodies were demanded from the surrounding tribes. Conquest rarely lasts long.

xiii

Spain: 1492

Thousands of miles to the east squatted the poor Catholic monarchies of Iberia, modern-day Spain and Portugal. Seven hundred years earlier, the righteous armies of Muhammad—the Moors—had invaded from North Africa, taking most of the peninsula for Islam. Muslim cities like Córdoba offered aqueducts with flowing water, libraries with tomes in philosophy and medicine, minareted mosques whose marbled interiors stretched under paint-striped arches. The region's Christians, Muslims, and Jews settled into the uneasy habits of peace and war. War and persecution prevailed. In 1469, two Catholic monarchs—Isabella of Castille and Ferdinand of Aragon—married, and from their union sprang the last expulsions of Muslims and Jews (though both were invited to convert instead of facing either the door or the sword). Muslim Granada fell to the Catholic armies in 1492, the same year an Italian sailor, Christopher Columbus, convinced Isabella to finance his chancy voyage to Asia. Everyone in Spain coveted silver and gold. They were the coin of the realm just about everywhere and could be traded for the Asian delicacies brought by Venetian traders. Columbus's voyages yielded centuries of gold for Spain, but he had actually gone in search of spices like cinnamon, nutmeg, and pepper, promising a direct route to these Asian-grown treasures, a way of cutting out the Italian middlemen. Columbus never saw the orderly civilization of the Aztecs. But the Spaniards who followed after him with their war hounds, metal armor, and crosses saw the Aztec cities and the Mayan pyramids farther to the South. These conquistadors largely forgot about cinnamon in their rush to conquer and convert.

Fusion: 1492 to Infinity

Who settled the "Americas" first? At least 30,000 years ago travelers from other shores descended: possibly by foot, possibly by boat, probably by both. They were the ancestors of today's indigenous peoples: Mayas, Mexicas, Navajos, and Eskimos. Later, waterproof Vikings in their high-prowed long ships sailed from Greenland to modern-day Newfoundland (on the cold coasts of northeastern Canada) sometime around 1000 CE. Maybe they stayed a long time, maybe only a few years, but Europeans and Americans began having contact—if only localized and infrequent—at least 500 years before Columbus and his disgruntled sailors showed up.

Columbus's voyages established a set of nasty precedents. The native Arawaks living in the Bahamas, the islands that Columbus first reached; the Incas of Peru; the Aztecs of Mexico: all these Native Americans either stood in the way of what Europeans wanted (gold and land) or became the objects of

European design, here to be traded with, enslaved, or converted to Christianity. Kinder, dissenting voices spoke up on behalf of the "Indians," but nothing could prevent diseases like smallpox from killing whole villages. In 1519 the Spanish-born administrator, adventurer, and killer Hernán Cortés illegally sailed from Cuba to Mexico, where within two years he and a small army subdued the Aztecs, partly with help from other native peoples, but largely because disease incapacitated Aztec society. The capital of a new colony, New Spain, rose on the rubble and streets of Tenochtitlán. (In 1821, the mestizo, or mixed-ancestry, heirs of Spanish-Indian contact took the original name of the Aztecs, "Mexica," and made it their own as they declared independence from Spain as the nation of Mexico.)

Spain enriched itself in the first 100 years of colonization. The other kingdoms of Europe watched and copied. With the help of coastal African nations, the Portuguese bought, brought, and sold African slaves. Then the Dutch and English muscled their way into the slave trade. Human bondage made the new economies possible. Plantation agriculture and mining became the models. This was colonial mathematics: coffers filling, taxes flowing, slave-filled ships floating, and missionaries counting souls. The other side of the equation did not look so good. By 1519, in Hispaniola (now Haiti and the Dominican Republic), about 3,000 Arawak Indians remained alive out of an original estimated population ranging from 200,000 to 300,000, most killed by European-derived diseases.[2] Often half of the slaves on a ship died during transportation to the planting, hoeing, shackled misery awaiting the survivors. Diseases from smallpox to measles crippled most native communities and cultures, accounting for perhaps 95 percent of the deaths that occurred due to contact with Europeans. Mortality rates from disease varied from one native community to the next, with inland communities sometimes gaining the chance to recover from an initial onslaught of smallpox.[3] Along the coast, typically anywhere from all to half the population died in first and subsequent rounds of disease. This made short-term and long-term repulsion of the Europeans next to impossible. Invaders could be resisted, but never turned back completely or for good.

As each European country planted colonies, success depended on either getting help from native populations or defeating them. In the title of his Pulitzer Prize–winning book *Guns, Germs, and Steel*, the scientist-turned-historian Jared Diamond points out three of the factors that enabled Europeans to dominate and defeat native peoples over a 400-year period. Tenochtitlán had perhaps 300,000 inhabitants at the same time London, England, had 200,000, and Tenochtitlán was cleaner, it had more potable water, and its citizens had better access to tasty food than their London counterparts. In measurable ways, the Aztecs had a more sophisticated, healthful civilization than anything to be found in Europe at the time. The Aztecs were successful fighters whose belief in the divine matched that of the Catholics, giving them equal access to the kind of holy gusto that makes armies believe a god is on their side. But Aztec arrows and immune systems proved unable to defend against Spanish steel swords or viral pathogens. Guns, germs, and steel made for European victories in battle, but so did the preexisting animosities between native peoples. Cortés's allies against the Aztecs were the Tlaxcalan people who had been at war for a century with Moctezuma and his predecessors.

From the southern tip of South America up to the far reaches of North America, more than 2,000 languages were spoken. The Aztecs spoke Nahuatl; the Onondaga of the Iroquois spoke a dialect of Iroquoian. Their languages would have been mutually unintelligible. A Spaniard would have had a better chance of understanding a Frenchman; both tongues descended from Latin. Speaking similar languages, however, was no guarantee of friendship or cooperation. These were intricate continents of peoples, languages, and cultures, and Europeans only complicated the picture. European use of Columbus's term "Indios" (i.e., "Indian") obscured the very real and vast differences between one native society to the next. Elaborately dressed Aztec priests and nobles demanded tribute from the regional farmers, setting up distinctions in wealth and leisure. Women were subservient, certainly in politics where they had no official capacity.

Far to the north, sometime before French or English explorers first encountered them, five upstate New York nations banded together to form the Iroquois Confederacy. Spread out over hundreds of miles of forests, rolling hills, and lake country, the Iroquois dominated trade and territory, often in competition with peoples like the Hurons to the north. Men hunted deer and trapped beaver while women raised the corn-bean-squash trinity. Iroquois women elected the men who served in the central governing council, and women could prevent war by refusing to supply food needed for a campaign. In centuries to come, Iroquois and Hurons sided with different European powers that were also in deadly competition. Native Americans gained and lost in their new associations with European immigrants: guns and allies helped overcome ancient rivals, but colonists and their semidomesticated pigs stepped into lands once reserved for hunting and farming. Ultimately, native societies adapted, often by grouping together in new political alliances and confederacies that better resembled the size and strength of the newcomers.

Competition between societies became the overarching force in the Americas. European countries and their satellite colonies battled incessantly for land. French Huguenots (Protestants) settled a prayerful little group on the Atlantic coast of Florida in the 1560s, only to be battered by stormy seas and executed by the Spanish. The Spanish presence in Florida was never much, but Spain kept enough soldiers there to dissuade the French and English from easily moving in. Spanish administrators did not so much care about Florida as they cared to keep foreign colonists from tromping into New Spain itself. Heavy-timbered Spanish galleons, hulls loaded with gold and silver, bobbed under their square sails—big white targets for English pirates like Francis Drake, who was commissioned by Queen Elizabeth to kindly relieve the Spanish of their excess fortune. England had to wait her turn to jump into the New World. Spain was the master of the seas until 1588, when England's underdog fleet blasted the Spanish Armada into retreat, further opening the Bahamas and North America to the British. And that is where this history of the United States begins: with Catholic Spain reduced and mostly Protestant England encouraged by the prospect of so much land and so much wealth waiting to be taken.

Notes

1. Bernardino de Sahagún, *The Florentine Codex: General History of the Things of New Spain*, trans. Arthur J.O. Anderson and Charles Dibble, 12 vols. (Salt Lake City: University of Utah Press, 1970), 11: 6.

2. Massimo Livi-Bacci, *A Concise History of World Population* (Molden, MA: Blackwell, 2001), 43.

3. A fascinating examination of Native American social and cultural change due to early contact with Europeans can be found in Alan Gallay, *The Indian Slave Trade: The Rise of the English Empire in the American South, 1670–1717* (New Haven, CT: Yale University Press, 2002).

American Stories

1

Colonial New England

Puritans pray at Thanksgiving dinner. *(Kean Collection/Getty Images)*

"The Country Is Not So As We Did Expect It."

By 1630, small English settlements dotted the coastline, close to Native American villages of Narragansetts, Massachusetts, and Wampanoags. Bouts of disease (probably smallpox brought by fishermen) had recently devastated the region's native population, leaving about 7,000 survivors where there had been 30,000. Then 102 sea-weary English had splashed ashore on Cape Cod in 1620. They soon relocated to a nearby, better-sheltered harbor, named Plymouth. Their Christian outpost was hundreds of miles north of the one other permanent English community in America: tobacco-growing Jamestown (built in 1607 for profit rather than salvation). The farther the better, decided the people of Plymouth. They were devoted to creating godly lives, which meant a full separation from the existing Church of England, headed by the popish King James I and tainted as it was with lingering reminders of Catholicism. This extremism had earned the Plymouth colonists the logical name "Separatists," although they are better known today as the Pilgrims.

These Separatist women and men were strict Calvinists (in their own way), adherents to the theories of John Calvin (1509–1564)—one of a few men, like Martin Luther, credited with inspiring and guiding the Protestant Reformation. From his seat in Geneva, Switzerland, black-capped Calvin taught the doctrine of predestination, the idea that God elects people for either salvation or damnation. Calvinists did not expect to earn a path into Heaven by doing good deeds, by following the liturgy, or by praying hard enough and right enough according to the Catholic practice. Instead, they devoted themselves to hard work, family, church, and scripture, hoping to find evidence in their success of divine election to heaven and salvation. Calvinism was revolutionary, a threat to the pope, as it was meant to be. For Protestants, the pope's power was not legitimate; some even considered him the Antichrist. No longer would half-educated village priests hold the keys to heaven. Protestants strove to know God through scripture and prayer, a more direct route than Catholicism offered. The English version of the Protestant Reformation went in a new direction in 1534, when stout King Henry VIII severed ties with the Vatican—so that he could sever ties to his Catholic wife—and created the Church of England (the Anglican Church). Under Henry VIII and his successors, the Anglican Church kept up old Roman Catholic liturgies, including penance, kneeling during administration of the Eucharist, and other traditions that Separatists (and other nonconformists) found contrary to the Bible. This was serious business because eternal human souls hung in the balance. The English Separatists had first emigrated to Holland. Fearing, however, that their children were becoming too Dutch, they decided to settle in the Americas, where they could make the world right.

4

The first seasons in America had been brutal, unyielding, and deadly. The winters were colder and the summers hotter than English folk had known, and farming prospects were mixed. There were good fields, but these were worked by Indians who regularly burned wide swaths of forest to make way for crops and to attract deer to the sweet grasses that sprang from the ashes. For the most part, the Indians helped, teaching colonists how to grow corn by using fish as fertilizer. Colonists had stowed some building supplies and personal effects on ships like the *Mayflower*, but at first the Pilgrims slept in caves and under makeshift branch-and-bark huts before they started building their houses. While the dream was to create a perfected England in a "new" land, the Pilgrims had to satisfy themselves with adapting to circumstances. The environment changed them as much as they managed to change it.

Rather than fashioning perfect Calvinist communities where only full church members could vote, where women stayed passive in public, and where religious heretics were chased away or killed, the Separatists, and their immediate followers, the Puritans, unintentionally made life so intolerably oppressive that religious freedom and outspoken women sprang up in their midst.

Roger Williams, the Narragansetts, and the Pequots

The Separatists of 1620 were followed by slow waves of migration until ten years later, when eleven ships arrived—bearing cattle, pigs, bricks, nails, beer, and nearly 1,000 cramped colonists under the governorship of long-faced John Winthrop, a born bureaucrat. Winthrop's fellow Puritans of 1630—named for their desire to "purify" yet remain in the Anglican Church—did not sail over choppy waters for two months in order to establish religious freedom. In their efforts to steer away from hellfire, Puritans had become justifiably known as serious, prone to sitting through four-hour sermons on Sundays *and* Thursdays. In their new colony of Massachusetts Bay, the Puritans were human in their days and nights: laughing, drinking alcohol (moderately), working, kissing, and fighting. But they did not joke about God or their worship of him. Rigid faith and piety explained their presence in America. Here the Puritan male leaders intended to conform to biblical law as they interpreted it, and no dissenting opinions or approaches would be tolerated. This inflexibility had earned them prison sentences and dismissals from ministries back in England. This commitment to a set of ideals also inspired freethinking, at least in a few.

In 1631, an odd, charismatic minister named Roger Williams joined the struggling colonists in Massachusetts. Williams was typically devout, but oddly open-minded. He settled as a pastor in Salem, north of Boston. The parishioners liked him well, but his deep-felt emotions on two subjects got him into trouble with the authorities in Boston. He believed that all Indian lands had been taken unjustly—that English-style colonization amounted to thievery. And he thought the local church ought not involve itself in politics or law. It seemed to Roger Williams that a person should be able to choose her or his own set of beliefs, even if that involved believing in no god at all. Williams advocated the separation of church and state right in the middle of a state that was, in essence, one giant church. In 1635, the central power in the colony, the General Court, exiled Williams. He received word that soldiers were on the way to arrest him and send him back to England. So in winter snow, forced to leave his two children and wife behind temporarily, he traipsed through the countryside for fourteen weeks, finally stopping about forty miles south of Boston on some land that the Narragansett people sold to him. He named this new settlement Providence Plantations. During his four years in America, Williams had learned local languages and befriended Narragansetts and Wampanoags. The type of friendship that he shared with Indians in the region was becoming more rare for white people as the seasons went by. Strife and discord escalated each year within communities and between communities.

Colonists and Indians needed each other, though at first the colonists were much more in need: running out of food; stricken by disease; shivering without good shelter; unable to fend off attacks from pirates, other groups of colonists, or Indians. Quickly, however, Native Americans grew to appreciate and depend upon European trade goods, especially guns, ammunition, and powder. Native peoples could acquire things like this only through trade, and because different tribes competed with and warred against each other, it became imperative to develop good and secure relationships with at least one group of colonists. Once a tribe or village was sufficiently weakened by disease and reliant on trade goods, colonists could begin to advance their own agendas if they wanted to, though not always with the desired results. As colonists pushed farther into the interior, they tripped over and became enmeshed in intertribal associations of conflict, peace, and uncertainty. Native American influenced colonist, and colonist influenced Native American.

The neighboring colonies of Plymouth and Massachusetts Bay were built in the midst of preexisting patterns of trade, war, and marriage. At the same time, other European nations were competing for trade and settlement in the region. The French headed north and started Quebec in 1608. The Dutch claimed New Amsterdam—modern-day New York—in 1609 and settled Manhattan island in 1625. Most were Christian of one stripe or another, so they had their sights fixed on eternity, but they intended to enjoy the good life while they were here. Southwest of Massachusetts flowed the Connecticut River, stocked with enough beaver and trees to make a poor man's heart skip a beat. Beaver pelts were all the rage in Europe and demanded a good price.

Lumber was the first major colonial export to Britain. And there was land aplenty for new settlements. The Dutch wanted in; the English wanted in. The Pequots, Niantics, and other Native American tribes already lived there. What would happen?

The Narragansetts lived to the east of the Connecticut River in present-day Rhode Island, where Roger Williams began Providence Plantations. The Pequots and Narragansetts were enemies, and both tribes hoped to use the English to their advantage. In the end, however, the English exploited the Narragansetts and the Pequots. Dutch colonists from Manhattan, Pilgrims from Plymouth, and Puritans from Massachusetts Bay all converged on the Connecticut country, erecting small forts and trading posts, sometimes living with a town of Pequots for a while. The Dutch were neither as numerous nor as pushy as the English in their attempts to take the area, and a large Pequot town welcomed some Dutch traders during the winter of 1633–1634. The townspeople suffered greatly for their openness. As William Bradford, governor at Plymouth, recalled, out of 1,000 Pequots living near the Dutch traders, 950 died from smallpox. "A sorer disease," Bradford explained, "cannot befall them . . . for want of bedding and [sheets] . . . they fall into a lamentable condition, as they lie on their hard mats, [the] pox breaking and mattering [oozing], and run[n]ing one into another, their skin cleaving to their mats they lie on . . . they die like rotten sheep." The Dutch did not get the pox, but they nearly starved to death. That left the Puritans, the Pilgrims, the Narragansetts, and the remaining Pequots to fight for the Connecticut country.

In 1634, a local Englishman named John Stone was killed by some Niantic Indians, who were subordinate to the Pequots, so the Pequots got blamed. Soon after, Governor Winthrop of Massachusetts Bay and the Pequots signed a treaty that was precipitated by Stone's murder. John Stone himself was not well liked, given his aptitude for getting drunk and having affairs with other men's wives. But he was English and Christian, and the Pequots were not. Already weakened by disease and by warfare with the Narragansetts, a Pequot delegation sent by the sachem Sassacus agreed to turn over Stone's killers to the English for punishment and give up lands along the Connecticut River in return for help settling disputes with the Narragansetts. Families from Massachusetts Bay outmaneuvered those from Plymouth and soon built towns in the Connecticut Valley. The Dutch had lost; Plymouth Pilgrims had lost; but now the Puritans and the Pequots would be living very close to each other. John Stone's killers were never turned over, and before long a new grievance settled into Puritan hearts.

In 1636, another colonist was killed—John Oldham, an Indian trader who had relocated to the Connecticut coast. Fear and rumors of further Pequot attacks circulated through Puritan colonies and towns. A small force of Puritans attempted to capture Oldham's killers, but failed to catch them. Instead, the Puritans burned Indian villages to the ground and destroyed crops, a tactic that would starve children as well as adults. The Pequots tried to persuade the Narragansetts and the neighboring Mohegans to join them in a war against the English. Instead, Roger Williams intervened, convincing the Narragansetts to remain neutral (and some fought alongside the Puritans). Right after Oldham's murder, Williams also tried to negotiate with the Pequots, but as he remembered it decades later, "Three days and nights my business forced me to lodge and mix with the bloody Pequot ambassadors, whose hands and arms reeked with the blood of my countrymen, murdered and massacred by them on Connecticut River, and from whom I could not but nightly look for their bloody knives at my own throat also." Roger Williams stridently opposed Puritan land-settlement policies and treatment of native peoples, yet he took sides with the English, thinking in terms of his "countrymen" and helping his English-speaking brethren who had already exiled him. A man's allegiance to his people and place of origin could be strong. The Mohegans, on the other hand (formerly part of the Pequot tribe), rather than helping their former Pequot colleagues, joined a combined Plymouth-Massachusetts-Connecticut army and attacked the Pequots in May 1637. The commonly used term "Indian" glossed over the vast differences between indigenous folk. Pequots and Narragansetts had no more love for each other at the time than did the English and French.

Fighting raged through July. The results were gory and decisive. At Fort Mystic, an enclosed Pequot settlement, colonists burned about 750 residents—children, women, and men—to death. Many who escaped were killed by Narragansetts waiting outside the circle of English fighters. At another battle in a swamp, the Pequots suffered equally disturbing losses. Colonists sold Pequot prisoners into slavery to either the islands of the West Indies or to other Indian tribes. From the east, Mohawks sent the skull of the sachem Sassacus as a present to the English colonists. Surviving Pequots were accepted into neighboring tribes. But as a distinct people—a unique society and culture—the Pequots were nearly erased. This has been referred to, debatably, as North America's first recorded genocide (though the word "genocide" was not coined until the 1940s).

The Pequot War offers an opportunity to reflect on the issue of Native American death at the tribal level. Some 150 years before the Pequot War, the Arawak people of Hispaniola, whom Columbus first encountered, all died within two generations, but the overwhelming majority died from disease rather than from warfare, as was the case throughout the Americas. Estimates of the total Native American population in North America circa 1500 CE vary wildly, and there is obviously no real way to derive an accurate figure. Were there 2 million or maybe 10 million North American Indians? According to census figures, by the end of the 1800s, there were 250,000 Native Americans—a possible population decline of 1,000 percent if the original high-end estimate of 10 million is accurate. How often, though, did European colonists set out intentionally to eradicate a whole population through murder, or prevent future births, or move children to live with a different people to stop a society from reproducing (three of the definitions of genocide)? The Pequot War can be a test case.

Writing in *Commentary* magazine in 2004, author Guenter Lewy said, "A number of recent historians have charged the Puritans with genocide: that is, with having carried out a premeditated plan to exterminate the Pequots. The evidence [argues against] this. The use of fire as a weapon of war was not unusual for either Europeans or Indians, and every contemporary account stresses that the burning of the fort [Mystic] was an act of self-protection, not part of a pre-planned massacre. In later stages of the Pequot war, moreover, the colonists spared women, children, and the elderly, further contradicting the idea of genocidal intention."[1] Lewy argues that the atrocities committed first by the Pequots precipitated the massacre at Fort Mystic. He says, "Fort Saybrook on the Connecticut River was besieged, and [Puritan] members of the garrison who ventured outside were ambushed and killed. One captured trader, tied to a stake in sight of the fort, was tortured for three days, expiring after his captors flayed his skin with the help of hot timbers and cut off his fingers and toes. Another prisoner was roasted alive." In other words, according to Lewy, war is horrifying, and the atrocities committed by one aggressor may cause like-minded retaliation and in fact justify that retaliation.

In direct opposition to Lewy, historians Laurence Hauptman and James Wherry say, "What befell the Pequots in 1637 and afterward clearly fits the most widely accepted definition of genocide, one set by the United Nations Convention on Genocide in 1948."[2] By way of contemporary evidence, Hauptman and Wherry quote a Puritan commentator who wrote in 1643, "the name of the Pequots . . . is blotted out from under heaven, there being not one that is, or (at least) dare call himself a Pequot." A man, Captain Underhill, who participated in the massacre at Fort Mystic, had this to say: "Many [Pequots] were burnt in the fort, both men, women, and children. [Other Pequots were] forced out, and came in troops to the [Narragansett] Indians, twenty and thirty at a time, which our soldiers received and entertained with the point of the sword. . . . We had sufficient light from the word of God for our proceedings."[3]

The near eradication of the Pequots happened during the spring and summer of 1637 as the English colonists shot, burned, dispersed, and sold into slavery every Pequot man, woman, and child they could find. These Pilgrims and Puritans demonstrated a willingness to do anything necessary to get what they wanted, in this case a feeling of safety and better access to land and beaver pelts throughout the green Connecticut River Valley. A handful of colonists disapproved of the war against the Pequots. One of these people was Anne Hutchinson, who in 1636 was about to have her own encounter with the power and authority of Massachusetts Bay Colony.

Anne Hutchinson and the Tradition of Dissent

Two questions: First, how did it happen that Anne Hutchinson, a forty-six-year-old mother of fifteen children, was excommunicated from her church, banished from her town, and set on the road to anywhere that would have her? Second, what were the seeds of religious freedom in America, and did Anne Hutchinson help to plant them?

November 1637 was cold, especially for Anne Hutchinson, who trudged five miles from Boston to the windowless, wood-frame courthouse in Cambridge, thinking that she might be pregnant (and she was)—with her sixteenth child. She, her husband William, and eleven of their children had sailed to America three years earlier, in 1634, because they had found the Anglican Church too Catholic, too focused on what Puritans called the "covenant of works" (things like penance), rather than the "covenant of grace" (interacting with God's words and waiting for the Holy Spirit to enter one's body). The leaders of the Anglican Church—King Charles I and the Archbishop of Canterbury, William Laud—had found Anne Hutchinson and people like her too radical, too dangerous to the religious, social, and political order in England. Anglican authorities had imprisoned Hutchinson's own father, Francis Marbury, three times for speaking out against Anglican teachings. While still in England, Anne and William had ridden two to a horse, twenty-four miles each way, to hear the spellbinding preacher John Cotton sermonize for hours at a time. Cotton was university trained, a captivating speaker, and a brilliant mind. Even his Anglican adversaries gave him credit for eloquence, sincerity of belief, and an uncanny knack for settling disputes in everyone's favor. Anne Hutchinson and John Cotton developed a mentor-acolyte relationship, and under his guidance she led weekly prayer meetings with other women at her home, examining scripture and reflecting on Cotton's moving speeches.

However, John Cotton attracted enough negative attention that even his persuasive charms could not keep him safe. Cotton felt that he knew whom God had elected for salvation, and these "Saints" became the focus of his sermons. The parishioners not considered "elect" in Cotton's eyes complained to church authorities. Although Cotton submitted and managed to keep his job, this first brush with trouble led to more. Cotton and the Hutchinsons soon felt enough

Anglican heat to spirit themselves 3,000 miles away in order to preach, pray, and live the way they thought right. For Puritans, running their own society in America was much different from banding together in England against the Anglican authorities, a common antagonist. Puritans like Francis Marbury, Governor John Winthrop, and John Cotton had stood on common ground in England while surrounded by crowds of Anglicans. But it turned out to be quite another thing to maintain such strict agreement about how to lead *the* proper godly life now that they were on their own. Interpretation of scripture naturally began to differ from one person to the next. In Massachusetts Bay Colony, religion and government were nearly one and the same; the very problem that had already caused tension with Roger Williams and that now dragged Anne Hutchinson into court on a cold November morning.

The courtroom in Cambridge was packed, mostly with people unfavorable to Hutchinson's cause. Governor Winthrop had convened this trial, and it was already his opinion that Hutchinson was dangerous to the well being of Massachusetts Bay, his primary concern and, perhaps, obsession. Obsessed or not, Winthrop was single-minded about protecting the colony, which he had referred to as a "City Upon a Hill," the virtuous beacon of godly living that Puritans would model for the rest of humanity. In his stiff, ruffled collar, Winthrop sat with a team of other ministers and called Hutchinson to stand (and not sit) before the judges. "Mrs. Hutchinson," he began, "you are called here as one of those that have troubled the peace of the commonwealth and the churches." As if troubling the peace were not bad enough, Winthrop scolded this matron and midwife for having "maintained a meeting and an assembly in your house that hath been condemned by the general assembly as a thing not tolerable nor comely in the sight of God nor fitting for your sex." Here it was: a woman had dared to step where only men were meant to tread, thus countering majority opinion in seventeenth-century English societies.

Societies have fairly clear expectations of male and female behavior, which are called gender roles. These cultural beliefs about how women and men should act and think can be felt so strongly that taboos develop to keep people within their "proper" spheres. Generally speaking, early colonial Englishwomen were expected to do certain things and absolutely not do other things. Giving birth; midwifing; maintaining hearth and home; gardening small vegetable plots for domestic use; weaving, sewing, and knitting; directing the servants; attending church and market; owning property; studying scripture; discussing scripture *at home* with family or other women: these activities were demanded or allowable. Custom expressly forbade disagreeing with a man in public uninvited, teaching the Bible to men, and criticizing a minister, ranging in order from bad to punishable. Anne Hutchinson had quarreled and bickered with a minister on the tedious sail to America, and she had been holding Bible lectures in her home since arrival in the colony (just as she had done in England after meeting John Cotton)—lectures that involved her preaching and teaching to men, along with scrutinizing whatever the ordained minister had said in church earlier that week. Hutchinson soon found herself accused of criticizing a minister. She had broken gender taboos, had acted, in Winthrop's opinion, "more bold than a man."[4] Within the four walls of home this behavior could be acceptable, but not in public.

Colonial spouses were known to love each other with tenderness and dreamy affection, but sweetness was not mandatory. As in society, so in the home: colonial households were supposed to be a mirror of the larger community, and vice versa. Cooperation was essential to survival because nearly everything a family needed had to be manufactured by husband, wife, children, and servants or slaves if they could be afforded. Colonists could purchase iron pots and skillets, carriages, nails, shoes, guns, glassware, fancy hats, and other occasional luxuries from local craftsmen and import merchants. Food, clothing, soap, candles, and some furniture were made at home. These were farm folk, mostly, or so they became out here on the English frontier (since a good many New England settlers had been city dwellers prior to emigrating). Within the Puritan family, sometimes referred to as a "little commonwealth," spouses did share responsibilities, and power also could be shared. But such equality as might be found depended on the man and woman in question. In public—both church and government—men demanded and kept all authority. This was biblical for Puritans. At home, however, men had to rely more on their wives than the surviving sermons and speeches and journal-jotted tavern talk indicate. Diaries, letters, and financial documents reveal homes where women discussed politics, helped balance meager budgets, and gave advice. As to be expected, in some families women had more power than in others. The Hutchinson home seems to have been such a place. In fact, Anne's husband accompanied her to the courthouse in Cambridge, sat silently through her two-day trial, and then accompanied her on the next phase of their life, as best we know without so much as a grumble. They were equals in an unequal world.

Anne Hutchinson listened attentively to the governor's accusations and plainly replied, "I am called here to answer before you but I hear no things laid to my charge." She had shown up, and she demanded that the judges either charge her with something specific and illegal or let her go. This was bold. Did her husband squirm, smile, or sit there impassively? We do not know, but Governor Winthrop wasted no time before claiming that Hutchinson had transgressed the "law of God and of the state." This was fine to say, but he had no proof. The governor and the woman sparred for hours, and she beat back every unfounded claim and insult thrown at her. With logic, scripture,

12

and sheer style, Hutchinson stood her ground in a mesmerized courtroom. The governor said that by leading these religious study sessions, Hutchinson was taking women away from their own homes: families were being "neglected" by their "dames," and Winthrop could "see no rule of God for this." He concluded this line of attack by saying "so what hurt comes of this you will be guilty of and we for suffering you." As "bold as a man," Hutchinson did not agree: "Sir, I do not believe that to be so." *How to respond to such a woman?* Winthrop must have wondered. He had called her here, given her a platform from which to speak her mind, and she was doing so, even though all Winthrop wanted to do was "reduce" her, put her in her place. But Hutchinson was not budging—that is, until she collapsed because of pregnancy and exhaustion.

Men rushed to her side and helped her up. Though the inquisitors offered her a break, she agreed to continue on with the trial. Accusations and defense lasted into the scattering autumn daylight. At one point, the deputy governor, Thomas Dudley, joined the attack. He got right to the point: "About three years ago we were all in peace. Mrs. Hutchinson, from that time she came hath made a disturbance, and some that came over with her in the ship did inform me what she was as soon as she was landed." The minister she had argued with aboard the ship had ratted on Hutchinson and gossiped about her. Dudley went on to say that he had immediately investigated Hutchinson's religious perspectives and found that "she held nothing different from us." However, within a year "she had vented divers of her strange opinions and had made parties in the country." Dudley was accusing Hutchinson not only of having a divergent understanding of God's laws (being opinionated), but of getting other people, "the parties in the country," to agree with her. Dudley claimed that Hutchinson was tearing the community apart. Building to a fearful crescendo, suggesting that she would knock the colony to pieces, Dudley concluded, "she hath a potent party in the country . . . she that hath depraved all the ministers and hath been the cause of what is fallen out."

In fact, there had been religious dissent within the colony, and Hutchinson had participated in the disagreements since the time of her arrival. Dudley's claims were accurate. Boston had only about 1,000 residents, and sometimes sixty of them showed up for Hutchinson's in-home sermons—nearly one-tenth the population under her sway. But had she actually done something illegal? By the end of the day, that was in question. This one housewife faced a wall of men, some with formal legal training and experience, and the day concluded with a draw. Governor Winthrop banged his gavel and said, "the time grows late, we shall therefore give you a little more time to consider of it and therefore desire that you attend the court again in the morning." Facing them on the next day would be a central issue: had she publicly accused all the ministers in the colony of being more in favor of a "covenant of works"

13

than the "covenant of grace" good Puritans were supposed to embrace? In other words, did Hutchinson claim that ministers other than John Cotton were preaching the Catholic doctrine?

Rather than walking the ten-mile trip home and back again, the Hutchinsons stayed at a nearby house. In the gathered dark, she burned candles to read transcripts of the trial. Throughout most of the next day's proceedings, her late-night studying paid off. Hutchinson requested that any minister who wanted to accuse her should take an oath before God attesting to the charges. Would they risk their souls just to get her out of the colony? No, they would not. Grown men squirmed and backpedaled, offering all sorts of reasons why swearing an oath was unnecessary. Finally, her good friend and counselor, John Cotton, took the floor. While he did not support her on every point possible, in the main he provided what should have been the last defense. "I must say," said Cotton, "that I did not find her saying that they were under a covenant of works, nor that she said they did preach a covenant of works." The only accusation that had trailed over from day one to day two of the trial was now dead to the law. Cotton professed that Hutchinson had not accused any other preachers of leaning toward Catholicism. She was safe.

Then she opened her mouth one more time, and what came out was her own exile. "If you please to give me leave I shall give you the ground of what I know to be true," Hutchinson proclaimed. Governor Winthrop almost stopped her, but thought better of it. Was she finally about to provide him the excuse he needed to get rid of her? Yes. Anne Hutchinson had not been afraid of the ocean, and she certainly would not be afraid to tell the truth. Unedited by fear, she said, "[Jesus] hath let me see which was the clear ministry and which the wrong. Since that time I confess . . . he hath left me to distinguish between the voice of my beloved and the voice of Moses, the voice of John the Baptist and the voice of antichrist, for all those voices are spoken of in scripture. Now if you do condemn me for speaking what in my conscience I know to be truth I must commit myself unto the Lord." Anne Hutchinson could hear God speaking to her.

Claiming to be a prophet was probably the most dangerous revelation she could have made. With talented argumentation, Hutchinson had emerged unscathed from a two-day trial. But for reasons the surviving documents do not answer, she said, when all seemed over, that God communicated with her directly—a position she must have known could be seen as heresy, since orthodox Puritans saw the Bible as God's final word. Governor Winthrop only had to let her speak and the case against her was won. A handful of ministers now took an oath against her, and they banished Anne Hutchinson from Massachusetts Bay Colony. For the duration of the winter she lived a couple of miles from home, under house arrest, where one of Winthrop's partisans kept careful watch over her. By April 1638, she was six months pregnant and had spent the winter being visited by the same ministers who disliked her personally and disagreed with her religious perspectives. John Cotton, her defender in court and old friend, turned against her during that winter, for at least one reason. Cotton's association with Hutchinson was not good for his reputation. Distancing himself from her had become politically and socially prudent—what had happened to her could happen to him too if he were not careful.

Anne Hutchinson had been legally exiled from the colony. Now, in April 1638, she faced the members of her church who had convened to choose whether or not to excommunicate her. Soon after she had disembarked in 1634, Boston church members had decided that Hutchinson was one of God's chosen, that she was "elect," and so they allowed her into full church covenant. Now they were meeting again, this time to decide if they should revoke her membership. Two more days of grilling and even more specific biblical interpretation led to the same kind of result as in the previous November: banishment. Anne Hutchinson was kicked out, excommunicated, from the Puritan church. In fact, she was called a "heathen" and an agent of the devil before she turned her own back on her former friends and neighbors and walked proudly out of the church, surrounded by a small group of friends. Hutchinson's trials were, in essence, the same trials that New England communities would endure for more than 100 years into the future. Societies founded with specific religious visions experienced numerous problems achieving their original goals when faced with challenges in America: diversity of opinion, warfare, disease, influxes of other faiths and denominations (like Jews and Quakers), and competition from a new value—capitalism.

Massachusetts Bay Colony initially established laws governing fair prices for goods and services and soon instituted sumptuary laws, which restricted poor people from wearing gaudy, expensive clothing. Although some Bay Colony settlers came over with more money than others (the Hutchinsons brought a purse of gold coins worth more than $1 million by today's standards), the divides between poor and wealthy were initially smaller than in Old England. Also, in America a person could gain prominence through luck and pluck, but in England there was a restricted nobility and advancement was more difficult. As each American decade passed, some citizens accumulated more cash, property, and possessions than others. This possibility of getting wealthy and hence gathering more liberty and power into one's own family became at least as tempting as following the strict social and economic rules of the Puritan community founders. By the 1700s, more and more people interpreted prosperity in the form of wealth as a sign of God's pleasure. New England's coastal towns, like Boston and Salem, embraced the far-flung Atlantic trade system. New values came bobbing in along with molasses from Barbados, slaves from Africa, and immigrants from Europe. Diversity accompanied trade.

In the same way that religious values intersected with the pursuit of money in Protestant society, religious intolerance—the very cornerstone of early New England—did not last in the same repressive form that Anne Hutchinson and Roger Williams faced in 1630s Massachusetts. Williams was chased out first, and one year later the Hutchinsons and some of their friends were exiled. They moved near to Providence Plantations, and during the next few decades a group of like-minded towns developed into what is now known as Rhode Island. These early towns set around Narragansett Bay included a radical element in their first sets of laws: religious freedom. This principle was inspired both by Roger Williams himself and by the persecution he and Anne Hutchinson faced in and around Boston. They instituted this right to freely worship by separating church from state so that one denomination or religion could not rule against others through the body of the government. Roger Williams stopped attending church entirely, unable to find even one that met his strict needs for Bible-guided accuracy. (When Connecticut incorporated as a colony in 1639, its leaders created a charter that allowed freemen who were not church members to vote, which was not yet the case in Massachusetts.) Experience had led to innovation. Experience led to the separation of church and state. This was one culmination in the Judeo-Christian tradition: a dawning recognition that reason and faith could coexist at a slight remove so that both might be promoted and protected.

Anne Hutchinson and her husband, William, were separated for six months in 1637–1638 so that he could get to Aquidneck Island ahead of her to begin building their new home. He lived in a simple hut at first, along with the other refugees, but soon the English pastoral scene was re-created: pasture for cattle, fields for corn, fences, solid wood houses with thatch and mud roofs. They reunited seven months into Anne's pregnancy, which quickened about six weeks early, and the baby was stillborn. Only three years later, in 1641, William died, aged fifty-five. It had been a relatively long life, for that era, and the last years had been trying. Anne Hutchinson interpreted her husband's death as a sign to uproot. The Dutch in New Amsterdam gave her permission to settle with them. In 1642 she arrived on Long Island with members of her now much-extended family. She was a grandmother. Then the autumn of her life bled into the autumn of 1643 when a group of Siwanoy warriors swept into her yard and killed her and her family.

And the World Kept On Changing

Anne Hutchinson died just as the New England colonial world that she and her family helped start began transforming into a series of fairly distinct colonies with their own rules and cultures. Virginia used African- and Native American slaves and white indentured servants—people who sold themselves for five to seven years in order to get passage to America. Virginia's economy flourished around the growth and sale of tobacco during the seventeenth century, and houses and plantations tended to be spread far apart, doing little to encourage church attendance or city life. Farther to the south, the Carolinas also relied heavily on slave labor, many of the slaves imported from British Caribbean islands (like Barbados) rather than straight from Africa. South Carolina's culture thus became a distorted mirror of the slave plantations of Barbados, where human life was cheap, entertainments ranked high, and society held fast to a hierarchy—some people were born to be better than others.

The Indian populations of the Carolinas and Georgia remained robust and powerful throughout the colonial period, in comparison to the devastation in numbers through disease and warfare that weakened the Narragansetts and Pequots of New England, as well as the Lenni Lenapes (Delawares) of Pennsylvania and Maryland. In the Carolinas, powerful confederacies of Catawbas, Creeks, Chickasaws, and Cherokees controlled the trade in deer hides, Indian slaves, and beaver pelts. These affiliations of clan- and tribe-related peoples could field thousands of warriors and played the competing European colonies and empires against each other. Colonial societies and cultures developed based on a complex alchemy of factors: existing populations of Native Americans, geographical features, and the particular groups of colonists who moved into a region.

Massachusetts, Connecticut, New Hampshire, Rhode Island: these were the original New England colonies, but of course their cultures did not literally stop at the map-edge between them and, for example, New York. People and people's ideas were fluid, in motion. By the 1700s, residents from the mid-Atlantic colonies (New York, New Jersey, Pennsylvania, Maryland, Delaware) and from the South (Virginia, North Carolina, South Carolina, Georgia) stereotyped New Englanders as religiously crazed Yankees. But it was not long before old-guard Puritans, the first generation, had to give way to their children, grandchildren, and immigrants—many of whom were not undergoing conversions, thus remaining outside of church membership. In 1662, the Half-way Covenant was adopted by many Congregational churches, allowing grandchildren of full church members to join the church on a limited basis (they could be baptized, but could not receive Communion until they testified to a believable conversion experience). Old ways were loosening.

Acceptance of altered piety did not happen immediately, and separation of church and state in a small corner of New England (i.e., Rhode Island) did not necessarily cause calmer heads to prevail. In 1692, the Town of

Salem (on the coast) and the Village of Salem (a few miles inland) started to persecute witches in their midst. Young girls flirted with magic to read their futures. Either magic is real, and the girls tapped into it, sending them into otherworldly visions and bodily tremors, or the girls only seemed to be afflicted by demons, spirits, and witches. Whatever the real nature of the world, European and colonial adults believed that devils and angels worked their wonders, while witches and warlocks flew around on brooms and met secretly to cast curses on their God-fearing neighbors.

The Bible is stocked with angels, and many Puritan divines—like the famous Cotton Mather, who was writing at the time about angelic visitations—accepted that it was humanity's lot to suffer the pull between Satan's minions and the beneficent gift of God's grace. It was up to people to choose, and some people chose the devil, if only through weakness. Only a few years before the witch trials began, Mather had recorded the following entry in his diary: "After outpourings of prayer, with the utmost fervor and fasting, there appeared an Angel, whose face shone like the noonday sun. His features were those of a man, and beardless; his head encircled by a splendid tiara; on his shoulders were wings; his garments were white and shining; his robe reached to his ankles; and about his loins was a belt not unlike the girdles of the peoples of the East."[5] For many colonial Puritans, the world around them was as stocked with angels and devils as the world they read about in their Bibles.

The Salem girls pointed fingers at community members—many of them single, middle-aged or old women—and adults believed the girls to be afflicted with evil curses. The local court put on trial and imprisoned men and women from the two Salems under suspicion of practicing witchcraft and hence holding the devil's hand. The trials admitted spectral evidence—essentially ghost stories. And one five-year-old girl, Dorcas Good, was imprisioned as an accused witch for eight months, during which her mother, Sarah, was hanged. These Salem witch trials are often called a hysteria for a variety of reasons, including the hanging of nineteen people and the crushing of one more under a stack of stones. By the summer of 1692, with dead bodies dangling on Gallows Hill, accusations were spreading outside of Salem. Even the governor's wife came under suspicion of collusion with the devil. This movement of indictments into adjacent towns and cities adds to a sense that this supposed outbreak of witchcraft was hysteria. Was everyone a witch?

The governor spoke forcefully against the proceedings after his wife was accused. The trials stopped. The remaining prisoners were set free in 1693. The Salem trials can be seen as commonplace when considered as part of a larger European-derived culture where literally thousands of people accused of witchcraft (about 80 percent of them women) had been executed. However, the Salem witch trials were actually an aberration in colonial America. They resulted in the only mass executions for witchcraft in the colonies. Colonial America had already become different from the European societies that spawned it.

Diversity was a reality, even if it was uncomfortable for many people to accept. Puritans settled in South Carolina as well as in Massachusetts. Quakers soon arrived in the colonies as well. The Christian spin-off denomination of the Society of Friends (Quakers) had begun in 1647 in England when its founder, George Fox, implored people to seek the "Inner Light" of Christ. Women and men were considered equal in Quaker meetinghouses, where people sat in long bouts of silence, punctuated by a Friend who felt moved by the Spirit to speak. Fox's methods and message soon spread to the colonies. Pennsylvania was founded in 1681 by William Penn on land he received as a gift from the king, partly to repay a debt to the Penn family, partly to get rid of the Quakers, who refused to take oaths to the state and who insisted on calling everyone "thee" and "thou," even bishops, earls, dukes, and knights who expected more honorific flourishes. Penn was a Quaker, and Pennsylvania became a haven for religious freedom, much like Rhode Island. (The Quakers dealt with local Native Americans more fairly and justly than any other colony, though relations did eventually fall apart.) But Quakers also went to New England and Virginia, where they encountered persecution. At first they were jailed, beaten, and run out of many towns. In 1660, authorities in Boston hanged Mary Dyer, a Quaker, for having been too rebellious, which was a roundabout way of saying that her Quaker ways would no long be tolerated. She had already been arrested numerous times for Quakerism, for "bearing witness to her faith." Another Christian group, Roman Catholics, congregated mostly in Maryland, initially a proprietary colony like Pennsylvania—a colony owned and run by a single person, family, or company. In other words, as much as the colonies developed individual characteristics, there was also much intermingling of peoples and traditions.

The colonies of North America were a mixed-up place: Muslims from Africa; Protestants, Catholics, and Jews from Europe; new languages (for example, the African-American dialect of Gullah, incorporating West African, Caribbean, and English); slavery; freedom. As the boat sailed or the horse trotted southward, the folkways of New England—with its rocky soils and cold winters—gave way slowly to the swamps and humidity of the coastal, tidewater South. Although English became the dominant language up and down the coast, and kings were toasted, and Christ was worshipped by his followers, life was different north to south and east to west. Time, augmenting the early differences, gave each colony a culture of its own.

Notes

1. Guenter Lewy, "Were American Indians the Victims of Genocide?" *Commentary*, September 2004, 58.

2. Laurence Hauptman and James D. Wherry, *The Pequots in Southern New England: The Fall and Rise of an American Indian Nation* (Norman: University of Oklahoma Press, 1993), 76.

3. Hauptman and Wherry, *Pequots in Southern New England*, 73.

4. Eve Laplante, *American Jezebel: The Uncommon Life of Anne Hutchinson, the Woman Who Defied the Puritans* (New York: HarperOne, 2004), 3.

5. Elizabeth Reis, "The Trouble With Angels," *Common-place: The Interactive Journal of Early American Life,* vol. 1, no. 3, April 2001.

2

The Colonial South

Ætatis suæ 21. Aº. 1616.

Pocahontas *(MPI/Getty Images)*

Jamestown: Pocahontas and John Smith

Founding colonies was big business. England's first successful colony started as a company town: James Town, Virginia, 1607. The profit motive kept hopeful, foolish, sometimes-greedy English settlers floating to this swampy spit of land on the James River long enough that their presence became permanent. In 1606, King James I (who commissioned an English translation of the Bible, the soon-to-be-popular King James version), in his "especiall grace" and "Royall goodnesse," generously granted a charter to a group of businessmen, the London Company, to make a colony in North America right in the middle of other people's territory—namely the Powhatan confederacy. The confederacy was named after its leader, Wahunsonacock, who also was called Powhatan, after his favored village. The London Company investors wanted gold and originally had no defined plans to start a new society (not a single woman went on the initial outing). They wanted to make some money. In line with the investors' wishes, the gentlemen gold diggers, day laborers, soldiers, sailors, and general adventure seekers first sent over were instructed to be cordial with any "naturals" who lived in the area, to live on uncontested land, and to comport themselves like civilized men. The stockholders assumed the local Indians would be happy to trade once they realized the English were there for that one purpose alone.

In the first ten years of Jamestown history almost everyone died horribly. Between starving to death, having the skin scraped off their living bones by Powhatan warriors using oyster shells, getting impaled on rock-tipped arrows, and in return burning villages, shooting drowning children in the head with muskets, and living in mortal fear, the residents of Jamestown were not doing well. Also, nobody could find any gold, though not for lack of looking. During the "starving time" winter of 1609–1610, about 100 people of 500 survived—if killing and eating your own wife, dining on rats, and digging up graves for brunch can be called "surviving." (The man who killed his wife was executed for the crime, though contemporaries had a twisted sense of humor about the incident. According to John Smith's indelicate summation, "now whether shee was better roasted, boyled or carbonado'd, I know not."[1]) There seemed reason to believe this venture would fail as dismally as earlier attempts in the area had—notoriously the short-lived 1585 and 1587 catastrophes on Roanoke Island, off the coast of present-day North Carolina. Some Roanoke colonists had starved; some had been killed; others had run off into the woods. A few had returned to England with Sir Francis Drake, recent slave trader, pirate, and circumnavigator of the world. Leaving the clue "Croatoan" scratched into a tree (likely a reference to the local Croatoan Indians), the Roanoke settlers met mysterious, deadly, or disappointing ends. Jamestown was turning out even worse.

Heroes make tragedy bearable. Jamestown provided two heroes-of-a-sort: the self-promoting Captain John Smith and Pocahontas. Smith was born a commoner in England's ranked society. In other words, leadership was unlikely. Pocahontas was a daughter of the *weroance* (i.e., emperor), Powhatan, who ruled a confederacy of many tribes spread across most of modern-day eastern Virginia. Pocahontas had dozens of siblings, yet Powhatan favored her, so she could have expected a good life. John Smith and Pocahontas met in 1607 when Pocahontas was about ten and Smith was about twenty-seven. He had already fought in European wars and escaped enslavement in Turkey by beating his owner to death, taking the man's clothes, and galloping home across most of Europe. Recently, Smith had sailed 3,000 miles to Virginia as the only lowborn member of the Jamestown governing council, a status that the other snobbish council members did not appreciate. Who was this man of no title or rank, other than the common tag of Captain, to be voicing an equal opinion in matters of state and consequence? Smith liked to think he was the only capable man around.

For three years, five-foot-four John Smith pushed the colonists to grow food, trade shrewdly for food, drill for combat, and act bold and brave enough to scare the local Indians into giving away more than they needed to in land and corn. There were literally thousands of warriors in the area beholden to the emperor Powhatan, and they easily could have overwhelmed the hundred-odd original colonists. Smith's natural curiosity and bravery led him to explore, which in turn led him into Powhatan's longhouse, bound as a captive. Powhatan measured Smith's importance and found it lacking. According to one of Smith's tellings, just as Powhatan's men were about to smash his brains with rocks, Pocahontas threw herself on top of him, daring the warriors to hit her first. Whether this act was staged for Smith's benefit or was really the intervention of a girl as brave and crazy as Smith, the results were the same. A fast friendship grew between John Smith and Pocahontas, and between Smith and Powhatan an uneasy truce developed, often maintained by bluster and threats. Smith returned to Jamestown with a reduced likelihood that the Powhatan fighters would attack and with improved prospects for his own future—early proof in the English colonies that a man could rise through his talents and skill.

Although Pocahontas was young, she had seen much. At Powhatan's capital, Werowocomoco, tribute in fur, copper, and corn was stored away for regular use and festivities. Messengers, diplomats, and visitors from neighboring peoples stopped by. In every sense, this was a busy place, even for Pocahontas. Although she was the ruler's daughter, Pocahontas did her part: planting in the fields, weaving, learning songs and dances, helping with the autumn harvest. Pocahontas was known to be mischievous, and well liked for it, perhaps the prerogative of nobility. She conferred special privileges on John Smith. By singling him out, by visiting him at Jamestown, by befriending him, Pocahontas coated him with at least the veneer of status. She could not, however, play any central part in her father's plans, and Powhatan was less than cheerful about the long-term prospects of an English presence in the area.

The London Company insisted that the colonists behave decently. Powhatan was under no such guidelines, and his confederacy of perhaps 20,000 people had been achieved as much through warfare as through the polite forms of diplomacy. Native American arrows were accurate well beyond the range of English muskets, and from the age of six, Powhatan boys learned to shoot. They could soon pick birds out of the sky. John Smith understood Powhatan's advantages and figured that only displays of strength would convince Powhatan and the neighborhood tribes to leave the English alone. During the first half of 1608, Smith and some men were out exploring when they were set upon by a group of Nansemond Indians in canoes. Smith scared off the Nansemonds, took their canoes, and began hacking them to pieces, an act equivalent to setting fire to an English sailing vessel and wasting all the work that went into it. The Indians asked him to stop, but Smith would yield only in return for favors and promises. With this one maneuver, Smith brought the Nansemonds under his sway and extracted a promise for future tribute in corn. Each time Smith did something like this, Powhatan learned about it, and each time Powhatan was forced to reconsider just how capable the English might be. John Smith was a realist, brutal at times, but seemingly no more brutal than any of the other people in the area, European or Native American.

Seventeenth-century punishments were physically harsh and quite public. There is no way to know for sure who introduced whom to scalping, but native and colonist alike sliced off enemies' scalps to use as trophies and as proof of victory. Sometimes victims were scalped before being killed. Some scalping victims survived. (In eighteenth-century Massachusetts, the colony paid money for the scalps of Indian children.) Powhatan fighters sometimes tied up a captive, flayed him, chopped up his body, and then burned him, all while the man was alive. At Jamestown, whipping was a basic punishment. In England, at least 200 crimes were punishable by hanging, including spilling a pail of milk if the act was done intentionally. Here is an example of the law code passed in 1612 at Jamestown: "That no man . . . curse . . . upon paine of severe punishment for the first offence so committed, and for the second, to have a bodkin [a thick, dull needle] thrust through his tongue, and if he continue the blaspheming of Gods holy name, for the third time so offending, he shall . . . receive censure of death for his offence." Lying was a major crime, too: "Hee that shall take an oath untruly, or beare false witnesse in any cause,

24

or against any man whatsoever, shall be punished with death." (One gets the feeling there was plenty of swearing and lying going on.) The Jamestown colonists brought a rack with them, a torture device dating back to Rome, on which a person was tied down so that the arms and legs could be stretched apart to the breaking point. John Smith once threatened a Powhatan prisoner with the rack, and the man quickly chose to talk instead. However, while violent punishments were considered appropriate, they were not supposed to be used without official, legal permission. Because the London Company wanted Indians to be treated gently, Smith's behavior struck some of his fellow colonists and their sponsors as unwarranted and excessive. This nasty reputation, along with his lower-class birth, would be used against Smith in months to come. Smith became governor in 1608. He informed the scraggly colonial masses that they would either work for food or starve—no more idling the time away panning for gold. Smith's bossiness, forced routines, and bartering for Indian corn with tribes like the Nansemonds kept Jamestown going through the winter.

Jamestown's survival nagged at Powhatan. Land, liberty, and life were at stake, definitely beginning with the first—land. English people claimed land through written contracts, with fences, and through "improvements" like felling trees, planting crops, and building houses. A king and his agents could give land away or sell it, at first in theory and later in practice. Native Americans in North America did not use written contracts prior to the arrival of Europeans because they had not invented writing, but native peoples did have their own versions of land ownership: they fought wars for land, planted crops, and lived in houses. While Native American territorial boundaries were not so mathematically outlined as those appearing on European maps, the land and its fruit were every bit as important to natives as to immigrants. And with every English ship that docked at Jamestown to let off another batch of colonists, Powhatan and his brother Opechancanough saw their land—and hence their liberty and lives—threatened. They also saw the colonists running chronically short on food and hence feeling weak and scared. So Powhatan fought back at exactly the same time John Smith returned to England.

In the summer of 1609, Smith received word that Sir Robert Gates was replacing him as governor. In the meantime, while Smith was in a boat attending to business, a flash gunpowder fire badly burned him. Convulsed by pain and removed from his post, Smith chose to go back to England. Other than as a historian and commentator, his departure concluded John Smith's involvement with Jamestown. Smith had nourished the colony with strict discipline and cunning—if also aggressive—relations with the region's native peoples. The next governors were less competent.

Governor Gates, Smith's intended replacement, was temporarily lost at sea, so the remaining 500 Jamestonians got stuck with a clothing-obsessed, twenty-nine-year-old nobleman named George Percy. He was not stupid, but he was not capable under the circumstances. Powhatan invited the colonists to Werowocomoco, where many of them were promptly killed and their ship almost taken. In response, Percy essentially closed Jamestown's gates and watched the apocalypse, the "starving time" that lasted through the winter of 1609–1610. When Governor Gates and his colonists arrived in April 1610 (after wintering as lucky victims of a shipwreck on Bermuda), they found the emaciated remnants of Jamestown, feces and garbage in the streets, and little to be thankful for other than an unexpected relief ship that arrived soon after them. As might be expected, bloody warfare followed this infusion of food and colonists. In retaliation for Powhatan's deceit the past winter, the English ruthlessly attacked a local tribe, the Paspaheghs. The killing continued on both sides for years.

With war afoot, Pocahontas kept away from Jamestown after John Smith's departure. Prior to 1610, she had been a welcome and curious visitor, by all evidence genuinely interested in English people and their culture. The sickening warfare of 1610, combined with the loss of her friend, John Smith, kept Pocahontas with her people. However, in March 1613, a ship's captain named Samuel Argall caught wind of Pocahontas's presence in a village he was visiting. Argall conned Pocahontas on board his ship and then held her captive. The colony's next governor, the draconian Sir Thomas Dale (author of the 1612 execute-you-for-swearing law code), upheld the kidnapping. Governor Dale demanded a prisoner swap: Pocahontas in return for all English prisoners and weapons stolen during recent hostilities. Powhatan sent back the handful of Englishmen and some broken guns, but he did not return all the implements his people had heisted. So Governor Dale refused to send Pocahontas back. The folk of Jamestown gladly took her in, converted her to Christianity, and encouraged her to feel at home.

John Rolfe had been one of the men shipwrecked on Bermuda a few years beforehand. Now safely settled at Jamestown, Rolfe spent time with Pocahontas and fell head over heels over tobacco in love with her. Apparently she liked him too, and they received permission to wed from everyone important. Powhatan consented and in his place for the nuptials sent an emissary, his brother Opechancanough (who got the opportunity to live firsthand with the English and study them). Pocahontas's marriage to John Rolfe reinstated the half-hearted goodwill that had once existed between the colonists and the Powhatans. Years of war turned into a few years of relative peace. The crucial diplomatic love affair between Pocahontas and Rolfe gave safe space for his ridiculously successful experiments in farming tobacco, that noxious weed that just about everybody loved and that local Indians already grew. If John Smith and Pocahontas saved Jamestown (and hence England's stab at empire building), John Rolfe's faith in smokable, snuffable vegetable leaves made sure that England had found gold after all—green gold. The nicotine was addictive, the profits were addictive, and now there was finally a good reason to move to Virginia.

Pocahontas's marriage was a success in many ways. She and John had a baby, Thomas. She became a devoted Christian and wore homespun dresses. She was, in essence, proof to English eyes that savages could be civilized: she even changed her name to Rebecca. In 1616, husband, wife, and baby (along with barrels of tobacco) sailed for England—on what author Tim Hashaw calls "a propaganda blitz to obscure bad news coming from the colony,"[2] namely the ongoing death rate and lack of success at making money. Many things awaited them: Shakespeare's plays; introductions to royalty; visits to London's bustling, noisy, coal-choked streets and chapels; and a brief, unexpected reunion with John Smith. He had recently returned to England after another trip to the Americas where he had had some more hair-raising adventures, including an escape from a Portuguese prison ship that sank right after he sloshed overboard in a small boat. In writing about these last escapades, Smith came up with the name "New England" for the region we now call . . . New England. Pocahontas died in 1617, just before embarking on what otherwise would have been a good sail back to Virginia. A lung disease took her, and John Rolfe left behind their young son, who was at the time also sick and unlikely to survive the voyage. The son lived into adulthood, and John Rolfe lived until 1622, long enough to keep planting tobacco and almost long enough to witness Virginia's next strategic butchery.

While it is tempting to credit the muscular, fearless John Smith with floating the colony through its first near-impossible years, Pocahontas deserves at least as much credit, if not more. However, to give them heroic credit would rest on a particular kind of perspective. Smith's and Pocahontas's twin roles in resuscitating Jamestown are also one early part of the larger history of the dispossession of Native Americans from most of their land. In other words, Pocahontas and Smith could as easily be called a traitor and a thief as a pair of heroes. The exportation of European peoples and culture was already ongoing by 1600. Neither Smith nor Pocahontas had anything to do with the roots or origins of colonization. They merely tried to act as best they could given the circumstances, which were tough by any reckoning. Jamestown's hero—John Smith—was, after all, Werowocomoco's villain. Perhaps it makes more sense not to call anyone a hero. And maybe at its best, history can help us see events from more than one perspective. One man's friend is another man's enemy.

Jamestown: Tobacco and Slaves

John Smith's and Pocahontas's lives may be entertaining, and they can illuminate early patterns of relationships between colonists and Indians, but the long
story of the colonial South has more to do with cash crops and forced labor.
English colonists borrowed some behaviors from the pioneering Spanish and
Portuguese, both of whom enslaved American Indians and Africans. Slavery
was older than the Bible and included in the Bible, and the practice itself was
widely accepted. However, each European empire implemented slavery in its
own way. The historian Ira Berlin points out two fundamental types of social
arrangements: "societies with slaves" and "slave societies."[3] The northern
English colonies became societies with slaves. Except for southern New York,
the agriculture of the North was not dependent on slave labor; and northern
economies in general relied on slavery only because northern merchants and
sea captains sold slaves. All the southern colonies, however, became slave
societies. Slaves and slavery defined the South, and were inextricable from
its social systems, economy, and culture. There are basic reasons for this, and
the earliest reason may have been tobacco.

Fiddling with tobacco varieties, John Rolfe hybridized one that tasted
good and could sprout in Virginia's soil and climate. Tobacco agriculture,
however, is labor intensive. And if the land is not allowed to rest and recover
its nutrients after a planting-harvesting cycle, the soil will soon lose the nutrients needed to grow much of anything, requiring that new land be cleared
and plowed. In the first few decades of Virginia's tobacco boom, Europe
could not get enough of the stuff, which meant that planters had yet another
incentive to put ever more acreage into use. Hence, the growing demand for
tobacco intensified the need for land and laborers. There were four options to
obtain workers. First, farmers paid their own way to Virginia and worked their
own land with the help of family members. Not many people came over that
way, and those who did soon wanted to make more money, so they needed
extra hands to help. Second, a majority of the Europeans who emigrated to
Virginia during the 1600s came over not as free people, but as indentured
servants—men and women who could not afford a ticket to the Americas
and who therefore literally sold themselves to the highest bidder. About 75
percent of all Virginia immigrants in the 1600s were indentured servants.
Their terms of indenture typically lasted from four to seven years; many
died before earning freedom, and many were brutalized while indentured. To
those who lasted, the colony gave a few acres, sometimes a gun, and some
corn to start a new, free life. Third and fourth, a farmer could buy either a
Native American slave or an African slave. Up front, a slave cost more than
an indentured servant, and until the late 1600s, there were many poor white

people seeking a way to get to the colonies. Both cost and availability made indentured servants more tempting.

However, by the late 1600s in Virginia and by the early 1700s in South Carolina (first colonized in 1670), slaves became the predominant form of labor. In fact, by the early 1700s, eastern counties in South Carolina had more slaves than free people. Why? And why did skin color and slavery eventually become synonymous? Instead of a slave system in which both black and white could be lifelong slaves, inheritable slavery became a condition only for African-Americans (and a dwindling number of Native Americans).

The first recorded colonial English purchase of African laborers was made in Virginia in 1619 when twenty "Negars [Negroes]" were bought from an English-Dutch warship, the *White Lion*, which had been in service as a pirate ship since the 1580s.[4] Befitting an era when opportunity rested on oppression and opportunism, the *White Lion*'s captain, John Colyn Jope, had seized the Angolan "Negars" from the diseased hold of a Spanish slaving ship after a fierce cannon fight at sea. So an English pirate, sailing with Dutch letters of marque (essentially a royal pirate license) stole slaves from a Spanish slave ship—poetic justice, except for the Angolans being passed from one European thief to the next. Even more poetically just, the seizure of Angolan slaves naturally angered the Spanish, who pressured King James to stop his subjects from blasting away at Spanish property. The king, sick of English pirates causing him diplomatic problems by using New World ports—like Jamestown—for their illicit business, revoked the London Company's charter in 1624. Now all the lands from modern-day Georgia to Maine would be open to other groups of English settlers not affiliated with the now-defunct London Company. In other words, piracy made Massachusetts Bay Colony possible as a separate and distinct entity.[5]

As for the status of the first Angolan African-Americans sold at Jamestown in 1619, it is not possible to say with certainty whether they were indentured servants or slaves. Certainly, through the 1640s and beyond, there were instances of indentured and enslaved black men and women becoming free, buying slaves of their own, and becoming quite prosperous. One Angolan man, Antonio, arrived not free in Virginia in 1621, having already been a slave in Africa. An Angolan woman, Maria, arrived in 1622 as a servant, and they wed, after which they changed their names to Anthony and Mary Johnson. Together they had four children, earned their freedom (or were freed by the colony), purchased plots of land in 1650, planted tobacco, bought slaves, had white servants,[6] and even sued white neighbors who were harboring one of their runaway slaves. The court ordered the slave to be returned to Anthony Johnson. In other words, skin color did not initially determine a person's fate.

Skin-color status started to change in 1662 when Virginia made it law that the child of a female slave would also be a slave—for life. There were indentured, white female servants in Virginia at the time, but seemingly no white female slaves, so the law was making slavery and African heritage one and the same. Anthony and Mary Johnson moved to Maryland in 1665 onto a 350-acre plantation. After Anthony died, in 1670 the courts in Virginia seized his old property, declaring that a "negroe" was by definition an "alien" and could not be guaranteed property rights. Slowly definitions of citizenship blended into definitions of skin color, restricting the rights and liberties of African-Americans, slave and free alike.

Colonial Virginia: 1622, 1676, and 1705

The morning of March 22, 1622, apparently started out like any other day in Virginia. Poor farmers and their poorer servants, and land-rich planters and their poor servants all set to work at their tasks. As was common, Powhatan men walked onto the riverside plantations to trade fish and hides for whatever valuables the English might be willing to exchange. Within hours, about 350 English men and women lay murdered. The Powhatan Indians under their new emperor, Opechancanough, had swept down upon the English in Virginia to wipe out the colony.

The Powhatans brought no weapons of their own so as to arouse no suspicions. Once on the farms and plantations, they grabbed whatever tools and weapons were accessible and struck. Most outlying houses were destroyed, along with cattle and crops. The English settlers fled to Jamestown, which remained safe, but which became overcrowded and more unsanitary than usual. In all, about one-fourth of the colony's population died in the attacks, soon to be followed by even more deaths from an epidemic that was exacerbated by the cramped living conditions in Jamestown. But Opechancanough underestimated the colonists' will to stay and fight, and fight back they did—first by giving poisoned wine to Powhatan peace negotiators.

Virginians had not recognized the extent to which the Powhatan confederacy resented and feared the expanding colonial population. In January 1622, the governor wrote to the London Company that he found "great amity" and "confidence with the natives." One month before the attack, a local proclamation celebrated the "happy league of peace" existing between "the English and the Natives" because "the fear of killing each other is now vanished away." Immediately following the massacre, however, colonists felt betrayed and began referring to local Native Americans as "beasts," "lions," and "dragons." In fact, by August 1622, all desire for friendship and equal trade had vanished. The colonists wanted to get rid of the local Indians and take their land. In a sort of revenge manifesto, Virginians declared that while their "hand[s] before were tied with gentleness and fair usage," they were now "set at liberty by the treacherous violence of the savages." Virginians who had for fifteen years tried to occupy what they considered only unwanted "waste" land would "now by right of war, and law of nations, invade the [Indians'] country, and destroy them who sought to destroy us." Virginians looked forward to "possessing the fruits of others' labours." This talk of possessing other people's labor fit together neatly with existing and expanding use of servants and slaves.

For the next forty years, the colonists of Virginia pushed farther westward, fighting only one more brief war in 1644 against one-hundred-year-old Opechancanough and his forces. He himself was captured, taken to Jamestown, and shot in the back by a colonist. The remaining Powhatan Indians were scattered. Conflicts over land and trade continued to flare up with tribes on the frontier, and in 1676, one more upheaval, known as Bacon's Rebellion, convulsed the colony. Not only was there bloodshed, but also the "rebellion" smacked the colony's leaders as the most dangerous sort of uprising. Frontier white and black men banded together with some disaffected Jamestown bigwigs to kill friendly Indians and to rid themselves of Governor William Berkeley and his ruling faction. Social and political order seemed doomed. Civil war was at hand.

Each colonial region developed a different social hierarchy. In New England, ministers and merchants commanded respect. After England took New Netherland from the Dutch in 1664 and renamed it New York, old Dutch families and select English families each gained thousands of acres throughout the Hudson River Valley, renting out land to tenant farmers. By the mid-1700s, slave labor was more common than free white labor in districts of the Hudson Valley, and New York City had a slave economy. New York's skilled craftsmen relied on slaves. Historian Ira Berlin points out "more than one-third of the immigrants arriving in New York between 1732 and 1754 were slaves."[7] In the South, immigrants who arrived with money in their purse and good connections to authority could acquire land, slaves, and servants without much difficulty. The Virginia headlight system awarded fifty-acre land grants based on the number of servants a person imported: the more indentures, children, and slaves a settler bought, the more land he got. In South Carolina, North Carolina, and Virginia, wealthy plantation owners became the planter class, the men who dominated the assemblies (like the Virginia House of Burgesses, started in 1619). Great planters led the militias and expected deference from the commoners.

Throughout the colonies, however, struggling commoners were not content to be lorded over, and friction between those with power and those without it sometimes created violent consequences. During most years, seventeenth-century Virginia taxed each free person with a poll tax, which was a fixed sum, usually a quantity of tobacco. In other words, the richest person in the colony paid the same sum as the poorest free man or woman, which seemed unfair to the poor. Using the House of Burgesses as a tool to dominate colonial Virginia, the great planters wrote laws to benefit themselves. These Tidewater planters wanted freedom of action for themselves but not for anyone else, whether white, red, or black. North American English-dominated colonies did not begin as places of equality, and if anything, in the South they became less equal as time passed.

Nathaniel Bacon Jr., cousin-by-marriage to Governor Berkeley, moved from England to Virginia in 1674. The governor gave Bacon both land and a seat on the elite Council of State. The hotheaded, well-educated Bacon moved out to the frontier, where colonial settlers were accusing the powerful Seneca and Susquehannock tribes of murder. War on Virginia's border seemed imminent. Then, in 1675, a devastating conflict broke out in New England when the Wampanoags and Nipmuks joined forces against colonists. Whole towns had to be emptied as the Indian fighters attacked. Word reached Governor Berkeley of King Philip's War (named after Metacom of the Wampanoags, called "King Philip" by the colonists). Berkeley feared that events in New England would influence affairs in Virginia, so he tried to halt frontier hostilities by restricting trade and contact between colonists and all Indians. But Nathaniel Bacon and some frontiersmen attacked friendly Indian tribes, especially those easy to prey on. According to historian Wilcomb Washburn, "Bacon and his men did not kill a single enemy Indian but contented themselves with frightening away, killing, or enslaving most of the friendly neighboring Indians,"[8] like the Pamunkeys—part of the reduced Powhatan confederacy. Berkeley declared Bacon a rebel, but not before Bacon and about 200 followers did more damage.

Local Occaneechees allowed Bacon and his men into their fort in early 1676 and raided a nearby settlement of Susquehannocks, apparently at Bacon's request. Bacon's men killed the captive Susquehannocks and then slaughtered the Occaneechees, perhaps taking some as captives to be sold as slaves. Not long after, contemptuous of the governor's decree that Bacon submit himself as a rebel, Nathaniel Bacon sailed to Jamestown to take a seat in the House of Burgesses, to which he had just been elected by elated frontiersmen pleased with his murder of the Occaneechees. Berkeley's forces apprehended Bacon, who was brought before the governor and pardoned. A twisted web of alliances sits at the heart of this story.

Governor Berkeley did not have the confidence of all the leading colonists, nor did he have the loyalty of frontiersmen, many of whom were poor and most of whom felt threatened by Indians. Bacon gained the support of both groups opposed to Berkeley. At the same time, the governor wanted to keep up good relationships with as many neighboring tribes as possible, partly because he made lots of money trading with them. Balancing these conflicted allegiances proved impossible for everyone involved, including Native American leaders, like the head of the weakened Powhatan confederacy, a woman named Cockacoeske. She was descended from Powhatan and Opechancanough and was herself a Pamunkey—the tribe initially at the heart of the Powhatan confederacy. Descended from chiefs and born into a culture where women could lead, Cockacoeske was a verbal match for any colonial leader.

Cockacoeske appeared in Jamestown during the summer of 1676, just as the House of Burgesses (the Assembly) faced the possibility of civil war. An observer in the House's meeting hall remembered Cockacoeske's entrance. Long black hair woven into a braid hung down her back, and a string of white beads circled her head "in imitation of a crown." She appeared "majestic" in a fringed deerskin robe, "graceful" to the point of "admiration." Though the Pamunkeys were much reduced from their former numbers, Berkeley and the Assembly wanted her to help fight against the Susquehannocks. Cockacoeske gave the colonists little of what they wanted and much they did not expect, particularly a lecture on the colony's refusal to offer "compensation" for her husband, who had died fighting alongside the Virginians against other native peoples in years past. Most members of the Assembly cared little for her loss, essentially ignoring her lecture and request for compensation. According to the observer, the "morose chairman" brushed past her innuendos and "rudely pushed again" for Cockacoeske to help the Virginians one more time. "What Indians will you now contribute?" asked the chairman. She offered six warriors and "rose up and gravely walked away, as not pleased with her treatment."[9]

Berkeley held onto Cockacoeske's allegiance (no thanks to his "morose" legislators and their rude attitudes), but Nathaniel Bacon continued to press for vengeance against any and all tribes. A small faction of leaders supported him, and together with a white and black militia, Bacon scared Governor Berkeley onto the safety of a ship. During the next two months, the governor raised an army of his own and marched on Bacon's forces, pushing them back out of Jamestown. Bacon encircled the city and defended his position by taking the wives of the governor's supporters, dressing them in white, and setting them in between the opposing armies, essentially as shields. Then Bacon cannonaded Jamestown and took it a second time. Afterward, in mid-September 1676, Bacon's hooligans burned most of Jamestown. Then, quite suddenly, Bacon died of dysentery (bloody diarrhea).

What has been termed "Bacon's Rebellion" highlighted the colony's internal weaknesses. Western settlers felt ignored, overtaxed, and underprotected by a governor whom they accused of passing political plums to his supporters. The governor and his supporters, however, saw in Bacon's militia only a rabble of poor whites and blacks directed by a few disloyal, sniveling Assembly members, many of whom Berkeley promptly hanged before he sailed back to England to defend his actions (where he promptly died).

Out of this chaos, some small hopes surfaced while other indications of future injustice emerged. Less than a year after Bacon's death, Cockacoeske led a delegation of tribes into a negotiation with Crown officials. The resulting 1677 Treaty of Middle Plantation reinforced Cockacoeske's dominion over the old tribes of the Powhatan confederacy, while cementing the Crown's dominion over her and other tribes. The treaty provided certain assurances to signatory tribes that their land rights would be respected, but they had to abide by colonial laws. Virginia and the king emerged victorious, at least on paper. At the same time, the House of Burgesses rewarded the colonial soldiers who had taken Indian captives with a grisly reward: they got to keep any captured Indians as slaves. Drawing a connection between domestic insurrection and slavery made sense from the legislators' point of view: Indians seemed dangerous and so did slaves.

The next two decades witnessed a rash of slave laws, all designed to tighten, strengthen, and define the meaning of slavery in Virginia. Runaway slaves could be beaten and even killed if they resisted arrest. Slaves had to have a pass to go out at night or to spend more than four hours at anyone's plantation other than their master's. In 1691, the word "white" was used for the first time to draw a legal distinction between Europeans and both Native Americans and African-Americans—in particular by banning from the colony any "English or other white women" or men who chose to marry "a negroe, mulatto, or Indian man or woman." The capstone of Virginia's slave codes came in 1705 with laws barring "negroes, mulattoes and Indian" slaves from testifying in court and declaring all of them to be "real estate" that could be appraised for financial value and passed through inheritance from generation to generation. Conversion to Christianity was no longer accepted as a method to gain freedom. The easy association of whites and blacks so common in the 1600s—the kind of connections that swelled Nathaniel Bacon's 500-man army with eighty black slaves—became scarce by the early 1700s. Virginia's laws drove wedges between people with different skin colors. The law gave an advantage to whiteness, where white and black had worked equally next to each other only fifty years before. Although Virginia was not the first colony to actually write slave laws—Massachusetts had done so in 1641—Virginia would become the most populous colony by the time of the Revolution in 1775. Its reliance on black slavery helped set the cement of race relations for America and later for the United States.

From Barbados to South Carolina: Trade, War, and Slavery

From any sane person's perch, places like early Virginia and Massachusetts were worthless backwaters. A Jamestown servant, Richard Frethorne, wrote a depressing letter home moaning about diseases ("scurvy and the bloody flux"), the mess that passed for food ("peas, and loblollie [water gruel]"), the friction of multicultural relationships ("For we live in fear of the enemy [Indians] every hour, yet we have had a combat with them . . . and we took two alive and made slaves of them"), and the general misery of the place ("I have nothing to comfort me, nor is there nothing to be gotten here but sickness and death"). After cataloguing his misery, Frethorne pleaded to his father, "for God's sake send beef and cheese and butter."[10] That was Jamestown. As for New England, the Puritans were orderly and long-lived, but from the start they had been disobedient. And what did they have to offer England except lumber, fish, cattle, and corn? At least the last two—cattle and corn—could be sent to England's one real treasure trove: the West Indies, the chain of island jewels that included Jamaica and Barbados, which grew sugar cane instead of food crops. True, Virginia did stuff England's coffers with proceeds from tobacco sales, but Barbados and Jamaica could exploit the sweet tooth. Sugar and slaves made English dreams come true in the Bahamas—bringing in much more money than the mainland colonies ever did. But until 1670 there was one big obstacle in Jamaica: the Spanish were already there. So England sent in the pirates.

Port Royal, Jamaica, was born in warfare and later licked clean by the sea. In 1655, the English sacked Jamaica and took it from the Spanish. The man who liberated paradise for England was Henry Morgan, privateer to some, pirate to others. (A privateer was simply a pirate with permission.) After helping himself to Jamaica, Morgan added a number of other items to his résumé, including more uninvited visits to Spanish colonies in Panama and Venezuela. He even perfected the use of nuns and priests as human shields while attacking defended positions. After establishing a dazzling reputation for carousing and lawlessness, Morgan became deputy governor of Jamaica in 1674. Ever since 1655, Port Royal had been a thriving, debauched, and frivolous city, home to a mixed-up batch of pirates, merchants, slaves, and planters. The status-conscious planters in Jamaica had a difficult time accepting a buccaneer for deputy governor, but the fortunes of pirate and planter were linked. Nearly 1,500 of Morgan's brigands provided protection for the sugar plantations. In any case, the upper-class planters who ruled Jamaica kept a vain eye on the latest London fashions, not always as concerned with laws and debates as with ruffles and buckles.

The debilitating irony of colonization was that Englishmen moved thousands of miles away (wherever opportunity beckoned) in order to live as if they were still at home. These Caribbean planters considered themselves true Englishmen, so they made sense of their new world by mimicking the trends of the mother country. But neither the genteel apparel, the alcohol guzzling, nor the less-than-helpful medical theories of merry old England were suited to Jamaica. The colonists imported the latest thick cotton jackets and pants, complete with hats and gloves, all for use in the noon-day sun of St. Nevis and Barbados. According to historian Richard Dunn, in 1688 Jamaica's governor drank so much one night while toasting the Prince of Wales that "he plunged into a fit of jaundice and shortly died."[11] As if heavy drinking and heavy clothes were not enough to bring the lords and ladies to their knees, at night they slept with the shutters closed, part of a medical regimen based on the notion that nighttime breezes brought swampy vapors—believed to be a major cause of disease. Unable to cool off, unable to properly sweat, they lay in their chamber tombs waiting for the morning's first drink.

More surprising than revelations of Englishmen who liked to drink (and eat fatty food) is Richard Dunn's theory about the relatively more healthful diets that England's Caribbean slaves had access to. While the islands' rulers lay passed out along the sides of roads from heat exhaustion and inebriation, the much abused and dreadfully overworked slaves usually drank rum only on Sundays (when they were allowed to), raised small plots of green vegetables for personal use, and ate tropical fruit. Life expectancies for Caribbean slaves were short (estimated at two to three years at the worst for the newly arrived), but for those who survived, their health may have rivaled their owners'. Diseases like yellow fever, tuberculosis, and leprosy slew indiscriminately, turning island paradises into multicolored graveyards. During the 1600s, the life expectancy for white people in the Bahamas was under thirty-five. Port Royal's wanton hedonism sank into the sea when an earthquake tore the city apart and a tsunami rolled over the remains in 1692. Hundreds, probably thousands, of people died, followed by disease and more deaths. The uneven Caribbean culture of Barbados was the basis of the first English colonization of South Carolina in 1670. South Carolina planters did not need Virginians to teach them about slavery.

Planters, slaves, pirates, and the promise of profit flowed the few hundred miles from island to mainland right into the middle of Spanish, French, Creek, Choctaw, Cherokee, and Yamasee power struggles. As it turned out, South Carolinians would find two main ways to get rich: slave trading and rice growing. And, of course, rice culture depended on slaves. Carolina, Florida, and Mississippi valley Native Americans were the dominant forces in the Deep South throughout the 1600s and into the early 1700s. They controlled access to other Native American slaves, animal hides, and land. They used Europeans and Europeans used them.

From 1670 to 1715, English, Scottish, and Scots-Irish settlers, both free and indentured, migrated to South Carolina, with the Scots settling at the very southern border: opportunity in return for sacrifice. The main settlements situated around Charles Town wanted loyal fighters between themselves and the Spanish in St. Augustine, Florida, so the Scots became a buffer. Slaves, masters, and servants lived in crude equality during Carolina's early years. There were no plantations to speak of, only swamps and insects, forests and river plains to tame. The usual assortment of cattle and pigs unceremoniously wandered ashore. African-descended slaves became the first southern cowboys, driving the herds and building enclosures for them.

Native Americans had slaves and traded slaves, just like the incoming English from Barbados. But more than anywhere else in eastern North America, Native Americans of the South raided and warred with one another to feed the slave hunger of colonists. In the ensuing decades, first the Westos, then the Savannahs, and finally the Yamasees entered into precarious arrangements with the Carolinian government. As the Lords Proprietors (the noblemen who owned the colony) sat in distant Britain dictating policy, colonists interpreted those policies as they pleased. This was much the same pattern that had occurred in Virginia. Harmonious intentions evaporated in the humid avarice of the South. Greed was not limited to Europeans, however. The landscape demanded a hearty work ethic of anyone hoping to survive. And all the cultures that met in the Deep South saw benefit and gain in trade. People became a commodity right alongside tobacco, rice, and deer. Southerners (of whatever skin color) communicated the same way, regardless of what languages they spoke. Trade was the shared language.

Every economy has its own moral standards. With live human bodies serving as the coin of the realm, friend and foe began to look alike: potentially anyone could become a slave. Suspicions and insecurities seeped into the relationships between Indians and colonists. The governors, the Commissioners of the Indian Trade, and the Lords Proprietors of South Carolina all tried to put limits on which tribes could, and could not, be enslaved. But the lure of profits undermined attempts to regulate the economy. A particular class of men known as Indian traders stretched the moral standards of South Carolina's slave economy to the breaking point between peace and war. Indian traders were a conduit between Native American societies and Charles Town. Traders like Eleazer Wiggan learned local languages, often had Native American wives, and spent half their time hiking through the hills and valleys, guiding pack animals loaded with deer hides one way and hats, blankets, shirts, cloth, bullets, powder, and guns the other way. Powder-haired rich men may have set trade policy while cooling themselves with salty Atlantic breezes in Charles Town, but the Indian traders were the men who mingled and mixed in the villages, who bartered and haggled. When Indian traders behaved greedily, war could result.

In 1715 the colony of South Carolina came close to annihilation. From towns and villages in the Creek confederacy, which could field perhaps 6,000 fighters, to the Yamasees, Catawbas, and Cherokees, grievances mounted that could no longer be calmed by reassurances from the colonial authorities. For more than ten years, a motley assortment of traders had been plying native peoples with liquor and then demanding impossible numbers of deer hides in exchange for European-made trade goods. By 1715, it was estimated that Cherokee hunters were 100,000 deer hides in arrears—a number that could never be provided, and sufficient cause to consider striking back at these immoral traders. Indians had other reasons to be upset. For example, in 1710 colonial authorities reported that the Indian trader Jonathan Crosley, "being jealous of a Whore of his," had "beat and abused" an Indian. When a white man named Jonathan Crocket tried to intervene, Crosley beat him too until Crocket spit blood. The trader Crosley, crass and violent, was behaving typically for men of his profession. By 1711, the Commissioners of the Indian Trade—all wealthy merchants, planters, and politicians—worried that "the utter Ruin and Desolation of the Government" might ensue unless all "Affairs between [the Yamasee Indians] and Traders" were settled.[12] The commissioners revoked traders' licenses, fined them, and generally tried to enforce laws against selling liquor to Indians and making slaves of friendly tribe members when deer-hide debts were not paid. Enforcement did not work, however, so the Yamasees took matters into their own hands.

In early 1715, Creeks, Catawbas, and Yamasees killed the traders in their villages. But the Yamasees and some Creeks went further, dashing into frontier houses and settlements and murdering every settler they found. Within days, hundreds of colonists were dead and the colonial frontier emptied into Charles Town, where frightened settlers huddled for safety much as Virginians had done at Jamestown in 1622. Historian Alan Gallay points out that there was more to these attacks than simple retaliation for years of abuse. Yamasee lands along the Savannah River were being invaded by land-hungry settlers. The tributaries of the Savannah could be dyked to flood fields for growing rice. By 1715, rice agriculture was becoming as much a staple of the Carolinian economy as were deer hides and Indian slaves. The Yamasees were defending their homes, their way of life, by striking at the frontier settlers. However, they could not win on their own, and the same group of Indian traders who had done so much to create friction were now called on to soothe the temper of the Cherokees, Creeks, and Choctaws.

Eleazer Wiggan's association with South Carolina extended back at least to 1711, when he established trade with the Overhill Cherokees, far to the north. But in 1714, he was convicted of causing trouble between some Cherokees and the Yuchi Indians. Apparently bribed by Wiggan and his partner, a Cherokee army decimated a Yuchi village. The Cherokees knew that a successful raid would provide them with captives whom they could then sell to Wiggan, thus absolving them of their debts to him. The killings threatened the stability of the region. Wiggan's partner ran off, and Wiggan got reprimanded and lost his trading license for a while. But his infamous reputation did not make him any less valuable to the colonial government. In fact, his familiarity with the Cherokees and Catawbas gave him special privileges.

Carolina's authorities knew they had to keep the Catawbas and Cherokees from joining the Yamasees and Creeks in a full-scale war against the colony. The colonial militia had about 2,000 men by 1716. The region's native peoples could have fielded a joint military exceeding 10,000 experienced fighters. Charles Town needed men like Wiggan, so in late 1716 the governor sent him as an emissary to the Catawbas and Cherokees to keep them from allying with the Yamasees and Creeks. The governor's gamble worked out. In early May 1717, Wiggan reported "that when he was among the Catabaw [sic], the Charikees [sic] sent a painted Stick to give them notice to join their Forces in the latter End of July next to prosecute the War with them against the Creeks." While the Creeks were raiding the colonists, the Cherokees were raiding the Creeks. Animosities between Native Americans once again prevented them from banding together against colonials, and now Wiggan had proof that South Carolina need not worry about the Catawbas. South Carolina could relax.

The Yamasee nation was destroyed, with survivors either enslaved or accepted into Creek families, who themselves moved farther west, away from the English and Scots of Carolina. As Alan Gallay expertly explains, "The Yamasee War was thus an end and a beginning. It reconstructed the South in a way that few events have—only the end of the Civil War compares—for this war marked the birth of the Old South, just as Appomattox later marked its death."[13] Although trade with the Indians continued, it excluded Indian slaves, focusing instead on animal pelts. And with this transition away from Indian slavery came a rush of African and Creole (people of African ancestry but raised in the West Indies) slaves. These slaves sweated and toiled in Carolina's burgeoning rice plantations. Virginia moved toward African-American slavery for reasons similar to those in South Carolina. Enslaving Native Americans caused too many problems, and black slaves could be more easily monitored and identified—their skin color set them apart. Just as Virginia began to tighten its slave laws after Bacon's Rebellion, South Carolina had begun to tighten its laws by 1720. Fear, tradition, and profit blended into a skin-color slave system, one that gradually developed full-blown theories about racial difference.

As for the Lords Proprietors of South Carolina, they had become an obsolete nuisance by 1719. Their feeble attempts at retaining control of the colony became threadbare and obvious during the Yamasee War. As was eventually to happen with all the colonies, South Carolina passed into royal hands in 1729. The king's colonial subjects had become substantial in numbers, with nearly 100,000 colonists living in Virginia alone by 1730. Colonial revenues mattered to the empire, and these growing societies were worth fighting for against the Spanish and French. It only made sense that as proprietors bungled and mismanaged the affairs of empire, the king and Parliament should step in to bring order and sense. Massachusetts had become a royal colony in 1692. Virginia had been taken over by the Crown in 1624, right after the first Powhatan War, though the House of Burgesses continued to control local matters. In other words, while colonial leadership developed, the British Empire brought all the English settlements within its dominion. Beginning in 1651, Parliament passed Navigation Acts (regulating trade and commerce) with the intention of keeping gold, silver, crops, lumber, and all manufactured items within a closed economic system. If the colonies had been founded rather haphazardly, this do-as-you-please attitude did not last forever.

An American Mosaic

More than ever before in the American or European traditions, peoples from different cultures came together to form new ones. Slaves and masters lived in close proximity. As the diary of a famous Virginian, William Byrd II, reveals, their daily routines got lumped together: "February 8, 1709. I rose at 5 o'clock this morning and read a chapter in Hebrew and 200 verses in Homer's *Odyssey*. I ate milk for breakfast. I said my prayers. Jenny and Eugene [slaves] were whipped. I danced my dance. I read law in the morning and Italian in the afternoon."[4] Milk, prayers, and whippings could all happen in the same breath. Little about the early 1700s would seem normal to a twenty-first–century visitor. William Byrd's diary shows the dream-angel, mystical world that colonists inhabited side by side with men and women simply referred to as "my negroes." He wrote:

> Some night this month I dreamed that I saw a flaming sword in the sky and called some company to see it . . . and about a week after my wife and I were walking and we discovered in the clouds a shining cloud exactly in the shape of a dart and seemed to be over my plantation but it soon disappeared likewise. Both these appearances seemed to foretell some misfortune to me which afterwards came to pass in the death of several of my negroes after a very unusual manner. My wife about two months since dreamed she saw an angel in the shape of a big woman who told her the time was altered and the seasons were changed and that several calamities would follow that confusion. God avert his judgment from this poor country.[15]

40

While kings and queens dreamed of colonial empires blanketing the globe, and colonists dreamed of big women angels, societal patterns emerged. The mid-1700s would be a time of definitions and prosperity in colonial America: a time for soul-fire religion; for slaves to embrace the freedom chant of Christianity while struggling to break the chains that bound them; for brick houses to line the streets of Boston and Philadelphia and for brick mansions to radiate elegance and power along the banks of southern rivers; a time for laws, colleges, and politics. Colonial Americans would broaden their vision beyond the boundaries of parish, town, and county, and they would see that their law, their habits, their essential interests were in need of protection from the same country that had birthed them. In reality, colonial America was birthed by Yamasees, Powhatans, and Wampanoags just as much as it was by English, Scots, and West Africans like the Ndongo—the twenty "Negars" sold at Jamestown in 1619.

Notes

1. John Smith, *The Generall Historie of Virginia, New England & The Summer Isles* (Glasgow, Scotland: James MacLehose, 1907) vol. 1: 204.
2. Tim Hashaw, *The Birth of Black America: The First African Americans and the Pursuit of Freedom at Jamestown* (New York: Carroll & Graff, 2007), 47.
3. Ira Berlin, *Many Thousands Gone: The First Two Centuries of Slavery in North America* (New York: Belknap, 2000).
4. Hashaw, *Birth of Black America*, 71.
5. Hashaw, *Birth of Black America*, 98–99.
6. Hashaw, *Birth of Black America*, 14.
7. Berlin, *Many Thousands Gone*, 179.
8. Wilcomb E. Washburn, *The Governor and the Rebel* (New York: W.W. Norton, 1972).
9. "The Beginning, Progress, and Conclusion of Bacon's Rebellion in Virginia, In the Years 1675 and 1676," *The Thomas Jefferson Papers*, Series 8: Virginia Records, 1606–1737, http://memory.loc.gov/ammem/collections/jefferson_papers/tm.html.
10. Susan Kingsbury, ed., *The Records of the Virginia Company of London*, "Richard Frethorne, letter to his father and mother" (Washington, DC: Government Printing Office, 1935), vol. 4: 58–60.
11. Richard S. Dunn, *Sugar and Slaves: The Rise of the Planter Class in the English West Indies, 1624–1713* (Chapel Hill: University of North Carolina Press, 2000), 161.
12. W.L. McDowell, ed., *Journals of the Commissioners of the Indian Trade, September 20, 1710–August 29, 1718* (Columbia: South Carolina Archives Department, 1955), 30 May 1711.
13. Alan Gallay, *The Indian Slave Trade: The Rise of the English Empire in the American South, 1670–1717* (New Haven, CT: Yale University Press, 2003), 338.
14. Kenneth A. Lockridge, *Settlement and Unsettlement in Early America* (New York: Cambridge University Press, 1981), 92.
15. Kenneth A. Lockridge, *The Diary and Life of William Byrd II of Virginia, 1674–1744* (Chapel Hill: University of North Carolina Press, 1987), 64–65.

3

Colonial Society

Benjamin Franklin relaxes at home. *(Stock Montage/Getty Images)*

William Byrd: Colonizing Nature

William Byrd II liked to have a good laugh. In 1728, Byrd, other colonials, and a Saponi hunter named Bearskin shared a tent in a pounding rainstorm. Bearskin "asked the Englishmen what it was that made that rumbling noise when it thundered." The English replied that their two gods, Indian and Christian, were exchanging musket volleys. According to Byrd, "The Indian, carrying on the humor replied . . . that the rain which followed upon the thunder must be occasioned by the Indian god's being so scared he [wet himself]."[1]

What was this refined and cultured gentleman doing out in the rain with an Indian? Byrd was an important man in Virginia who could afford to be easy with his humor, owned vast plantation estates, and sat in the governor's Council of State. Byrd had coins in his pockets, slaves in their quarters, and looked every bit the gentleman in his oil-on-canvas portrait: thick brown wig, its tight coils touching the lapel of his gold-accented, blue silk coat; slender, delicate fingers resting casually at the waist; and a penetrating gaze, looking out at the viewer, as if to say, "Yes, I can afford to loaf about having my portrait painted, but don't mistake me for a fop because I get things done." Given his wealth, Byrd could have sailed just about anywhere. He could have gone to India, where Britain's East India Company was taking over, running a foreign nation for profits in tea and opium. But India was in the opposite direction from his ambitions, at home in Virginia. He could have lived in England comfortably (which he did for over half his life), but although he considered himself English, William Byrd was a Virginian. He was born there, and in Virginia William Byrd had opportunity for fame and influence. In 1728, along with a few others, Byrd set out to survey the dividing line between Virginia and North Carolina, which is how he ended up in the rain, in a tent, with a man named Bearskin, laughing about gods wetting themselves.

The handful of colonial cities had only handfuls of people in the 1700s: Philadelphia had 10,000 to 15,000 by 1740; Boston, New York, and Charles Town had even fewer. The cities were exciting places, if also dirty and dangerous. The British navy sometimes sent its sailors to impress colonists into the service, forcible enlistment to the most dangerous job around. Housewives and tavern keepers dumped buckets of slop (old food, feces, and whatever else ended up in the chamber pot) directly into the street. Pigs rooted around, and when children were not doing chores they were rooting around too. Benjamin Franklin (future inventor, statesman, writer, publisher, and all-around rascal) remembered a boyhood incident in Boston when he and his fellow conspirators stole bricks from a half-built house so they could make a pier by the river. They got caught. Rich families had black slaves in white gloves to open coach doors and brush down the horses. In Charles Town, white people complained that black women scared them silly with verbal harassment in the vegetable market, which the black women unofficially ran. Blacks and whites from the countryside brought fruits, vegetables, and meats into town for sale, one of the few ways they could make a dollar. Commerce, trade, and travel between cities and country were common, but it was in the country that most people, like William Byrd II, lived.

The English ideal was to tame nature. The whole point was not to sail to America, set up a tent in the wilderness, and live like the stereotype of an Indian, which Byrd succinctly spelled out in some cutting remarks about Bearskin: "This was the substance of Bearskin's religion and was as much . . . as could be expected from a mere state of nature, without one glimpse of revelation or philosophy." A "mere state of nature" not informed by intellectual traditions like formal philosophy would, in Byrd's opinion, leave a man misguided and ignorant. "Indeed, the Indian notion of a future happiness is a little gross and sensual, like [Muhammad's] Paradise. But how can it be otherwise," Byrd asked rhetorically, "in a people that are contented with Nature as they find her and have no other lights but what they receive from purblind [defective] tradition?"[2] Byrd did not just pick on Indians; he picked on anyone who lived too much in a "state of nature."

Throughout his spring and autumn dividing-line survey, William Byrd and his company always stopped so that the chaplain might baptize or christen the bedraggled children of poor white folk. Byrd made a clear distinction between upper-class gentlemen (like himself) and the backcountry squatters whom he depicted as typically living without Christianity—in other words, like Bearskin. Byrd implied that a tendency toward slothful and immoral living had ample room to flourish in the backwoods of North Carolina, in particular. He lamented what he saw as North Carolina's liberal government, which seemed to encourage too much independence. Lack of restrictions and regulations, Byrd believed, made people daily more unproductive and useless, whatever their ethnicity. As he sarcastically put it, "A citizen here is counted extravagant if he has ambition enough to aspire to a brick chimney."[3] Proper patriarchal, authoritarian government and Christianity—the two hallmarks of Byrd's brand of civilization—could reclaim people gone over to, or born into, nature. Without the drapings of English culture and order, poorly bred people would remain unenlightened and unredeemed. Great Tidewater planters like himself had bested and tamed nature. He and his class set the mark for everyone else—white, black, mulatto, or Indian. It only made sense, then, that the Byrds, the Carters, and other plantation owners should rule. Without them at the helm, it was assumed, nature would conquer reason, God, and civilization. The plantation owners did not have far to look—nature was right out the back door.

45

Most colonists did not bathe often, if at all. The soft soap made from ashes and animal fat got used on clothes, which did not get cleaned often either. The number one cleaning solution for the home was vinegar. Nobody had a bathroom, so people scampered to the outhouse or into the bushes when the urge hit. Flies, mosquitoes, and mice had free run in most houses. It generally took about fifty years to clear a hundred forested acres, so every time a family moved farther west, they could expect to live in the shadow of trees for years, if not a whole lifetime. Until Benjamin Franklin invented the lightning rod, houses and whole neighborhoods had no fire protection whatsoever when thunderstorms rumbled overhead. Southern plantations and even smaller households were expected to feed, entertain, and house any drop-by visitors, a kind of hospitality that pleased many a lonely housewife, but never failed to remind the cultured few just how many people still lived in a "mere state of nature."

Jonathan Edwards, George Whitefield, the Great Awakening (and Benjamin Franklin, Too)

If William Byrd II worried about people's lack of Christianity, he was not alone in his fears. Scientific inquiry (called "natural philosophy" at the time), the ongoing revival in studying ancient Greek thinkers like Socrates and Plato, and the loosening of tradition that happened on the frontier was making America a less God-centered place. Old-school fire-and-brimstone Christians had to tolerate worrisome doctrines like deism. Deists essentially argued that God had created life and then retreated to some divine spa, leaving humans to work out their issues alone. Earthquakes could be explained through inquiry and reason. So could the flow of the oceans; in fact, the colonies' best-known deist, Benjamin Franklin, was the first person to write a convincing explanation for the flow of ocean currents. Dismayed church leaders wondered what was to be done.

People are emotional. Puritan churches attracted sober-minded, wordy pastors, like Cotton Mather, who wrote scores of books and sermonized for hours on end. Puritan pastors dwelt on the Word, examining scripture with infinite care and dedication—much the same way Anne Hutchinson and John Winthrop had sparred over the Bible in 1637. It was difficult to get the masses worked up about a sin-centered, verbose, solemn spirituality and religion. Enter John Wesley, Jonathan Edwards, and especially George Whitefield.

To sink into people's souls, what Christianity needed, apparently, was more singing, more extemporaneous preaching, more gut-wrenching, heart-tearing, joyful—and fearful—in-your-bones worship. John Wesley studied at Oxford University in England, along with a devoted core of students, one of whom was George Whitefield, a gifted speaker. Harvard University in Massachusetts (founded right after the Anne Hutchinson scare), Yale in Connecticut, and Oxford all had their origins in training clergy. While Wesley was at Oxford earning for himself and his students the name "Methodist" (meant at first as a mild insult) for his development of rigorous study habits, Jonathan Edwards was attending Yale, an original springboard for Puritan preachers. Edwards—son of a minister—held onto the Anglican Church, but his approach diverged radically from established church practices. During the 1730s, Edwards began to embrace the heightened emotions and body-rocking ecstasy of the nascent revival movement. He described the conversion process like this: "Persons are first awakened with a sense of their miserable condition by nature, the danger they are in of perishing eternally." Some who sensed their own "miserable condition" felt "their consciences . . . suddenly smitten, as if their hearts were pierced through with a dart." After suffering through this painful awakening, the born-again convert achieved "comfortable evidences of pardon and acceptance with God."[4] The process was challenging, but it led to inner peace, in Edwards's opinion. George Whitefield arrived at the same conclusion in England, where he too had been experimenting with new styles of preaching, in particular outdoors. As one can imagine, Whitefield and Edwards upset some other preachers.

In 1735, John Wesley came to the colony of Georgia, established three years earlier by an Englishman named James Oglethorpe. Georgia's original laws forbade slavery and tried to maintain good and fair relations with local Indians, making the colony an oddity in the South. Georgia was intended to be a haven for poor people who had few other options. Wesley stayed for two years, during which time he became enchanted with Moravian immigrants who stressed a personal relationship to God. This individualist spirituality fit together well with the small student assemblies Wesley had pioneered at Oxford. Although Wesley returned to England, he first wrote to Whitefield and suggested Georgia as a ripe field for Whitefield's captivating sermons. Whitefield set sail for Georgia even as Wesley was preparing to go back to England in 1737. They were on the water at the same time, heading in opposite directions. While John Wesley went on to found the Methodist Church and to ordain its first North American ministers in the 1780s, it was George Whitefield and Jonathan Edwards who had the bigger impact on colonial American society.

One way to measure a person's importance is to gauge the anger she or he attracts. George Whitefield excited listeners to shriek and call, holler and whoop, to fall to the ground infused by the Spirit. His opponents felt just about as much passion, but for different reasons—they distrusted his methods. Whitefield's and Edwards's detractors became known as "Old Light" ministers, counterpoints to the "New Lights" who followed in Whitefield's footsteps. Charles Chauncy was an Old Light minister from Boston who had the opportunity and, in his opinion, the misfortune to watch Whitefield at work. In 1742, he wrote to a British colleague to complain about Whitefield's emergent popularity. "When [Whitefield] came to town," Chauncy wrote, "he was received as though he had been an angel of God. . . . He was strangely flocked after by all sorts of persons, and much admired by the vulgar, both great and small." As disturbing to Chauncy as common people's admiration for Whitefield was the "veneration" of other ministers, who invited him to preach before their congregations. Before long, Chauncy complained, "Evening lectures were set up in one place and another; no less than six in this town, four weekly, and two monthly ones, though the town does not consist of above 5,000 families." In other words, just about everybody in Boston went to hear Whitefield speak, and many felt pulled into his words, so that the "great business of the town [was] to run from place to place," chasing after Whitefield.

Why would a fellow minister have a problem with such successful evangelizing? Chauncy asked the same question in his letter, knowing his British friend would be wondering the same thing. "And here you will doubtless be disposed to inquire," wrote Chauncy, "what was the great good this gentleman was the instrument of." For starters, Chauncy thought people were spending too much time at sermons. They were neglecting "all other business" in favor of Whitefield's "*new way.*" The italics were Chauncy's, an ink-on-paper sneer. Worse yet, although a few sinners were saved, "so far as I could judge," Chauncy continued, "the town, in general, was not much mended in those things wherein a reformation was greatly needed." Whitefield's audience—the whole town of Boston, essentially—still held onto "the same pride and vanity, the same luxury and intemperance, the same lying and tricking and cheating as before [Whitefield] came along."[5] Charles Chauncy was convinced that George Whitefield was a charlatan, whatever his intentions.

Benjamin Franklin, on the other hand, although a deist, became a lifelong friend of Whitefield's. Franklin encountered Whitefield in Boston and marveled at his audience, who "admir'd and respected [Whitefield], notwithstanding his common abuse of them, by assuring them that they were naturally half beasts and half devils." In fact, Franklin attended a sermon "in the course of which I perceived he intended to finish with a collection, and I silently resolved he should get nothing from me." Franklin was notoriously tightfisted with his money and did not intend to give Whitefield any of it. However, "as he proceeded I began to soften, and concluded to give the coppers. Another stroke of his oratory made me asham'd of that, and determin'd me to give the silver; and he finish'd so admirably, that I empty'd my pocket wholly into the collector's dish, gold and all." Unlike Charles Chauncy's scathing reviews of Whitefield, Franklin found him a "perfectly honest man, and methinks my testimony in his favour ought to have the more weight, as we had no religious connection."[6]

The more that ministers like Chauncy denied their churches to Whitefield, the more Whitefield preached outdoors. And the more time he spent in non-traditional settings, the more unconventional the revival meetings became: the more emotional, the more physical, and the more open to sudden preaching by African-Americans and women. Although England's North American colonies offered greater opportunity for financial and social advancement than was available in England at the time, the colonies were still socially stratified—with a thin skim of wealthy and powerful leaders on top making the laws for everyone else. Whitefield's and Edwards's revival meetings blurred such social distinctions. In Virginia, for example, women often sat segregated from men during Anglican services, and the few slaves allowed in church were even further segregated in special seats placed farthest from the pulpit.[7] It was typical for the wealthy male planters to walk into church a little bit late, enjoying the chance to strut their fine clothes and show a disdain for the timeliness expected of others. Outdoor, camp-style meetings did not allow for such easy segregation or pretensions. Furthermore, as African-Americans converted to Christianity in great numbers at the revivals, slavery itself came under new scrutiny. One Whitefield disciple, Samuel Davies, made it his mission to evangelize slaves in the South (clearing the path for Methodists and Baptists to become dominant there). For generations, Christians had been uncomfortable enslaving other Christians. Granted, Virginia dealt with this issue before Whitefield came along by saying that a slave was a slave, regardless of her or his religion. Slave owners whose entire livelihood and social status depended on black slaves resisted giving up their money and stature for religious reasons. Although only about 2 percent of slaves were converted at the time of the War of Independence, increasing conversions prompted owners to find new ways of justifying slavery—perhaps one factor in the emergence of racial theories that white people latched onto as scientific "proof" that blacks were inherently inferior.

The religious enthusiasm, the spawning of new denominations (like the Methodist Episcopal Church), the sense that untrained individuals could feel God's spirit and communicate it to others on the spot, and even more radically the suggestion that all people's souls were equal before God (espoused by at least a few New Lights) came to be known as the Great Awakening. George Whitefield sailed to the colonies seven different times, traveling through the North and the South. He stoked Christian fires, and certain churches' memberships soared—namely, Presbyterian and Baptist. Not all colonials, however, fell under the sway of fundamentalist preachers.

Neither Whitefield's elegance nor Edwards's invocation of an "angry God" convinced everyone to worry about their salvation. Benjamin Franklin, again, provides a thoughtful antidote to the anxiety of New Lights and Old Lights alike. In 1728, living in Philadelphia and running his own print shop, Franklin penned his thoughts on the nature of divinity and humanity's relationship to the divine: "I believe there is one supreme, most perfect Being, Author and Father of the gods themselves." Notice that Franklin did not refer to "God." Beyond this use of metaphor to describe the divine ("author and father"), Franklin could not agree that humans sat at the top of the chain of life: "For I believe that man is not the most perfect being but one, but rather that there are many degrees of beings superior to him." Ever the scientist, Franklin literally looked to the cosmos for his answers and inspiration: "When I stretch my imagination through and beyond our system of planets, beyond the visible fixed stars themselves . . . then this little ball on which we move seems, even in my narrow imagination, to be almost nothing, and myself less than nothing, and of no sort of consequence." Franklin's humility came not from Biblical commands and injunctions, but from reason, from thought.

As for the duty Franklin thought people owed to the "Father of the gods themselves," his obligation differed drastically from the obedience preached by men like Jonathan Edwards. Franklin wrote, "I imagine it great vanity in me to suppose, that the Supremely Perfect does in the least regard such an inconsiderable nothing as man." In other words, Franklin's god was not overly interested in people. Franklin could not "conceive otherwise, than that He, the Infinite Father, expects or requires no worship or praise from us, but that He is even infinitely above it." If the "Infinite Father" did not notice people, why would he be interested in worship? Franklin, always a student of human character, understood, however, that "there is in all men something like a natural principle which inclines them to *devotion*, or the worship of some unseen power." The puzzle for him, then, was to figure out what the "Supremely Perfect" would want from people. Franklin's answer was this: "He has created many things, which seem purely designed for the delight of man, I believe He is not offended when He sees His children solace themselves in any manner of pleasant exercises and innocent delights; and I think no pleasure innocent that is to man hurtful . . . let me resolve to be virtuous, that I may be happy, that I may please Him, who is delighted to see me happy. Amen!"[8] Franklin was saying that overindulgence was no good, but that a little partying was godly in moderation. Abstinence is one form of excess, and for a while Franklin was a vegetarian, abstinent in his avoidance of meat. However, aboard a ship departing Boston, he watched as sailors cut open fish bellies, preparing for a feast. Noticing that the large fish had smaller ones in their bellies, Franklin thought to himself, "If you eat one another, I don't see why we mayn't eat you," and he joined the feast.[9]

William Byrd II and Benjamin Franklin were not so very far apart in some ways, but worlds apart in others. Both men reveled in the gifts of their world, enjoying the luxuries their wealth permitted, and both men worked hard to shape society into a sensible order. However, Byrd was a Virginian who remained committed to African-American slavery and to the tight-knit, planter-ruled counties of the South. He died in 1744, a few decades before widespread antislavery sentiments began to sweep through America. Benjamin Franklin organized fire-fighting brigades, started the first lending library in the colonies, invented bifocal glasses, and published the colonies' favorite almanac, *Poor Richard's*. These imprints of his orderly mind drew on the scientific, rational traditions of Europe and America. But Franklin differed from Byrd on matters of theology and natural philosophy as they pertained to nature and civilization. Shortly before dying in 1790, Franklin signed up for the first antislavery society in the United States. He had come to believe that all men were indeed created equal, a notion that he arrived at without the influence of Protestant revivalism. Franklin was every bit the product of European-born civilization, much like William Byrd II, but in their opinions of other peoples they could not have been less alike.

Byrd characterized Native American religion as "gross and sensual" and said that Indians were "contented with Nature," suggesting that they did not organize their societies beyond the crudest state. Franklin could not have disagreed more. He had studied the Iroquois system of government and found it worked very well; in fact, he may have borrowed from it for his contributions to the Constitution. He wrote, almost pointing at Byrd, "SAVAGES we call them, because their manners differ from ours, which we think the perfection of civility; they think the same of theirs." Both colonists and Indians could be cultural bigots, in other words. In the end, Franklin thought all people, of whatever origins, capable of "politeness" and "rudeness," of good manners and bad. Franklin did not think that Native Americans lived in some caveman, throwback state of nature. Rather, he saw that they had sophisticated governments in which men and women participated: "for all their Government is by Counsel, or Advice, of the sages; there is no Force, there are no Prisons, no Officers to compel Obedience, or inflict punishment." Besides providing a civil society, the Iroquois governing councils were models of polite behavior compared to the House of Commons in Britain, where "confusion" reigned and the speaker had to shout himself "hoarse" to establish order. When an Iroquois wanted to say something, Franklin explained, "he that would speak, rises. The rest observe a profound Silence."[10]

William Byrd and Benjamin Franklin worked hard to create civil societies, but it may be that Franklin preferred the civil societies of North America that were here first. At least he said it that way to get his point across. If Franklin was uncommonly deistic, uncommonly friendly to Indians, and uncommonly contented about the pleasures of the flesh, he was not entirely alone in his opinions. The cultural seesaw that he and Byrd rode together illustrates the similarities and divides in the colonial mind.

Elizabeth Lucas Pinckney

On a late spring day in 1742, Elizabeth Lucas ("Eliza") was feeling worn out and older than her years. "I shall begin to think my self an old woman before I am . . . a young one," she wrote to her friend, Mary Bartlett. [11] Eliza had had few easy years to speak of and had no particular reason to think she would ever have children or even get married. Eliza's future husband, Charles Pinckney, was twenty-two years older than she, and in 1742 he was married to someone else. Eliza liked to go to the Pinckneys' house in Charles Town, South Carolina, to socialize and to read their fine collection of books—that is, when she was not absorbed in the business of running her own plantation about seventeen miles overland from Charles Town. At the age of twenty, Eliza Lucas already had more financial responsibility than probably any other woman on the continent.

Four years before Eliza grumbled about work-induced premature aging, she and her family had arrived in South Carolina from one of England's Caribbean islands, Antigua. A dead relative had left Eliza's father some South Carolinian property—three separate plantations. Before her father, George Lucas, could settle down to the partriarchal life of a gentleman farmer, he was recalled to Antigua to help defend England's far-flung empire against Spain. His turnaround left the mosquito-ridden, malaria-infested tree and rice plantations in sixteen-year-old Eliza's hands. Her mother was sick, her sister was even younger, and somebody had to keep the family inheritance profitable. Eliza turned out to be ready for the challenge. She was naturally gifted, and she had gone to school in England, unusual for young colonial women, whose education rarely exceeded learning their letters at home. Gifted as Eliza was, she reminded a correspondent that she had "the business of 3 plantations to transact, which requires much writing and more business and fatigue of other sorts than you can imagine."

If constant labor, disease, Indian wars, and internal squabbling were not enough to keep colonists busy, there were always the wars for empire fought between England, Spain, and France on and off from the late 1600s through the American Revolution. The first of these land-grab wars between the empire-states of Europe (sometimes collectively called the French and Indian Wars) was known to colonists as King William's War (1689–1697). It was followed by Queen Anne's War (1702–1713). Other than some fighting in

Charles Town, these two conflicts had been confined mostly to the North, with Britain and its Indian allies fighting back and forth with France and its Indian allies. Quebec in Canada and sites in Massachusetts, Maine, and New York regularly suffered during these more than twenty years of bloodshed.

The latest war was known to the colonists as King George's War (1744–1748). Limited warfare had actually begun during 1738 when a British captain named Jenkins claimed that the Spanish had cut off part of his ear. He exhibited a pickled ear in front of Parliament, which immediately declared war on Spain—giving the first part of the war the obvious name, the War of Jenkins's Ear. The war was part of a larger European conflict that spilled over into the North American field when the French went after Nova Scotia. Colonial cities like Boston got flooded by refugees, many of them women escaping from Indian and French raiders, their husbands killed and children in tow. At first, places like Salem and Boston tried to help war widows, but support networks were not adequate to handle literally thousands of needy mouths. Boston, Philadelphia, and New York City experimented with various types of welfare. In 1748, Boston opened a workhouse for widows and orphans where all day long they were put to spinning cloth in return for a pittance. About one-third of Boston's women were widows. (Another upshot of these wars was the constant maintenance of well-trained militias throughout New England. This tradition of farmer soldiers contributed to the colonists' ability to fight successfully against the British in the early years of the American Revolution.) Though war never reduced Eliza Lucas to the ragged status of a pauper, England's colonial conflicts did give her both new responsibilities and new freedoms.

In 1739 Eliza's father George Lucas sailed back to Antigua, leaving his family behind near Charles Town. Eliza had lots to do to ensure that the family's plantations succeeded. She wrote to her father and the various agents who sold the farms' produce. She supervised the overseers and daily work around the Wappoo plantation where she resided. She experimented with crops like indigo (an expensive dye used for cloth), ginger, cotton, and cassava (a starchy tuber that formed the basis of Caribbean diets, but that could kill if traces of cyanide were not carefully taken out of the tuber's meat). Times were troublesome; privateers and pirates sailed the high seas, raiding the merchant vessels that carried the Lucas family's crops. Eliza recorded one instance, in July 1740, of a "large ship" that was captured by Spanish pirates. Unfortunately, the captain was a Quaker who "would not fight." But an unlucky colonel aboard, named Braithwait, "undertook to fight" the Spanish buccaneers when his Quaker captain would not. As Eliza explained the incident, the British ship did not have enough gunpowder. The Spanish captain boarded the ship and found Colonel Braithwait "comforting his wife who was greatly frighted."

Because Braithwait had led the resistance, the Spanish captain shot him "dead in her sight." Although Eliza's father survived the war, her mind skittered with thoughts of the danger he could be in. "The dangerous situation you are in," she wrote to him, "terrifies us beyond expression."

As a young lady with prospects, it was expected that Eliza would want to marry. Her situation was fairly unusual. Women throughout the colonies were legally entitled to run businesses (farms included), and women could inherit property; middle-aged or old widows regularly ran inns and taverns, and all midwives were women. But few young women operated plantations on their own. Grown men and women assumed that a young lady not yet twenty would benefit from the worldly vision, guidance, and mentoring of a husband—preferably older, given the peculiarities of Eliza's circumstances, or so her father must have thought when he proposed an eligible suitor early in 1740. Eliza had absolutely no problem saying no. "As you propose Mr. L. to me," she flatly informed her father, "I am sorry I can't have Sentiments favourable enough of him to take time to think on the Subject." The wooer, "Mr. L.," was obviously not much of a catch, age having something to do with the mismatch. "As I know tis my happiness you consult," Eliza wrote, "[I] must beg the favour of you to pay my thanks to the old Gentleman for his Generosity." Niceties aside, Eliza was sure that "the riches of Peru and Chili if he had them put together could not purchase a sufficient Esteem for him to make him my husband."

Young people in the English colonies had been taking more control over their marriage prospects and choices during the 1700s. For one thing, while premarital sex remained technically punishable in many places, instances of teenage pregnancies were on the rise. The best way for parents to make a single, young, pregnant woman socially acceptable was through marriage—hopefully to the impatient buck who had impregnated her, and preferably before anyone outside the families found out about the impending baby. All along the coast, fresh farmlands became scarce during the 1700s, and young people were faced with two choices if they wanted independence: move farther west to clear out space of their own, or get pregnant, which would lead fast to marriage and the possibility of scoring a prized chunk of inheritance early. Sex paved the road to property. While love was not a necessary precondition for marriage, amorous feelings were becoming a more important part of the process. In the same letter that Eliza turned down "Mr. L.," she also reminded her father that she would not be made "a Sacrifice to Wealth." In other words, even if Mr. L. could have brought wealth of his own and a keen eye for managing plantations, that was not as important to Eliza as her happiness. Eliza concluded the issue in the definite tones her father must have expected. "Give me leave to assure you, my dear Sir, that a single life is my only Choice and if it were not as I am yet but Eighteen, hope you will [set] aside the thoughts of my marrying yet these 2 or 3 years at least." As history best knows, George Lucas stopped suggesting husbands to his daughter. And no wonder: she was doing expertly all on her own.

For the next four years, until 1744, Eliza's life settled into certain routines. With the Pinckneys' home in Charles Town open to her, Eliza found the port city a "polite, agreeable place. The people live very Gentile [genteel] and very much in the English taste." Wealthy planters, their families, the colony's bureaucrats, and a general assortment of laborers, shopkeepers, servants, slaves, and sailors congregated in Charles Town. Native Americans frequented the town, usually on trade or diplomatic business of their own, and the Indian traders who followed in the footsteps of Eleazer Wiggan still brought their pack trains heaped high with animal hides. The brick houses along the harbor buzzed at night with excited talk of scandals, philosophy, affairs of empire, and the latest crop yields. Music drifted out into the streets. It was the age of Johann Sebastian Bach, after all. Eliza sometimes stayed with the Pinckneys for three weeks to a month at a time, but the demands of Wappoo Plantations would soon call her back.

Eliza undertook all tasks that crossed her path. In early 1741, she wrote to her friend (and future husband) in Charles Town, Charles Pinckney, to say that spending time with him and Mrs. Pinckney would be "a much pleasanter prescription" than whatever drugs the local doctor had just given her. Indeed, a visit from friends would have been far better than most of the opium, alcohol, and quackery that passed for medicine in the 1700s. Eliza had already survived smallpox, and it is possible she contracted malaria in South Carolina, given her symptoms: headaches that got worse in hot weather, "acute pain," and sickness in her stomach. Bloodletting and purgatives were two medical favorites, both more likely to dehydrate and weaken a sick person than heal or help. Besides seeking medical care for herself, her family members, and the slaves, Eliza also ran a home school. "To follow my inclination at this time," she wrote, "I must endeavour [not] to forget I have a Sister to instruct and a parcel of little Negroes whom I have undertaken to teach to read." Slaves rarely learned the art of letters. An eighteenth-century owner could choose to teach slaves to read, though a 1740 South Carolina slave law stipulated a fine of "one hundred pounds, current money" for teaching writing to slaves. Doctoring was a common side occupation for a plantation master. Eliza was simply doing her duty in that instance. However, agriculture was the mainstay of plantation business, and Eliza Lucas grew one crop that altered the future of South Carolina more than any other innovation until the introduction of the cotton gin in 1793.

Sometime in the late spring of 1741, Eliza wrote to her father that "we had a fine Crop of Indigo Seed upon the ground . . . [but] the frost took it before it was dry. I picked out the best of it and had it planted, but there'is not more than a hundred bushes of it come up . . . I make no doubt Indigo will prove a very valuable commodity in time." Part of the pea family, indigo plants, with their eight-foot stalks, yielded a deep blue dye. As Eliza's remarks indicate, indigo was already a Caribbean success. South Carolina up to the 1740s had exported slaves, rice, and naval stores (masts, pitch, and tar). The exportation of slaves virtually ended after the Yamasee War, and while naval stores were both necessary and valuable, plantations devoid of trees obviously could not produce them. That left rice farming, which was time-consuming, labor-intensive, and wholly dependent on the security of the Atlantic. Eliza and her father decided to diversify, but for four years either the indigo plants did not grow well enough or the dye-making expert her father sent over did more harm than good (perhaps even sabotaging Eliza's efforts).

Eliza's experimentation did not keep her too busy to jump into family discussions or to muse in self-reflection. In 1741, she implored her eldest brother, George, not to join the army. Eliza began the letter by slyly apologizing for "presuming" to lecture an older brother about "false notions of honour." She thought George was making poor "distinctions between Courage and rashness, Justice and revenge." Eliza thought it was imperative that with "his first entrance into [adult] life," George should be careful "of his duty to his Creator, for nothing but an early piety and steady Virtue can make him happy." Neither age nor gender prevented Eliza from trying to persuade her brother that a more gentle course than war could better honor God and lead to happiness, a state of mind not always available to her either. Once, after returning home from visiting the Pinckneys, Eliza sent them a letter struck through with what might be called teen angst in the twenty-first century. In melancholy ink she wrote, "At my return hither everything appeared gloomy and lonesome. I began to consider what alteration there was in this place . . . but found the change not in the place but in my self, and it doubt-less proceeded from that giddy gayety and want of reflection which I contracted when in town." Charles Town was exciting and "giddy," but Wappoo Creek was "lonesome." True to her own philosophical nature, Eliza cured the doldrums not with whiskey or distractions; instead, she picked up a volume of the philosopher John Locke's writing and immersed herself "to see wherein personal Identity consisted and if I was the very same self." Her thoughtfulness helps explain why Eliza Lucas did so well at whatever she tried.

The year 1744 marked the next major change in Eliza's life. Her father had recently been named lieutenant governor of Antigua and asked his wife and daughters to move back to be with him in the Bahamas. Eliza was spared the move by an all-too-common colonial tragedy, early death: Charles Pinckney's wife died. Pinckney was the speaker of the Assembly and was now an eligible bachelor. Eliza and Charles's five-year acquaintance made them ideal mates, and they married in 1744. For almost a decade they made a happy life. Two of their three children, Charles Cotesworth Pinckney and Thomas Pinckney, went on to become Patriot leaders during the War of Independence. The third child, Harriott Pinckney, married a wealthy plantation widower named Daniel Horry in 1768 at the age of nineteen. Harriott Horry went on to run the plantation after Daniel's death and write a cookbook that is still in print, primarily for its insights into colonial living. In 1747, the year of her father's death, Eliza's indigo plants began to do very well. In part she accomplished this by giving away seeds to other planters in the area, ensuring that the plant would become vital to their interests as well. Indigo became South Carolina's second-biggest export after rice. Charles Pinckney's political ambitions were thwarted, however. As William Byrd II had learned in Virginia a generation earlier (when he failed to secure a governor's seat), it was nearly impossible for colonists to ascend into the highest government jobs. Executive appointments went almost exclusively to men literally closer to the king, which meant that aspiring and successful colonists were held back from achieving full local authority because of the imperial system itself. Increasingly, governors and elected assemblies disagreed and wrestled over matters of taxation, defense, and the like. In 1753, the Pinckney family boarded a ship for England where Charles, having been removed (against his will) from his brief tenure as chief justice of South Carolina, was to be the new representative of the colony. Now thirty-one years old, Eliza Lucas Pinckney was the mother of three children, the wife of a colonial agent, and an experienced businesswoman.

Her two sons entered English schools, just as Eliza had done, and Charles took on his new responsibilities. Within one year, however, matters once again beyond her control aimed Eliza in a colonial direction. In the 1750s the land known today as Canada was in French hands. Although there were few French settlers there compared to the number of people in the English colonies, the French were influential with Native Americans to the north and west of the English colonies. Powerful confederacies like the Hurons in the north and the Cherokees on the borders of Carolina saw the looming threat in Britain's presence. Every year more slaves and more Europeans arrived. Every year more farmers, slaves, and trappers pushed farther into the interior, competing with Indians for land, hides, and power. Deer hides and beaver fur had been in vogue in Europe. And although fashion is by nature fickle, deer leather maintained its place in the eighteenth-century European fashion market. Large stretches of eastern woodlands and meadows had been transformed into deer graveyards by intensive hunting over the past 100 years. So colonial and Native American hunters and trappers had lately been concentrating their efforts in the vast Ohio Valley, which stretched westward from the Appalachian Mountains to the Mississippi River. The Ohio country was contested ground, and in 1753 the French declared their intention to take control of it, in part by building a line of forts north to south. The French had nearly every Native American tribe and confederacy on their side, except for the Iroquois League of upstate New York, probably the most powerful native league on the entire continent.

Even as Eliza Pinckney wrote from her new home in England to say, "I thank God we have been all perfectly well . . . the children have not had even a common cold," the continent of North America moved toward war. In late 1753, an up-and-coming Virginia plantation owner and militia officer, George Washington, rode west to parlay with a French commander, insisting that the French leave the Ohio country immediately. Washington returned to Virginia and informed Governor Robert Dinwiddie that the French were well positioned and meant to stay. In 1754, Washington returned to the Ohio country with a group of militiamen and proceeded to unintentionally spark the French and Indian War by twice clashing with French troops. Although captured in the second encounter, Washington was allowed to return to Virginia, after which he distinguished himself as a colonial officer, displaying a special talent for leading successful retreats. In 1756, the war took on global proportions when France and Britain formally declared war on each other and fought sea and land battles from India to Europe to North America. Fighting lasted just long enough that the struggle became known as the Seven Years' War. In North America, the French and their Indian allies were defeated, and the consequences were momentous. With the exception of a few islands and New Orleans, all of France's colonial territories in North America were transferred to British hands, as was Florida, which had been controlled by Spain. Great Britain claimed North America from the Atlantic to the Mississippi.

In the process of orchestrating its victory, Great Britain had sown the seeds of its own demise in North America. In 1754, representatives from seven colonies and the Iroquois League met in Albany, New York, to discuss exactly how they should repel the French threat. Benjamin Franklin presented a plan for unity, a kind of colonial congress. Although the plan got rejected by almost everyone other than the Albany delegates, this was the first suggestion that the colonies could band together as one. Furthermore, fighting a world war against the French proved more costly than any campaign Britain had ever undertaken. A particularly shrewd politician, William Pitt, convinced king and Parliament to go further into debt to fund the war. The extra money made the difference, but it left Britain's coffers empty. And with new territory came new headaches that British officials would deal with during the next twenty years: paying off the debt, keeping colonists from intruding into Native American lands, protecting the expanded empire, and ultimately dealing with unruly colonists who had developed a taste for governing and taxing themselves. While in England, Charles Pinckney had felt the sting of worrying about his own property, and in 1757 he decided to return to South Carolina to take care of affairs there, right during the heart of the war.

In February 1757, Eliza told a correspondent "upon our continual alarms from abroad Mr. Pinckney came to a resolution to return to Carolina for two Year." With the two sons remaining behind to complete their educations, Eliza, her daughter Harriott, and her husband went back to Charles Town in 1758 so that he could sell most of their plantations, which were under threat. Their boat sailed into Charles Town's harbor in May, and Charles Pinckney died of malaria only a few weeks later. Eliza's first letter in months broke the news of Charles's death to the children. "How shall I write to you! What shall I say to you! My dear, my ever dear Children! But if possible more so now than Ever, for I have a tale to tell you that will pierce your tender infant hearts! You have mett with the greatest loss, my children, you could meet with upon Earth! Your dear, dear father, the best and most valueable of parents, is no more!" Taking solace in her husband's stoic end—"He met the king of terrors without the least terror or affright"—Eliza Pinckney hoped she would meet him "in Glory never never more to be separated." In the meantime, planet Earth held firm under her feet, and Eliza returned to the duties of hearth, home, plantation, and business.

Eliza Lucas Pinckney lived until 1793, long enough to suffer through the Revolution, to read her son Charles's name etched into the Constitution as one of its signatories, to take pride in South Carolina's one-term governor, Thomas Pinckney, and to live out the last eight years of her life with the widowed Harriott. Eliza died in 1793 in Philadelphia, where she had gone to seek a cure for cancer. Her two sons were better known to contemporary Americans than she was, but her surviving letters, her introduction of indigo agriculture, and her outstanding qualities have endeared her to history. The local newspaper of Charleston (as Charles Town was renamed in 1783) knew what to say about the pleasure of spending time with Eliza Lucas Pinckney: "Her understanding, aided by an uncommon strength of memory, had been so highly cultivated and improved by travel and extensive reading, and was so richly furnished, as well with scientific, as practical knowledge, that her talent for conversation was unrivalled." Those who knew her held her in the "highest veneration and respect."[12]

Changing Identities

When the French and Indian War ended in 1763, colonial America was prosperous. The very prosperity of society made America diverse in culture and diverse in ethnicity. Some people came for opportunity. Other people were forced to immigrate. By 1710 in South Carolina, there were more black slaves than free white people.[13] Black outnumbered white, but white owned black. Ownership, however, was a relative truth. In 1739, just south of Eliza Lucas's property, nearly one hundred slaves fought valiantly for their freedom in a brief insurrection called the Stono Rebellion. White militias killed and captured the freedom fighters, though a few made it to Spanish Florida. Their aggressive resistance to owners' power was not unusual, but it did lead to more punitive and restrictive slave laws. Black American slaves struggled to loosen their bonds, and white American slave owners responded by tightening the bonds. Slave and master lived right next door. Slave quarters were never far from the plantation's big house, and in cities like Charles Town, domestic slaves had huts in the back yard of their owner's brick mansions. White families waited impatiently at dinner tables for black slaves to deliver platters of food from kitchens typically separated from the house. Blacks and whites lived in each other's shadow and probably spoke *to* each other as often as they spoke *around* each other. England owned North America, but English was only one out of many languages to be heard from Georgia to New England. The slave dialect Gullah emerged as a fusion of West African languages, Caribbean Creole, and English. Meanwhile, Arabic, Germanic, Irish Gaelic, and Hebraic dialects were spoken up and down the coast, along with Algonquian and Iroquoian derivatives. But by 1730, the Indian population south of Virginia dipped below the combined numbers of black and white colonists.

Because of disease and war, Native American coastal populations were small but remained vibrant. The overall Native American population in the South declined from perhaps 200,000 in 1685 to about 65,000 in 1730, nearly all from disease epidemics. Peoples like the Cherokees and the Creeks had fought against British America during the French and Indian War, and though they lost, they were not defeated. But Native Americans had become relatively dependent on trade goods by the mid-1700s. Guns were necessary for hunting and war; cloth and wool had largely replaced animal hides. Native women, who had once farmed and enjoyed political status and power, increasingly lived like white women: keeping to the home and staying out of the fields. Colonial men, long uncomfortable with women who lived like men, had tried for generations to alter Native American societies to resemble colonial societies, in religion, gender roles, language, dress, and mannerisms.

For nearly 200 years, natives and newcomers had done a variety of dances together, delicate and indelicate. Existing societies ended and adapted, and new societies formed. While old struggles between native and newcomer would continue on into the 1800s, the years from 1763 to 1775 tested colonial America in a way previously impossible. Great Britain now ruled a large part of the continent from Canada to Florida. Just as colonists' slaves worked hard to be free, the colonists themselves gradually sensed that their own liberties were endangered by the same imperial system that had recently given them so much security.

Notes

1. John Spencer Bassett, ed., *The Writings of Colonel William Byrd of Westover, Esq* (New York: Doubleday, 1901), 144.

2. Bassett, ed., *The Writings of Colonel William Byrd*, 143.

3. Bassett, ed., *The Writings of Colonel William Byrd*, 709.

4. Jonathan Edwards, *A Narrative of Many Surprising Conversions in Northampton and Vicinity* (Worcester, MA: Moses W. Grout, 1832), 22–23.

5. Charles Chauncy, "A Letter from a Gentleman in Boston, to Mr. George Wishart, One of the Ministers of Edinburgh, Concerning the State of Religion in New-England" in Richard L. Bushman, ed., *The Great Awakening: Documents on the Revival of Religion, 1740–1745* (Chapel Hill: University of North Carolina Press, 1969), 116–119.

6. Charles W. Eliot, ed., *The Autobiography of Benjamin Franklin* (New York: Collier, 1909), 105.

7. For a fuller examination of the Anglican religion in colonial Virginia, see John K. Nelson, *A Blessed Company: Parishes, Parsons, and Parishioners in Anglican Virginia, 1690–1776* (Chapel Hill: University of North Carolina Press, 2001).

8. Albert Henry Smyth, ed., *The Writings of Benjamin Franklin Volume II, 1722–1750* (New York: Macmillan, 1905), 92–94.

9. Eliot, ed., *The Autobiography of Benjamin Franklin*, 36.

10. Edmund S. Morgan, ed., *Not Your Usual Founding Father: Selected Readings from Benjamin Franklin* (New Haven, CT: Yale University Press, 2006), 52–53.

11. Letter and diary quotations can be found in both Harriott Horry Ravenel, *Eliza Pinckney* (New York: Charles Scribner's Sons, 1896) and Elise Pinckney, ed., *The Letterbook of Eliza Lucas Pinckney, 1739–1762* (University of South Carolina Press, 1997).

12. Elise Pinckney, ed., *The Letterbook of Eliza Lucas Pinckney*, xxv–xxvi.

13. Peter H. Wood, *Black Majority: Negroes in Colonial South Carolina from 1670 Through the Stono Rebellion* (New York: W.W. Norton, 1996), 131.

4

The Coming of the Revolution

Abigail Adams *(MPI/Getty Images)*

On the Road to Revolutions

The colonial world was largely provincial. Most people were farmers, and few traveled more than twenty miles from their homes in the whole course of their lives. People were typically committed to family, church, and visible community. Yet trade, ideas, religion, war, and the occasional wanderer also linked settlers across the lines that separated the colonies. Lately it had been war, but the French were now defeated and Great Britain was the victor, so most displaced people and militiamen returned to their hometowns or struggled westward, looking for new lands and opportunities.

Therefore, to understand how America's colonists came to the point of revolt, we have to understand not only why discontent became so palpable, but also how a sense of unity developed among the colonies—in fact, how a sense of confederation was born.

In 1765 delegates from different colonies met for the Stamp Act Congress, the first time that the colonies got together in opposition to something Britain had done. In September 1774, fifty-six delegates met as the First Continental Congress in Philadelphia to declare their opposition to Britain's tax policies. They recessed and then reincarnated as the Second Continental Congress in May 1775. Most of the representatives were not at first ready to separate from Britain. They simply wanted their fears addressed and allayed. Colonial delegates took more than a full year after the shots were fired at Lexington and Concord in April 1775 to agree upon the Declaration of Independence. The publication of this document was the pivotal moment, an irrevocable step into the unknown.

Once the delegates signed the Declaration on August 2, 1776, they became, as far as Britain was concerned, outright traitors. They had sealed their names to the future. Henry Laurens from South Carolina, John Adams from Massachusetts, and Benjamin Rush from Pennsylvania were the rebel leaders. Behind them, however, were the mass of citizens, the farm families, the blacksmiths and seamstresses, the thinkers and writers who supported the rebellion. Without the genuine interest of most of the colonists, the leaders would have had no one to lead.

About one-fifth of the population of Britain's North American colonies was enslaved. African-Americans did not write newspaper editorials, deliver thundering orations in the brick-clad assembly halls of the South, or elect anybody to the Continental Congress, but they did sometimes write petitions to local assemblies requesting freedom. The slaves expressed their revolutionary ideology in the tracks their feet left on the way to join the British and Continental armies—both armies promised freedom to slaves who joined their ranks—and in the few petitions that have survived. The many advertisements offering rewards for the return of runaways were a sure sign that these women and men knew what freedom meant and were willing to make their own declarations of independence by leaping over plantation boundaries and giving liberty a running chance.

Abigail Adams

To know Abigail Adams is to know how America became independent. Born the daughter of a New England Congregational minister, Abigail grew up in a family with a history of service to the community. Dedicated to the duties of hearth and home, she was a loyal British subject who became an advocate of American independence at the same time that she began arguing for a larger share of equality for women. Abigail supported the efforts of her husband, John Adams, to establish a new American government, one that was less revolutionary than she would have preferred. The words and deeds of Abigail Adams—ardent patriot, loyal helpmate, and tireless contributor to the cause of separation—represent women's contributions to the formation of a new nation. Without her and her American sisters, there would be no United States.

Abigail was born in 1744 in Weymouth, a few miles south of Boston, the boisterous, teeming market of Massachusetts. A somewhat sickly child, she received an education at home. The women in her family were strong and more independent than was common, and these traits became evident in Abigail even at a young age. She spoke her mind. At the age of nineteen, during their courtship, she needled John Adams with the following tease: "You was pleas'd to say that the receipt of a letter from [me] always gave you pleasure. Whether this was designed for a complement (a commodity I acknowledge that you very seldom deal in) or as a real truth, you best know."[1]

In 1759, Abigail Smith had met John Adams, a young, Harvard-educated lawyer whose services her father requested. Within two years, by the time Abigail was seventeen, the two were courting, and because they lived a few miles apart, they had to write letters, many of which have survived. They continued to correspond even after they married in 1764 because John rode the court circuit, going as far as Maine to represent his clients' interests. The future for Abigail and John looked bright and free of troubles. John was a well-reputed lawyer, and they had expanded the size of their farm. On July 14, 1765, after their first child was born, Abigail wrote to her friend Hannah Green that the Adamses were "Bless'd with a charming Girl whose pretty Smiles already delight my Heart, who is the Dear Image of her still Dearer Pappa." In the four years of correspondence prior to this letter, Abigail mentioned never a word about empire or political liberty. John's and Abigail's early letters to each other and to their acquaintances reflect a stable world and an interest in friends, family, and local matters. The Stamp Act changed all that.

Starting in 1765, John became immersed in the colonists' protests against British laws and policies. Later in his life, John Adams said that the real revolution took place before any bullets flew, that the "change in the principles, opinions, sentiments, and affections of the people was the real American Revolution."[2] Abigail's letters reveal this crucial change. Her developing attachment to the cause of America appears in the surviving letters she wrote to John, to her friend Mercy Otis Warren (an author who was the wife and the sister of other luminous Patriots), and to other relatives and friends.

At the end of the Seven Years' War in 1763, Britain had decided that the business of running colonies was costing enough that the colonists themselves ought to help pay the war debt. In March 1765, therefore, Parliament passed a tax—the Stamp Act—on certain paper products, like mortgages, deeds, playing cards, and almanacs, items used by a wide variety of colonists, especially educated colonists. The colonists were not happy about this tax, and at town hall meetings, during sessions of legislatures, and in broadsides and pamphlets they expressed their opposition.

Although none of John's or Abigail's letters from 1765 still exist, historians have unearthed newspapers and other publications that flooded the colonies from Georgia (the only colony to obey the Stamp Act) to New Hampshire. Besides reading such accounts, Abigail probably had other, firsthand sources of information as well. James Otis (brother of Mercy) and Samuel Adams (John's cousin) were instrumental in creating the Sons of Liberty in 1765 and the local committee of correspondence in 1772. The Sons of Liberty organized protests against the Stamp Act, including an attack on Andrew Oliver, who was nominated an agent of the British government—to sell the offensive stamps—without his own knowledge or consent. Oliver's house was pelted with stones and his effigy was publicly burned, leading him to quit the job before it ever began. James Otis proposed, in the Massachusetts Assembly, that a group of representatives from the thirteen colonies should meet in New York to decide upon collective agreement and action against the tax. At this Stamp Act Congress, the delegates resolved that only elected bodies could tax the colonists and that Parliament was not such a body for them. These colonists were beginning to conceive of themselves as distinctly American.

These events in far-off New York were matched locally when in the same month, October 1765, John Adams wrote a document for his hometown of Braintree that declared taxation without representation unjustifiable and unconstitutional according to the traditional British system. The document was soon adopted by forty other towns throughout Massachusetts. John had made his entrance into the debates, and Abigail went along with him. Although Parliament rescinded the stamp tax in 1766, at the same time Parliament declared its absolute legislative authority over the entire British Empire in all matters.

This claim, the Declaratory Act, aroused little ire in the colonies at the time, but it established the basis for the unstable relationship between Britain and America that would continue for the next eight years. And now Americans had developed a willingness to work together. Opposition was giving them something in common.

In July 1766, Abigail was still writing of domestic affairs, declaring that she would not follow her sister Mary's "practise of rising by 4 oclock. It does not agree with my inclination to Laziness." In October, she wrote again to Mary, announcing, "We do pretty much as We used to of old. Marry and give in Marriage, encrease and multiply all in the old fashiond way. . . . My Good Man is so very fat that I am lean as a rale." Abigail took pride in John's fame and the attention he gained from participating in the protests against the Stamp Act, and now she could laugh at his paunch. Life resembled its old patterns. Once again, however, events outside of Braintree would pull the Adams family into what were to become national concerns.

In 1768, the Adams family moved to Boston, where John was doing the bulk of his law practice with the General Court. Soon after their move, a detachment of British soldiers landed, and during the following three years Abigail developed a dislike for the British Empire. The soldiers turned the Commons into a rowdy camp where troops marched and drilled. The soldiers were not paid much, so they took local jobs in their off-hours, which did not please the city's working poor. Fights often broke out between the British soldiers and the citizens of Boston.

Compounding this animosity, in 1767 a new Parliamentary law, the Townshend Acts, imposed a set of taxes on many items, including tea. The already organized colonies passed nonimportation agreements to boycott British manufactures. Without full cooperation from colonial women, who managed the household economy, this boycott would not have worked. Men wrote the political treatises in opposition to the Townshend duties, but women did much of the labor, making many of the goods that were no longer being purchased from Britain. For example, they spun wool and distributed it to the needy. The boycott eventually succeeded in getting all the duties removed except for the one on tea.

By January 1770, Abigail would write to a cousin, Isaac, "When you left us, you did not tell me, nor did I know till a few days agone, that you designd a visit to our (cruel) Mother Country, shall I say." Her labeling of Britain as "cruel" spells out the first bitter word she was to use for her "Mother Country." In 1771 Isaac wrote back to the Adamses, "Capt. Preston will be reimbursed in the expences of his prosecution and meet with some further compensation for his confinement." This Captain Preston stood in the middle, literally, of the next problem between Britain and Boston.

On the evening of March 5, 1770, Boston locals had clashed with a few British soldiers led by Preston. As one participant, George Robert Twelves Hewes (a shoemaker), remembered it, a British officer had refused to pay a barber for a shave. Later that evening, a restless crowd gathered around the house where the officer was staying. A British sentinel refused to let the barber's message boy talk to the stingy officer to demand payment for the shave. The crowd became angry. Captain Preston arrived. Next, according to Hewes, "The captain of the guard then said to [the crowd], if you do not disperse, I will fire upon you, and then gave orders to his men to make ready, and immediately after gave them orders to fire. Three of our citizens fell dead on the spot . . . and two, who were wounded, died the next day; and nine others were also wounded."[3] This event became known as the Boston Massacre. An engraver and silversmith named Paul Revere soon designed (or possibly plagiarized) a drawing of the event. Revere's picture shows British soldiers standing in a neat line firing into a confused crowd, many with their backs turned toward the British redcoats. The image was intentionally deceiving, a bit of propaganda. The soldiers look like they had a plan, and the Bostonians look entirely like victims, not at all like an angry crowd who had initially surrounded a lone sentry.

Although John Adams opposed many imperial policies, he soon took on the defense of the British soldiers who were accused of murder. John Adams believed in the rule of English law and wanted the colonies to seem like law-abiding, orderly communities. John got the British soldiers and Captain Preston acquitted, and his reputation actually improved. In fact, he was elected to the General Court. The people of Massachusetts appreciated his values. In a letter to Isaac in 1771, John laughed, "if C. Preston is to be reimbursed his Expences, I wish his Expences, at least to [me] had been greater." While he could joke about being an underpaid lawyer, John Adams recognized the seriousness of his choices. In a diary entry, he described his perception of Abigail's feelings when she learned that he would join the court and defend Preston. "That excellent Lady," John wrote, "who has always encouraged me, burst into a flood of Tears, but said she was very sensible of all the Danger to her and to our Children as well as to me, but she thought I had done as I ought, she was very willing to share in all that was to come and place her trust in Providence."[4] The labors of John Adams were also the labors of Abigail Adams. Not only did she support him emotionally, but also she ended up with four children to raise, a household to run, and finances to manage during his increasing absences from home.

By April 1771, Abigail was back in Braintree, soon to be followed for a short while by her husband. She informed Isaac that since "Infancy" she had wanted to visit England, but due to its "unnatural treatment" of the colonies, her desire was diminished. As well, she knew that women were "considered as Domestick Beings" and that married women "have generally speaking obstacles sufficent to prevent their Roving." While her husband and Isaac traveled, she never went more than a few miles from home, having plenty of "obstacles" to keep her there. By 1772, John would tell Abigail, "This wandering, [itinerating] Life grows more and more disagreeable to me. I want to see my Wife and Children every Day, I want to see my Grass and Blossoms and Corn." Yet belief in their natural rights and liberties meant that both Abigail and John would continue to make sacrifices, she by staying home, he by leaving home.

The political heat in America rose and fell from 1765 to 1775, and in public very few colonists advocated full independence until 1776. For ten years, most colonists tried to get Parliament and the king to recognize the difference between the right to regulate trade—which the colonials readily granted to Parliament—and the right to impose taxes, which many colonials believed was the responsibility of their locally elected legislators. After the Boston Massacre, peace and union seemed possible for a time, but once again, the logic of empire as reasoned in pounds sterling and pounds of tea would come to outweigh any good sense Britain's lords might have had. In this mercantilist economy, Britain wanted its colonies to buy items like tea and molasses only from registered British ships and merchants. The East India Company had loads of tea in its warehouses and no one to buy it. So Parliament and the East India Company shipped the surplus tea to American colonists, who realized they could just as easily drink coffee as tea. In late December 1773, some colonists decided that since they were not drinking the tea, it might do better at the bottom of the ocean than sitting on British ships in Boston's harbor.

Samuel Adams, son of a brewer and the leading force to remove British troops from Boston, is credited with dreaming up the Boston Tea Party as a protest against Parliament's choice to force colonists to buy the East India Company's taxed tea. Three teams of men dressed like Mohawk Indians silently boarded three British ships, carefully opened hundreds of crates of tea, dumped the tea leaves into the water, and claimed the act in the name of the Sons of Liberty. Crowds of happy Bostonians watched from the pier. When one of the faux Indians tried to cram some tea into his pockets, his friends stripped him naked and sent him home through the winter streets in shivering shame. The tea party took place on December 16, 1773. However, more than a week earlier, on December 5, Abigail had written to her friend Mercy Warren to say, "the Tea that bainfull weed is arrived. Great and I hope Effectual opposition has been made to the landing of it . . . The proceedings of our Citizens have been United, Spirited and firm. The flame is kindled and like Lightning it catches from Soul to Soul. Great will be the devastation if not timely quenched or allayed by some more Lenient Measures." It is unlikely that Abigail knew of her cousin-in-law Sam's plan for the tea, but she knew people's feelings well enough to generally predict what would happen. Abigail's own rebellious sentiments were hardening. She closed that same letter by referring to the role of slave master that she saw Britain adopting for itself. "There was a Report prevaild that to morrow there will be an attempt to Land this weed of Slavery." While her mind was "shocked at the Thought of sheding Humane Blood," Abigail believed that if a "civil War" occurred, "very Many of our Heroes will spend their lives in the cause." In her mind, the protest against the tax on the tea would be the act of "Heroes."

The colonists expected Parliament to respond harshly, and it did with the Coercive Acts, known as the Intolerable Acts in the colonies. Bostonians would have to repay the value of the tea or have their port closed indefinitely. The seat of government was moved to Salem, and the royal governor was replaced by General Thomas Gage. Martial law was established. Worse yet, the Quebec Act expanded the boundaries of Canada into the Ohio Valley, essentially cutting off the hopes of American land speculators. Besides, Quebec was Catholic, and the colonies were mostly Protestant. As historian Pauline Maier has said, "The American independence movement grew in part from suspicions that official British 'softness' on Catholicism signaled the decay of English freedom."[5] During this year of 1774, Abigail Adams resolved on independence for her country, in February telling her friend Mercy, "What a pity it is that so much of that same Spirit which prompted Satan to a revolt in heaven should possess the Sons of men and eradicate every principal of Humanity and Benevolence." In Abigail's mind, Britain had become possessed by the "same Spirit which prompted Satan."

In June 1774, John Adams galloped off to the Continental Congress, set to convene in Philadelphia. On his way, he stopped in New York City and informed Abigail by letter, "I find more Persons here, who call the Destruction of the Tea, Mischief and Wickedness, than any where else. More Persons who say that the Duty upon Tea is not a Tax, nor an Imposition because we are at Liberty to use it or not." New York would become known in ensuing years as the seat of Loyalist sympathy in America, a sentiment John noticed. On July 1, he wrote to say, "I must intreat you, my dear Partner in all the Joys and Sorrows, Prosperity and Adversity of my Life, to take a Part with me in the Struggle," and indeed she would—though at a distance. Abigail rarely saw John for the next ten years. He was a member of the First and Second Continental Congresses, in far-off Philadelphia, and he twice went to Europe: as an ambassador to France and then to Britain. As Abigail would frequently say, "We have had but little of his company he has been so much engaged in the affairs of the State." She herself was also engaged in the affairs of state, but from the vantage of home where she and her Patriot sisters raised the first generation of republican Americans. Abigail's eldest son, John Quincy, became the sixth president of the United States, following his father, who became the second.

American women warmed to the spirit of rebellion alongside their men, equally determined to protect their "natural" liberties and rights. Though John Adams has gone down in history as one of America's premier political theorists, Abigail's was just as intelligent and independent a mind as his. As the Congress deliberated during the autumn of 1774, Abigail informed John of the events in Braintree and Boston that he was missing, and she understood the elements of strategy. "Indeed," she wrote, the residents of Boston "have not the advantages, nor the resolution to encourage our own Manufactories which people in the country have. . . . As for me I will seek wool and flax and work willingly with my Hands." These, then, were women's contributions to disunion: debating the finer points of theory with husbands and friends, expressing indignation and anger at Parliament's decisions, supporting the activities of liberty, and working willingly with their hands. Women were equal players in the Revolutionary struggle of the 1770s, and as John drafted the new documents of government, Abigail told him in March 1776 to "remember the Ladies" because she knew that "all men would be tyrants if they could." A revolution for home rule, for a time, still left men ruling at home.

The Declaration of Independence

On June 28, 1776, at the Pennsylvania State House in Philadelphia, about fifty wig-wearing men from the colonies gathered in yet another secret session of the Second Continental Congress. The colonies had been at war for more than a year without ever having declared independence. Up to this point, they had been fighting to force King George III and Parliament to respect the traditional rights and liberties of his British colonists. A committee of five colonists was now ready to present a written declaration to the entire assembled Congress. The other delegates, well-dressed men betting their lives on this document, were prepared to debate and edit the words of liberty and independence. Words were their weapons, along with other men's bodies and the faint hope that France and Spain might join in the fight.

The finished Declaration of Independence, soon to be written on a piece of parchment made of animal skins, had been drafted primarily by Thomas Jefferson. Benjamin Franklin, America's favorite celebrity and one of the only men in America with an international reputation, was supposed to have worked on the first draft, but he had retired to a nearby house in order to recuperate from a painful attack of gout, so he had sent only last-minute editorial suggestions. Short, stocky John Adams, a forceful public speaker and perhaps the greatest advocate for independence in the Congress, was also on the drafting committee. But for two reasons Adams had deferred to the shy yet fame-driven Jefferson: Jefferson was a Virginian—the support of the South was needed, and Jefferson was better with words on the page. So Jefferson, who suffered from crippling headaches throughout his years in public office (the headaches stopped as soon as he retired), had done most of the writing, often sitting in bed to compose the Declaration on a wooden lap desk of his design. In the spacious second floor of a brick mason's three-story house on a Philadelphia street corner, Jefferson's servants and slaves brought him what food or drink he needed while he worked.

The Congress kept no official record of its debates. Modern historians have tried to reconstruct them based on a few diary entries made by members and their subsequent recollections, along with some notes Jefferson apparently jotted down at the time. Figuring out what happened—who said what—is guesswork held together by journal fragments, memoirs, letters home, and hearsay. On June 28, someone read the Declaration aloud to the assembled delegates, pausing for effect throughout the reading, turning it into a kind of one-man theater performance, as was the style of the day.[6] These were some of America's brightest and best-trained scholars, and they knew the power of ceremony.

In a letter to Abigail, John Adams called July 2, 1776, the "most memorable Epocha, in the History of America." He was off by two days. The Congress did vote for independence on July 2, but the delegates wanted more time to play with the language in Jefferson's draft document. Then, on July 4, the assembled delegates voted almost unanimously to adopt the Declaration and have it printed throughout the colonies, where it was to be read to local assemblies, to the armies, and wherever people congregated. The decision to create a sovereign nation, to finally proclaim what had already been made obvious by armed conflict, had not been easily arrived at. The delegates to the Continental Congress were Englishmen who until recently had meant to remain that way. A few things changed their minds.

On May 15, Virginia's convention in Williamsburg had voted that "the Delegates appointed to represent this Colony in General Congress be instructed to propose to that respectable body to declare the United Colonies free and independent States." Virginia's instructions to its delegates in the Congress set in motion the train of recommendations and debates that led to the decision of July 4. But why had Virginians wanted to gain independence from Britain? They were far away from the troubles in Boston, and as in all of the thirteen colonies, the standard of living of the average white person in Virginia was actually better than the standard of living for the average person in Britain. The king's subjects in the colonies had been steadily and effectively working to improve the physical quality of life, so why revolt?

The delegates to the First Continental Congress had met briefly, late in 1774, to express their desire to be treated properly "as Englishmen," to enact a nonimportation agreement, and to maintain their rights to "life, liberty, and property." Then they had disbanded and gone home. Their promise to meet again early in 1775 had gotten an unexpected jolt from battles at Lexington and Concord in Massachusetts on April 19. Ever since 1774, New England farmers had been gathering by the hundreds, and even thousands, to take matters into their own hands when their friends faced imprisonment for debt or unpaid taxes. With muskets in hand, they would surround incoming royal-appointed judges and prevent them from opening court sessions, sometimes going so far as to make them sign letters of resignation on the spot.[7] From the perspective of General Thomas Gage in Boston, the country farmers had gone crazy and dangerous. He wanted to take away their guns, and he sent a column of troops northward to confiscate ammunition. On the morning of April 19, 1775, these troops of British regulars had apparently fired first on local militiamen assembled in Lexington's town square, a "battle" to be followed later in the day by a clash at Concord. In the late afternoon, taking cover behind trees and sturdy New England stone walls, farmers-turned-fighters shot at the redcoats as they scrambled back to Boston, wounded and exhausted. Local militias then surrounded the town and kept the redcoats penned in. These first musket balls of the war proved to the congressional delegates that the British would kill to keep their empire and that the citizens of the colonies would fight back.

In a way, as many people at the time said, Britain itself kept pushing the colonists toward revolution. Although the Continental Congress became the presiding voice of the colonies when it took charge of the militia army arrayed outside Boston, the delegates still meant to remain loyal to King George of Britain. They sent him an "Olive Branch Petition" during the summer of 1775. The king would not even look at it. Between the king stating in October that the colonists were in open rebellion that had to be suppressed with force and the royal governor of Virginia, Lord Dunmore, offering freedom to any black slaves who would fight for England, neither the king nor his representatives were doing anything to make it easy for the colonists to stay loyal.

Every month, some new grievance enraged colonial assemblies and caused them to protest Britain's rule. According to the Quebec Act of 1774, the border of Quebec was extended south to the Ohio River, introducing into the region thousands of formerly French Roman Catholics, committed to what the Protestant colonists considered blind obedience to the pope.

Thousands of British troops were quartered in the colonies to keep the colonists from exercising their rights as English-born citizens to protest taxes they had not agreed to. And now black slaves (property!) were being invited to run away from their masters and help the British oppressors enforce their tyranny. Britain's grievous excesses in Massachusetts were only an example of what other colonies thought they could expect. Britain itself was uniting the colonies, exactly the opposite of what the king and Parliament wanted.

Still, despite all that provocation, most of the delegates in Philadelphia had explicit instructions from their colonial governments *not* to vote for anything that smacked of independence. Then Tom Paine wrote *Common Sense*.

Thomas Paine was born in 1737 in a small English city. He got seven years of schooling, learned the trade of making hoops out of whalebone for corsets, and for a time held a minor position as a tax collector. He wrote a single political pamphlet, to which few paid attention. Paine also met Benjamin Franklin, who was serving as a colonial agent for a number of colonies in England. The two men shared an interest in natural philosophy (science). Still, this was not exactly the young adulthood out of which great statesmen were made—except in America, which is where Paine headed in 1774 after both his second divorce and the loss of his job as a tax collector. His thirty-seven years in England had nurtured an awareness that the common people had a hard time moving up in the world.

According to historian Eric Foner's description, "The Philadelphia where Paine arrived in the fall of 1774 was 'the capital of the new world.' With a population of some 30,000, it was the largest city in English America . . . tiny by modern standards—it covered an area of less than one square mile."[8] The city bustled with industry on a colonial scale. Mechanics, artisans, and merchants filled the warehouses, wharves, and shop stalls with every kind of goods and services to be found in British America. From hatmakers to shoemakers, from brewers to carpenters (who made the round-backed, spindled Windsor chairs that the members of the Congress sat on), all manner of craftsmen toiled with iron and wooden tools in the natural light that filtered through the English-made panes of glass in their shops. These were an educated and political lot. They employed apprentices, slaves, and indentured servants (probably half the workforce) and could therefore see the difference between their servants' and slaves' lack of freedom and their own liberty. New British taxes and royal courts set up to enforce those taxes made a deep impression on colonial merchants and artisans. They did not want to become tax slaves. Commerce was their livelihood and in many ways the political spark that seized their attention. Many merchants and artisans were displeased with Parliament, its taxes on their property, and the suppression of their liberty that these taxes insinuated. But what did they think of the king, the symbol of the empire? A majority of colonists seem to have stayed loyal to the king until some time in early 1776.

Thomas Paine fit right into the rowdy, articulate citizenry of Philadelphia. He was an artisan, a skilled worker. His mind raced with politics, and he was developing ideas of his own about the king. Paine spoke the dialect of his age, the language of the people, in a way that compelled others not only to listen, but also to act. He stepped off a ship's deck in late November 1774 with a letter of introduction from Ben Franklin, the favorite man of Philadelphia's working class, and went to work as a newspaper editor, the perfect platform for his emerging talents.

A full year passed, during which Paine met the leaders of the Continental Congress. At the end of 1775, Dr. Benjamin Rush, a member of the Congress, asked Paine to write a pamphlet about the American crisis. From corsetmaker to tax collector to editor, Paine had tried his hand at three skills. Now he would change how colonists felt about the king. On January 9, 1776, his *Common Sense* was published, and it set the rebellion on fire with republican flames. Paine wrote, "The cause of America is in a great measure the cause of all mankind." In passage after passage, Paine took aim at the idea of monarchy and blasted it to pieces. "A thirst for absolute power is the natural disease of monarchy," he wrote; "of more worth is one honest man to society, and in the sight of God, than all the crowned ruffians that ever lived." Paine concluded his booklet saying; "Nothing can settle our affairs so expeditiously as an open, and determined declaration for independence."[9] Six months later, the colonists' affairs were settled exactly that way.

It has been estimated that enough copies of *Common Sense* were sold throughout the colonies (at least 150,000) so that every literate man and woman could have read it. Although the pamphlet's popularity did not entirely please men like John Adams, who thought Paine's language "flowing from simple Ignorance, and a mere desire to please the democratic Party in Philadelphia,"[10] others recognized the value of Paine's contribution. On April 1, 1776, George Washington wrote to Joseph Reed of Pennsylvania, "My countrymen I know, from their form of government, and steady attachment heretofore to royalty, will come reluctantly into the idea of independence, but time and persecution bring many wonderful things to pass; and by private letters, which I have lately received from Virginia, I find 'Common Sense' is working a powerful change there in the minds of many men."[11]

Early in 1776, men met in taverns, coffeehouses, churches, and syna-gogues to talk about the affairs that engulfed the colonies. Women met and talked at spinning bees and at birthings. In the evenings, husbands and wives conversed with each other. Paine's words were on their lips, and warfare was coming closer to more peoples' homes. The British troops evacuated Boston in March 1776 and sailed to Canada. In Virginia, the combined forces of Loyalists, British regulars, and escaped slaves under Lord Dunmore's command bombarded towns and skirmished with colonial militia. In June, the Continental Congress received word that a Patriot attack on Quebec, led in part by Benedict Arnold, had turned into a fiasco, with most of the American troops killed, captured, or in flight.

So by June 1776, with the Congress receiving regular dispatches about all these conflicts, its members wanted to take bolder measures to make the cause clear and worth the sacrifices being suffered. But the assemblies of New York, New Jersey, Pennsylvania, Delaware, South Carolina, and Maryland had not assented to a declaration of independence. In early June 1776, the Congress had to wait for everyone to agree. Then Jefferson began to write. From late June through July 4, his draft was debated and a few changes were made. The most notable, perhaps, was the deletion of a passage referring directly to the "execrable commerce" of slavery. The Congress scratched out, "he [the king] has waged cruel war against human nature itself, violating its most sacred rights of life & liberty in the persons of a distant people [Africans], who never offended him, captivating and carrying them into slavery in another hemisphere, or to incur miserable death in their transportation thither." No one now knows exactly which delegates insisted on removing that passage, but according to Jefferson, the "clause . . . reprobating the enslaving the inhabitants of Africa, was struck out in complaisance to South Carolina and Georgia, who had never attempted to restrain the importation of slaves, and who on the contrary still wished to continue it. Our northern brethren also I believe felt a little tender under those censures; for tho' their people have very few slaves themselves yet they had been pretty considerable carriers of them to others."[12] With these concessions to slaveholders and slave traders and a few other phrases omitted or reworded for elegance, the delegates voted to adopt the Declaration of Independence on July 4.

On that same day, John Dunlap, a local printer, produced the first broadsides of the Declaration, some of which were shipped to state assemblies. One ended up in George Washington's hands. Twenty-four of these original printings still exist. By July 6, a copy of the Declaration appeared in the *Pennsylvania Gazette*, and over the next few weeks, newspapers throughout the states printed it, though not always on page one.

The residents of New York City heard the Declaration of Independence read out loud by brigade commanders of the Continental Army on July 9, 1776. The *Pennsylvania Journal* reported that the reading "was received everywhere with loud huzzas, and the utmost demonstrations of joy." The happy

"Sons of Freedom" wanted to do more than cheer, so they yanked down a giant statue of King George III sitting pompously astride a horse and left it "prostrate in the dirt—the just desert of an ungrateful tyrant!" Better yet, the *Journal* explained, "the lead wherewith the monument was made is to be run into bullets, to assimilate with the brains of our infatuated adversaries, who, to gain a pepper-corn have lost an empire."[13]

Life, Liberty, and the Pursuit of Happiness

Historian David McCullough writes about an incident when John Adams was gone from home and Abigail Adams was left to supervise the farm, raise the children, and deal with community matters as she saw fit. It came to her attention that local white people were unhappy to discover their children were attending school with a young black boy named James Prince who worked for her. Abigail chided the parents and children and quickly got them to relent. James Prince stayed in the school, and the disgruntled whites stayed quiet. This deft maneuvering came from the same woman who told her husband to "remember the Ladies" while drafting the nation's founding documents. The congressional delegates, however, chose to remember neither the ladies nor the black people of the United States of America.

If legal conditions stayed relatively unimproved for free African-Americans, over the next few decades they worsened for slaves. African-American slave women and men had essentially five options: stay on the plantation, petition their home state for freedom, run away to join the British army, join the Continental Army or state militia, or simply run away. Two of these options were available because of the war. Slaves had always had the options to stay or run away and to petition, but in November 1775, Virginia's last royal governor, Lord Dunmore, declared that all slaves and indentured servants were "FREE, that are willing and able to bear arms; they joining his Majesty's troops . . . for the purpose of reducing this colony to a proper sense of their duty to his Majesty's crown and dignity." An unknown number of slaves took Dunmore up on this offer, and many more found their way to the lines of the British army during the next eight years.

The *Virginia Gazette*, for example, on November 4, 1775, ran the following advertisement for a fugitive slave: "RUN away from the Subscriber . . . a small new Negro Man named GEORGE, about 40 Years of Age, with a Nick in one Ear, and some Marks with the Whip. He was about Williamsburg till last Winter, but either went or was sent to Lord Dunmore's Quarter in Frederick County, and there passes for his Property. Whoever conveys him to me shall have 5 [pounds]. Reward."[14] On the seventeenth, the *Gazette* ran another notice about a slave escaping to Lord Dunmore's protection:

RUN off last night, from the subscriber, a negro man named CHARLES, who is a very shrewd sensible fellow, and can both read and write. . . . He is very black, has a large nose, and is about 5 feet 8 or 10 inches high. . . . There is reason to believe he intends an attempt to get to lord Dunmore; and as I have reason to believe his design of going off was long premeditated . . . I am apprehensive he may prove daring and resolute, if endeavoured to be taken. His elopement was from no cause of complaint, or dread of a whipping (for he has always been remarkably indulged, indeed too much so) but from a determined resolution to get Liberty, as he conceived, by flying to lord Dunmore. I will give FIVE POUNDS to any person who secures him.

These ads, though written by white slaveholders, suggest a good deal about the probable intentions of the escaped slaves. In their owners' minds, at least, the slaves had become familiarized with the reigning word of the day: "Liberty." And the slaves believed liberty could be had at the side of Lord Dunmore. News traveled rapidly through slave quarters, between rows of tobacco plants and wheat stalks, and from the mouths of white colonists into the ears of black freedom fighters who committed themselves to the one side willing to offer them independence in Virginia in 1775. These African-American men voted for freedom with their bodies.

In Massachusetts, slaves used another tactic, offering further proof that the public sloganeering, legislative rumble, and dining-room conversations of whites were not lost upon their slaves. In April 1773, four African-American men sent a letter to the town of Thompson's representative in the Massachusetts assembly. Noting that the "divine spirit of *freedom*, seems to fire every humane breast on this continent," they urged the legislature to assist them out of their "deplorable state" of slavery. The writers argued that since "the people of this province seem to be actuated by the principles of equity and justice," the petitioners "cannot but expect" that the legislators will "take our deplorable case into serious consideration, and give us that ample relief which, *as men*, we have a natural right to." Finally, the letter writers noted that they were planning to "leave the province, which we determine to do as soon as we can, from our joynt labours [procuring] money to transport ourselves to some part of the Coast of *Africa*, where we propose a settlement."

In their petition, the writers—Peter Bestes, Sambo Freeman, Felix Holbrook, and Chester Joie—also referred to the proceedings of the legislature, the policies of the Spanish Empire, and the religious sentiments of Puritan-influenced New England. They knew what philosophers, ministers, and politicians were talking about and debating. The petition echoes with the slogans of the Revolution: liberty, freedom, justice, and natural rights. Rather than running away or waiting for Providence to deliver them—the petitioners

THE COMING OF THE REVOLUTION

acknowledged "the wise and righteous governor of the universe has permitted our fellow men to make us slaves"—the letter writers worked the legal system, just as any citizen could do, though they were not citizens. As far as history knows, their petition was never answered.[15]

Advertisements for fugitive slaves and the petition of four slaves for "equity and justice" reveal that black men and women enunciated the need for freedom in the same way their white owners did. Black slaves and free blacks used the arguments of the white owners against them. Consequently, both state legislatures and the Continental Congress debated their own hypocrisy. They fought for freedom while denying it to others. Even though freedom for slaves nationwide lay nearly a hundred years into the future, black men and women worked to create change. In 1791, Benjamin Banneker, an African-American scientist and farmer, sent a letter to Thomas Jefferson. Banneker questioned how Jefferson could write about the "equal and impartial distribution of . . . rights and privileges" to all while simultaneously "detaining by fraud and violence so numerous a part of my brethren, under groaning captivity and cruel oppression." Here Banneker pinpointed the enduring paradox that Jefferson and other Revolutionary leaders "should at the same time be found guilty of that most criminal act, which you professedly detested in others"—the "great violation of liberty" for enslaved African-Americans.[16]

States throughout the North began providing for the gradual emancipation of their slaves, partly, at least, in response to the petitions written by African-Americans, the sacrifices made by about 5,000 black soldiers who fought against Britain in the Revolution, and the shared efforts of multiracial abolitionist societies. In the Revolutionary era, few people were passive, the banners of many causes were lifted, and the social world of America changed along with its political system.

Notes

1. Unless otherwise noted, all correspondence between Abigail and John Adams can be found in L.H. Butterfield, Marc Friedlaender, and Mary-Jo Kline, *The Book of Abigail and John: Selected Letters of the Adams Family, 1762–1784* (Cambridge, MA: Harvard University Press, 1975).

2. Charles Francis Adams, *The works of John Adams, second President of the United States: With a life of the author, notes and illustrations Vol. X* (Boston: Little, Brown, 1856), 283.

3. James Hawkes, *A retrospect of the Boston tea-party: With a memoir of George R.T. Hewes, a survivor of the little band of patriots who drowned the tea in Boston harbour in 1773* (New York: S.S. Bliss, 1834), 30.

4. John Adams autobiography, part 1, "John Adams," through 1776, sheet 13 of 53 [electronic edition]. *Adams Family Papers: An Electronic Archive.* Massachusetts Historical Society, www.masshist.org/digitaladams/.

5. Pauline Maier, *The Old Revolutionaries: Political Lives in the Age of Samuel Adams* (New York: W.W. Norton, 1990).

6. Jay Fliegelman, *Declaring Independence: Jefferson, Natural Language, and the Culture of Performance* (Stanford, CA: Stanford University Press, 1993), offers a full discourse on the ceremony of public speech and writing in the age of the Declaration.

7. A full and lively description of farmers' rebellions can be found in Ray Raphael, *A People's History of the American Revolution: How Common People Shaped the Fight for Independence* (New York: Harper Perennial, 2002).

8. Eric Foner, *Tom Paine and Revolutionary America* (New York: Oxford University, 1976), 19.

9. This is a public domain document.

10. John Adams autobiography, part 1, "John Adams," through 1776, sheet 23 of 53 [electronic edition]. *Adams Family Papers: An Electronic Archive.* Massachusetts Historical Society, www.masshist.org/digitaladams/.

11. Worthington Chauncey Ford, ed., *The Writings of George Washington Vol. 4* (New York: G.P. Putnam's Sons, 1889), 4.

12. Thomas Jefferson, *Autobiography* (Philadelphia: University of Pennsylvania Press, 2004), 33.

13. Frank Moore, *Diary of the American Revolution: From Newspapers and Original Documents Vol. I* (New York: Charles Scribner, 1860), 270–271.

14. Both this advertisement and the one following were taken from Lathan A. Windley, *A Profile of Runaway Slaves in Virginia and South Carolina from 1730 Through 1787* (New York: Garland, 1995), vol. I, 172; vol. I, 333.

15. Dorothy Porter, *Early Negro Writing, 1760–1837* (Baltimore: Black Class, 1995), 254–255.

16. Howard Zinn and Anthony Arnove, *Voices of a People's History of the United States* (New York: Seven Stories, 2004), 58–61.

5

The American Revolution

George Washington *(MPI/Getty Images)*

An Overview

The French and Indian War, which ended in 1763, resulted in the surrender of France's claims to New World territory. England reigned supreme, and most American colonists felt content. Only thirteen years later, however, many of these same colonists proclaimed the "absolute Tyranny" of King George III, issued the Declaration of Independence, and thereby announced the emergence of a new nation: the United States of America.

King and Parliament had other ideas about the goings-on in America—namely, that men like Thomas Jefferson and Benjamin Franklin were traitors who ought to dangle from a tall tree. Franklin knew the danger he and his friends faced. "We must, indeed, all hang together, or most assuredly we shall all hang separately," Franklin said with a wry laugh at the final signing of the Declaration on August 2, 1776.[1] Franklin did not lose his sense of humor, and he hoped not to lose his head, though the hangman's noose seemed awfully close. By July 1776, Great Britain had the world's most powerful navy, a corps of 30,000 tough troops landing at Staten Island, and plenty of money to hire mercenaries. The American revolutionaries had no navy, no money, and not much of an army. How, then, did residents of thirteen distinct and often quarrelsome states actually fight Great Britain and win?

Colonists no longer, a few million farmers, philosophers, midwives, tavern keepers, laundresses, lawyers, and businessmen—now calling themselves Patriots—turned a war of ideas into a war of lead musket balls, bayonet charges, and never-ending marches. The Continental Congress fielded a small, determined army, led by George Washington, throughout the war. But the Continental Army suffered too little pay, too little food, and too few shoes. The men got so desperate they even tried selling what few clothes they had, a move that General Washington snorted about in a General Order issued in June 1777: "A soldier shall not presume to sell any part of his cloaths on any pretence whatever."[2] The individual states had their own troubles and did not want to give much power or money to Congress. Men joined state militias and fought alongside Washington's army and then went home to their families and farms. Without enough men, muskets, or money and with Britain's navy blockading the coast, these united Americans needed help, and soon. Luckily for the rebel Patriots, France and Spain remembered their wounds from the Seven Years' War and joined the American fight for independence.

From 1776 through 1781, the Continental Army, the French and Spanish navies, and eventually a French army faced British troops and German (Hessian) mercenaries in battle. Most of the major confrontations took place in the middle states because that was where the Continental Army roamed. British generals chased the Continentals from New York to New Jersey to

Pennsylvania. But General Washington mastered the art of retreat and of surprise attack. Just when it looked like the British would trap his army in early 1777, Washington ordered more wood thrown onto the evening bonfires to make the camp look lively and settled. Then he and the troops slipped away under cover of the cunning subterfuge. Washington understood the nature of guerrilla warfare. He needed to wear down the British public's will to fight. That meant surviving.

Armies need more than guns and glory to survive. Alongside Washington's half-barefoot, flea-ridden, smallpox-scarred, diarrhea-weakened men strode hundreds of women: prostitutes, servants, slaves, soldiers' wives. They cooked the meals, mended what passed for uniforms, tended the wounded, and provided whatever comforts they could. Washington felt uneasy about their presence—in a General Order of August 1777 he fumed that "the multitude of women in particular, especially those who are pregnant, or have children are a clog upon every movement"—but he knew he needed their help. A few women, like Deborah Sampson, dressed in men's clothes, enlisted, and served not as seamstresses but as soldiers. Sampson served for more than a year until she got caught, but she still received a lifelong veteran's pension from Massachusetts. However, most women and men in the struggling states who sided with the movement for independence made their contributions by donating food, clothing, and shelter and by maintaining farms and businesses while armies and militias clashed and camped across the countryside.

During the War of Independence, not everyone in America wanted to break away from Great Britain. Loyalists, perhaps one-fourth of the overall population, honored King George and wanted to remain part of the British Empire. Once the British seized New York City in the summer of 1776 and sent Washington's army scurrying for New Jersey, Loyalists flocked to Manhattan to enjoy the safe company of their peers and to avoid the abuse of their irate Patriot neighbors. Throughout the colonies, Patriots confiscated the property of Loyalists, applied hot tar and feathers to Loyalists' naked bodies, and in general did much to demean and harass them. In June 1778, Louisa Susannah Wells and her Loyalist family slipped out of Charleston, South Carolina, on a ship bound for New York. A British warship intercepted them, took them prisoner, and put them before a tribunal to determine the nature of their loyalties. The judge recognized the family's loyalty to the Crown, set them free in New York City, and returned their possessions. Louisa Wells remembered that "my spirits were so high, and I felt myself so happy, at being in a country, where I could hear so much about Great Britain, that I believe they thought me half-crazy."[3] Eventually she and about 100,000 other Loyalists sailed for Britain, never to return to America. While the Wells family stayed together, other families were torn apart by the Revolution. Benjamin Franklin and his son William, the royal governor of New Jersey, had a falling-out during the war. William remained true to England and was thrown into Simsbury prison in Connecticut, an abandoned copper mine referred to as the "Catacomb of Loyalty," a hellish place from which he was released in a prisoner swap in late 1778, after nearly two years of confinement.[4] William Franklin stayed in New York until 1782, at which point he sailed for England. Benjamin and William Franklin saw each other one last time in 1785, but their relationship never regained the joy of earlier years. The Revolution was their undoing.

Although British and American representatives did not sign a peace treaty until 1783, all major combat ended in 1781 at Yorktown, Virginia. There a combined American-French army surrounded and defeated Lord Cornwallis's fortified troops while a French navy sat in the harbor, preventing the British fleet from providing help or rescue. During the next two years, however, minor but bitter skirmishes raged throughout the South, where Loyalist and Patriot partisans attacked each other in some of the war's most ugly encounters. Roving bands of thieves and thugs looted farms, stole cattle, and created general mayhem, often by hiding behind false loyalties to one side or the other. In the South, especially, the Revolution was as much a civil war as a contest for political independence, and the tit-for-tat vengeance killings ended only after George Washington dispatched General Nathanael Greene to calm the chaotic backcountry by offering everyone amnesty in return for peace.

For eight years, from 1775 through 1783, amateur American armies and militias—made up of black and white soldiers—contended against the swagger and discipline of Europe's finest regiments, all for the establishment of political freedoms that American leaders denied to more than half the residents of the territory encompassed by the new United States. Nearly all African-Americans were slaves, women could not vote, and the new nation guaranteed Native Americans very few rights and considered most Indians as already conquered peoples at war's end. Out of this confusion of warring interests and warring armies emerged a victorious squabble of states that framed documents freely expressing what was not always freely given, the rights of "Life, Liberty and the pursuit of Happiness." In the front parlor of almost everyone's mind during the war and after sat the valiant figure of a Virginia planter and slave owner, George Washington—the nation's first general and first president.

George Washington: Man of Contradictions

By the time he died in 1799, George Washington had become something new in America, a man for all causes: peace and war; a leader of a national army representing colonies that had bickered as often as cooperated; independent owner and master of 300 slaves whom he freed not during his life but as the

84

final act of his life; and first president of a country suspicious of the accumulation of power in the hands of one man. In each case, he stood at the apex of contradictions, and he seems to have surmounted them all.

Born in 1732 to a prosperous family as the first son of his father's second marriage, George Washington initially inherited little of his family's vast fortune, though while still a boy he was bequeathed ten slaves. Thanks to ambition, the inheritance of the family's plantation, Mount Vernon, after an older brother's death, and an advantageous marriage to the wealthy widow Martha Custis, by the late 1750s George Washington stepped fully into the role of gentleman planter he had so longed to enjoy. Washington's service in the French and Indian War earned him a high reputation for valor and skilled leadership. Brimming with status, in 1758 he resigned his militia commission and returned to civilian life and election to the House of Burgesses. He divided his time between politics, plantation management, and family. Though he and Martha had no children together, George helped raise her two children from her first marriage. Love them as he did, Washington's business life occupied most of his time.

George Washington was a Virginia planter, part of the landed elite, a seller of fine tobaccos and lately of wheat. Washington was a man of the soil, having roamed the backcountry as a surveyor while in his teens, but it was slaves who tilled the land Washington inherited. He owned and worked 300 slaves at the time of the Revolution. With his experience in the militia, Washington was also a man of war. One part of George Washington's life prepared him for another: commander of slaves, commander of soldiers.

What remains of George Washington's thoughts can be found in his thousands of surviving letters. It was his formula not to record sensitive details or feelings in his diary. Those thoughts he reserved for correspondence and conversation, which he enjoyed with an evening's glass of imported Madeira wine. Washington's soul was in the soil and the saddle, and his personal writings reflect the dual nature of his past. At some of the most crucial moments, he wrote not one jot of high-minded, patriotic rhetoric; instead, he wrote about cherries. On March 15, 1775, he traveled to Richmond to attend the Second Virginia Convention, "the Independant Company there" that protested Parliament's shuttering of Boston's port in retaliation for the Boston Tea Party of December 6, 1773. A diary entry written while at the Convention recalling March 10, only days prior to his departure for Richmond, reveals not a care for liberty, muskets, or marching men: "when the cherry buds were a good deal swelled, and the white part of them beginning to appear, I gathered the fatter . . . cherries." While he debated liberty, he thought about fruit.

Once the fighting started, however, the diary entries ceased, probably reflecting the growing miseries around him. What time was there to record the fatness of cherries or the temperature when independence seemed to hang by a memory of hope?

From June 1775 through September 1783, George Washington led the Continental Army, which at first was little more than a homespun collection of some 20,000 citizen-soldiers—most white, a few black, and many signed on for a year or less. The colonies had no permanent armies, only militias like the minutemen of Massachusetts who had fought against the British at Lexington and Concord in April 1775. They could shoot well, and they were fighting for their homes, but they had crops to harvest and calves to midwife, so they could not afford to be off soldiering indefinitely. Somehow these freedom-minded, New England militiamen would have to be fused with un-disciplined farmer-fighters from the other colonies into a trained army willing to stay in the field for years. That was one small part of George Washington's mission in June 1775 when he arrived at the outskirts of Boston, where the feisty minutemen had ensnared the British redcoats.

After drilling and accepting Washington's brand of military discipline, the Continental Army scared the British out of Boston in March 1776. During that previous long, cold winter, Washington's officers had talked him out of an all-out assault on the entrenched redcoats. With the extra time, he planned and executed a secretive movement of troops and cannons to Dorchester Heights, from which lead balls could have been lobbed at the Brits. Rather than getting blasted to pieces, the British chose to sail away. Washington's victory at Boston invigorated the Patriot cause, as did the publication of Tom Paine's *Common Sense*, the booklet that condemned King George III as a tyrant who denied the natural rights of Americans. Independence was declared on July 4, 1776.

Declaring independence and getting it were not, however, the same. Washington played a pivotal part in making independence possible. Somehow, in the scramble and scurry of military operations, Washington became an icon of strength and republican virtue around whom his countrymen could rally. He became their bedrock, their symbol, their lightning rod, even if some of his early strategies did not work well at all.

From Boston, Washington led the army to Manhattan in New York, where he hoped to defend an indefensible city. About one-fourth of his men had smallpox, many New Yorkers were Loyalists, and the British fleet that arrived in early July 1776 had more than 30,000 men crammed aboard what looked like a sea of trees, the masts were so many. Under General Lord Howe, the British stormed the Continental Army's positions and drove them into retreat toward New Jersey.

With New York City and the surrounding area lost to the Americans, Washington displayed one of the qualities that made him effective: great courage.

By Christmas time, winter weather set in; ice and snow blanketed the land. The opportunity was ripe for a surprise. So on December 26, 1776, Washington took his now more seasoned troops across the Delaware River and sprang a cold and furious attack upon German mercenaries at Trenton, New Jersey. Washington and his few thousand remaining Continentals—some trudging shoeless and bloody-footed through the snow and sleet—proved they had the daring and ability to win a fight. When the shooting started in the slick streets of Trenton, unprepared Germans stumbled into Washington's ambush, and more than a thousand surrendered. It had been quite a year: a victory at Boston, the loss of New York, and then victory at Trenton. Yet few Continental soldiers remained, and those who stayed were sick and weary. Then, during 1777, the British marched an army from New York to Philadelphia and occupied the very city where the Declaration had been written. Congress fled. Independence rested on a precipice.

Seasons of war lay ahead, and during those years, though Washington could be a master of delegation, he also knew how to gallop into the thick of the fight, a general literally among soldiers. After the Continental Army endured a six-month stay at Valley Forge, Pennsylvania, where one-fourth of the troops died from disease and exposure during the winter of 1777–1778, the British decided to evacuate Philadelphia and return overland to New York. Washington's troops attacked the British forces between the two cities at the Battle of Monmouth, the last major battle in the North. One soldier recalled that Washington "after passing us . . . rode on to the plain field and took an observation of the advancing enemy. He remained there some time upon his old English charger, while the shot from the British artillery were rending up the earth all around him."[5] Washington personally rallied the troops as they retreated, pulling them back to face the British. Such bravery was typical of this six-foot-three, robust Virginian who went unscathed during a nearly ten-year war that killed about 25,000 American soldiers.

Washington obviously could not be everywhere at once. In 1777 he missed a series of decisive battles near Saratoga, New York. The British wanted to cut New England off from the rest of the colonies, and Major General John Burgoyne was marching from Canada through upstate New York to implement the British strategy. Opposing Burgoyne, Major General Horatio Gates led a small force of Continentals and merged them with both local militiamen and other Continental forces already in the area under Major General Benedict Arnold's command. About 9,000 British and Hessian soldiers died or surrendered near Saratoga, while the Americans lost fewer than 500 men. The success of the combined forces of Continental regulars and militiamen sent a clear message to the Americans, the British, and the French that independence could be won. The victory helped bring the French into fully supporting the

American cause. However, Gates did not directly inform Washington, his commanding officer, of the victory as would have been customary. Instead, Gates sent a message to Congress. This irked Washington, who accurately suspected that Gates wanted a position with more status, namely Washington's job. On October 30, in sarcastic tones, Washington berated Gates for not minding his place: "I cannot but regret, that a matter of such magnitude and so interesting to our General Operations, should have reached me by report only, or thro' the Channel of Letters." The war was a personal matter for Washington, who would not let this slight to pride and protocol stand.

For the Continental Army to function properly, Washington needed loyal commanders. Ironically, although Gates thought more highly of himself than of Washington, Gates did serve loyally, if impudently. The other prominent general at Saratoga, Benedict Arnold—a more daring and effective commander than Gates—later turned his name into a synonym for "traitor." Arnold's treachery stemmed from a sense that he was underappreciated. He passed military secrets to the British and then joined them in September 1780 after being passed over for promotion and after his contact, the spy John Andre, was captured and hanged. (Washington refused to have Andre executed by pistol shot—a more honorable death typically befitting a gentleman. To Washington, a spy was a spy.) After he went turncoat, Benedict Arnold helped the British burn Richmond, Virginia.

Washington needed more than trustworthy officers to defeat the British; he needed an army willing both to suffer for a dream and remain loyal to him and to the impoverished Continental Congress. By January 1781, small mutinies had already fizzled, but the officers and soldiers of the Pennsylvania Line decided they could serve no longer, would sacrifice no more. Many had already been in the army for three years. Some of them had not been paid for a year, either by the Congress or by the state of Pennsylvania, and clothing was typically inadequate. General Washington headquartered some distance from the main army, which was encamped at Morristown, New Jersey. The commander on the spot was General Anthony Wayne. On the evening of January 1, 1781, members of the Pennsylvania Line began to mutiny, forcing hesitant comrades to join in by firing cannon volleys over their heads. One night later, the entire Line—thousands of men—revolted and marched toward Princeton, New Jersey, and hence toward the British, whom Washington feared the mutineers might join. General Wayne managed to slow them down and got them to negotiate. Washington sent a letter to Congress and to a number of states' governors, imploring them to send necessary funds: "The . . . distresses that have resulted from the total want of pay for nearly twelve months, the want of clothing at a severe season, and not [i]nfrequently the want of provisions, are beyond description. The circumstances will now point out much more forcibly what ought to be done, than any thing that can possibly be said by me on the subject." After days of bargaining, a deal was reached in which half of the Pennsylvania Line soldiers (more than 1,200 men) were allowed to retire, and all were pardoned. It seemed General Washington could be fierce in battle yet gentle with his troops.

Only days later, about 300 members of the New Jersey Line tried their luck at a mutiny, perhaps hoping to receive back pay or be discharged like their comrades from Pennsylvania. Instead, Washington ordered other troops to crush the mutiny, and then he executed its two leaders, having them kneel in the snow before a firing squad. Washington was lenient only up to a point. He had not meant gentleness to be an invitation to chaos. In his words, ever since the twin executions "the spirit of mutiny seems now to have completely subsided and to have given place to a genuine repentance." While he was not always callous, Washington was calculating, willing to use the powers granted to him by Congress as needed.

While the war officially stretched into 1783, it effectively ended at Yorktown, Virginia, in 1781 when a French fleet, French troops, and an American army ensnared British general Charles Cornwallis's force of more than 8,000 men. In the weeks leading up to the surrender, American engineers had tightened the noose of ditches around the neck of British fortifications. At one point a common soldier, Joseph Plumb Martin, was digging late at night in the rain and encountered Washington himself, risking his neck for an up-close look at the situation: "There came a man alone to us, having on an [overcoat]." In the pitch dark, the stranger asked how to find the engineers, and then "the stranger inquired what troops we were, talked familiarly with us a few minutes, when, being informed which way the officers had gone, he went off in the same direction." Martin marveled at the mortal danger they all were in and finished the story by saying, "In a short time the engineers returned and the afore-mentioned stranger [came] with them. They discoursed together some time when, by the officers often calling him 'Your Excellency,' we discovered that it was General Washington. Had we dared, we might have cautioned him for exposing himself too carelessly to danger at such a time, and doubtless he would have taken it in good part if we had. But nothing ill happened to either him or ourselves." Such stories of Washington's nerve were common. As at the Battle of Monmouth, he was known to sit on his horse in the midst of musket volleys with soldiers falling all around, not a shot hitting him.

Washington could not avoid all kinds of pain, however. War can be as much a story of what a soldier misses, as it is a story of what he does. Since 1759 Washington had been married to a woman whom he had probably first courted for advantage and then came to love: Martha Custis. George had written to Martha back in June 1775 to tell her about his appointment to the post of general: "My Dearest: I am now set down to write to you on a subject, which fills me with inexpressible concern, and this concern is greatly aggravated and increased, when I reflect upon the uneasiness I know it will give you." Reaching to quiet her fears, Washington said he would feel "no pain from the toil or the danger of the campaign; my unhappiness will flow from the uneasiness I know you will feel from being left alone."

George and Martha were not always separated during the war, however. They spent the war's winters together—for example, at Valley Forge, where the Washingtons enjoyed much finer, warmer, and better-provisioned quarters than the troops. During the cold months, other officers' wives also encamped, like Lucy Greene, whose husband Nathanael was a prized addition to Washington's staff. Martha and Lucy clinked cups of wine to toast birthdays and holidays, but they also held sewing circles and diligently worked as hard as the other thousands of female food foragers, cannon cleaners, and laundresses who marched (and sometimes fought) with the Continental Army. Still, George and Martha spent much of the eight years apart. In 1784, after the ratification of the peace treaty with Britain, George returned to Mount Vernon, where he and Martha stayed until his election to the presidency in 1789. Then he rode to the capital in New York, garlanded in the adoration of the nation he had shepherded through its ordeal. Once again, Martha followed soon after.

Mary Jemison: Seneca and Loyalist

On the Pennsylvania frontier in 1758, during the French and Indian War, fifteen-year-old Mary Jemison's parents and siblings were killed by Shawnee Indians who took Jemison captive and gave her to another tribe, the Senecas, part of the Iroquois nation. "My dear little Mary," her mother said at their last farewell, "I fear that the time has arrived when we must be parted forever . . . remember my child your own name."[6] Soon after this parting, Mary had watched the Shawnees prepare her parents' scalps by "putting them, yet wet and bloody" on hoops to be scraped and dried. Jemison was then taken to Fort Duquesne (later Pittsburgh), where she was given to two Seneca women who soon became her adoptive sisters. Years later, Jemison noted that her Seneca sisters always treated her like a "real sister," in part because she had replaced their dead brother and filled a needed spot in the extended family. In little more than a few days, by way of murder, capture, and ritual, she had become someone new. This was the first revolution in Mary Jemison's life.

After an adoption ceremony, which she remembered as "a most dismal howling, crying bitterly, and wringing their hands in all the agonies of grief for a deceased relative," Jemison was given the name "Dickewamis," which signified "a pretty girl, a handsome girl, or a pleasant good thing." Mary

90

Jemison had become Seneca. Throughout the colonial period, hundreds of children, women, and men were abducted by Native Americans and adopted. Many of these colonists chose to stay with their new families even when offered the choice to return to their first homes. On and off for six more decades, Dickewamis had the opportunity to return to white society, but she always chose her adopted Seneca lodgings.

Just as with other people living in eastern North America, the events of the 1770s forced Native Americans to take sides. During the Revolution, most of the roughly 150,000 remaining Indians of the East Coast sided with the British, sometimes because they inaccurately read the future (where they mistakenly saw British victory), at other times because Indian peoples knew that white colonists intended to take their land while Parliament had lately attempted to protect it (with the 1763 Proclamation Line). Most Iroquois sided with the British after considering the opinions of a British delegation and then listening to the persuasive speeches of Joseph Brant, a Mohawk and fierce British partisan.

Jemison had a memory of that council at which most Iroquois decided to fight with the British, and she recalled that the British addressed the Iroquois' "avarice, by telling our people that the people of the states were few in number, and easily subdued . . . that the King was rich and powerful, both in money and subjects." Seneca women, unlike colonial women, could attend diplomatic councils, where they helped choose the men who represented their interests at the Iroquois congress. It was not long before Mohawks, Senecas, Cayugas, and Onondagas began fighting against the rebellious colonists. According to Jemison, "In May following, our Indians were in their first battle with the Americans. . . . While they were absent at that time, my daughter Nancy was born." Although Seneca women involved themselves in affairs of state, they were not soldiers. As Dickewamis, Jemison attended to child rearing and the other labors common to women of the Iroquois, namely farming.

Another of Mary Jemison's remarks about the war is also typical of women's experiences, white and Indian: "During the revolution, my house was the home of Col's Butler and [Joseph]Brandt, whenever they chanced to come into our neighborhood as they passed to and from Fort Niagara, which was the seat of their military operations. Many and many a night I have pounded samp [i.e., corn] for them from sun-set till sun-rise, and furnished them with necessary provision and clean clothing for their journey." White colonial women also recorded such additional labor, as they not only ran family farms while husbands were camped elsewhere, but frequently provided clothing and food for the troops. Indian and white women had much in common during these years: extra labor, husbands and sons frequently gone and killed, flight from homes that were ransacked, starving as food ran out. Eliza Pinckney, near Charles

Town, South Carolina, during the war, related in a letter her own reduced circumstances: "I have been robbed and deserted by my slaves; my property pulled to pieces, burnt and destroyed. . . . Such is the deplorable state of our Country from two armies being in it for nearly two years. . . . Crops, stock, boats, Carts gone, taken or destroyed." Mary Jemison lived through equally trying times during 1779 when an expedition of 3,000 colonial militiamen under General John Sullivan—one of Washington's favored generals—burned whole fields of corn in order to subdue the Indians by starving them.

When Sullivan's forces made their way westward to Seneca lands, the women and children moved toward Buffalo, and Jemison recalled, "At that time, I had three children who went with me on foot, one who rode on horse back, and one whom I carried on my back." Before leaving, they stashed a portion of their corn harvest, intending to rely upon it after their return. However, General Sullivan made it a point to destroy every morsel of food he could find. After the militia left, the Senecas returned. Jemison found that Sullivan's troops had "burnt our houses, killed what few cattle and horses they could find, destroyed our fruit trees, and left nothing but the bare soil and timber . . . there was not a mouthful of any kind of sustenance left, not even enough to keep a child one day from perishing with hunger."

A war that united the colonies separated many Indian nations. The Revolution amplified preexisting animosities in the Mohawk Valley. One of Mary Jemison's memories underscores the way in which the Revolution tore families apart. After a battle at Conesus Lake, two Oneida brothers encountered each other, "one in the capacity of a conqueror, the other in that of a prisoner." The brother fighting for the British had captured his brother, who had lately led General Sullivan to the Seneca villages. The victorious brother addressed the other: "Brother! You have merited death and shall have your deserts. . . . When those rebels had drove us from the fields of our fathers to seek out new homes, it was you who could dare to step forth as their pilot, and conduct them even to the doors of our wigwams, to butcher our children." The victor continued, "But though you have merited death and shall die on this spot, my hands shall not be stained in the blood of a brother. *Who will strike?*" A man named Little Beard "struck the prisoner on the head with his tomahawk," killing him instantly. Flight, hunger, burned homes, and stories of death made up a large parcel of Mary Jemison's memories of the Revolution.

One part of the Declaration of Independence accuses the king of England of having "endeavoured to bring on the inhabitants of our frontiers, the merciless Indian Savages, whose known rule of warfare, is an undistinguished destruction of all ages, sexes and conditions." Scathing rhetoric like this exemplified many colonials' opinions about Indians, making it little wonder that most Native Americans who participated in the war sided with the British, who seemed to offer the best hope. If the Revolution was an attempt to redefine what it meant to be an American, if the Revolution crafted a new kind of citizen, it did so by both inclusion and exclusion: not everyone obtained the full rights of American citizenship once the peace was signed.

In peace treaties of 1784, the United States considered the Indian allies of the British as "subjugated" and gave them small parcels of land to live on. These Indian peoples and their descendants would wait until 1924 to be granted citizenship in the United States. There were exceptions, like Mary Jemison, who was given citizenship by New York State in 1817, but she was already an exception, a white Indian, and she lived out her days passing back and forth between Seneca and white communities. In 1783, more than 2 million white Americans gained a new kind of freedom—relative self-determination. White Americans then used that freedom to dominate the rest of the continent in the ensuing decades. The American Revolution reshaped the world. It was also a War of Independence for the Iroquois Confederacy, the Delawares of Pennsylvania, the Cherokees and Catawbas of the South, but they did not win, even though, in the words of Colin Calloway, "Indians remained a force to be reckoned with at the war's end."[7]

Joseph Plumb Martin: A Common Soldier in the Continental Army

Joseph Plumb Martin enlisted in the Continental Army in 1776. He endured gnawing hunger and the near-constant searching for his next meal through-out the war. Martin did fight, but his day-to-day experiences boiled down to missed meals, the scabrous misery of smallpox, and a sense for the way that Washington's army moved through communities that were not thrilled to have thousands of ravenous men feeding off their fields and livestock.

Patrick Henry and Thomas Jefferson of Virginia, Samuel Adams of Mas-sachusetts, and Benjamin Franklin of Pennsylvania were influential men who risked their lives for the cause of independence, but none of them actually fought in the Revolution. They all could have been hanged as traitors, but none of them hefted a smoothbore musket that had to be precisely loaded in the midst of a battle, using an oxen powder horn to tip in the powder. The armies of the United States were made up predominantly of the poor, who enlisted at first out of patriotism, but as the years went on, for promises of signing bonuses and land grants. Rich men could pay substitutes to fight in their place.

Joseph Martin was about sixteen when he first enlisted. He recorded in a later memoir that after the battles of Lexington and Concord in April 1775, he listened to the "conversation and disputes of the good old farmer politicians"

93

and thought himself "as warm a patriot as the best of them." Accompanying some of his friends to an enlistment camp, he made "a woeful scratch on the paper" and became on the instant an enlistee. The soldier's life immediately took him by ship to New York, where he was quartered "opposite . . . a wine cellar." He and some other lads broke in and helped themselves to the wine, one flask of which he removed to the "safety" of his room. Although they were found out and scolded, no true punishment came of the affair. Joseph Martin's time in the army began on a tipsy note. Before long, new realities set in.

After the army had spent a few months in New York, the British forces attacked. By the middle of September 1776, British warships began bombarding American positions, and troops were clashing. As Martin remembered, "seeing we could make no resistance," the Continentals retreated. "We had to advance slowly," he recalled, "for my comrade having been some time unwell was now so overcome by heat, hunger, and fatigue that he became suddenly and violently sick." Martin himself had not eaten for more than a full day, and the weather was "exceeding hot." He "waddled on as well and fast" as he could. They managed to escape, but about one-quarter of the army was out of commission at the time due to dysentery and smallpox. Disease and hunger were more deadly foes than the British.

October 1776 found the situation more dire, and as British troops took one American fortification after another, Continental soldiers went to reconnoiter the enemy's movements. At one such moment, Martin told a sergeant he was too sick for scouting, though all he really needed "was a bellyful of victuals." When the sergeant began looking for a different scout, Martin realized it would be easier to find food while scouting in the country than to sit hot and hungry in camp. During the scouting expedition, he and a "messmate" bumped into a farmer and his turnip field. The man demanded some kind of payment for the tubers, so they agreed to help pick the turnips in return for some of the harvest, but "after the good man had sat us to work and chatted with us a few minutes, he went off and left us. After he was gone and we had pulled and cut as many as we wanted, we packed them up and decamped, leaving the owner of the turnips to pull his share." There was nothing unusual in this. When food was scarce and local farmers were just as likely to sell at high prices to the British as they were to offer provisions to the Continental Army, it became a necessity to take what could be had.

In May 1777, Martin received a smallpox inoculation, part of a program instituted by General Washington. The inoculation induced a mild form of the disease, leading Martin to quip that he "had the smallpox favorably as did the rest, generally." As the reduced pocks began to show, he and a comrade went to a river, undressed, and slipped into the water, where they fished and "continued at this business three or four hours, and when we came out of the water the pustules of the smallpox were well cleansed." He was on the road again sixteen days after the inoculation, but soon broke out in a second round of boils, this set much worse than the first. He had eleven boils on one arm alone, "each as big as half a hen's egg." Apparently, the rest of his "carcass" was in no better shape. Martin survived the disease, however, as did increasing percentages of the Continental Army once General Washington's inoculation orders worked their way through the veins of the troops.

The "trouble, fatigue, and dangers" of the soldier's life made up the larger story of the War of Independence, but common soldiers received little ac- claim. To highlight this oversight, Martin summarized a failed attempt to defend Fort Mercer in New Jersey during November 1777: "Here ends the account of as hard and fatiguing a job . . . as occurred during the Revolutionary War." According to Martin, the defeat of Cornwallis in 1781 was "no more to be compared with [Fort Mercer] than the sting of a bee is to the bite of a rattlesnake." Yet little attention was paid to incidents like the defense of Fort Mercer because "there was no Washington . . . there. Had there been, the af- fair would have been extolled to the skies." As history would have it, "Great men get great praise; little men, nothing."

The uncommon exertions of common folk won the war. The soldiers regu- larly got "a little beef, but no bread" and continued "starving and freezing." Those like Martin who survived the experience lived with more than memories of hunger and marching because it was also a soldier's duty to fight. At the battle of Monmouth Courthouse in 1778, Martin tried to shoot an enemy soldier yet hoped he had not. As he recalled it, the British troops "were retreating in line, though in some disorder. I singled out a man and took my aim directly between his shoulders. . . . He was a good mark, being a broad-shouldered fellow. What became of him I know not; the fire and smoke hid him from my sight. One thing I know, that is, I took as deliberate aim at him as ever I did at any game in my life. But after all, I hope I did not kill him."

As Martin wanted the reader to remember, "Whosoever has the patience to follow me to the end of this rhapsody, I will confess that I think he must have almost as great a share of perseverance in reading it as I had to go through the hardships and dangers it records."

Anthony Allaire: A New York Loyalist in the Carolinas

British and Hessian troops fought because it was their job. Many Native Americans fought because they felt pushed into it from both sides—old al- liances with Britain strengthened by the abuses of colonial aggression. And there were Euro-American Loyalists, too, those men and women who fought for what Anthony Allaire called "King and country."[8] The Patriots like Joseph

95

Martin, whom Allaire called "rebels" and likened to a "camp . . . of horse thieves," had their reasons for fighting, and so did the Loyalists.

Allaire wrote a diary from March through November 25, 1780, during which time he walked hundreds of miles, was involved in the capture of Charleston, South Carolina, and fought in the decisive battle of King's Mountain, where the Loyalist forces were routed and all 1,000 troops killed or captured in sixty-five minutes. Allaire gives the scope of war from the diarist's perspective: one part strategy, the other part daily observation. Allaire's time as a marching soldier had to do with what eyes, ears, and skin could find—unexpected visitors or "a piece of low ground covered with magnolias in full bloom, which emitted a most delicious odor."

Allaire first steps out of his own pages in early March 1780, counting the number of men he traveled with—about 1,500 in all—and recounting how he "smoked tobacco and drank grog with . . . two devils incarnate," a pair of Indians called John and James who were assisting the king's forces in the South. As March passed underfoot, small encounters and near-misses with rebel forces occurred in the midst of days that were alternately pleasant and miserable, the weather making the difference. The damp and chills of a spring campaign, however, did not prevent Allaire from having a wry laugh at an enemy's expense. On March 14, Allaire and his fellow soldiers "found several horses . . . Continental stores and ammunition, hid in a swamp by one John Stafford, a sort of Rebel commissary who lives at Coosawhatchie and is, by the by, a cursed fool, which alone prevents his being a d[amne]d rogue."

Allaire soon encountered eighty rebel militiamen who tried to prevent the Loyalists from crossing a river. After he had been "amused" by some cross-river gun fire, the "bayonet was introduced" by a group of Allaire's partisans who had crossed the river elsewhere. Allaire's men captured four badly hurt rebels, and his companion, Dr. Johnson, applied bandages to the captives' wounds. Although soldiers and civilians were sometimes ruthless—the tarring and feathering of Loyalists in the northern colonies, the beating and arrests of men in taverns who dared speak favorably of King George—not all were unkind. Bandages often followed bayonets.

Allaire soon reached a "Rebel" settlement. Even though he had reason to regard the community with disgust, "the women were treated very tenderly, and with the utmost civility, notwithstanding their husbands were out in arms against us." The treatment of women by armies and militias followed the larger pattern of civility and brutality. Women, often thought of as a form of property, were usually treated well when of the upper class, but were abused at will by the British and their Loyalist colonial allies otherwise. For example, a Pennsylvania newspaper reported that a "girl of thirteen years of age was taken from her father's house, carried to a barn about a mile, there ravished, and afterwards made use of by five more of these brutes."[9] The Patriot troops were equally capable of such deeds, as Allaire testified on April 14 (by which time his men had met up with General Cornwallis and General Henry Clinton on their way to storm the city of Charleston). A house caught fire and casks of powder exploded. "This confusion was scarcely over when three ladies came to our camp in great distress. . . . A plundering villain had most shockingly abused them. Lady Colleton badly cut in the hand by a broadsword, and bruised."

April passed in the company of the British generals and their red-coated regulars. In 1776, the Patriots of Charleston had rebuffed the British. The redcoats returned to the land of tobacco, slaves, and uncertainty in 1778, hoping to isolate the South much as they had tried to quarantine New England until the British loss at Saratoga in 1777. Now Allaire and his commanders were headed to Charleston for a second try at this seat of southern rebellion. By May 8, 1780, the British had taken Fort Moultrie, and on May 12 Charleston surrendered to the king's forces after a few days' bombardment from the harbor. After a brief respite, Allaire was back on the move, this time headed northwest, ultimately to cross the border into North Carolina. As was common, the march began at 2 AM, but a wearying day's hike was improved when Allaire and Dr. Johnson "dined with . . . the ladies we protected in their distress when we were here the fourteenth of April."

For the next seven weeks, Allaire would see little combat. On June 4, Allaire's unit rested in the woods outside a rebel's plantation, passing around flasks of confiscated "prized wine." Feeling tipsy and satisfied, Allaire scribbled in his diary that it had been a "very convenient time to drink his Majesty's health." After the toast, the Loyalists found "two modest country women" who "afforded some merry scenes," though not to the "satisfaction" of Allaire. This encounter suggests the lack of respect given to "country women" compared to the chivalry shown to the "ladies" of April. Even in war, distinctions of social class pervaded combatants' behavior and attitudes. Loyalists were not fighting to change the world; they were fighting to keep it the same.

July and August saw minor skirmishes and many early mornings of getting "in motion." The Continental forces in the area were under the command of Horatio Gates—the recent victor at Saratoga—who was unable to repeat that earlier success. On August 16, Cornwallis defeated Gates's army, which Allaire found to be "agreeable news." However, he received "the disagreeable news" that he was "to be separated from the army, and act on the frontiers with the militia." He recorded an even more disagreeable sight in early September: "Here was a Rebel militia-man that got wounded in the right arm. . . . The bone was very much shattered. One Frost, a blacksmith, took it off with a shoemaker's knife and carpenter's saw. He stopped the blood with the

97

fungus of the oak, without taking up a blood vessel." Whether the man lived is unknown; at least half of all soldiers' deaths during the eight war years happened because of disease and infection. This amputee would have been lucky to live many days beyond the operation.

Getting close to what would become known as the Battle of King's Mountain, Allaire and company routed a small force of what he sarcastically termed "Congress heroes." He managed to keep his sense of humor until October 7 at "Little King's Mountain, where we took up our ground." The fighting commenced, smoke from musket volleys clouding the tangled cavalry charges and rattling saber thrusts. Soon fifty of Allaire's seventy-man detachment had been killed or wounded. After the fierce melee, all 1,000 Loyalists were either dead or captured, including Allaire, who described his brief captivity in the hands of "villains" whose idea of a joke was to give "five old shirts" to nine men. Rude practical jokes escalated into unbearable evenings of threats and beatings. Dr. Johnson, who had upheld his Hippocratic oath by tending to friend and foe alike, did not receive comparable gifts from his Patriot captors. A Patriot colonel named Cleveland insulted and beat Dr. Johnson "for attempting to dress a man whom they had cut on the march." Under the lash of such mistreatment, Allaire and Johnson eventually escaped and made it back to Charleston on November 29, after which Allaire served more time as a Loyalist soldier. After the war he settled in Canada, dying in 1838.

The War of Independence was a time of principles often expressed in unprincipled ways. For the common soldier like Allaire, most days were spent marching, an endless trudging over swollen rivers and through insect-infested lowlands. While Patriots and Loyalists alike were hanged, beheaded, and shot for adhering to their respective causes, and while homes were ransacked and heads scalped, not all morals were left with dead bodies to rot in the swamps. Allaire recounted breaches of decency, but he also revealed that his own commanders and he himself spent much energy trying to behave well. Allaire's soldiering days were one sliver of the southern campaign that pitted neighbors against each other and that ended with the defeat of Cornwallis's forces at Yorktown in 1781. After Washington replaced Horatio Gates with General Nathanael Greene as commander of southern policy and engagement, Greene found ways of taming the cycle of chaos and vengeance and eventually brought back into the fold many of the men like Allaire who had fought for what they deemed the true "Government": Britain. Allaire, however, stayed true to the cause of British hegemony in North America, once commenting sadly in his diary, "many good friends to Government have suffered much by the Rebels"—a sentiment borne out by the tales he told.

Perceptions: African-Americans and the War of Independence

Why did all these people fight and sacrifice? Did Washington and Jefferson really think that the Stamp Act, the Declaratory Act, the tax on tea, and the stationing of troops in Boston were violations of the colonists' "natural rights"? Were the colonial leaders also (or only) fighting to strengthen their own dominance at home, to keep the English from interfering? The debates are ongoing, with a recent addition by writers Alfred and Ruth Blumrosen, who show that a 1772 decision of the British courts to free a slave named James Somerset caused colonial slave owners to fear for their right to do as they pleased with their "property."[10] If African-American slaves were, perhaps, one cause of the war, what of their role in it?

African-Americans served in northern state militias and were part of the minutemen companies from Massachusetts so long renowned for their true American spirit and sacrificial patriotism. African-Americans fought in every major engagement in the north, including the battle at Monmouth Courthouse in which General Washington turned defeat into victory by spurring his horse through the crowd of retreating soldiers and admonishing them to fight back. Black soldiers were also in the Patriot ranks at Yorktown, where a German adviser, Baron von Closen, watched the Continental Army pass by and remarked, "three-quarters of the Rhode Island regiment consists of negroes, and that regiment is the most neatly dressed, the best under arms, and the most precise in its maneuvers."[11]

Participants in the American Revolution had a variety of opinions about "negroes." Mary Jemison was sympathetic, and after recalling the starving time that followed General Sullivan's attack on her village, she added, "At that time, two negroes, who had run away from their masters sometime before, were the only inhabitants of those flats. They lived in a small cabin and had planted and raised a large field of corn." They hired her to husk, and she remembered that "I have laughed a thousand times to myself when I have thought of the good old negro, who hired me, who fearing that I should get taken or injured by the Indians, stood by me constantly when I was husking, with a loaded gun in his hand." Jemison looked white, and the "old negro" must not have known that she was also Seneca or he would not have feared for her capture by the very same Indians she considered family.

Jemison's fond reminiscence of these African-Americans is countered by Joseph Plumb Martin's unkind memories of black people he met while campaigning. Martin sarcastically recalled that a house where he "was quartered had a smart-looking Negro man, a great politician. He quickly began to upbraid me about my opposition to the British." Martin commented, "I had no inclination to waste the shafts of my rhetoric upon a Negro slave." Martin

99

also told of a garrison of "fugitive Negroes," one of whom the Continentals sent back to "his master." In biting and unsympathetic words, Martin said that upon returning to his master, the runaway "no doubt . . . got a striped jacket [whipped] as part of his uniform suit." Finally, in language that equated black men with cattle, Martin remembered seeing "in the woods herds of Negroes" outside of Yorktown. For Joseph Plumb Martin, the War of Independence was meant to be a revolution in governmental style, not in race relations.

African-Americans of the colonial period rarely read or wrote in English because most masters did their best to prevent book learning. Free black people and some slaves did, however, become literate, and though few in number, their own revolutionary yearnings stand out from the records they left. At the beginning of the war, the celebrated poet Phillis Wheatley wrote a poem in praise of General Washington, which read in part:

> Proceed, great chief, with virtue on thy side,
> Thy ev'ry action let the goddess guide.
> A crown, a mansion, and a throne that shine,
> With gold unfading, WASHINGTON! be thine.[12]

In 1776, Washington replied, "If you should ever come to Cambridge, or near Head Quarters, I shall be happy to see a person so favoured by the Muses, and to whom Nature has been so liberal and beneficent in her dispensations. I am, with great Respect, etc." Though Wheatley praised Washington, in 1774 she had written a letter to Samson Occom, a Mohegan preacher, which demonstrated how clearly she saw the hypocrisy of the leaders of the growing rebellion: she wanted to "convince" the Patriot leaders "of the strange Absurdity of their Conduct whose Words and Actions are so diametrically opposite. How well the cry for liberty, and the reverse disposition for the exercise of oppressive power over others agree—I humbly think it does not require the penetration of a philosopher to determine."[13]

Wheatley herself had been granted freedom by her owners in 1774. There were other options available for gaining freedom. One was to serve in the militia or Continental forces, which sometimes gained a black man emancipation. Another route to independence was to join the British forces, and though some slaves were returned to their owners, many thousands did get freed this way. The final method, which had larger implications, was first employed with success in 1781 in Massachusetts by a woman named Mum Bett, who sued her owner for freedom after getting burned by a "fire shovel" he swung at Mum Bett's sister. Historian Gary Nash points out that even though "Mum Bett's own husband had fallen on a Massachusetts battlefield" fighting for independence, it took a lawsuit to gain her freedom in 1783.[14] Soon after Mum

Bett's case, a man named Quock Walker sued his owner for freedom and for damages following a severe beating. In Walker's case, the chief justice of the Massachusetts Supreme Court ruled, "I think the idea of slavery is inconsistent with our own conduct and Constitution; and there can be no such thing as perpetual servitude of a rational creature, unless his liberty is forfeited by some criminal conduct or given up by personal consent or contract."[15] While Pennsylvania was the first state to pass a law ending slavery (though gradually), Walker's case set a judicial precedent. Emancipation was happening at the state level, not the national level.

The white residents of the thirteen colonies had banded together to fight for their political independence, and some African-Americans and Native Americans joined them. Both Indians and blacks were sensitive to the half-measures of freedom being doled out by the sons of liberty who did not consistently treat their brothers and sisters to the same new rights of "Life, Liberty, and the pursuit of Happiness" they had so lately proclaimed. But the American Revolution did change the racial politics of America, and northern people soon began to spread the wealth of freedom. Quaker abolition societies would blossom, and states would pass laws ending slavery. The Revolution would not change everything, but it was a start.

Notes

1. Quoted in Walter Isaacson, *Benjamin Franklin: An American Life* (New York: Simon & Schuster, 2004).

2. Unless otherwise noted, all George Washington quotations are taken from *The George Washington Papers at the Library of Congress* (Washington, DC: Library of Congress, Manuscript Division). http://memory.loc.gov/ammem/gwhtml/gwhome.html.

3. Louisa Susannah Wells, *The Journal of a Voyage from Charlestown to London* (New York: New York Times and Arno, 1968), 29.

4. Wallace Brown, *The Good Americans: The Loyalists in the American Revolution* (New York: William Morrow, 1969), 141.

5. Unless, otherwise noted, all quotes from Joseph Plumb Martin can be found in George F. Scheer, ed., *Joseph Plumb Martin, A narrative of some of the adventures, dangers and sufferings of a Revolutionary soldier* (New York: New York Times and Arno, 1968).

6. All quotations pertaining to the life of Mary Jemison, unless otherwise noted, were taken from James E. Seaver, *A Narrative of the Life of Mrs. Mary Jemison* (Canandaigua, NY: J.D. Bemis, 1824).

7. Colin G. Calloway, *The American Revolution in Indian Country: Crisis and Diversity in Native American Communities* (New York: Cambridge University Press, 1995), 272.

8. All of Allaire's comments can be read in "Diary of Lieutenant Anthony Allaire, of Ferguson's Corps: memorandum of occurrences during the campaign of 1780," appearing in Lyman C. Draper, *King's Mountain and Its Heroes* (Cincinnati, OH: Peter G. Thompson, 1881), 484–415.

9. Quoted in Ray Raphael, *A People's History of the American Revolution* (New York: New Press, 2001), 168.

10. Alfred W. Blumrosen and Ruth G. Blumrosen, *Slave Nation: How Slavery United the Colonies and Sparked the American Revolution* (Naperville, IL: Sourcebooks, 2005).

11. Lt. Col [Ret.] Michael Lee Lanning, *The African-American Soldiers: From Crispus Attucks to Colin Powell* (New York: Citadel, 2004), 11.

12. Hilda L. Smith, *Women's Political and Social Thought: An Anthology* (Bloomington: Indiana University Press, 2000), 129.

13. Phillis Wheatley, in Betty Wood, *Slavery in Colonial America, 1619–1776* (Lanham, MD: Rowman & Littlefield, 2005), 118.

14. Gary B. Nash, *The Unknown American Revolution: The Unruly Birth of Democracy and the Struggle to Create America* (New York: Penguin, 2006), 407.

15. Nicholas J. Santoro, *Atlas of Slavery and Civil Rights: An Annotated Chronicle of the Passage From Slavery and Segregation to Civil Rights and Equality Under the Law* (Lincoln, NE: iUniverse, 2006), 17.

6

The Constitutional Period

Benjamin Banneker *(MPI/Getty Images)*

Washington and Madison: At the Constitutional Convention

By the middle years of the 1780s, men like George Washington and James Madison (a fellow Virginian and member of the Continental Congress) considered the Articles of Confederation—the original governing document of the United States, ratified in 1781 during the war—weak and incapable of holding the thirteen states together. The central government had no authority to demand taxes, to prevent the separate states from dealing individually with foreign nations, or to field a conscripted army if necessary. In late 1786 in rural Massachusetts, an army of indebted farmers led by Revolutionary War veteran Daniel Shays closed courts and marched on a federal arsenal before they were stopped by a state militia—the central government being unable to field a force. These farmer-veterans were the new revolutionaries, accusing the government of suppressing the same liberties that Adams, Jefferson, and Washington had felt the British were besieging ten years before. The "founding fathers" had become conservative—wanting to protect the new government—but the citizens remained inflamed, revolutionized. Reading about the events in far-off Massachusetts at his Virginia plantation, Mount Vernon, George Washington sensed an "impending storm." At a meeting held in Annapolis, Maryland, in September 1786, James Madison and Alexander Hamilton (a Revolutionary War officer who had served with Washington) urged Congress to appoint delegates to meet the following spring in Philadelphia in order to "revise" the Articles of Confederation.

When representatives of the states met at the Constitutional Convention in Philadelphia in May 1787, Edmund Randolph of Virginia submitted a plan (largely written by Madison) for totally re-creating the government, a much bolder move than had been advertised. With many modifications but few major changes, Randolph's plan was adopted on September 17, 1787, by the convention delegates as the new Constitution of the United States, though it would take two more years before all thirteen states ratified it.

Along the way, James Madison—thirty-six, slender and short, with pale skin and a voice so soft that other people would move toward him and gather around as he spoke—sat in the thick of the fifty-five members of the Constitutional Convention and took story-filled notes on what his comrades said. These lawyers and planters wore wool-fiber coats in the blazing heat of a building sealed shut to the public eye and ear. During those four hot months, aging Benjamin Franklin often snoozed in the back row, but when he did speak up, his sentiments helped soothe other members' flaring tempers and doubts. One month into the debate, on June 28, Franklin suggested that each day's session should start with a prayer. Delegates from large and small states were clashing over how to determine representation, and Franklin thought that without divine "aid, we shall succeed in this political Building no better than the Builders of Babel." John Adams would probably have approved of Franklin's suggestion, but in 1787 he was overseas serving as minister to Great Britain. Years later, Adams would write that for seventy-six years he had been "a church-going animal." The idea to have a daily prayer never went anywhere, probably because the money could not be raised to hire a minister. The government and the convention were broke.

On June 10, Madison—who would become the principal drafter of the Constitution—sent a letter to his friend James Monroe, who was back in Virginia. Madison wrote that one "of the earliest rules established by the Convention restrained the members from any disclosure whatever of the proceedings." Madison thought the rule against press leaks would "save both the Convention and the Community from a thousand erroneous and perhaps mischievous reports." With George Washington sitting as president of the convention (humbly and usually silent), Madison, Franklin, and company locked themselves away inside the State House with guards outside and created the rules to bind a nation. They kept the citizens, the "Community," from participating initially, but in the end, it would be the states, the white men with property, who would have to agree to what these authors of the nation wrote.

During the ratification process, citizens worried about many elements of the proposed Constitution, especially whether the federal government might become too powerful and thereby endanger common people's liberties. Would sheriffs have the right to search people's homes without a warrant? Would people be allowed to meet publicly to demonstrate and air their grievances? In other words, citizens worried about what was *not* in the proposed Constitution. They saw no guarantees for freedom of speech or of the press, for example. As for religion, the only reference appeared in Article VI, which stated that "no religious Test shall ever be required as Qualification" to hold a federal office. The delegates at the convention in Philadelphia had not wanted to deal with religion at the national level and preferred to let the states make their own religious rules. For most citizens, however, the delegates had not gone far enough. In fact, many Americans wanted the Constitution to ensure one religious freedom alone: the right to worship as one chose without governmental interference, oversight, or establishment. Protestants did not want Catholics telling them how to worship, and vice versa; and Jews feared oppression from their Christian neighbors. (In 1790, in response to Jewish people's fears, President Washington pledged that the republic would offer "to bigotry no sanction, to persecution no assistance.") Due to all these anxieties coughed up by publication of the proposed Constitution, with its implied powerful government, people demanded, as Madison knew they would, certain safeguards, now called the Bill of Rights. The history of the Constitutional Convention and of the ratification process is the story of the end of the Revolution. It is the history of learning to balance competing needs. The federal government had to be strong enough to protect the nation and keep its economy running, yet well enough designed that the people in power could never become tyrants or interfere with "Life, Liberty, and the pursuit of Happiness."

The Constitution: Debating the Future

The Constitution did not create a democracy. It created a republic. It was to be a republic that enshrined the rights of the states in careful balance with the power of the federal government, created by men who did not all or always believe in the wisdom of the common person. Edmund Randolph, a few days into the debates, said, "Our chief danger arises from the democratic parts of our constitution . . . the powers of government exercised by the people swallows up the other branches. None of the [state] constitutions have provided sufficient checks against the democracy." Randolph wanted a stronger government, but not one that would exert the pure will of the people. That was exactly what he feared—too much of the common man.

This fear of "the democratic parts of our constitution" was not shared by all leading men in America. Ben Franklin, for one, favored the wisdom of the people. Franklin, according to James Madison, "was understood to be partial to a single House of Legislation," wanting no checks on popular sovereignty. After all, the Senate was created as a place for the well born, well educated, and well to do, who were supposedly less likely to give themselves over to passion, emotion, or any of the other hobgoblins of the average mind that could be soaked with false ideas. The Senate was also meant to be a place where the aristocratic designs of America's elite could be channeled into some useful purpose. In fact, the Constitution could not become law unless ratified by the states. The people got a chance to review the document, debate it formally and informally, and white men chose for themselves whether or not it would replace the Articles of Confederation.

In Massachusetts, the state ratifying convention met early in 1788, and a few days into the debate, a Dr. Taylor stood up to voice his opinion on the need for frequent elections of congressional representatives: "Mr. President, I am opposed to biennial, and am in favor of annual elections . . . [yearly elections have], indeed, sir, been considered as the safeguard of the liberties of the people; and the annihilation of it, the avenue through which tyranny will enter." In other words, Dr. Taylor disagreed fundamentally with Edmund Randolph. For Taylor, the way to "safeguard the liberties" of the people was to make congressmen as responsive as possible to the will of the electorate:

voters would get a chance every year to kick out congressmen. Taylor and Franklin were not too far apart.

The argument between men like Edmund Randolph of Virginia and Dr. Taylor of Massachusetts was going on everywhere across the United States during 1778 and 1789 as citizens considered the best form of government they could hope to get. From these arguments came a movement toward compromise. Nearly everyone in the country agreed that the United States needed to have a viable government, and nearly everyone with a vote agreed that the exclusive liberties of white men needed to be protected. The question was how to implement the proper safeguards so that a strong central government could regulate commerce, lead the nation in war if necessary, but not trample on the freedoms of the citizenry. There were a few major sticking points: the continued existence of slavery and how it would factor into the nation, the relative power of small states versus large states, and the way the branches of government would look (one president or two? one legislature or more?).

Slavery was a controversial national issue. South Carolina had more slaves than free people, and Virginia's slaves made up about 40 percent of its total population. Serious money was invested in human property, and not many owners were willing to part with their investments. (However, from 1782 to 1792, Virginians did voluntarily free about 10,000 slaves.) If the North and the South were to stay part of the same nation, they would have to compromise on slavery. After all, by 1790, there were no slaves at all left in Massachusetts, and in 1780 Pennsylvania passed a law for gradual emancipation of all slaves. Rhode Island and Connecticut followed suit in 1784 with their own laws for gradual emancipation. The cultures of the North and South diverged widely with regard to slavery, causing friction that became a significant sticking point during the Constitutional Convention.

Issues surrounding slavery blended naturally into issues of state representation in Congress. Southern delegates wanted their slaves to count toward the number of representatives that southern states would send to Congress, an idea many northerners found patently dangerous and unfair. This major disagreement was settled by giving the South most of what it wanted. Written into the Constitution was a clause counting slaves as three-fifths of a person, and that in turn determined the number of congressmen a state would get in the House of Representatives. Southern slave owners, in effect, got more than one vote, and the North had to stomach that clause if it wanted the Constitution to be ratified, if it wanted the nation to remain whole. As Madison reported the words of a Virginia colleague, George Mason, "From the nature of man we may be sure, that those who have power in their hands will not give it up while they can retain it."

107

The settlement of the new western territories factored prominently into the proceedings—land represented a power that many wanted. West to the Mississippi River, north to the Canadian border, and south to Florida and Louisiana, the United States could expand. That would involve the further dislocation of native peoples, but few white Americans cared much. The one kind of lasting payment the government could offer Revolutionary War veterans was land, and the good land on the Atlantic coast was long since taken. The West beckoned. But how would these new territories be settled? The delegates in Philadelphia and the members of the Continental Congress in New York had to decide if slavery would be allowed to extend its influences into the Northwest Territory.

Madison himself spoke to the convention about the twin issues of power and slavery on June 30, 1787. On that day, while he sat scratching down notes with a quill pen, he heard James Wilson pointing out that the small states north of Pennsylvania would not be happy if states got representation in both houses of Congress proportionate to their population (i.e., states with small populations getting both fewer congressmen and fewer senators than states with large populations). Commenting on a Connecticut delegate's desire to have equal representation in the Senate, Wilson said this would "enable the minority to controul in all cases whatsoever, the sentiments and interests of the majority." Consequently, Wilson could imagine that "a separation must take place," a crumbling of the new nation, if something were not done to redress the fears of both large and small states. Wilson asked the convention, "Can we forget for whom we are forming a Government? Is it for *men,* or for the imaginary beings called States?" Madison, however, recognized that the central difficulty had more to do with slavery than with representation in Congress as a function of population.

Writing about himself in the third person, Madison recorded his own speech of the day: "he [Madison] contended that the States were divided into different interests not by their difference of size, but by other circumstances . . . principally from [the effects of] their having or not having slaves." This difference formed "the greatest division of interests in the U. States . . . it lay between the Northern & Southern." Madison himself had been "casting about in his mind" for a solution, which was "proportioning the votes of the States in both branches, to their respective numbers of inhabitants computing the slaves in the ratio of 5 to 3." It was an effective solution to a vexing problem, though he could not have known that it would later be one of the major contributing factors to the Civil War. The three-fifths compromise became a short-term way to keep the North and the South together in one nation.

Figuring out how to tax slaves and give votes to their owners for congressional representation did not answer the question of slavery's expansion. It was really the Continental Congress that found that solution rather than the Constitutional Convention delegates. With land speculators from Georgia to the Canadian border purchasing vast tracts of land and hoping to sell those domains to settlers, the pressure was on to establish orderly rules of settlement. Other than negotiating treaties with Indians—and many negotiations were made at the tip of a gun barrel—some ordinance had to be made for slavery. Once again, a man from Virginia seems to have proposed the solution, which was fitting because southerners would have been unlikely to accept any diminution of their slave-holding rights proposed by a northern, morally starched Yankee. On June 13, 1787, Congressman Richard Henry Lee (having just stopped off on his way to New York to talk with members of the Constitutional Convention in Philadelphia) proposed to his peers in the Continental Congress that slavery should not be permitted to expand north of the Ohio River, and this choice was unanimously agreed upon in Congress. Consequently, the slave interests in Philadelphia at the Constitutional Convention were assured that the entire Southwest would fill with cotton, slaves, and promises of money on their southern terms.

Though the hairsplitting debates spun on for two more months, a working document was signed on September 17. The hypnotizing rhetoric of Benjamin Franklin can be seen at work, calming the worries of the other delegates, preparing the way for approval. No delegate could be happy with all the provisions in the Constitution, but Franklin wanted his fellow statesmen to see how remarkable it was, given how many conflicting interests had been balanced through compromise. Using his usual doses of allegory and anecdote, Franklin offered his wisdom to men not lacking in it themselves. Not feeling up to reading his own prepared speech, Franklin got his fellow Pennsylvanian James Wilson to read it for him, in Wilson's Scottish brogue:

> Mr President, I confess that I do not entirely approve this Constitution at present, but Sir, I am not sure I shall never approve it: For having lived long, I have experienced many Instances of being oblig'd, by better Information or fuller Consideration, to change Opinions even on important Subjects, which I once thought right, but found to be otherwise. It is therefore that the older I grow the more apt I am to doubt my own Judgment, and to pay more Respect to the Judgment of others. Most Men indeed as well as most Sects in Religion, think themselves in Possession of all Truth, and that wherever others differ from them it is so far Error. Steele, a Protestant in a Dedication tells the Pope, that the only Difference between our two Churches in their Opinions of the Certainty of their Doctrine, is, the Romish Church is infallible, and the Church of England is never in the Wrong. But tho' many private Persons think almost as highly of their own Infallibility, as of that of their Sect, few express it so naturally as a certain French Lady, who in a

little Dispute with her Sister, said, I don't know how it happens, Sister, but I meet with no body but myself that's *always* in the right . . .

In these Sentiments, Sir, I agree to this Constitution, with all its Faults, if they are such; because I think a General Government necessary for us. . . . I doubt too whether any other Convention we can obtain, may be able to make a better Constitution: For when you assemble a Number of Men to have the Advantage of their joint Wisdom, you inevitably assemble with those Men all their Prejudices, their Passions, their Errors of Opinion, their local Interests, and their selfish Views. From such an Assembly can a perfect Production be expected? It therefore astonishes me, Sir, to find this System approaching so near to Perfection as it does . . . Thus I consent, Sir, to this Constitution because I expect no better, and because I am not sure that it is not the best. The Opinions I have had of its Errors, I sacrifice to the Public Good . . . Much of the Strength and Efficiency of any Government in procuring and securing Happiness to the People depends on Opinion, on the general Opinion of the Goodness of that Government as well as of the Wisdom and Integrity of its Governors . . . On the whole, Sir, I cannot help expressing a Wish, that every Member of the Convention, who may still have Objections to it, would with me on this Occasion doubt a little of his own Infallibility, and to make *manifest* our *Unanimity* put his Name to this Instrument.

By January 1788, four months later, five states had ratified the Constitution, out of the minimum of nine needed for its implementation. State conventions in Delaware, Pennsylvania, New Jersey, Georgia, and Connecticut had approved it, and intense newspaper debates continued in the other eight states. People opposed to the Constitution were styled Anti-Federalists—a reference to their fear that the central government described in the Constitution had too much power. Those in favor of the Constitution were known as Federalists. Massachusetts, Maryland, South Carolina, and New Hampshire followed with the remaining four ratifications needed. Virginia, the state with the largest population, did not ratify the Constitution until June 1788. Virginians held out until assured that better safeguards of individual liberty—now known as the Bill of Rights—would soon be added.

The apprehensions and disagreements that characterized the constitutional debates were not cured by the document that was produced. Slave owners from the South worried about maintaining their way of life; private citizens wondered sometimes if the federal government was not infringing too much on personal liberty. But women and men of the United States—free and slave—set out to fashion a society that the Constitution provided for: one based in commerce, shared enterprise, compromise, free speech (and lots of it), and the chance to alter government and society as each new generation saw fit.

Mary Dewees: Heading West

Philadelphia was one of America's premiere cities, the one with the largest population, the one where the founding documents were written. The United States was, however, a republic of farmers, who constituted 95 percent of the population according to the first census in 1790. In 1787, just as the Constitutional Convention was meeting in the grandiose State House, many families were setting off for the far West, to the frontiers of Kentucky and Franklin (later called Tennessee) to homestead and farm. To a nation of immigrants and the descendants of immigrants, the West represented a new chance: sometimes to create a perfect society, at other times simply to do well for oneself.

At five in the afternoon on September 27, 1787, ten days after representatives from New Hampshire to Georgia signed and agreed to disseminate the Constitution, Mary Dewees, along with her children and husband, left Philadelphia and bade "a last farewell" to good friends before setting "off for Kentucky."[1] Although some members of the family were "sick the greatest part of the way," as Mary Dewees explained in her journal, the family traveled six miles that day. Five wagons full of people, biscuits, and ham were on their way over the Allegheny Mountains (as the Appalachian range is called in Pennsylvania), bound for the fields of Kentucky, there to take advantage of the western lands being doled out to the farmland gamblers of America.

How these flat fields fit for corn and wheat had lately been made available to white settlement was of no concern to Mary, but she did detail the "excessive" sickness that plagued her for days. After a slow recovery, and after seeing some of the quaint towns around Lancaster—with elegant houses and gardens—the Dewees family began to ascend the foothills of the Alleghenies.

Only twenty years prior to this journey, the lands of western North Carolina, Virginia, and Pennsylvania were not known as "Tennessee" or "Kentucky." They were Shawnee hunting grounds, also claimed by France, Spain, and Britain. The French and Indian War and the Revolution created new maps and new owners, where before there had been fields, rivers, herds of buffalo, and salt licks for deer—the very things to attract hunters, trappers, and speculators. In the late 1760s, Daniel Boone—a paradoxically self-promoting loner—had blazed trails on the other side of the Cumberland Gap, a natural pass through the same Appalachian Mountains that Mary Dewees would face in 1787. Thousands of trappers and farmers had followed Boone. By the mid-1770s, there were roughly 50,000 colonists living west of the mountains—illegally, according to Britain's Proclamation Line of 1763 that was supposed to prevent any colonization of that territory. By 1784, the peace treaty with Britain had been ratified, leaving these far western lands for the taking. The states ceded their claims to the federal government, which in turn

111

passed laws like the Northwest Ordinances, providing for orderly establishment of towns and government, minus slavery north of the Ohio River after 1787. From the perspective of a distant observer, all was in order. From the perspective of a "pioneer," most days were tiring hard work, interspersed with the pleasures that scenery, towns, and forts could offer.

For about two weeks during mid-October 1787, the Dewees party clattered over stony mountain roads that were "very tedious." At one point, Mary Dewees compared her family to a "parcel of goats." As the adults trudged, afraid of falling off the mountain, the children ran on ahead, "jumping and skipping, some times quite out of sight." The family slapped together log cabins "with a few slabs for a roof, and the earth for a floor." Mary Dewees and company had all become "amazing dirty," and she moaned how lucky it would be to "escape being 'flead' alive." They were hosts to both wheat-field dreams and fleas, and Mary could finally say, "I think by this time we may call ourselves mountain proof."

By October 18, they were on the Monongahela River, rafting to Pittsburgh, where she "saw a very handsome parlor, elegantly papered and well furnished. It appeared more like Philadelphia than any I have seen since I left that place." European-descended migrants wanted to export their culture and happily looked for signs of it wherever they went. Few people headed into the wilderness intending to leave it wild. On October 25, the Dewees party left their new Pittsburgh friends "not without regret" and continued on toward Wheeling and finally Lexington.

Throughout this account of her journey westward, Mary Dewees remained buoyant of spirit, whether she was recounting the sublime vistas or the work and amusements of men and women, which fell into the gender-segregated categories to be expected:

> Our men went to give refreshment to the Horses. We females having had a good fire made up, set about preparing supper which consisted of an excellent dish of coffee having milk with us; those who chose had a dish of cold ham and pickled beats with the addition of bread, butter biscuit, and cheese made up our repast. After supper, sister, the children, and myself, took up our lodging in the waggon. The men with their blankets laid down at the fireside, the wind being high with some rain, disturbed our repose until near day light.

"The weather," she recorded, "much in our favour. It rained all day. Sewing and reading, and when the weather is fine, walking, are the amusements we enjoy. The gentlemen pass their time in hunting of deer, turkeys, ducks, and every other kind of wild fowl with which this country abounds." What Mary saw as "amusements" were becoming the marks of a kind of enslavement for other women. The Revolution had used a bold new language, asserting the innate rights of "man," though many women construed that word broadly to include both sexes. Even as Mary Dewees wrote contentedly in her journal, other women were preparing to assert their right to do more than cook, read, and sew. Two years later, in 1790, Judith Sargent Murray published an essay in *Massachusetts Magazine* titled "On the Equality of the Sexes." Murray stated in plain language, "Yes, ye lordly, ye haughty sex [men], our souls are by nature equal to yours; the same breath of God animates, enlivens, and invigorates us; and . . . we are not fallen lower than yourselves."[2] While Murray went on to write a book, *The Gleaner*, championing women's right to equal education as needed preparation for their roles as dispensers of virtue in the new Republic, Mary Dewees had already settled in Lexington, Kentucky, carrying on an unbroken tradition of women as helpmeets. This tradition did not, in Dewees's case, cause any recorded concern whatsoever. Women in the United States were starting to define their public and family roles differently.

After a few arduous months of traveling, Mary Dewees concluded her journal with what can be called, simply, relief. "I can assure you I have enjoyed more happiness the few days I have been here than I have experienced these four or five years past. I have my little family together and am in full expectations of seeing better days." Judith Murray was also married, with children to raise. Murray's feminist yearnings were meant to be an amendment to the role of wife, mother, and individual within a changing society. As the states ratified the Constitution and added the first ten amendments, the Bill of Rights, Mary Dewees made her own choices about the freedoms she would enact, all of which seem to have been in the tradition established before her by generations of women who did not regularly challenge the patriarchy of manners, customs, and laws in colonial America. But this subservience, willing and unwilling, was not long to last in a revolutionized America. A contemporary diarist, Nancy Shippen, jotted a favorite line from a novel (*The History of Emily Montague*) into her diary: "I cannot agree [that] Women are only born to suffer & to obey—that men are generally tyranical I will own, but such as know how to be happy, willingly give up the harsh title of master for the more tender & endearing one of Friend. Equality is the soul of friendship; marriage, to give delight, must join *two minds*, not devote a slave to the will of an imperious Lord."[3] Whether or not Mary Dewees would have agreed about the need for equality in marriage, she was thankful for her life: "May I ever retain a great full sense of the obligation due to the great Creator for his amazing goodness to me, especially, who had every reason from the first of the journey to fear quite the reverse."

Benjamin Banneker

Like Mary Dewees, Benjamin Banneker spent most of his life laboring over the common tasks of their era: tending to farm and family. However, Banneker also had a streak of assertive defiance, much like Judith Sargent Murray—an unwillingness to passively let white men in power truncate his potential. The specific details of Benjamin Banneker's life are not easy to come by; researchers have chased after the scattered remnants of his story for decades, looking to letters that mention him, the oral histories of family friends, and the few remaining testaments that Banneker himself left.

He was a farmer, first and foremost, if a person is defined by the hours spent at one task more than others. By itch and inclination, however, Banneker was a scientist and a writer, though in a society that discouraged black men from such pursuits. Banneker was an assistant surveyor for the District of Columbia, chosen as the nation's capital in 1789. He also wrote a series of almanacs in which he recorded his insights and described with great precision the movements of the moon and planets.

Born free and black in Maryland in 1731, Benjamin Banneker grew up an unusual young man in an unusual family. His grandmother, Molly, was a white woman from England who had been sent to the Americas as an indentured servant in the late 1600s, a penalty for having spilled a bucket of milk. After serving out the seven-year term of her servitude, Molly received a few acres from the colony and set to planting the corn she had also been given, but her own labors were not enough, and with anguish she purchased two slaves to help her, intending to soon set them free. Molly did just that, and promptly she and one of the men, Banneky, married each other, in direct violation of the racial laws of Maryland. White and black were meant to mingle, not mix. Laws were not always enforced, however, and they lived out their lives in the successes of land and children.

Benjamin Banneker's father carried on the family tradition of tilling the soil, raising tobacco for sale and food for eating. The Banneker farm was not large, about 100 acres, but it was enough to sustain the family with constant labor. Raised in his family's free fields, Banneker watched his father build furniture by hand, simple yet sturdy, and these habits of competence inculcated in Benjamin the wherewithal to persevere. His father and grandfather died at relatively young ages, leaving him in charge of affairs, with less time for book learning than he likely would have enjoyed.

Banneker's first teacher was his grandmother, who taught him to read and write, often from her prized, thick Bible; later he gained the rudiments of a schoolhouse education as well. After getting down his letters, it was back to the fields for many years, during which time he tended to occupy his few leisure hours playing songs on his violin and flute, while his sisters would sometimes sing along if they knew the tune. And when the chance arose, Banneker would read what literature came his way.

The eighteenth century was an age of print: books, pamphlets, Bibles, and newspapers fairly flew out print shop doors and into taverns, homes, and meeting houses of America's unusually well-educated populace. The almanac was the favorite form of print. Ben Franklin's own *Poor Richard's Almanack* was the best known and liked, but there were innumerable competitors, each offering a blend of commentary, advice, and astronomical observation and prediction. Almanacs blended the practical and the folksy sides of the developing American character—"Early to bed and early to rise makes a man healthy, wealthy, and wise," proclaimed Ben Franklin. Benjamin Banneker was known to sift through the pages of what material he could find, and these often political, frequently rowdy, and sometimes intelligent tracts seem to have induced him to add his own name to the list of published authors.

However, long before Banneker would have the chance to prove himself with words, he had already made a name for himself otherwise. By the time he was twenty-two, Banneker had literally cut and whittled a working clock—made almost entirely of wood (with the occasional bit of metal). Using carving tools and a file, and working from pictures and a clock loaned for modeling, he made a timepiece that was reputed to have remained accurate for fifty years, though he had no training in watch making, a skill typically learned during a lengthy apprenticeship. Up to that point, he had been recognized locally as intelligent, but chatter about the clock spread his reputation. The wooden wonder brought visitors to his house, and his own sharp mind drew him out to view engineering projects in the vicinity—where, until the 1770s, solitude had been his companion.

A family, the Ellicots, bought some acreage not far away where they designed and built a fully mechanical mill powered by river water. Their designs, store, and friendliness brought Banneker into their orbit, and a young member of the family, George, quickly recognized Banneker's sharp mind. A lasting friendship between the black man and the white man developed. George Ellicot lent a few books to Banneker on astronomy and mathematics. Though without any field experience, Banneker learned the book-basics of surveying, so when George's cousin Charles Ellicot was appointed lead surveyor for the District of Columbia by Secretary of State Thomas Jefferson, Banneker was in turn recommended by the Ellicots as an assistant, to which Jefferson agreed. Thus began the relationship between Banneker and Jefferson, one not in the end entirely to Jefferson's liking or advantage.

Banneker worked for months in a tent where he took celestial measurements day and night to make sure that the camp clock—used in the surveying—stayed true. But the sleeplessness of the labor and the winter's cold wore into Banneker's sixty-year-old frame, and he returned to his farm before the surveying was complete. He surely would have been acquainted with the slaves who did the grunt work on the project. Congress had decided to build the new capital closer to the South than the nation's original capital, New York City, in order to better represent the union of the nation and also serve as the continuing symbol of a commitment to slavery. Slave trading remained a reality in Washington, DC, until 1850, and indeed it was largely slave laborers who built the new Capitol building, the slaves being rented out from nearby plantations for five dollars a day.

Soon after getting home, Banneker wrote a personal letter to Secretary of State Jefferson. Jefferson had published sentiments in favor of ending slavery, and Banneker wanted to push him into action. In the mid-1780s, in his *Notes on the State of Virginia*, Jefferson had written, "half the citizens [trample] on the rights of the other. . . . Indeed I tremble for my country when I reflect that God is just: that his justice cannot sleep for ever." Jefferson made plain his hope that slavery would be ended "with the consent of the masters" because "the spirit of the master is abating, that of the slave rising from the dust." To Banneker, these shots at slavery seemed hopeful.

Banneker's letter, soon widely published (along with Jefferson's short reply), began by admitting to "that freedom, which I take with you on the present occasion." Free black men did not upbraid the secretary of state publicly or privately. It just was not done. Banneker did it. Then he continued:

> I suppose it is a truth too well attested to you, to need a proof here, that we are a race of beings who have long labored under the abuse and censure of the world; that we have long been looked upon with an eye of contempt; and that we have long been considered rather as brutish than human. . . . Sir, I hope I may safely admit . . . that you are measurably friendly, and well disposed towards us; and that you are willing and ready to lend your aid and assistance to our relief, from those many distresses, and numerous calamities, to which we are reduced.

In short, Banneker wanted Jefferson, lately his employer, to now become his ally as an abolitionist.

Jefferson thanked Banneker for the letter (one can imagine through gritted teeth and a clenched pen) and for a copy of Banneker's soon-to-be-published almanac. "No body wishes more than I do," Jefferson replied, "to see such proofs as you exhibit, that nature has given to our black brethren talents equal to those of the other colors of men; and that the appearance of the want of them, is owing merely to the degraded condition of their existence, both in Africa and America." Jefferson informed Banneker that he would send the almanac to a respected French scientist, which Jefferson did.

While the clock making had got Benjamin Banneker noticed, the almanac was his greatest recognized achievement. The publishers of Banneker's almanac, on its first page, expressed "themselves gratified in the Opportunity of presenting to the Public . . . what must be considered an extraordinary Effect of Genius—a complete and accurate EPHEMERIS for the Year 1792, calculated by a sable Descendant of Africa, who, by this Specimen of Ingenuity [demonstrates] that mental Powers and Endowments are not the exclusive Excellence of white People, but that the Rays of Science may alike illumine the Minds of Men of every Clime." The politics of race were now being moderated by science. The new methods of measurement (whether of the boundaries of the nation's new capital, the movement of stars, or the clicking of a clock's pendulum in approximation of time) were grasped by men of learning to argue that indeed "all men are created equal," a point that Banneker also made to Jefferson in the 1791 letter.

The United States was an experiment, a result of new ways of thinking—philosophy applied to government, not by nobles and clergy, but by educated citizens. The scientific "revolutions" of the preceding centuries were having their effects, and although the free African-American population of Maryland in 1790 was small—about 8,000—its best-known representative, Benjamin Banneker, excelled at mathematics and sciences, proof to a creative United States citizenry that African-descended Americans were equally capable of learning and inventing and that they too could help to change the world. Banneker himself grew up on a wilderness farm where his ex-slave father built a house and its early furniture with simple hand tools—a craftsman and farmer. These traditions of freedom and industry marked Benjamin Banneker and made him a true son of America's promise.

The Constitution: Intentions and Consequences

According to historian Edmund S. Morgan, after declaring independence, "the important thing was not to reform society but to keep government subordinate to it."[4] For the men who met in Philadelphia during the summer of 1787 to draft the Constitution, that may have been true. They were wealthy plantation owners, businessmen, and lawyers. Life was good. Society was working out well for them. The framers of the Constitution needed the kind of government that would protect the economy, protect the nation from invasion, and provide domestic tranquility. George Washington, who presided over the debates, James Madison, and Charles Cotesworth Pinckney had all literally fought during the Revolutionary War against a government they believed was trampling on a noble, industrious, and relatively free society. Government was necessary, they believed, but government should be constrained in its powers and responsive to the will of the people. Part of that constraint was to be internal: the checks and balances between the different branches of government. Part of that constraint was to be external: the play of powers and responsibilities between state governments and the federal government, with citizens, the people, voting legislators and executives in and out of power.

Defining "the people" consumed some of the debate at the Constitutional Convention, and it consumed much of people's energy in the decades after the Convention. As provided by the Constitution, individual states were left to establish their own requirements for political enfranchisement, rules for who was and who was not allowed to vote. Only New Jersey gave women the vote, but only a few women and for less than a decade. All the states required that a person be free in order to vote, and most states maintained a minimum property requirement for decades. These rules enabled some African-Americans in the North to vote. Before the Civil War, however, women essentially did not vote, and black men's votes effected few elections. Only in the ten years before the start of the Civil War in 1861 did even a few women start to publicly demand voting rights, and the supermajority of African-Americans in the nation lived as slaves in the South, where they were defined as property, and property does not vote. In terms of the basic citizen's right to cast a ballot, society did not reform for women or for many African-Americans after the War of Independence. But in many other ways, society did reform, regardless of any desires the framers of the Constitution may have had.

If the Constitution did not grant equality to the masses, subsequent additions have brought new generations closer to the implications enshrined in the opening phrases, "We the People of the United States in order to form a more perfect Union . . ." With each passing generation, more people have been considered "the People." And the Constitution is itself a revolutionary document because it allows for amendments, for change. The Constitution can adapt to a changing society.

Notes

1. Diary of Mary Dewees in Elwood Roberts, ed., *The Dewees Family: Genealogical Data, Biographical Facts and Historical Information* (Morristown, PA: William H. Roberts, 1905), 107–126.

2. Sharon M. Harris, ed., *Selected Writings of Judith Sargent Murray* (New York: Oxford University Press, 1995), 8.

3. All quotations from Nancy Shippen in chapters 6 and 7 were taken from Ethel Armes, *Nancy Shippen, Her Journal Book: The International Romance of a Young Lady of Fashion of Colonial Philadelphia with Letters to Her and About Her* (Philadelphia: J.B. Lippincott, 1935).

4. Edmund S. Morgan, *The Birth of the Republic, 1763–89* (Chicago: University of Chicago Press, 1993), 88.

7

Politics and Society in the Early Republic

Alexander Hamilton *(Hulton Archive/Getty Images)*

Of Midwives and Monarchs

Who have been more important in history, the common people with little power individually or the presidents, kings, philosophers, popes, and generals? Perhaps the elites have been more responsible for laws, wars, and religious perspectives, and genius writers like Thomas Jefferson have turned words into revolutions while Bach and Mozart turned passion into melody. Elites have wielded the blunt power of command and force, and they have used words and images to vast manipulative effect. However, maintenance of traditions year to year has been the work of countless midwives, bakers, storytellers, herbalists, carpenters, and sailors. Commoners have harnessed the energy of vegetables and cotton to feed and clothe the armies that they, their sons, and their fathers have filled. If nothing else, history has recorded the names of many leaders and few followers. We know the stories of Abigail and John Adams, but who remembers the name of their blacksmith or midwife?

Even though the elites have been important, there is a numerical reality to history, which suggests that if 95 percent of everybody was a farmer in 1790, history students should study the lives of farmers 95 percent of the time. However, farming techniques had hardly changed for centuries, so to study a farmer in 1790 is not much different than to study a farmer in 1690—with a few exceptions. First, by 1790 the hard-rock soils of New England had been cleared for generations. Young men who inherited their father's fields did not have to labor over giant tree stumps and more rocks than roots. Local roads leading to towns were safer, making markets more accessible and social contacts fuller, more diverse. In the South, white people had adjusted to the murderous temperatures, diseases, and other natural hardships that had kept their grandparents' life expectancies so low, and labor shortages had been worked out—to the disadvantage of African-Americans. By 1800, northerners and southerners could both expect, on average, to live to be about forty-five if they survived the plague of childhood illnesses. But high infant mortality dragged down the average, and it was not uncommon for people to live into their seventies. Life had become somewhat easier, even for farmers.

Voting rights were restricted, decreasing the political power of poor people. And women could not vote anywhere except in New Jersey—and there only from the late 1790s until 1807. In most districts, white men had to own property to vote, although the required value of the property was lower than it had been. Politicians in New York campaigned with gusto. For the mayoral elections in New York City, Aaron Burr went door-to-door, playing to each constituent's interests. And in Virginia, politicians learned that without enough whiskey and pork doled out generously to the electorate, the opposition candidate would win. In other words, the middling classes had their opinions, and shrewd politicians learned how to appeal to men with the vote.

While lawmakers shaped the nation with rules and regulations, preachers worked from the pulpit through the spirit, tugging consciences in new directions. In the 1730s and 1740s, George Whitefield had stormed America with his fiery calls for salvation through rebirth. He had infused Americans with a new passion for Christ and in the process altered the social dynamics of the colonies. Occasionally, black men called "exhorters" now stood in front of mixed congregations and rocked the spiritual house. Some white people began to see that all souls were equal, a recognition that led to the formation of abolition societies and schools for black people so they too could learn to read the Bible. Whitefield had written to some southern slave owners to say, "Blacks are just as much, and no more, conceived and born in sin as White men are."[1] Even so, he had urged converted slaves to remain obedient to their masters, and he himself had purchased at least twenty slaves. By the 1790s, however, fewer Americans were going to church than ever before, perhaps as few as one in fifteen. It is hard to know what caused this drop, though a movement toward a more rational, scientific mind-set could have been influential. Although church membership was temporarily reduced, religion remained important, particularly in African-American communities—enslaved and free—where so much evangelizing had been done as a result of the Great Awakening. America's first black priest was Absalom Jones, recognized and embraced by the Episcopal Church, elected a deacon in 1795 and a priest in 1804. Jones helped to establish the Free Africa Society in Philadelphia, a dedicated community service organization. Jones became a leader, but not because he was born into the position. He worked relentlessly in Philadelphia, first to free himself from slavery, then his wife, and then his community. This was accomplished less by the influence of laws than by the efforts of people on the street. Religion was a seedbed for democracy.

In the era of the young republic, men and women faced different limitations. The stories of Alexander Hamilton and Nancy Shippen demonstrate some of the limits that a commoner and a wealthy woman faced. Hamilton was a poor immigrant who made good on the shores of revolution and in the corridors of politics. Hamilton's story seems to confirm the boundless potential of this nation that allowed an unknown young man to craft policies and visions that still guide the country today. Nancy Shippen was a privileged woman who, although enjoying most of the advantages of her station, was defeated by the unequal power given to men in the early republic.

Alexander Hamilton

Born on the West Indian sugar island of St. Croix in 1755, Alexander Hamilton led a short, meteoric life. His father left the family while Hamilton was still a boy, and his mother was unable to offer much by way of support. At about ten years old, the precocious boy was put to work in a mercantile business and quickly distinguished himself. After a devastating Caribbean storm, some fancy hurricane journalism got him noticed—one phrase reading, "the prodigious glare of almost perpetual lightning"[2]—and a benefactor sent Hamilton to school in New York in 1772, just in time for the Revolution.

As with so many men of his generation, the war made him. Serving in an artillery company, Hamilton valiantly defended his position against the British onslaught in the battle for New York in 1776. General Washington noticed Hamilton and made him a lieutenant colonel and trusted adviser. Of equal and lasting significance, in 1780, Hamilton married the daughter of one of New York's wealthiest families, Elizabeth Schuyler, who would be by his side until the fateful end.

By war's conclusion, then, Alexander Hamilton had the makings of greatness: a quick mind, a veteran's credentials, the friendship of George Washington (the nation's first citizen), and a loving, well-connected wife. Add to this Hamilton's own burgeoning career as a lawyer, and there seemed little to stop him. In fact, for years nothing did stop him.

Hamilton and his growing family settled into the fast-talking, politically excited atmosphere of New York City, the nation's first capital, where he set up an office on Wall Street, got his red hair braided and powdered most mornings, took a wide range of cases, charged his clients reasonable fees, and immersed himself in the business of banking and governance. For the next twenty years, Hamilton promoted a vision of America that joined government, the people, and finances in a secular trinity of such lasting significance that his face appears today on the ten-dollar bill and his mark appears in the strength of the federal government. George Washington was the most beloved of Americans, but Hamilton may have done more than anyone else to carve this nation in the image of his charged imagination.

His service in the Congress during the 1780s only convinced him of the need for a more robust federal union, leading him to advocate for the Constitutional Convention. Though his role in the Convention was small, Hamilton joined forces with James Madison and John Jay to write the most convincing and vigorous essays in support of the Constitution. These *Federalist Papers* established Hamilton as a premier political theorist and ensured the ratification of the Constitution. Between that achievement and his role in building the Bank of New York, Hamilton became a natural choice for secretary of the treasury. In thirty-odd years he had traveled from a clerk's job on the slave-dominated shores of the Caribbean to a cabinet position in Washington's first administration (where one-fifth of New York City's population was still enslaved). Known to his detractors and enemies as a bastard, both figuratively and literally (his mother having become pregnant by a man other than her husband), Hamilton was entering into an American political scene where the hurricanes of smear tactics buffeted all contenders more violently than the raging winds and "perpetual lightning" of his youth. Political life in the early United States was nasty.

As a recent biographer, Richard Brookhiser, pointed out, the "one American activity [Hamilton] never quite mastered . . . was politics."[3] Ironically, the arena he never really left was politics; it offered him the best opportunity for implementing his vision. The United States had its freedom, and its citizens had their republican virtues. Many people questioned how to keep these virtues from being corrupted.

Ninety-five percent of people lived on farms or in towns with fewer than 2,500 people, and trade and commerce were necessary. Virginians could not eat their tobacco, and Connecticut Yankees could not smoke their apples or maple syrup. Under the new Constitution, the federal government could set taxes to raise revenues, but internal taxes were the devil that had set off the Revolution, so Congress was shy of them. Because the United States still imported many of its luxury goods from Europe, it was natural that tariffs (taxes on incoming goods) should make up the bulk of the government's revenues (in fact, by the early 1790s, tariffs made up 90 percent of the government's income). This much most statesmen agreed upon, but Hamilton thought in larger terms. While he supported close ties with Great Britain, Hamilton believed that the United States needed to literally build its own fortunes by promoting manufacturing, banking, and trade on an expanded scale. This policy set him firmly at odds with Thomas Jefferson, the first secretary of state, who wanted Americans to till the earth, dabble in small sciences, and stay clear of the vices of corruption, aristocracy, and degradation he saw as the inevitable products of cities, trade, and manufacturing.

For years, it became Jefferson's unlucky fate to live in Hamilton's shadow. During Washington's two terms as president, from 1789 to 1796, Hamilton proposed a series of programs that Congress and President Washington adopted: the Bank of the United States (1791), the assumption of all state and national debts that arose from the War of Independence (1790), close relations with Britain and weaker relations with France, an excise tax on liquor of 7 cents per gallon (1791), and expanded presidential powers. The merchants and traders of New England, along with their less numerous southern counterparts, were seen as the primary (if not the only) beneficiaries of Hamilton's manufacturing and debt plans. Indeed, most of Hamilton's programs appealed to people from the middle states and New England, but tasted bitter to southerners. The sectional differences between North and South that had surfaced during the Constitutional Convention continued to afflict the nation, and in many ways Hamilton and Jefferson came to represent the two sides. In 1792, in a letter to Washington, Jefferson referred to Hamilton and his supporters as "Monarchical federalists," likening them to kings and the supporters of kings, a pack of vampires set on draining the blood of goodness from the nation. Jefferson begged Washington to stay on for a second term, thinking that only Washington's heroic stature could keep the union together in the face of the dissent and disagreement that were increasingly coming to characterize the nation's politics. "North & South will hang together, if they have you to hang on," he implored. Jefferson believed that with Washington's "presence" at the helm for another four years, new attempts could be made "not inconsistent with the union & peace of the states."[4]

If Americans of the early twenty-first century think that the duels between liberal and conservative commentators are something new or unusual, they only need to look at the all-out newspaper warfare of the 1790s. Hamilton published essays in newspapers that were nothing but a mouthpiece for his ideas and a cannon for his attacks on naysayers. Jefferson matched Hamilton by setting up poet Philip Freneau with a government job so Freneau could afford to publish the *National Gazette*, the mouthpiece for Jefferson's ideas and counterattacks. These partisan rags were typical of the era, mixing fact with fury and regularly printing allegations about various politicians' sexual appetites. Jefferson, for example, was publicly accused of sleeping with his slave Sally Hemmings (which he probably did), who happened to be his wife's half sister, though no one in the family would admit to it. Hamilton was also accused of cheating on his wife (which he did). Scandalous personal details and deep ideological commitments mingled in the newspapers of the day, leading to the one thing that no politicians seemed to want: the formation of political parties.

By the turn of the century, two political parties existed in America: the Federalists (Hamilton's side), and the Democratic Republicans (Jefferson's). Slowly these protoparties began to involve everyday people, just as had happened during the Revolution, and in fact the everyday people were helping to create the parties. When exactly the parties solidified cannot be said with certainty, but they had their roots in the debates over ratifying the Constitution and then blossomed during the 1790s over such issues as relations with Britain and France, public financing of debt, a national bank, and the strength of the federal government in relation to the states (and later the Alien and Sedition Acts). All these issues pitted supporters of a strong national government against those who feared that a robust federal power would lead to tyranny. By 1792, the deferential, elitist politics of the day were shifting toward somewhat more direct involvement by the "people," who were becoming interested in the issues and influenced by masters of rhetoric like Hamilton.

During the middle years of the decade, more than forty Democratic Republican societies formed throughout the country, attracting equally the common people and the high living. Often opposed to the administration's policies and willing to say so, these societies were stocked with pro-French citizens (many recent arrivals from that country), who supported the French Revolution, in all its head-removing excesses, as the continuation of the American Revolution. Washington himself was coming under attack in the press. In a 1793 letter, Jefferson told James Madison that Washington was "extremely affected by the attacks made & kept up on him in the public papers. I think he feels those things more than any person I ever yet met with."[5] Washington mistakenly blamed these societies for stirring up what came to be known as the Whiskey Rebellion of 1794.

Hamilton's 1791 excise tax on liquor spurred people living west of the Appalachian Mountains to agree with Jefferson that the federal government was too strong. Westerners were prevented by Spain from trading through New Orleans at the southern tip of the Mississippi River, and they could not afford to transport their grains across the mountains in any form other than whiskey. They had next to no cash on hand, so the excise tax of a few cents a gallon was not only exorbitant but also impossible. In addition, farmers living in western Pennsylvania had to travel about 300 miles to Philadelphia to be tried there in court if they broke the law and did not pay the tax. The liquor tax turned out to be one sure way to get the common people involved in politics. By 1792, these western whiskey farmers had formed committees of correspondence, much like those of the pre-Revolutionary days, and were not bashful about attacking tax collectors when letters failed. Rather than raising an army to crush these insurrectionists, Washington simply issued an appeal for them to desist, and his reputation was still golden enough that they desisted.

U.S. citizens did not like paying taxes, but the government needed tax revenue. In 1794, Washington and Hamilton issued warrants for sixty distillers to appear in court in Philadelphia for nonpayment of taxes. Instead of going to court, the distillers set fire to the home of General John Neville, the loathed excise inspector. After taxing his house with flames, these whiskey rebels decided to pay an armed visit to Pittsburgh. Washington finally got on his horse, raised a militia of nearly 15,000 from four states, and sent Hamilton along with Virginia's governor at the head of the army to crush the rebellion. Sheer numbers alone convinced the rebels to yield, and ultimately no one languished in jail; the only two found guilty were quickly pardoned.

Hamilton believed that this martial display of force was exactly what the federal government needed to be able to do, though Jefferson thought the whole affair had led to a "detestation of the government."[6]

Though Hamilton and Jefferson did not always agree, they had been able to agree during the first years of Washington's administration. For example, they had willingly compromised to locate the nation's capital permanently on the Potomac River in exchange for passage of Hamilton's request to have the government assume the public debt (so it could pay off its international creditors and get some much-needed credit). Yet their relations had already soured by 1792, as shown by Hamilton's remark in a letter to a friend that Jefferson had a "womanish attachment to France, and a womanish resentment against Great Britain."[7] This schoolyard swing at Jefferson was precipitated by their basic disagreement about the proper form of government: should the United States be more like France or England?

Thomas Jefferson had once said, "The tree of liberty must be refreshed from time to time with the blood of patriots and tyrants."[8] The French took him at his word during the 1790s. When they cut off the heads of their king and queen in 1793, men like Hamilton came to believe even more strongly that Great Britain offered the only sane alternative; besides, Britain alone represented 75 percent of the United States' foreign trade—a big inducement to stay friendly. Jefferson retired from his cabinet job at the end of 1793 to sink into a much-desired seclusion with his books, experiments, crops, and slaves at Monticello, his estate in Virginia. Hamilton departed Washington's presidential side in 1795, to resume his law practice. However, Jefferson's retirement was short-lived; he was elected vice president when John Adams became president in 1796. To the consternation of both men, Hamilton virtually controlled the secretary of state, Timothy Pickering, whom he had chosen for Washington and whom Adams kept on in his job as a token of his esteem for Washington.

Adams's tenure as president was beset not only with problems at home, but also with international wars that dragged the United States into a quasi war with France (see Chapter 8). Adams responded to this crisis with the Alien and Sedition Acts. The first law, though never used, could have caused "males of the age of fourteen years and upwards, who shall be within the United States, and not actually naturalized . . . to be apprehended, restrained, secured and removed, as alien enemies." This law was directed at the French, causing a storm in Jefferson's pro-French emotions. By this point, 1798, Jefferson and Adams were no longer speaking, their political differences having got the better of them. The Sedition Act permitted a $2,000 fine and two years in prison for anyone who wrote, printed, uttered, or published "any false, scandalous and malicious writing or writings against the government of the United States, or either house of the Congress of the United States, or the President of the United States, with intent to defame." In other words, anyone who criticized the administration could go to jail, and though this law seemed to laugh in the face of the Bill of Rights, the country was at war, and the law was passed.

The Sedition Act was used twelve times to imprison publishers who criticized Adams and his policies. Freedom of the press vanished for two years.

The states of Virginia and Kentucky passed resolutions declaring their firm opposition to the laws, with Kentucky asserting a right to "nullify" (cancel) federal laws of such abhorrence and seeming unconstitutionality. Jefferson had drafted the Kentucky resolution, putting himself more firmly at odds with Adams. While U.S. merchant ships battled French privateers on the high seas, Vice President Jefferson and President Adams had their own quasi war.

Meanwhile, Adams lost any affection he once had for Alexander Hamilton. They both were Federalists, but they did not necessarily see eye to eye. In the 1796 election, Hamilton had cast his influence against both Adams and Jefferson by urging New England electors to vote for Thomas Pinckney (Elizabeth Pinckney's son). Although Adams beat Pinckney, he took Hamilton's exertions as a personal affront. Hamilton continued to prove himself an able agitator but blind to the sensitivities of politics, as likely to offend as to make a needed friend. Hamilton can probably be excused for some of his mistakes; the alliances of these national leaders were tangled, and favoring one person was sure to upset another.

Government makes laws, but it is made up of politicians. The laws and choices they make frequently stem from backroom dealings. In the late eighteenth century, the backroom was often a letter, and in the election of 1800, Alexander Hamilton's pen struck at the presidential hopes of Aaron Burr, a charmer, formerly a senator from New York, and now a free-spending, woman-chasing lawyer with whom Hamilton sometimes worked. With only a few exceptions, the people who knew Burr well did not trust him. Hamilton ranked first among them; he once said of Burr, "As a public man, he is one of the worst sort—a friend to nothing but as it suits his interest and ambition. . . . In a word, if we have an embryo-Caesar in the United States, [i]t is Burr."[9] So when Burr tied Jefferson for the presidency in 1800 with seventy-three electoral votes each, Hamilton was faced with an unusual choice. Should he throw his political weight behind his regular enemy of the last ten years, Jefferson? Or should he support Aaron Burr? Hamilton chose Jefferson, partly because Jefferson secretly promised not to mess with the financial system Hamilton had built. After voting thirty-five times, the House of Representatives (at that time the arbiter of ties) chose Jefferson too, largely because of Hamilton's behind-the-scenes advocacy. According to the old rules of the Constitution, Burr became vice president, having received the second-highest number of electoral votes. Hamilton's meddling in this affair, combined with his less-than-diplomatic public utterances, would cost him, in the end, more than all the defeats he inflicted on others.

The ideological boxing of politicians and their partisans in person and in the newspapers sometimes crossed into a third dimension: physical violence. Honor and pride mingled in these men's minds, and when newspaper comments crossed the threshold between criticism and character libel, a challenge to settle matters in a "gentlemanly" manner often followed. In other words, to defend their reputations, these giants of society would duel. In 1803, William Coleman (the editor of the *Evening Post*, a newspaper Hamilton had started in 1801) killed the harbormaster of New York, mainly in defense of Hamilton's reputation. Dueling was illegal in New York, so the duelists would row across the Hudson River to Weehawken, New Jersey, to do battle. While illegal in most places and excoriated by many critics as immoral, dueling was treated by its participants as necessary and honorable. Combatants verbally downgraded duels to "interviews," a casual label for a potentially deadly affair.

Duels ended in death about 20 percent of the time because the smoothbore pistols used were not accurate beyond a few paces. The protocol of the system required the duelists' seconds (friends who accompanied and supported the duelists) to try to avoid the duel beforehand by soothing emotions and proposing ways for the injured parties to simultaneously apologize and save face. These mediations did not always work. Such was the sad case with Hamilton's nineteen-year-old son, Philip, in 1802, when he dueled with a lawyer, George Eacker, who had earlier insulted Alexander Hamilton, suggesting in an Independence Day speech that Hamilton would support armed revolution against Republicans. Philip took his last breaths in his father's arms.

By 1804, then, Hamilton had lost his son to a duel and witnessed the recent erosion of Federalist popularity (in the aftermath of the Alien and Sedition Acts) to Jefferson's Democratic Republican Party. On top of that, Hamilton was barely treading water against the fast stream of his own monthly expenses, and Aaron Burr was busy campaigning for himself for governor of New York, knowing he would neither replace Jefferson as president in the forthcoming elections nor even remain as vice president. From his home on the outskirts of New York City, Hamilton settled into his old habit of reducing Burr's ambitions. Just before the election, at an anti-Burr meeting convened at a tavern, Hamilton made some damning remarks about Burr, calling him a "man of irregular and unsatiable ambition."[10] Two spies who were hiding under a bed in the next room overheard the remarks. Burr's spies told him what they had heard, and soon similar scathing remarks attributed to Hamilton were printed in a newspaper. Burr lost the election for governor and could see his own political fortunes sinking with little hope of resurrection outside of miracles. Since no heavenly forces were interceding on his behalf, Burr went about creating his own miracles, a dangerous game, especially for a man with his history.

In certain circles, there had been recent talk of breaking the New England states off from the rest of the United States, not least because of the votes that southern slave owners garnered from the counting of their slaves toward federal representation and hence toward the election of presidents. Many northerners feared this growing "slave power." Although Hamilton had begged off from the secessionist scheming, Burr was intrigued. He needed the glamour of such a grandiose political scheme to keep his political career going. Burr had promised his co-conspirators that if elected governor of New York, he would take the state into the planned secession. Now with these hopes sunk, Burr turned his spite on Hamilton, who offered a ripe grievance with his recent slanders of Burr.

Wasting no killing time, Burr sent Hamilton a letter in June demanding "acknowledgment or denial" of the recently reported slanders attributed to Hamilton. Burr either expected Hamilton to admit to the slanders or apologize. Hamilton decided to admit in a rather roundabout fashion, though he did conclude by saying that if Burr could not agree with his explanation, "I can only regret the circumstance, and must abide the consequences."[11] Hamilton was willing to duel, but in no hurry, soon declaring himself "opposed to the practice of duelling" on religious and moral grounds.[12] But neither he nor Burr in subsequent letters could settle matters with words, so they submitted the final ruling to a brace of pistols.

On July 11, 1804, the two men were rowed separately by their seconds to Weehawken through a morning fog. They cleared away brush together, though Burr did most of the work, having got there first. They took out their pistols, agreed upon the rules, and walked about thirty paces apart. Hamilton had already declared an intention not to fire actually *at* Burr; he meant this display to be manly but not lethal. Burr shot at Hamilton and hit him, the bullet passing through his abdomen, cutting the liver and damaging the spine. The doctor who accompanied the duelists administered what care he could, which amounted to getting Hamilton back to the city. Hamilton died the next day, attended by doses of laudanum (liquid opium), his family, and the reluctant ministrations of a priest who scolded Hamilton for not attending church and hence not properly preparing his soul for death.

Fifteen years into the Constitution, the third vice president of the United States shot and killed the former secretary of the treasury. Burr spent the remaining thirty-two years of his life involved in further bizarre schemes to enrich himself and to invade Mexico and make it part of the United States. He was indicted more than once for crimes—both murder and treason—but managed to escape punishment.

Hamilton's death was mourned by the nation, even by those who had disliked him and his policies. His longtime friend, Gouverneur Morris, delivered the funeral oration in a cloudburst of tears. Morris told the assembled throng,

131

"I will struggle with my bursting heart to pourtray that Heroic Spirit, which has flown to the mansions of bliss."[13] John Marshall, the chief justice of the Supreme Court, rightly commented in a biography of George Washington, "seldom has any minister excited the opposite passions of love and hate in a higher degree than Colonel Hamilton."[14] Contemporaries' love and hatred for Hamilton revealed the emotional pull of politics. Emotion—as expressed in moral and ethical terms of right and wrong—guides politics, central to the election of legislators and to the laws they pass. Lawmakers have had their philosophies and theories of government from the first moments of the first struggles at the nation's founding. Yet politics is a human affair, in all its many dimensions: intellectual, emotional, and physical—a balance that Alexander Hamilton did not get quite right.

Nancy Shippen

Alexander Hamilton lived and died according to public rules written by men. Nancy Shippen, though wealthy and well loved, also had to abide the rule of men as a daughter, a wife, and a mother. Having been the belle of Philadelphia society and the darling of her family, Nancy Shippen was subjected to the whims, caprices, and authority of her father and her husband. This is her tragedy, a personal history that shows how the colonies were bound together by marriage and how marriage bound women to a fate over which they had little control.

The United States was stepping onto the world stage, and the first player to recognize the official presence of the States was France, followed by Spain. This new American country of farms and small cities was something of a novelty to the aristocrats of Europe. The distinctions between gentry and commoner were not as easy to see in the United States as in the castles, manors, and palaces of France or Britain, where gold dust was sprinkled on fruit and where princes and princesses commissioned great works of music from the likes of Bach and Mozart. One of the few U.S. emissaries to Europe, Benjamin Franklin, wore a cap of raccoon fur, not because he was a woodsman, but in order to play to the image of the American frontiersman that Europeans expected. There were, however, genteel exceptions, like Nancy Shippen.

Her father, Dr. William Shippen Jr., was descended from the first mayor of Philadelphia, and her mother was the sister of Richard Henry Lee of Virginia, who had suggested to the rest of the Continental Congress on June 7, 1776, that it was time to declare independence. Dr. Shippen was the director of hospitals for the Continental Army, so Nancy's mother's and father's families traveled in the same patriotic circles, and their three-story house in Philadelphia often served as unofficial headquarters for the new nation's leaders. George

Washington liked to come by for tea, and Richard Henry Lee had wandered around the house, his eyes catching the flames of candles reflected in polished wood floors, the night before his momentous speech to the Congress. Nancy Shippen grew up here, surrounded by excellence and attention.

Love and war drew the world together and tore it apart. Nancy's first love was the symbol of the new nation's first overseas affair, and his name was Louis Otto, a Frenchman assigned as an aide to the French legation. She called him Leander, a classical reference to a mythological young Greek who swam across the Dardanelles nightly to be with his love. Louis Otto was young, promising, and entirely hers. They met during the waning days of the war, a year before Cornwallis surrendered, when full independence was only a treaty (and some southern civil war) away. Otto would walk by the windows of Shippen House and cast his eyes over the company, searching her out. Then he would write to her and describe what he had spied: "Miss Nancy before the tea table, in an artfully neglected Dress, her hairs flying a little upon her neck . . . changing her Seat several times, but allways pretty far from the candel: and looking however *as lovely as an Angel.*"[15] Nancy's affections were caught, as her father could tell: Nancy "loves [Otto] first. . . . On Tuesday evening when O[tto] comes he is the angel."[16]

In fact, after a yearlong flirtation and friendship—when Nancy and Louis would entertain elite company, her voice accompanied by his harpsichord— the young Frenchman proposed marriage. Otto's courtship was smooth: "I am allways at a loss how to express myself with you. There is something so heavenly in my soul when I begin to write that I should not be able of expressing it even in my own language." But really he was not at a loss for words. "When I look on you," he jotted, lovesick, "the Symbole of the most perfect mind . . . I press my lipps upon your hand from which I would never be separated."[17] In early 1781, Nancy Shippen accepted, which elicited Louis Otto's exuberant reply: "Was it a dream, my dear Nancy? Or did I really hear you pronounce that heavenly *yes!*"[18]

Louis had heard correctly, but Nancy's words and wishes were less important than her father's. Dr. Shippen loved his daughter dearly, but he had more concerns on his mind than her romance. Someone else had also been courting her, Henry Livingston, a colonel in the Continental Army and an heir to the vast, feudal estates and fortunes of the Livingstons of New York. Their many thousands of acres had been a seventeenth-century gift from William Penn. Henry Livingston had money, which Louis Otto did not, and Nancy Shippen's father was increasingly cash-poor. The war had wreaked havoc on his finances, as it had for many. While serving as a doctor with the army, Dr. Shippen had had to neglect his own medical practice at home, and the economy was slumping right along with the ever-depreciating value of the Continental dollar, which Congress had issued in vast quantities to cover its unmanageable bills. As Nancy's father said, "L[ivingston] has 12 or 15,000 [pounds] hard."[19] This simple number became the arithmetic of her marriage.

Once Dr. Shippen was certain of Henry Livingston's interest in Nancy, he used the power that an eighteenth-century father had over his daughter's affairs by ordering Louis Otto not to come around for four weeks. In the absence of her true love and in the company of a seemingly charming man and hero, and under the pressure of her father's wishes, Nancy Shippen consented to marry Henry. The wedding took place on March 4, 1781. This was the manipulated choice that would break her happiness.

Soon after marrying Henry Livingston, Nancy gave birth to a baby daughter, called Peggy by the family. In April 1782, Nancy wrote in her journal, "I have the sweetest Child that ever was born—in her I shall be most blest."[20] And though she could describe dressing her "Angel Child" and having "kiss'd her a hundred times," these would be nearly the only tendernesses in Nancy's life for the rest of her days.[21] Her husband was prone to violent rages and desperate jealousies, and he took out his passions on Nancy, "persecuting [her] with his reproaches." Within his own wealthy family, who exhibited all the decorum and good manners befitting their elevated status, Henry was known as a brute and a cheat. Henry's own mother wrote to Nancy, "Oh what a malignant heart has he."[22]

Men of this era could be brutal and get away with it, even in the courts, and this was particularly true as values shifted during and after the War for Independence. Women were no longer seen as lusty maids barely able to restrain their own urges. Now women were increasingly thought of as sexually dormant, the protectors of morality and virtue. As the nation underwent transformations, so too did expectations of women's behavior. Any woman who seemed to stray from this new code of behavior was treated as unworthy, beneath contempt. An infamous court trial in 1793 in New York testified to the lack of civic and legal support for women in cases where gender and sexuality met. When a young seamstress named Lanah Sawyer was raped by wealthy Henry Bedlow, the facts of the case were never in question. But during the trial Lanah Sawyer's character was called into question as Bedlow's lawyers asked why she repeatedly accompanied him (on three dates) if not for sex. The all-male jury acquitted Bedlow in less than twenty minutes, arguably not wanting to encourage other women to challenge male authority. After the rapist was found not guilty, the red-light district of Manhattan saw three nights of rioting in which bordellos were sacked, perhaps a way for poorer men to strike back at the places where rich men like Henry Bedlow preyed on disadvantaged women. In the early republic, it was easier for poor men to indirectly lash out than it was for women to assert equality.

Although Nancy Shippen never actually did anything wrong, her husband's accusations about her loose nature gave him a kind of power over her—despite Nancy's discovery that he had sired children with a number of different women and was thinking about bringing them all to live under one roof, along with her little Peggy! It was not many months before Nancy chose to leave him and his mother's New York estate in order to return to her parents' home in Philadelphia.

In itself, leaving her in-laws' home was a bold move for a young woman with a baby in the 1780s, and the law was not on her side in the coming years. Dr. Shippen's finances continued to slump, and though he did not approve of the accusations Henry Livingston made about Nancy's behavior—namely that she remained in love with Otto (true), communicated with Otto (false), and flirted with other men (false)—Nancy's father informed her in early 1783 that she would have to send Peggy, now seventeen months old, to live with her paternal grandmother, Henry's mother. The Livingstons could offer Peggy the kind of future that made sense to the untitled aristocrats of the United States.

Even as Nancy Shippen prepared to take Peggy back to New York to leave her there, Nancy remained faithful to the husband who emotionally abused her. In her journal, a few nights before departing, Nancy wrote, "Leander [Otto] went past the window while we were at Tea—he look'd in—his Eyes told me he wou'd be happy to join us—but I did not ask him—prudence forbid it . . . because it wou'd displease my husband."[23] Nancy nursed the fruitless hope that a reunion with Henry would mean that she could stay near her daughter, but this never came to pass. Nancy stayed at the Livingston estate long enough to realize that Henry would not visit her (as he was not at home when Nancy arrived with baby Peggy). Nancy wrote him a parting letter: "tho I return to my parents I return not *all*; All that is now dear to you, I leave to you; But what in this case will be your greatest happiness, will be to me, in the pangs of parting & continued separation, unspeakable Anguish."[24]

Having been prodded by her father to marry Henry Livingston, Nancy was now forced by her parents and in-laws to leave Peggy, the one joy in her life to the same new family that was the source of her sorrows. Years of separation followed, during which mother and daughter saw each other infrequently and often secretively. Henry sought to control Nancy by threatening to take Peggy to live with him in Georgia (a threat he used as leverage for a divorce). By the laws of the eighteenth century, Henry was legally entitled to keep his daughter with him, regardless of his own infidelities and the little time he had spent with her.

Louis Otto remained Nancy Shippen's steadfast friend in these years, throughout a marriage of his own. Decorum outweighed their continuing love, however. Because she was married to a man who would not grant her an amicable divorce, because the legislature of New York would have to pass a special bill allowing her to get divorced (a law that Henry's lawyers contested), Nancy spent her days caring for an ailing mother, pining after Peggy, and engaging in the tea parties, house visits, and forest walks that made up the hours of the well-to-do.

During the late 1780s, Henry Livingston's mother began to allow Peggy to return to Nancy for intermittent summer visits. Peggy was becoming well educated and adored by those who knew her, just as Nancy had been, but the vigorous spirit was long since drained from Nancy Shippen. She lived out the rest of her life in a kind of semi-seclusion, cocooned in the weary heartbreak that had afflicted her for the fifteen years that Peggy lived in far-off New York, which took long enough to reach by coach, but which was a legal galaxy away.

The politics of gender in the United States were changing. Just as the language of liberty infused life into the antislavery movement, the same currents began to flow slowly toward women. In 1796, women gained the right to vote in New Jersey (for about a decade). Schooling for girls became more available, and women began to teach. It became women's duty to provide the moral underpinnings of the new republic, and in this educator's role they gained a kind of independence from men. Nancy Shippen, however, did not enjoy many of these new opportunities. Now a teenager, Peggy, of her own volition, returned to Nancy's side in 1797, six years after Nancy's last entry in her journal: "It is certain that when the mind bleeds with some wound of recent misfortune nothing is of equal efficacy with religious comfort."[25] Nancy Shippen turned her attention toward God, fell prey to the financial pleas of religious charlatans, and became something of a secular nun, although her fondest hope during the summer years of her youth had been to marry the Frenchman, Louis Otto, who demonstrated the loyalty and kindness that her own husband never offered.

John Marshall's Supreme Court

Alexander Hamilton played his part in holding the nation together, making every attempt to interpret the Constitution in broad terms that would strengthen the country by strengthening the federal government whenever necessary and appropriate. For instance, in a 1791 letter to President Washington, he argued that the Bank of the United States, which is not mentioned in the Constitution, could be incorporated based on implied powers. Article I, Section 18, of the Constitution says that Congress has the power to "make all laws which shall be necessary and proper" for executing its listed duties. Based on the phrase "necessary and proper," Hamilton argued, "*necessary* often means no more than *needful, requisite, incidental, useful* or *conducive to.*"[26] In other words, what the government needed would be the proper thing to do, after taking into consideration all the other restrictions of the Constitution. Hamilton said the constitutionality of a law could be tested by asking whether the law would support the obvious "end[s]" of the Constitution, those objectives which it was written to accomplish. If the law were a "means" to that "end," then it was constitutional.[27]

Not everyone agreed with Hamilton, but early in 1801, on his way out the door, President John Adams appointed a new Supreme Court justice who did: Chief Justice John Marshall. Born the eldest of fifteen children in a wilderness family on Virginia's western frontier, Marshall served under Washington at Valley Forge and watched local farmers sell produce to his starving army at the highest prices possible. These experiences convinced him that the nation needed a strong federal government, which he found legal justification for in Article I, Section 8, of the Constitution, which said that the purpose of Congress was "to provide for the common Defense and general Welfare." Marshall thus agreed with Hamilton, and until his death in 1835, he worked to empower the Supreme Court and to give the federal government jurisdiction over the states. The writers of the Constitution created the Supreme Court, but John Marshall gave it authority.

Marshall corralled his fellow justices so effectively that he had to write only one dissenting opinion in thirty-four years on the bench. A handful of his decisions set precedents that are still with us today. The first and most fundamental of these was handed down in 1803 in the famous case of *Marbury v. Madison*. President John Adams had made a few "midnight" appointments on his way out the White House doors, and one of them was given to William Marbury, a lawyer who was to be made justice of the peace for Washington, DC. But the appointment, though signed and sealed, was accidentally left on Adams's desk and never actually delivered to Marbury. Thomas Jefferson, the newly elected president, was appalled at Adams's last-minute appointments, especially because the appointees were all ardent Federalists, so Jefferson refused to have Marbury's appointment delivered. To make a living, Marbury had to go back to work as a lawyer, but he secured a writ of mandamus, a judicial command, to have his appointment delivered. The case made it to the Supreme Court.

Chief Justice Marshall was in a bind. The Supreme Court had a generous writ of power in the Constitution, but up to that point it had exercised little authority. Marshall had no leverage to enforce any decision his court might hand down, and he was sure that Jefferson would not honor a ruling in Marbury's favor. So he ruled that the Judiciary Act of 1789 exceeded Congress's powers and that the Supreme Court had no constitutional authority to issue a writ of mandamus—that, in essence, Marshall could not force Jefferson to deliver the appointment. This was a technicality, and although the decision seemed to restrict the Court's powers (to the delight of Republicans), Marshall was actually setting the precedent that the Supreme Court could rule over the constitutionality of laws passed by Congress. This power is known as judicial review, and even though the process is not spelled out in the Constitution, it has been a central role of the Supreme Court ever since 1803.

In John Marshall's long career, he helped establish the authority of federal law over state law, especially in 1818 in *McCullough v. Maryland*, when the Supreme Court prevented the State of Maryland from taxing a branch of the Second Bank of the United States. Marshall also gave corporations a new kind of life, imbuing them with the rights of an immortal individual in the eyes of the law in *Dartmouth College v. Woodward* in 1819. Marshall prevented the State of New Hampshire from taking control of Dartmouth College, which the trustees had argued would break the original contract. Marshall's opinions were controversial in his day and angered no one more than Thomas Jefferson. However, Jefferson could be a good sport. He said that the chief justice was so persuasive that if Marshall asked him if it were daylight outside, the reply would be "Sir, I don't know, I can't tell!"[28]

Marshall was a man of simple manners and tastes, and stories told about him reflect early nineteenth-century customs and republican values. His wife was sickly, so Marshall did the food shopping, walking to the market stalls to pick through seasonal produce and squawking fowl. One day (as related by Leonard Baker, a recent biographer), a young man, worried about his own reputation but under instructions from his mother, fretted about having to carry a turkey home from the market like a common servant. John Marshall, dressed as usual in casual attire and thus looking like a servant himself, offered to carry the turkey part way for the young man. When they reached Marshall's door, Marshall announced that he was home and handed over the turkey. The young man stammered out, "But this is the home of the Chief Justice of the United States," and Marshall, without missing a step, smiled and said, "I know."[29]

Notes

1. Frank Lambert, "'I Saw the Book Talk': Slave Readings of the First Great Awakening," *Journal of African American History,* 87 (Winter 2002): 12–25.
2. Richard Brookhiser, *Alexander Hamilton, American* (New York: Free Press, 2000), 20.
3. Brookhiser, *Alexander Hamilton, American*, 9.
4. Paul Leicester Ford, ed., *The Writings of Thomas Jefferson* (New York: G.P. Putnam's Sons, 1895), 6: 5.

5. Ford, ed., *The Writings of Thomas Jefferson*, 6: 293.

6. Ford, ed., *The Writings of Thomas Jefferson*, 6: 518.

7. Henry Cabot Lodge, ed., *The Works of Alexander Hamilton* (New York G.P. Putnam's Sons, 1886), 8: 259.

8. Thomas Jefferson Randolph, ed., *Memoir, Correspondence, and Miscellanies, from the Papers of Thomas Jefferson* (Charlottesville, VA: F. Carr, 1829), 268.

9. Henry Cabot Lodge, ed., *The Works of Alexander Hamilton,* (New York: G.P. Putnam's Sons, 1904), 8: 285.

10. Brookhiser, *Alexander Hamilton, American,* 207.

11. Lodge, ed., *The Works of Alexander Hamilton* 10: 463.

12. Lodge, ed., *The Works of Alexander Hamilton,* 10: 471.

13. Harold G. Syrett, ed., *The Papers of Alexander Hamilton* (New York: Columbia University Press, 1979), 26: 325.

14. John Marshall, *The Life of George Washington* (Philadelphia: James Crissy, 1832), 2: 356.

15. Ethel Armes, ed., *Nancy Shippen: Her Journal Book* (Philadelphia: J.B. Lippincott, 1935), 113.

16. Armes, ed., *Nancy Shippen,* 101.

17. Armes, ed., *Nancy Shippen,* 98.

18. Armes, ed., *Nancy Shippen,* 105.

19. Armes, ed., *Nancy Shippen,* 101.

20. Armes, ed., *Nancy Shippen,* 140.

21. Armes, ed., *Nancy Shippen,* 141.

22. Armes, ed., *Nancy Shippen,* 271.

23. Armes, ed., *Nancy Shippen,* 28.

24. Armes, ed., *Nancy Shippen,* 159.

25. Armes, ed., *Nancy Shippen,* 294.

26. John C. Hamilton, ed., *The Works of Alexander Hamilton* (New York: Charles S. Francis, 1850), 4:109.

27. Hamilton, ed., *The Works of Alexander Hamilton,* 4: 113.

28. Quoted in Jean Edward Smith, *John Marshall: Definer of a Nation* (New York, Henry Holt, 1996), 12.

29. Leonard Baker, *John Marhsall: A Life in Law* (New York: Macmillan, 1974), 755.

8

The United States on
the World Stage

Sacagawea and the Corps of Discovery *(MPI/Getty Images)*

Money, War, and Power

The United States was an unusual country. It had no nobility. Monarchies and empires dominated the rest of the world. Like Europe's nobility, however, Americans were discovering the loaded joys of money. The majority of farmers and the minority of merchants, lawyers, and other professionals simply wanted the other nations of the world to open up their markets, sell reasonably priced manufactured goods to the United States, and buy American produce. U.S. citizens were sure that prosperity was their inalienable right.

Europeans and North Africans had other ideas. Great Britain, not happy with having lost 4 million colonists and a chunk of land bigger than England itself, restricted U.S. merchants from trading in the financial fun houses of the Caribbean. France more or less liked the United States, but it wanted its money back, having lent a hefty fortune to finance the War for Independence. Then there were the four North African Barbary States of Tripoli, Tunis, Morocco, and Algiers—infamous for their pirates. These tiny nations helped themselves to other countries' ships, gold, silver, and citizens. Piracy was business in Barbary. After a successful capture, the Barbary rulers would demand ransom money and "tribute" payments if Europeans and Americans wanted to continue sailing past the Strait of Gibraltar, which led from the Atlantic into the Mediterranean. It seemed that nobody else was going to serve up as much life, liberty, or pursuit of happiness as U.S. citizens wanted.

George Washington wryly described the feeling of going to his first presidential inauguration in 1789 as "a culprit who is going to the place of his execution."[1] For the people of the United States, the more than twenty years following 1789 were akin to a fraternity hazing party masquerading as a debutante ball at which all the guests arrive bearing poisoned daggers and demands for cash. The United States' international choices influenced the choices made at home: political parties formed partly in reaction to world events; a navy was built; and like it or not (some did, some did not), the United States had to fight for its right to trade and be respected.

From the beginning, this new nation of people entwined in their own internal struggles was part of a larger map. The peace treaty signed in 1783 extended the borders of the United States westward to the Mississippi and south to the northern edge of Florida, although New Orleans remained in the hands of the Spanish. These boundaries basically left two-thirds of the continent up for grabs, as far as many white people were concerned; however, hundreds of thousands of Native Americans lived in these "unclaimed" western expanses. Thomas Jefferson wrote a government check for $15 million, bought the Louisiana Territory in 1803 (doubling the land mass of the United States), and sent Lewis and Clark's Corps of Discovery into the wilds to meet Indians and establish a claim to the far West. The Corps of Discovery was a kind of international diplomacy, which Sacajawea—a Shoshone—made eminently easier by becoming the go-between for the peoples of the West and the small party of scraggly Americans representing the acquisitive might of a numerous people.

By 1790, the United States was an independent nation. But what did that amount to?

Citizen Genet: French Diplomacy with a Twist

The United States had no fangs. George Washington had kept the underpaid Continental Army drilling until the peace treaty with Britain was signed. Then the soldiers were promptly sent home to poverty and farming. With only the pretense of a military in the early 1790s—about 5,000 soldiers in all—the republic had to rely on goodwill, diplomatic finesse, and bluffs in its negotiations with England and France.

In 1789, the people of France plunged into chaotic revolution. In 1793, French revolutionaries beheaded their king, Louis XVI, and his Austrian-born wife, Marie Antoinette. Regicide was soon followed by war with England and Spain, the Reign of Terror (during which public beheadings served as sport), subsequent terrors (more beheadings), and the dictatorship of Napoleon Bonaparte, who exported France's liberty, equality, and fraternity at gunpoint. The United States wanted to stay out of the way, neutral, but continue to trade. The French wanted help, at least financially, so they sent a promising diplomat who sizzled with revolutionary zeal: Citizen Edmond Genet ("Citizen" being the new prefix in France, suggestive of the new social equality).

Genet landed in Charleston, South Carolina, on April 8, 1793. The American minister to France, Gouverneur Morris, had already sent ahead a cutting letter of introduction to President Washington. Morris wrote, "I have seen M. Genet. . . . He has, I think, more of genius than ability, and you will see in him at first blush the manner and look of an upstart."[2] In the midst of a weeklong series of parties and dinners thrown in his honor by the grandees of Charleston society, Genet did his best to live down to Morris's remarks. Within days, Genet hired five U.S. captains and their ships to prey on British vessels. In a fit of ego, he even had one of these privateers named after himself: the *Citizen Genet*. Out of his many flimsy schemes, this was the only one that met with even limited success: the privateers did immediately begin capturing British ships. However, Genet's use of American ships as his own personal pirate fleet stirred up more problems than it solved, and it underscored the ways in which the United States' national sovereignty was not respected by other nations in that age of empires.

During the month of April, Citizen Genet traveled north in a processional of American cheers and hurrahs for him and the republicanism that he seemed to represent. Meanwhile, Congress and the president deliberated the best course to take in the developing war between France and England. They chose outright neutrality, though Secretary of State Thomas Jefferson did manage to get the word "neutrality" stricken from the official decree. Jefferson leaned toward France, and Genet could have accomplished a lot for France if he had had an ounce of subtlety. But Genet's pushy behavior caused his own downfall. He also managed to create one of the final fissures between the U.S. government's pro-British faction, centered on Secretary of the Treasury Alexander Hamilton, and the pro-French "republican" faction, generally led by Jefferson. At the time, Jefferson wrote, "It is impossible for anything to be more affectionate, more magnanimous than . . . [Genet's] mission." Then Jefferson accused Hamilton's partisans of wanting "to make a part in the confederacy of princes against human liberty" by supporting Britain at the expense of France.[3] Hamilton wanted to support Britain (the "princes"), Jefferson did not, and at first President Washington chose the middle path between these two cabinet secretaries.

Genet reached Philadelphia after a month, long enough to have become confused by the enthusiasm many U.S. citizens showed him and deluded by his own hopes. Though unhappy about American neutrality, Genet still hoped to secure advanced payments on the debt that the United States owed France. But Congress and the president thought it unwise to give what little money they had to the French government, which was regularly cutting off its own citizens' heads. The guillotine lopped off up to 400 heads a day in Paris, and the ruling clique rarely lasted a year. Besides, Genet's privateers were not only capturing British ships, but also doing it in U.S. territorial waters, breaking the United States' newly stated neutrality.

On July 11, 1793, the president wrote to Jefferson in exasperation. Genet seemed to be steering U.S. policy right alongside his captured British prizes of war. "What is to be done," Washington wondered, "in the case of the Little Sarah [a captured British frigate being fitted out as a privateer], now at Chester? Is the Minister of the French Republic to set the Acts of this Government at defiance, *with impunity?*" During the spring and summer, as the U.S. government became less willing to work with Genet, he threatened to use newspapers and agents to urge the American populace to intervene on France's behalf, in spite of congressional neutrality. President Washington knew Genet had "threaten[ed] the Executive with an appeal to the People. What must the World think of such conduct, and of the Governmt. of the U. States in submitting to it? These are serious questions. Circumstances press for decision." Washington wanted to know Jefferson's "opinion upon them, even before tomorrow, for the Vessel [the *Little Sarah*] may then be gone."[4]

In flagrant disregard of the order that the *Little Sarah* not be allowed out of Virginia, Genet renamed it the *Little Democrat* and sent it into the Atlantic as a privateer. Genet had some leverage to ignore U.S. law because of the treaty signed between France and the United States in 1778, during the American Revolution. France had helped birth the United States, and now it expected help in return. Genet could point to treaty documents that seemed to guarantee America's commitment. While working defiantly in plain sight, Genet also worked clandestinely. But he underestimated both the strength of the presidency and the support of the people for George Washington. According to one contemporary's account, Genet "seem[ed] to have expected that the popularity of his nation would enable him to overthrow [the presidency], or to render it subservient to his views."[5] If Congress and George Washington were not willing to share in the bloody work of forcing liberty onto the peoples of Britain and Spain, Genet would look to the American people for help. Genet participated in "democratic societies," modeled on the revolutionary clubs of France, where fans of France (often French-born opponents of Washington's administration) could intrigue and complain. Though next to nothing was accomplished in these meetings, they seemed nefarious to President Washington.

Meanwhile, in the midst of thoroughly offending the United States' number one hero, George Washington, Genet got busy with a scheme to free Louisiana from the monarchs of Spain. The Spanish were preventing white settlers in frontier states and territories from trading through the port of New Orleans, and Genet hoped to exploit the ill will created by this impediment. A Revolutionary War hero, George Rogers Clark (lately impoverished), had secretly offered his services to the French. So Genet put into motion a scheme to float a liberating Kentuckian army into Louisiana, where he assumed the largely French populace would smash the tiny Spanish garrison. Jefferson gave his blessing, but commented in a diary entry that Genet—without manners or any good sense—had called him "Mr. Jeff" rather than "Sec[retary] of state." Genet, it seemed, lacked both courtesy and brains. Jefferson did not want U.S. citizens to get hanged as traitors for their part in an illegal assault on Spanish New Orleans. Otherwise, Jefferson said, "I did not care what insurrections should be excited in Louisiana."[6] Jefferson, who already had his eyes on the West, realized that if Genet could somehow dislodge the Spanish from New Orleans, it would be good for the United States.

Until the late summer of 1793, Jefferson continued to believe that Genet would *not* ruin France's reputation in the United States. This confidence in Genet slipped along with each of Genet's missteps. In mid-July, a fleet of French warships arrived in Baltimore's harbor, carrying some 10,000 refugees from the island of Haiti, recently engulfed in a slave revolt. Assuming that

145

the fleet freed him from U.S. interference, Genet believed he could invade Canada, Florida, and Louisiana and release all the peoples of the Americas from outdated European kings and queens. Genet wanted to usher in the dawn of universal justice. Of course, the British ambassadors demanded that the United States disassociate itself from the fanatical French. But far as Jefferson was concerned, France was "the only nation on earth sincerely our friend."[7] He did not want to give in to British demands, and his resistance increasingly put him at loggerheads with Hamilton. By the end of the year, Jefferson and Hamilton's domestic supporters were also at odds. Foreign policy had further driven American politics into two separate camps, two parties: the Federalists and the Democratic Republicans.

By the start of August 1793, Washington and his cabinet agreed that Genet would have to leave the country. They requested his recall, though Genet did not find out about this until September. Then he began to worry. It would be bad enough to lose his job, but it would be suicidal to tell his new bosses, the Jacobins, who were in the process of killing his old bosses, the Girondins, that he had failed in his mission. After a flurry of letter writing in defense of his behavior, Genet appealed for asylum. The most unlikely person stepped forward to accommodate him: Alexander Hamilton—defender of Britain, archrival of Jefferson. Hamilton could distinguish between Genet and Genet's mission. Besides, Hamilton had recently said, "if all the people in America were now assembled, & to call on me to say whether I am a friend to the French revolution, I would declare *that I have it in abhorrence*."[8] What better stab at an abhorrent government than to refuse the return of one of its citizens, for whom the Jacobins had issued an arrest warrant.

Edmond Genet, now citizen of the United States, married Cornelia Clinton, daughter of the governor of New York. He lived out his days as a farmer, settling into the greenery of a state that would soon witness some of the roughest contests of political animosity to beset the young republic. Genet's mission to the United States drew out an intensity of intellect and emotion at the highest levels of government and from the plainest quarters of the public. During the late autumn of 1793, James Madison and James Monroe (two future presidents) got into a pen-and-ink newspaper duel with Hamilton and his supporters concerning the proper place of the United States in the contests of European powers. Great decisions were soon made. In 1794, the United States signed a peace treaty with Britain and then in 1795 signed one with Spain that opened the Mississippi to free trade. Genet had failed on all accounts. However, even if he had not been an incompetent bungler, the desire of the ascendant Federalists to secure free trade with Great Britain probably would have sunk France's ship of desires in any case.

Soon, naval battles with the Barbary pirates and with France's own navy would begin to establish America's hard-won right to trade freely in the Atlantic world. These same conflicts would also further separate Federalists from Democratic Republicans, ultimately giving triumph to Jefferson and some of his ideas.

The Barbary Wars: 1784–1805

On January 31, 1804, Commodore Edward Preble handed a set of instructions to Lieutenant Commandant Stephen Decatur. They were anchored off the coast of Syracuse on the Italian coast, two oceans away from home. Preble instructed Decatur to "take command of the…*Intrepid*, and prepare her with all possible despatch for a cruise of thirty days . . . for *boarding and burning the Philadelphia* in the harbor of Tripoli . . . enter that harbor in the night, *board the Philadelphia, burn her*, and make good your retreat."[9]

Two weeks later, on February 17, Decatur wrote a letter "at sea" from his cabin on the *Intrepid* to inform Preble that he had carried out his duty. After entering the Tripoli harbor disguised as a pirate ship, at nine o'clock in the evening Decatur and sixty men had boarded the *Philadelphia* and "after a short contest, carried her." Decatur declared his men "brave fellows" whose "coolness" in battle he trusted "will ever characterise the American tars." Only one American seaman had been slightly injured, and the daring raid had been pulled off without a single gunshot, even though twenty Tripolitan corsairs had been killed, all in the flash of swords on the quarterdeck. Decatur's men had made a lot of noise boarding the *Philadelphia*, and the clash of their swords had caused "a general alarm on shore." The Tripolitans had, he reported, "commenced a fire on us from all their batteries on shore, but with no other effect than one shot passing through our top-gallant sail."[10] The U.S. mariners had set the *Philadelphia* on fire, and Decatur's two remaining ships had barely escaped from the harbor because "a gale commenced immediately. . . and it was with difficulty the ketch was got out of the harbor."[11] Behind them, flames had blazed on the sinking *Philadelphia*.

What had the tiny squadron of U.S. Navy vessels been doing in the Mediterranean, sailing brazenly into Barbary ports and burning a U.S. ship?

In 1804 America's navy was less than ten years old, and it had been commissioned only in response to the aggressions of other powers. George Washington himself thought that a standing army would eventually suppress liberties, that America should "avoid the necessity of those overgrown military establishments, which under any form of government are inauspicious to liberty, and which are to be regarded as particularly hostile to republican liberty."[12] Federalists and Democratic Republicans alike preferred the additions of trade to the subtractions of war, unwilling to waste money on munitions and battles when it could be spent outfitting new merchant ships to carry tobacco, cotton, and naval stores to the markets of the world. As early as the late 1780s, however, the Barbary States of North Africa had attacked U.S. merchant ships, enslaving the prisoners and demanding ransom and future tribute payments as security against more raids. Debates within the United States began immediately as to the proper response, with most people begrudgingly admitting that tributes were a cheaper price to pay for commerce than navies and wars. Thomas Jefferson, on the other hand, wanted to fight back, but he retired from public office at the end of Washington's first term as president, so his opinions stopped carrying official weight.

Piracy is a business that other nations do not like, but even the powerful Spanish, French, and British made regular payments to the rulers of Barbary. A Spanish fleet had tried to defeat the Algerine corsairs at the port of Tangiers in 1784 but was repulsed, so the United States knew it would have no chance. Algiers, Morocco, Tunis, and Tripoli were essentially poor countries, outposts of the Ottoman Empire, and they subsisted as the toll masters of the Mediterranean. European countries paid in gold, silver, and warships and munitions. Europeans literally gave the pirates the weapons they needed to keep on fighting.

One nation's pirate is another nation's privateer. For centuries, England had outfitted private captains to prey upon the treasure ships of Spain. Queen Elizabeth had knighted Francis Drake for his plunders of Spanish bullion. And during the War for Independence, because Congress had no real navy, it issued orders for privateers to waylay British ships, which is what John Paul Jones did off the coast of England. Naturally, the English called Jones a pirate.

The Moroccans captured their first U.S. ships in 1784, right after Algiers had defeated the Spanish. Ironically, the Moroccan leader, Sidi Muhammad, had offered diplomatic recognition of the United States back in 1778, when he had requested negotiations for trade and friendship. U.S. officials took years to respond because either they were too busy fighting the Revolution or their appointed negotiators kept dying before they could go to Morocco. By 1784, Sidi Muhammad was done waiting for the trade talks, so he started a little early bargaining by capturing the *Betsy*, taking its crew to Tangiers, and demanding ransom. Jefferson, the minister in Paris, wanted to fight for the crew's release, but John Adams thought that sparring over tokens of pride was not worth the cost, and Congress agreed with Adams, appropriating $80,000 to buy the freedom of the *Betsy*'s crew. By 1787, the United States and Morocco had signed a trade agreement, and conditions had improved, though not for everyone.

Other Barbary nations learned from Morocco's example, and Algeria took two U.S. ships in 1785. The ruler of Algeria wanted ransom money, but

Congress was broke. The Constitution did not yet exist, and the states were not ponying up money. The United States' credit was in shambles, its war debts unpaid, so it could not afford much, certainly not the new million-dollar ransom demanded.

One of the ships captured by Algeria was the *Dauphin* (out of Philadelphia), and its captain, Richard O'Brien, languished as a slave until 1795, when the United States and Algeria finally signed a peace treaty. O'Brien's case became a publicized cause in U.S. newspapers. He sent letters to prominent Americans—including Thomas Jefferson in Paris—pleading for release. A year after being taken captive, O'Brien informed Jefferson that a recent American negotiator, John Lamb (really just a merchant given the job in a pinch), had been horribly insufficient, exhibiting "ungentleman like behaviour" and being "a very uncapable man." Not shy with his words, O'Brien even called Lamb "unworthy of his commission & the cloth he wore." It is no surprise that O'Brien was upset. As he said, "it is impossible for us to be content whilst we are under the character of slaves, . . . Captain Stevens & Coffin have families . . . I have an aged mother, brother & sister [whose] whole dependance & subsistence was on me." Some of the captured seamen labored like slaves in the American South, with violence imminent and hard work constant. O'Brien pointed out that "Delays breed danger & opportunity once lost is not easily recovered, and our captivity will become an old affair and here we shall remain."[13] Ten years of captivity proved him right, even though people in the United States felt sympathy for his plight. The *Newport Mercury,* for example, reported on October 30, 1786, that a British diplomat in Algiers had "clothed several of the American captives, who were almost naked; and, in behalf of the States at large, has used all his interest, though in vain, with the councils of Algiers, respecting the demands for the ransom of American slaves."[14]

Between 1785 and 1793, conditions alternately worsened and improved. More U.S. ships were captured by Barbary pirates and the crews enslaved. This had the effect of pushing Congress to act and even influenced the Constitutional Convention, as leaders and commoners alike saw the need for a more capable central government. Beginning in the early 1790s, the desire for a robust response to piracy strengthened Alexander Hamilton's call, as secretary of the treasury, for a national bank of the United States and for the establishment of credit. In other words, Hamilton wanted U.S. citizens and foreign nations to invest in the United States, thereby bonding the people to their government and other countries to the interests of America. To the fury of Jefferson's Republican partisans, Hamilton's proposals were enacted, giving the federal government more money and power to act in emergencies.

In 1793, the Algerians took eleven American vessels. Something had to be done, and in early 1794 Congress ordered a naval fleet of six vessels. The small fleet was not ready until 1797, when new dangers had arrived. Britain and France remained at each other's throats, neither allowing the United States to remain truly neutral, each attacking U.S. merchant ships. In 1798, three U.S. diplomats in France were told that the new French government would open a friendly diplomacy for a few pricey bribes. In the diplomats' dispatches to Congress, the French negotiators were listed as X, Y, and Z. This XYZ Affair, along with French attacks on more than 300 U.S. merchant brigs, led to what has been known as a quasi war with France, which took up all available naval energies. In short, the United States was either too broke, uninterested, or unable to deal with the Barbary States and their privateers.

Things changed with the election of Thomas Jefferson as president in 1800. Jefferson now had at his command a battle-tested, veteran fleet of more than twenty warships, some with seventy-four guns, ready to defend what the president perceived as America's honor. For a decade Jefferson had wanted to put a decisive end to the Barbary troubles, and this was his time to act. In summer 1801, Jefferson dispatched the fleet, and the small schooner *Enterprise* defeated a Tripolitan corsair in three hours of heated gun battle, with the warriors within pistol shot of each other. But because Jefferson had no permission from Congress to fight an offensive war, the Tripolitan ship had to be set free (with twenty of its crew dead and its guns dumped overboard). On December 8, Meriwether Lewis, the president's personal secretary (and future leader of the Corps of Discovery), read a presidential message to the House of Representatives, in which Jefferson stated that Tripoli had once again declared war on the United States. Jefferson insisted "the style of the demand admitted but one answer": he wanted Congress to authorize the use of offensive force as a defensive measure, and Congress complied.[15]

Rather than marauding all over the Mediterranean seeking battle with the Tripoli pirates, the U.S. fleet settled on a blockade, but that did not work because the smaller Tripolitan vessels could hug the coastline at night, undetected, and soon the other three Barbary States either declared war or postured menacingly, demanding more tribute. Jefferson appointed a new commander for the naval squadron in the region, Commodore Preble, who set sail with seven vessels to enforce the porous blockade. In the Tripolitan harbor, the battleship *Philadelphia* ran aground in shallow water. Over 300 crewmembers were seized, and the Tripolitans now had a modern ship, equivalent to the best in the water. So the raid by Stephen Decatur was settled upon as the only way to keep the Tripolitans from using the *Philadelphia* against the United States. In order to slip into the harbor undetected, Decatur captured a Barbary vessel familiar to Mediterranean eyes and renamed it the *Intrepid*. He and his crew sailed in disguise, like true pirates themselves.

It took one more year to coerce a peace treaty from the ruler of Tripoli, Yusuf Qaramanli. Getting the peace treaty involved joint land and sea operations. Decatur's bravery provided the motivation to proceed with these attacks against Tripoli. In the process, Decatur won the adulation of the nation, and the nation gained a belief in its own military ability. In August 1804, in cooperation with Qaramanli's ousted brother, Hamet, who wanted the throne of Tripoli for himself, the United States began bombarding Tripoli and its warships. Decatur led the successful attack. When his brother was killed in the fierce battle, the young commander sailed back into the harbor and fought his brother's killer in one-to-one combat: Decatur's sword against the other man's spear. In the struggle, Decatur's sword broke. Before his opponent could kill him, Decatur pulled a small pistol from the pocket of his trousers and ended the fight. Newspapers chronicled the duel, adding to Decatur's fame.

From August 1804 through June 1805, the U.S. naval fleet increased in size and pressed its newfound advantage against a weakened Tripolitan flotilla. In early 1805, an American commander named William Eaton, a force of eight marines, and many Arabs set out with Hamet Qaramanli across North Africa. In June, they successfully pressured Yusuf Qaramanli to concede to the forces arrayed against him. The hard-won peace earned a respite for U.S. shipping in the Mediterranean, but it would not be until the middle of the next decade that matters were settled with the Barbary States.

As for matters at home, the treaty with Tripoli did not gain Jefferson the applause he might have anticipated. The leader of the overland strike, William Eaton, criticized the peace treaty as a sellout for money that got paid to the Tripolitans in exchange for the prisoners from the *Philadelphia*. Eaton was equally incensed by a decision to abandon Hamet and his forces. The Federalists harnessed Eaton's hostility and used it to politically attack Jefferson. War policy became the cudgel for politicians to wield at home, each side accusing the other of poor decision making and weakness. In the United States, unity floundered. Past political feuds and deep-seated disagreements about how the government should be run kept Federalists and Republicans at odds. While temporary peace had been established in the Mediterranean, problems continued at home. Congress was in agreement, however, about the need to establish dominion in the West.

Sacagawea and the Corps of Discovery

At the falls of the Missouri River on June 29, 1805, the Corps of Discovery—led by Meriwether Lewis and William Clark—woke to a prairie "so wet as to render it impossible to pass."[16] Sergeant Ordway, one of the thirty-three members of the Corps, struggled along with everyone else to move tons of dry goods up and around the falls. These explorers were headed into the unknown, there to make maps, seek out an all-water route across the continent, catalogue the plant and animal life, stake an American claim to the far West, and establish new relationships with the Indian peoples they met. This circumventing of the falls was a Herculean task. In his journal, Ordway noted that the slave York, the French-Canadian trapper Charbonneau, and his "Squaw," Sacagawea, accompanied Clark on the day's task.[17] Although Ordway had met Sacagawea more than half a year earlier, this was his first mention of her in his journal, as she had not yet contributed decisively to their journey. However, another member of the expedition, Lieutenant Patrick Gass, had commented in April 1805, "we expect she [Sacagawea] will be of service to us."[18] For the next year and more, Sacagawea—whose name means "Bird Woman"—would take a more prominent place in the journals of those members who kept them, and she secured herself an indelible place in what is arguably the United States' favorite story.

Thomas Jefferson's foreign policy involved dealing with the Barbary pirates and the excesses of Napoleon Bonaparte, but it also involved a diplomacy of more consequence for the future: the acquisition of the Louisiana Territory. Napoleon was a young man when he brought order to the decay of the French Revolution in 1799, and by 1803 he had embroiled Europe in wars of unimaginable scale as he marched here and there with an army of 800,000 troops. Paying for the army was its own feat, and to raise the needed money, he sold the Louisiana Territory to the United States for approximately $15 million—never mind what the Indians living there thought.

Jefferson did mind what the Indians thought. He knew Native Americans could be either obstacles or advantages to his scheme for creating an "Empire of Liberty" stretching across the Great Plains, where he hoped to offer land to a nation of virtuous, republican farmers for untold generations to come. The purchase secured Jefferson's popularity and gave him the chance to hatch a plan he had had for some years. The tribes of the Mississippi and Missouri rivers carried on an extensive trade with French and British traders, who traded clothing, ironware, and guns and ammunition in exchange for animal pelts. Not only did Jefferson want to displace these foreign traders and let the Indian nations know that the United States was on the scene, but he wanted to put an end to the intertribal warfare of the Plains. In particular, Jefferson knew that certain tribes of Sioux, particularly the Brules and Tetons, had a stranglehold on trade along the northern Missouri into the Dakotas. Jefferson wanted to arrange a peace between the Arikaras, the Mandans, the Kiowas, and others, so these tribes could form a coalition powerful enough to check the Sioux and enable U.S. traders to do an uninterrupted business on these rivers that were the veins of trade.

Meriwether Lewis was born in 1774, at the onset of the Revolution, and grew up hearing many tales of glory and adventure. Born into the planter class of Virginia, Lewis received a backwoods education and enough book learning to be an able explorer and writer. Jefferson had known Lewis from the latter's boyhood and recognized him as a young man of ability. Having served in the militia raised to quell the Whiskey Rebellion of 1794 and later as an officer in western posts and forts, Lewis was acquainted with the entirety of the small army and with the river systems of the interior. Early in his administration, Jefferson invited Lewis to be his personal secretary. Soon after, Jefferson asked Lewis to lead an exploratory party west. Lewis requested William Clark, whom he had met in the military and who had a deserved reputation for strength of mind and spirit, as his co-commander, and Jefferson agreed.

In June 1803, Jefferson wrote Lewis a letter detailing the many objectives he had in mind for the Corps. Notably, Jefferson wrote, "The commerce which may be carried on with the people inhabiting the line you will pursue, renders a knowledge of those people important." Zeroing in on "commerce," Jefferson underscored one of his chief obligations: to provide for the economic welfare of the nation. Jefferson instructed Lewis to "treat [the Indians] in the most friendly & conciliatory manner which their own conduct will admit." Lewis should also "make them acquainted with . . . our dispositions to a commercial intercourse with them." In the long run, Jefferson hoped to "civilize & instruct them."[19] The president believed little in the capacities of African-Americans, but thought that Native Americans could be educated as the moral and intellectual equals of whites.

The Corps of Discovery was small, initially fewer than thirty men. Although they were a military party—armed with the latest Kentucky rifles, a small swivel cannon set on the bow of their keel boat, and a variety of other weapons—they would have been no real match for any of the large tribes they passed, be they Teton Sioux or Mandans. Lewis, Clark, and their men were entering an environment where existing trade networks, alliances, and animosities intertwined as much as they did in Europe. To understand the diplomacy of the Plains took a thorough knowledge of local history and languages, none of which the original members of the Corps of Discovery possessed. Lewis and Clark represented a growing power, but to prove that would take skill.

During 1804, the Corps traveled up the Missouri River from St. Louis to the Mandan villages in modern-day North Dakota. Along the way, the two commanders signed on additional members, mainly trappers and traders who had the needed knowledge. George Drouillard was fluent in the sign language of the region, allowing him to communicate across spoken barriers. An untrustworthy figure named Jusseaume was contracted for a time because he knew the northern tribes: the Otos, Mandans, and others. It was, however, on November 4, 1804, "a fine morning," that William Clark recorded the arrival of a "Mr. Chaubonee [Charbonneau]," interpreter for the Hidatsa people. Along with Toussaint Charbonneau came two slave "wives." Sacagawea was one of them, and since she was a Shoshone from far to the west, Lewis and Clark wanted her to accompany them as a potential guide, interpreter, and emissary. Though she would be with the Corps of Discovery for the next year and a half, her contributions did not become essential until the spring and summer of 1805. However, the presence of a woman with a military party gave it a peaceful aura.

As soon as the Corps arrived at a collection of Mandan villages where they would spend the winter, they set to building a winter camp: "at work at the Fort," in Clark's words. The temperature regularly hovered around negative thirty degrees Fahrenheit, often plunging into the minus forties. Sacagawea was about sixteen, and she was pregnant. Before leaving the Mandans and heading westward with Lewis and Clark, Sacagawea gave birth, on February 11. It was thirty-eight below zero when Lewis woke up, and by 4 PM it had risen to a balmy fourteen below zero. Although Lewis had not mentioned her prior to this day, he said, "It is worthy of remark that this was the first child which this woman had." It was worthy of remark because of how arduous the birthing was: "tedious and the pain violent." The trader Jusseaume informed Lewis about a local labor aid, "the rattle of the rattle-snake," which he assured Clark "had never failed to produce the desired effect . . . hastening the birth of the child." Two bits were put into water, which Sacagawea drank, and the baby came right out, though Lewis admitted, "whether this medicine was truly the cause or not I shall not undertake to determine."

The mortality rate for women in labor and their infants during the colonial and early republic periods accounts for the fear that Lewis had for Sacagawea and his desire to administer some kind, any kind, of medicine. As the noted historian Laura Ulrich points out, there is no sure way to know what the overall averages were for the time, but estimates for some English villages suggest "ten to twenty-nine maternal deaths per thousand births," while in some "London and Dublin hospitals, maternal mortality ranged from 30 to 200 (!) per thousand births."[20] These numbers are offset by the success of a Maine midwife, Martha Ballard, who had only five women out of a thousand die in labor; only 2 percent of the infants that Ballard midwived were stillborn. The medical care provided by even the most noted physicians of the day included bloodletting for nearly everything and the administration of very strong purgatives, both of which had the effect of weakening a patient more often than curing. Every member of the Corps survived the trip except one, who probably died of appendicitis, which was wholly incurable at the time, the surgery being unavailable.

While the birth of Sacagawea's baby did not defy all odds, it was difficult, and the cold probably did not help. More impressive than a subzero birth was her sojourn with the Corps, baby Jean Baptiste along for the ride on her back. From April through June 1805, the party traveled the Missouri to the base of the Rocky Mountains, where they got bogged down in the nearly month-long portage around the falls. There, on June 29, the day Ordway described as too wet to pass over the prairie, Clark, Sacagawea, and her baby nearly lost their lives.

After a light morning rain, the day cleared, and Clark set off for the falls to gather more of the luggage, taking with him Sacagawea, her husband, and York. Ominous clouds gathered swiftly, "threaten[ing] im[m]ediate rain." Clark spied a sheltered ravine and led the small party into its security, from which they watched the rain, fierce winds, and finally hail the size of fruit (which knocked three men off their feet and bruised many others). A torrent of water came tearing at their position, washing away everything in its path. Clark took his gun and shot pouch in his left hand, and "with the right scrambled up the hill pushing [Sacagawea] (who had her child in her arms) before [him]." Charbonneau tried "to pull up his wife by the hand much scared and nearly without motion." Now safe, they rushed back to camp to get new clothes for the baby, whose own had been torn off in the flood. Clark, however, was worried for Sacagawea "who was but just recovering from a Severe indisposition, and was wet and Cold." For days prior, she had suffered from a feverish sickness that he had feared would be fatal. He declared himself "fearfull of a relaps."

While this may have been the most dangerous moment of the journey for Sacagawea, it was emblematic of the rigors and dangers that the entire party faced as they trekked through each pass in the Rocky Mountains and along the Missouri and Columbia river systems. The expedition imperiled them all, not only because of the unexpected, sudden dangers (rock slides and bear attacks), but also because of diseases (malaria and dysentery), frequent lack of food, and endless toil. The daily dangers of the trail, however, were countered by the pleasures afforded by fiddle playing, nightly drinks of whiskey, and such curiosities as prairie dog towns.

For Lewis and Clark, diplomatic relations with the many Indian nations were crucial, and here Sacagawea became key. To get to the other side of the Rockies, they needed horses, which the Corps counted on getting from the Shoshones, Sacagawea's birth tribe, whose territory they entered in July. By early August 1805, they were canoeing through serpentine waterways, which slowed travel, but the game they hunted remained relatively plentiful. Each man ate almost ten pounds of meat daily when it was available. During this time, Lewis and a small contingent of men went ahead to scout out the Shoshones, of whom no sign had been spotted. The Corps was nearing the Continental Divide (from where waters spill either east or west out of the Rockies), which Lewis and three other men crossed on August 12. The next day, Lewis and Drouillard encountered a variety of Shoshones. The men and women alike were scared, but through Lewis's alchemy of soft demeanor, gift giving, and painting of Shoshone women's faces with red vermillion—"which with this nation is emblematic of peace"—the Shoshones became "composed" and agreed to take Lewis to meet the rest of their band.

Soon after meeting sixty of their warriors on fine horses, Lewis wrote, "we wer all carresed and besmeared with their grease and paint till I was heartily tired of the national hug." Lewis met the band's leader, Cameahwait, who led them back to a camp where Lewis followed his host's lead: smoking a peace pipe, sitting on "green boughs and the skins of Antelopes," eating berry cakes, and watching the Shoshones dance. It had been a fine evening and augured well. However, all communications had been made through Drouillard and sign language, so complex conversations would have to wait for Sacagawea.

The next day was spent finding out about the passages through the mountains and about Shoshone relations with other Indian peoples. Cameahwait indicated that the Shoshones had an impossible time getting guns from Spanish traders, but that the Arikaras and Hidatsas were well armed. Lewis tried to allay the chief's fears by having Drouillard sign that neighboring Indians had promised to act respectfully toward the Shoshones. Waking "very early and as hungary as a wolf" on August 15, Lewis and a small party of Shoshones set out back along the trail to find the rest of the Corps. Cameahwait signed that others in his band did not trust Lewis or Drouillard, thinking them in league with enemies of the Shoshones. This lack of trust endowed the two-day trip with an edge of worry, though the fear was alleviated by the killing of a deer, whose meat was devoured uncooked and "most ravenously" by Cameahwait's brethren, leaving them in a "good humour." When they reached the rendezvous point, Clark and company were not there. Lewis gave Cameahwait his rifle as a token of security, and his men followed suit. They were now unarmed in the midst of an anxious party of Shoshone warriors, and Lewis had no idea what evil might have befallen Clark.

August 17 brought success. Brushes with rattlesnakes and the terrain had impeded Clark, Sacagawea, and the rest of the Corps. Now, as the two groups met up, Sacagawea shared a joyous greeting with a young Shoshone woman who had been a captive of the Mandans but who had already made her way back to the Shoshones. Their joy dispelled the nervousness Lewis had perceived among his Shoshone guides. Better yet, it turned out that Cameahwait was Sacagawea's brother. Fortune smiled.

True talks began (with a six-stage labyrinthine translation through Indian languages, French, and English), during which Lewis stressed the strength of the United States and President Jefferson's disposition to trade with the Shoshones. Commerce was their shared vocabulary expressed through the awkward medium of language. During these days, the Corps handed out trinkets like flags, shirts, and medals to the various chiefs; often one would feel shortchanged, leading Lewis to give another gift. Such exchanges were customary and expected, but they led to changes in Native American societies. In particular, white emissaries tended to single out one chief as the primary leader, even if this had not necessarily been the case beforehand. European-Americans were used to dealing with a single leader, like a president or a king. Lewis noticed that a chief's authority grew from "the influence which . . . his own examplary conduct may have acquired him in the minds of the individuals who compose the band." The mere treatment given Cameahwait by Lewis and Clark may have disposed his people to see him in an "examplary" light.

On August 25, the Corps set out again with many Shoshones along for part of the ride. Ultimately only one guide, Old Toby, would lead them through the mountains and onto the plains of the Columbia River, where their next significant encounter, with the Nez Percés, took place. Sacagawea and the Corps of Discovery made it to the Pacific Ocean and wintered there in damp, coffeeless misery until the early spring of 1806, when they began the return journey to the East.

The years spent on the trail were, from the perspective of Thomas Jefferson, a success. Descriptions of new animal and plant species filled entire books while taxidermied carcasses filled museum shelves, leading to the incorporation of western nature into the language of science, part of the process of colonization. The journey of the Corps of Discovery, then, is a story of the encroachment of civilization on nature. And the story of Indians in whites' eyes is an account of seeing nature in the red man. Sacagawea brings these threads together: an Indian woman sold to a white man (Charbonneau), both of whom helped other white men in their conquest of nature. As the modern Spokane author Sherman Alexie has said, "If the U.S. is Eden, then Sacagawea is Eve."[21]

By the time Lewis and Clark made it back to St. Louis in 1806, increased trade on the Missouri was noticeable. They had brought the Northwest into the fold of the United States. Chiefs of some tribes went to visit Jefferson in Washington, DC, and the process of moving the boundaries of the United States outward continued. Meriwether Lewis lived only until 1809, when he killed himself violently—perhaps not surprising to those who knew him best. Even on the trip across the continent, fellow expedition members had noted a deep melancholy in Lewis. William Clark lived until 1838, during which time he served as superintendent of Indian affairs and helped to raise Sacagawea's two children, including Jean Baptiste, whom Clark affectionately called "Pompy." Sacagawea's experiences after the expedition are not easy to ascertain. It has been argued that she lived until 1884, but most historians agree that she died in 1812, at the age of twenty-five.

Foreign Policy: Transatlantic and Transcontinental

The United States reeled itself into overseas adventures through a combination of its own desire to have a healthy commerce and the aggressive behavior of other nations. Citizen Genet came to the United States in 1793 to get money, and to take Florida and the Mississippi region away from Spain. His fumbled efforts at diplomacy were only the start of American hostilities with France that lasted for more than ten years. Britain's habit of harassing and attacking American merchant vessels, for an even longer period of time, became one of the major causes of the War of 1812.

The United States took itself into the west of this continent, however, without prodding from any external forces. While the movement of British explorers and traders into the Oregon country in the late 1790s did make Jefferson anxious, those movements were not aggressive to the United States. Jefferson undertook the purchase of the Louisiana Territory and the expedition of the Corps of Discovery for reasons germane to the character of the American mind. In particular, new land was considered necessary for the expansion of agriculture, commerce, and (it was believed) liberty.

The United States' involvement in the world altered the United States. American commerce and industry would benefit from an increasingly assertive foreign policy, but Native Americans and African-Americans would suffer so that others might gain.

Notes

1. George Washington to Henry Knox, April 1, 1789, *The George Washington Papers at the Library of Congress* (Washington, DC: Library of Congress, Manuscript Division), http://memory.loc.gov/cgi-bin/query/r?ammem/mgw:@field(DOCID+@lit (gw300225))2.

2. Anne Cary Morris, ed., *The Diary and Letters of Gouverneur Morris: Minister of the United States to France: Member of the Constitutional Convention; etc.* (New York: Charles Scribner's Sons, 1888), 2: 25.

3. H.A. Washington, ed., *The Writings of Thomas Jefferson* (Washington, DC: Taylor & Maury, 1853), 3: 563.

4. George Washington to Thomas Jefferson, July 11, 1793, *The George Washington Papers at the Library of Congress* (Washington, DC: Library of Congress, Manuscript Division), http://memory.loc.gov/cgi-.bin/query/r?ammem/mgw:@field(DOCID+@ lit(gw330013))#N0040-11.

5. John Marshall, *The Life of George Washington* (Philadelphia: James Crissy, 1832), 2: 265.

6. Thomas Jefferson, July 5, 1793, Edmond C. Genet Meeting Notes, *The Thomas Jefferson Papers Series 1. General Correspondence. 1651–1827*, http://memory.loc. gov/ammem/collections/jefferson_papers/mtjabout.html, 1090.

7. Paul Leicester Ford, ed., *The Writings of Thomas Jefferson* (New York: G.P. Putnam's Sons, 1892), 1: 267.

8. Ford, ed., *The Writings of Thomas Jefferson*, 1: 268.

9. *Documents, Official and Unofficial, Relating to the Case of the Capture and Destruction of the Frigate Philadelphia at Tripoli, on the 16th February, 1804* (Washington: John T. Towers, 1850), 17–18.

10. *Documents, Official and Unofficial*, 14.

11. *Documents, Official and Unofficial*, 15.

12. Frank Moore, *American Eloquence: A Collection of Speeches and Addresses by the Most Eloquent Orators of America*, "Farewell Address" (New York: D. Appleton, 1857), 1: 256.

13. *Naval documents related to the United States wars with the Barbary powers . . . [microform]: naval operations including diplomatic background . . . / published under direction of the Secretary of the Navy; prepared by the Office of Naval Records and Library, Navy Department, under the supervision of Dudley W. Knox, U.S. Navy (ret.)* (Washington: Government Printing Office, 1939–1944) "To Thomas Jefferson, U.S. Minister to Paris, France, from Richard O'Brien, Algiers / Algiers June 8th 1786."

14. *The Newport Mercury* [microform] (Newport, RI: J. Franklin, October 30, 1786).

15. Ford, ed., *The Writings of Thomas Jefferson*, 8: 117.

16. All quotes from Captains Lewis and Clark can be found in Reuben Gold Thwaites, ed., *Original Journals of the Lewis and Clark Expedition, 1804–1806* (New York: Dodd, Mead, 1904–1905), vols. I–VII.

17. Milo M. Quaife, ed., *The Journals of Captain Meriwether Lewis and Sergeant John Ordway Kept On The Expedition of Western Exploration, 1803–1806* (Madison: Wisconsin Historical Society, 1916), 211.

18. *Lewis and Clarke's Journal to the Rocky Mountains In the Year 1804,–05,–06: As Related by Patrick Gass, One of the Officers in the Expedition* (Dayton, OH: Ells, Claflin, 1847), 73.

19. H.A. Washington, ed., *The Writings of Thomas Jefferson* (Washington: Taylor & Maury, 1854), 8: 487–489.

20. Laura Thatcher Ulrich, *A Midwife's Tale: The Life of Martha Ballard, Based on Her Diary, 1785–1812* (New York: Vintage, 1991), 172. Accurately ascertaining actual infant or maternal mortality rates in the colonial period is essentially impossible. Scholar Judith Walzer Leavitt concurs with Ulrich on this point in both Judith Walzer Leavitt *Brought to Bed: Childbearing in America, 1750–1950* (New York: Oxford University Press, 1986) and Judith Walzer Leavitt, "Science Enters the Birthing Room: Obstetrics in America since the Eighteenth Century" *The Journal of American History*, vol. 70, no. 2 (September, 1983), pp. 281–304. In the latter, Leavitt comments, "Although statistics do not exist to measure these dangers precisely, women's fears were not unfounded. By all accounts maternal and infant mortality rates were high" (282).

21. Sherman Alexie, "What Sacagawea Means to Me (and Perhaps to You)," *Time*, July 8, 2002, 56.

9

The War of 1812

Dolley Madison *(Hulton Archive/Getty Images)*

Irritations, Aggravations, and Failed Diplomacies

What causes nations to fight? Some people might argue the reason is simple: greed. Others might say nationalism and pride play a leading role. And sometimes one side fights a defensive war, responding rather than instigating. The best answer is typically a combination of factors, and that was the case with the War of 1812, known as the "American War" in Canada. On June 1, 1812, President James Madison asked Congress to declare war against Great Britain since everyone could "behold" that Britain was already in "a state of war against the United States." This was, in Madison's opinion, a matter of defense. Britain had been violating the United States' neutral rights for years, he said, and the "savages" of the western frontier had been "influenced" to attack the United States.

Britain and France had been seizing American ships on and off since 1793. After a nearly two-year break from 1801 to 1803, European warfare resumed in late 1803 when Napoleon Bonaparte seized supreme power. From 1804 to 1812, Britain and France took roughly 1,400 U.S. ships. Both nations wanted to stop the United States from trading freely in a war zone where strategy relied on choking off the supply of goods like cotton and wheat to one's adversary.

In June 1807, a British war vessel looking for naval deserters stopped the *Chesapeake*, a U.S. ship. The British navy paid poor wages and offered abominable conditions, not the least of which was incessant warfare, so any number of British seamen had fled to U.S. ships. In response, Britain claimed the right to "impress" its own sailors back into service, and that included taking them off the decks of American trading ships. Like dolphins swept up in tuna-fishing nets, Britain often wrongfully impressed U.S. sailors as well, contemporary estimates ranging into the thousands. When the captain of the *Chesapeake* refused to let British marines aboard, the British fired their cannons, leaving twenty-one men dead. After the barrage, the British boarded the *Chesapeake* and took four men off. As it turned out, three were U.S. citizens; the fourth actually had deserted from the British navy. The British soon hanged their deserter. One of the Americans died in custody; the other two were released in late 1811. In response to the Chesapeake affair, regular impressment, and the taking of ships, the United States declared a total embargo in 1807, which achieved little more than to cripple the domestic economy, leaving wharves in Boston and Charleston full of unemployed sailors and stocked warehouses.

The embargo hurt Britain, but did not alter its behavior. Once Madison was elected president, Jefferson rescinded the Embargo Act as a parting gesture and signed the Non-Intercourse Act (a name that would not get used today, though the word already had sexual connotations by the late eighteenth century). The law permitted trade with anyone other than Britain or France. But with the economy in a perilous descent, Congress reopened trade with both nations in 1810. However, proposed legislation called Macon's Bill No. 2 (named sarcastically after Senator Nathaniel Macon of North Carolina, who opposed it) stated that if either Britain or France ended its aggravating policies, trade would halt with the other nation.

Napoleon was shrewd. Although he was not really willing to let U.S. goods flow freely into British ports, in November 1810, he *said* that he would allow open trade. Congress responded by enacting Macon's Bill No. 2 into law, freezing all trade with Britain in March 1811. These trans-Atlantic diplomacies coincided with warfare in the West between the militia led by Indiana Territory governor William Henry Harrison and the followers of two Shawnee brothers, Tecumseh and Tenskwatawa. Though Harrison routed the Shawnees, people in the West blamed Native American aggressiveness on the British in Canada. Now westerners wanted to invade Canada, and eastern Republicans wanted to stop British naval actions. Only the Federalists counseled continued negotiations. In violation of the embargoes and nonimportation acts over the years, Federalist merchants had been able to find loopholes in the law, and many had simply smuggled goods either by water or overland through Canada and Mexico. Most Federalists did not want war with Britain, as it would be no different from drilling holes in their own hulls.

What caused this war, then? For years, the primary instigators were Britain and France, though their policies toward U.S. shipping were not surprising. After all, why let the enemy get supplied? Once more, the interconnections of the world through trade led America into war.

As 1811 turned into 1812, Britain tried to parley. Britain offered to allow the United States a share in the trade with continental Europe on a fifty-fifty basis. Britain also offered to repay the United States for the *Chesapeake* and return the two remaining captive sailors. On June 16, 1812, Britain even rescinded its Orders in Council that had imposed the blockade of French-held Europe, a few days too late. News of the repeal of the orders took so long to reach American shores that Congress had already declared war on June 18. Besides, as historian Donald Hickey explained, problems had "festered so long" that these kinds of patches "gave little satisfaction to most Americans." Returning impressed seamen, said the Baltimore *Whig,* was like "restoring a hair after fracturing the skull."[1] Except for the entirety of Federalist legislators who voted against the war measure, most Americans thought of the fight against Great Britain as a kind of second War for Independence.

Dolley Madison

Long before the Quaker-raised Dolley Madison stepped into her role as the United States' first lady in March 1809, the nation's capital in Washington,

DC, was known as a backwater. Dolley did what she could to polish its image. Thomas Jefferson had been the first president to occupy the city and the "Palace" (now called the White House) for his whole time in office, and he had an odd sense of etiquette. Jefferson's wife had already died, leaving him to entertain visiting dignitaries by himself. Jefferson favored a republican simplicity. He did not take a coach to his own inaugural. He let people seat themselves "pell-mell" at the dinner table with chairs up for grabs, rather than placing guests according to their old-world status. Jefferson once greeted the British minister in torn pants, slippers, and a housecoat—an intentional snub. However, James and Dolley Madison had accompanied Jefferson to DC, where James served as secretary of state. Dolley had served as Jefferson's surrogate first lady, helping him to host parties and functions, gracing the company with her charm and manners, and taking advantage of Jefferson's two terms to polish her routine.

Abigail Adams, the second presidential wife, had arrived in Washington in 1800, just at the end of John's term. Although the White House and surrounding buildings had been under construction since 1792, Abigail found only "here and there . . . a small cot, without a glass window, interspersed amongst the forests, through which you travel miles without seeing any human being." Though she called the house "grand," she could not find a single log to burn for heat, there being no one available to cut or carry wood. Though "habitable," only a few rooms were furnished, leaving Abigail an "unfinished audience-room" where she hung up clothes to dry. Washington in 1800 was, according to Abigail, a city "only so in name."[2]

The capital had few residents: 3,210 according to the 1800 census. For those interested in refinements, relocating to the District of Columbia was like a prison sentence. While Congress was in session, its members could hear the report of gunfire; there was good bird hunting in the vicinity. Congressmen brought dogs with them into the chambers. Members of the Supreme Court roomed together in a boarding house, and they officially met in the basement of Congress. Justices of the Supreme Court regularly drank wine while at work. Pennsylvania Avenue, the main thoroughfare, remained an often-muddy dirt road until 1832, though during winter months the muck did freeze. A friend of Dolley's reported to her in a February 1804 letter that "we found the roads better than we expected" on a coach ride home to Virginia.[3] It was, all in all, a frontier capital for a frontier nation.

Frontiers are noted for their relaxed attitudes toward male and female behavior. Most congressmen left their families at home during the congressional sessions, making this a masculine environment. Although public speaking and politics were closed to women in early nineteenth-century America, the unusual nature of the new capital gave women an importance they enjoyed nowhere else. As author Sarah Luria pointed out, a "fuzziness between the personal and the political . . . gave women a wider scope than men."[4] Dolley Madison's surviving correspondence provides evidence of the way "the personal and the political" came together for her. Men of republican inclinations considered patronage—the blatant handing out of jobs based on personal connections—inappropriate. When, for example, John Adams appointed his son, John Quincy Adams, ambassador to Russia, carping critics complained. Society, on the other hand, encouraged women to operate based on social contacts and personal feelings. Hence, men could request government jobs indirectly by appealing to the right woman, like Dolley Madison.

For example, in February 1812, writer George Watterston wrote to Mrs. Madison to request her help getting a government job as a tax collector. Watterston slavishly promised to "ever esteem and admire" Dolley if in some spare moment or other she "mentioned" his request to Albert Gallatin, secretary of the treasury. He assured the first lady that "no motive other than that of necessity, [could] . . . have induced me to make this request."[5] Watterston did not get the tax job, but President Madison did make him librarian of Congress in 1815. Later in life, Watterston initiated the building of the Washington Monument. Dolley Madison may have made his work and accomplishments possible. While no letter of hers survives concerning Watterston's request, in a letter to President Madison in 1813, Watterston made reference to an excellent pedigree of recommendations that accompanied his application for the tax job. Perhaps Dolley's was part of the stack.

More pressing matters than diplomatic niceties, patronage, and dirty roads closed in on the Madisons' attention by the time of James's election to the presidency in 1808. As relations with Great Britain had worsened after the resumption of Napoleon's European wars in 1803, a few grievances (and a few desires) led the United States to declare a war of its own. But with only a small peacetime military, the United States began the War of 1812 with about 10,000 troops. A bigger problem would soon show itself—the lack of competent generals. For example, General James Wilkerson, commander of the forces in the Southeast and an old hero of the Revolution, had for more than a decade been on the payroll of Spain as a spy, and he tended to spend government funds on himself rather than on his duties. Secretary of the Navy Paul Hamilton was usually drunk by noon; Representative Nathaniel Macon Tuttle called him "about as fit for his [job] as the Indian prophet would be for Emperor of Europe."[6] Such were two of America's top military leaders.

Not only did President Madison have to deal, then, with a reluctant Federalist Party, with poor military leadership, and with a small army and virtually no navy, but also most states wanted to organize large militias that would be under their own commands. And of course, almost no one wanted to pay taxes to fund the war—this was the United States, after all. In essence, these were the same conditions that had faced colonists in the War for Independence.

In March 1812, three months before warfare would begin, Dolley Madison wrote to her younger sister, Anna Cutts, to talk politics and parties. "The world seems run[n]ing mad, what with one thing or another," Dolley scribbled. The Federalists had "refused" to attend presidential dinners or other functions. Dolley, however, concocted a plan to woo the feuding congressmen back together. She threw such big parties, "crowded with republicans," that the disgruntled Federalists got "alarmed" by the fun they were missing and returned to the fold.[7] Although congressmen from each state tended to room together during these years, thus isolating themselves inside their own factions, social functions hosted by Dolley Madison could bring the battling factions back together into a larger orbit. The first lady had the power to reunite.

Half a year later, in mid-October 1812, Dolley found herself "in the midst of business & anxiety." U.S. and British armies had already tangled, and she believed "prosperity & happiness would attend [the] Country" now that the "disgraceful" General William Hull (a celebrated Revolutionary War veteran) had been replaced by the "Brave" General Harrison. Writing that the war had been "forced" on the United States, Dolley turned toward William Henry Harrison for victory.[8]

In July 1812, General Hull had taken a force of some 2,000 men into Canada to destroy Fort Mulden, the key to the Canadian interior in the West. However, the British captured Hull's dispatches, figured out what he was doing, and cut off his supply lines, forcing the larger U.S. army to retreat to Detroit. Seen as cowardly throughout the nation, Hull made his retreat even worse when he submitted to phony threats of vicious Indians in the vicinity. Hull ended up crouching alone inside the fort at Detroit with tobacco juice dribbling into his beard. He sent up a white flag and sacrificed the campaign in the West to his own fears. The "Brave Harrison" mentioned by Dolley was William Henry Harrison, who had command of Kentucky's militia and was readying his forces to flatten the British. Though Dolley described herself as "full of hope,"[9] her optimism would have deserted her had she known that Stephen Van Rensselear—commander in the East—was about to lead a botched campaign across the Niagara River in a bid to take the city of Queenston. Getting across the river became more difficult than usual when an officer went down the river taking all the oars with him. Though Winfield Scott, only a lieutenant colonel, led a successful assault across the river two days later, the New York militia refused to go, saying that their job was to defend the state, not to invade a foreign nation, a stance the Kentucky militia had already taken with General Hull. In general, Dolley Madison's "hope" had little basis in reality.

During the brief fighting season of 1812, the only real victories for the

166

United States lay at sea. A British newspaper snubbed the U.S. Navy as "a few fire-built frigates, manned by a handful of bastards and outlaws,"[10] but this weak slap in the face was about the best Britain could do after such U.S. captains as Stephen Decatur (recent hero against Tripoli) captured the *Macedonian*—which netted him and his crew $200,000 in prize money and became part of the U.S. Navy for twenty-plus years. American privateers captured 450 British ships in the first six months of the war. The U.S. naval forces humbled the mighty British navy, and Canada's defenders routed the United States' own numerically superior ground forces. All in all, the state of war seemed to be tipped in Britain's favor at the close of 1812.

During 1813, U.S. forces fought on Lake Erie against the British navy, in Canada against the Shawnee Indians, and in the Southeast against the Creek Indians. Dolley Madison stayed informed. However, she spent the better part of 1813 receiving pleas for employment from various men, like William Lee. With flying flattery, Lee—a U.S. agent in France who sometimes shopped for the first lady in Paris—called Dolley "the Queen of the peoples hearts." Trying his best to be both nonchalant and humble, Lee asked her to consider him "if any thing should occur in which my feeble talents could be employed." Not surprisingly, if such a situation arose he would be "the happiest mortal living."[11] Nothing occurred in the short run, so William Lee kept on shopping.

Although the White House was previously shielded from the immediate dangers of war, the year 1814 would turn safety on its head for Dolley Madison, leaving less time to answer job requests. The British, having defeated Napoleon at the Battle of Leipzig in October 1813, could now devote its full might to the American War. Events in the South would prove critical.

At Fort Mims, near Mobile, Alabama, in August 1813, Creek warriors had killed about 250 women, children, and militiamen. Southern whites boiled for revenge. Early in 1814, at the Battle of Horseshoe Bend on the Tallapoosa River, a rising southern star, Andrew Jackson, led a vengeful slaughter—his men killed 800 Indians in retaliation for the massacre at Fort Mims. Murder was the parent of Jackson's reputation. The Treaty of Fort Jackson, signed in August, took 20 million acres away from the Creek nation, fully half its territory. But Dolley Madison did not live in Jackson-controlled Alabama. She lived on the coast, which the British had effectively blockaded. In 1813, the British burned Frenchtown, Maryland, and pillaged and raped in Hampton, Virginia. Suffering stalemates in huge land battles along the Niagara River during 1814, the British concentrated their naval efforts on the Chesapeake River cities of Baltimore and Washington, DC, where their expectations of success proved reasonable.

As the United States and Great Britain spent the first half of 1814 in combat, their ambassadors lamely negotiated. Until July 28, 1814, Dolley Madison wrote to acquaintances without any real note of concern. On that day, however, she wrote to her stylish friend Hannah Gallatin that the British were within twenty miles of the capital and that the local citizens were threatening her and James if they abandoned the city. "In case of an at[t]ack," Dolley wrote, "they will stop him & [say] that he shall fall with it." Dolley reported feeling "perturbed" though not "the least alarmed at these things, but entirely disgusted" and was resolved to stay by her husband's side. Continuing with confident flourishes, she wrote to her son a week later that "the British on our shore's are stealing & destroying private property, rarely coming to battle, but when they do, are allways beaten."[12] "Allways" proved to be the wrong word.

General William Winder, recently released from British captivity after suffering a strategic flop in the summer of 1813 at the Battle of Stoney Creek, theoretically had control of the defenses around the District of Columbia. Unable or unwilling to deal with the responsibility of drilling troops and preparing fortifications, Winder rode around the DC area for weeks on end, making himself so unreachable that a letter bearing new instructions took three weeks to catch him. Had Dolley Madison known about Winder's incapacity, she might have been less optimistic. Writing again to Hannah Gallatin on August 6, Dolley Madison teasingly suggested that if peace descended, Hannah might like "to be in Europe, as Minister." Dolley continued, "Oh that I could see you my beloved friend, that I might tell you, & hear from you many things." On a more realistic note, Dolley wanted to make sure Hannah had "an active agent to take care of [her] furniture," in case the British arrived.[13] Although afraid of losing furniture, Dolley did not lose her sense of humor as the British throngs closed in.

Arrive they did, and in her best-known letter (though the surviving copy is an edited rewrite touched up years later), Dolley Madison described the days of August 23 and 24, 1814, when the British burned the White House and the Capitol building to the ground. James had left Dolley to visit General Winder and the troops. The temperature soared to 100 degrees. James wrote with a pencil to inform her "the enemy seemed stronger than had at first been reported, and it might happen that they would reach the city, with the intention of destroying it." In response, she stuffed a carriage full of paper-filled trunks. Unable to get any wagons, Dolley Madison was going to have to "sacrifice" most of their belongings, furniture included. With the personal guard of 100 soldiers gone to the river, on the 24th she turned her "spy glass in every direction, and watch[ed] with unwearied anxiety, hoping to discover the approach of [her] dear husband."[14]

Through her telescope, Dolley witnessed the British rout General Winder's few forces at Bladensburg Bridge, only to have two dust-covered messengers come to her side, bidding her to "fly." Ordering a servant to break the glass on a canvas painting of George Washington, which he rolled up and gave to her, Dolley wrote, "And now, dear sister, I must leave this house, or the retreating army will make me a prisoner in it, by filling up the road I am directed to take."[15] Not even two decades old, the capital was left to British troops, who showed up hoping to find a ranking official who might be able to negotiate. With no such person there, they ate the president's dinner (still sitting on the table) and burned most of the official buildings. Dolley and James Madison escaped to safety and the war continued.

From the larger perspective, only two more major battles took place: one at Maryland in September 1814, which led to the writing of "The Star-Spangled Banner," and one outside New Orleans in 1815. Peace efforts had been ongoing during 1814, and the Treaty of Ghent was signed on December 24. However, it took weeks for such news to travel the ocean. Just as the war might have been prevented by quicker communications in 1812, this last great battle might have been avoided. If, however, the Battle of New Orleans had not happened, the drumbeat of nationalism and pride would have been fainter, and Andrew Jackson would have had a lesser dose of fame, possibly keeping him out of the White House.

Dolley Madison wrote to Hannah Gallatin on January 14, 1815, "The fate of N. Orleans will be known to day—on which so much depends."[16] Fighting in the vicinity had been ongoing for three weeks. General Jackson led forces of Indians, regulars, and militia into the swamps and lakes surrounding New Orleans to harry and pick at the approaching British army, some 10,000 strong. Most of the fighting was hit and run, but on January 8 Americans killed record numbers of British; on January 15, at the actual Battle of New Orleans, seventy U.S. soldiers died in comparison to 1,500 dead and wounded British. Thomas Baker Johnson, postmaster of New Orleans, wrote to Dolley to describe the carnage, victory, and loss of the preceding days. Spurred on by the watchwords "booty and beauty," the redcoats had tried to take the city, but once within twenty yards, the defenders had opened fire with guns and muskets, "leaving the ground strewn with [British] dead and dying." Johnson added that with the invaders in retreat, "The city is in a ferment of delight. The country is saved, the enemy vanquished, and hardly a widow or an orphan whose tears damp the general joy. All is exultation and jubilee."[17]

Dolley soon rejoiced in "our glorious Peace" and took no time in outfitting the Madisons' new home, across the street from the remains of the White House. "Do you know of any easy french Chairs to be sold in Philadelphia for a reasonable price?" she asked Hannah Gallatin. "In short any handsome furniture . . . would answer for us." All was not gaiety and ease, however. Congressmen had been flooding her house, and "in truth ever since the peace my brain has been turn'd with noise & bustle," she moaned.[18]

James Madison remained in office until 1817, when he and Dolley retired to Montpelier, their plantation in Virginia, a country retreat that left her with less bustle than she had grown accustomed to, but no shortage of responsibilities. James lived until 1836, and Dolley survived until 1849, spending the last thirteen years of her life back in Washington, DC. She left the plantation, its slaves, and her finances all in the fumbling, gambling, drunken hands of her one son: John Payne Todd. His mismanagement left her nearly destitute in the city of her former glory, where she nonetheless entertained statesmen, presidents, and cultural heroes until her own final days. For Dolley Madison, the War of 1812 was but one turbulent episode in her eighty-one years, during which she established a new etiquette for Washington society and helped stitch together the nation through the roles made available to women of her generation—roles that Dolley helped to create. Prior to the arrival in Washington of Eleanor Roosevelt in 1933, Dolley Madison was the most important first lady this nation had known.

Tecumseh: Independence Lost

Tecumseh, a Shawnee, was born in 1768, the same year as Dolley Madison. By the time of his birth, the family was living on a tributary of the Ohio River, part of the western domain the British government wanted to set aside for the Indians, the very same land white Americans dearly wanted. Warfare decided ownership. However, Christianity, frontier fighting, treaties, broken treaties, liquor, and disease were the lesser tools of settlement. During Tecumseh's forty-five years, he worked to band native peoples together into an intertribal confederacy that could stop the conquest of their lands. He was killed in 1813 near the Thames River in Canada, an ally-by-necessity of the British, and his death broke apart the last good chance for Native American resistance in the Great Lakes region.

Tecumseh was a handsome man and almost six feet tall. Both allies and adversaries agreed about his character. William Henry Harrison, long-term governor of Indiana Territory and antagonist to Tecumseh, said, "The implicit obedience and respect which the followers of Tecumseh pay him are really astonishing and more than any other circumstance [prove] him one of those uncommon geniuses which spring up occasionally to produce revolutions and overturn the existing order of things . . . wherever he goes, he makes an impression favorable to his purpose." Tecumseh's purpose, in his own words, was to prevent Indians from being "scattered as autumnal leaves before the wind."[19] Tecumseh spoke those words in 1811, on a journey he took southward into Choctaw and Chickasaw territory to convince those tribes to join his confederacy in a last attempt to hold onto land.

170

Like his people the Shawnees, who were spread out from the Deep South up to the border with Canada, Tecumseh traveled widely. In 1774, colonists had taken lands in western Virginia away from Shawnees, and Tecumseh's father died by white men's hands. Tecumseh saw the War for Independence in Indian country, watched the decimation of native forces, and fought in skirmishes toward the war's end, which was soon followed by a flood of white settlers, such as the Dewees family, into the Ohio Valley. Taking the lessons of the Revolution with him, Tecumseh began an opposition to U.S. armies and settlers in the early 1790s.

In the old Northwest, fragments of the Iroquois, Shawnee, Wyandot, Delaware, Miami, and other Native American tribes inhabited a vast region also home to British and French fur traders and a mixed-up host of dreamers and schemers. Political and social arrangements were complex in an environment so ripe with cultural differences, each group manipulating others for advantage.

There was no real centralized, intertribal leadership for Native Americans, so when one group made a treaty, it did not represent others' interests or feelings. U.S. negotiators used this fact to their advantage, giving presents, liquor, and money to the willing, who would in turn sign for the unwilling. In the 1780s, Indians of the Northwest signed a series of treaties, like the Treaty of Fort Harmar in 1789, a weak treaty signed by a few out-of-favor war leaders and discredited chiefs who represented few but themselves. Such treaties asserted U.S. sovereignty over the whole Ohio Valley, but a series of Native American victories caused the United States to backtrack in the 1790s, officially recognizing Native American ownership of the lands north of the Ohio River. White settlers, however, paid no attention to paper agreements and forced Indian peoples to either move farther west or fight for their lands.

During the 1790s, the British, sitting secure in Canada, encouraged Indian resistance to U.S. settlement. Britain had not abandoned its frontier forts, like Fort Mackinac, as the 1783 Treaty of Paris had required. The British demanded full repayment of Loyalist losses from the Revolution in return for deserting the posts. In reality, they enjoyed their continued dominance in the fur trade and wanted various Indian nations to act as a buffer between Canada and U.S. land hunger. The aggressiveness of U.S. citizens reinforced the alliance between the Native Americans and the British.

After the United States suffered military defeats against Shawnee-led armies in the early 1790s, General Anthony Wayne trained a disciplined force, his "American Legion." In 1794, the Legion departed for the interior, where Tecumseh waited. Although Native Americans fought each other as often as they fought European-Americans and Europeans, there was some history of intertribal unity. Within living memory, an Ottawa named Pontiac had banded

Great Lakes tribes together in 1763 to lead a resistance movement against colonists. More recently, in the late 1780s, Joseph Brant—the fiery Mohawk and British ally whom Mary Jemison knew—had been part of an attempt to bring the Great Lakes region into the fragmented Iroquoian League. Although the effort failed after the 1789 Treaty of Fort Harmar discredited the league's power, this kind of networking kept open channels of communication that Tecumseh used for the next two decades.

By 1794, Tecumseh had proved his worth in battle, namely at a place dubbed "Fallen Timbers" (because of trees that had toppled in a tornado). At Fallen Timbers, General Wayne defeated the Shawnees, but people had seen Tecumseh wherever the fighting was thickest. The Indians fled to nearby British Fort Miami, but were not let in. After this battle, Tecumseh held long memories of British betrayal and U.S. brutality. In the Treaty of Greenville, which followed the Battle of Fallen Timbers in 1795, most of present-day Ohio and portions of Indiana were ceded to the United States, but the U.S. government promised to respect remaining Native American territorial rights. Soon enough, the federal government would again show itself too weak (and not really interested enough) to stop cycles of frontier vengeance, the flow of liquor, and the stampede of settlers. Tecumseh refused to sign the Treaty of Greenville.

Lalawethika was one of Tecumseh's brothers, and until 1805 he was a terrible drunkard. Alcohol had lately stolen the vitality of many Great Lakes Indians, given its increased availability from the rising numbers of American corn farmers and increased sales from Canadian merchants. In 1805, Lalawethika had a vision that convinced him to give up liquor and preach to his people the removal of Christianity, alcohol, and other tainted shards of European-derived culture in a bid to return to a half-remembered, traditional way of living. Renaming himself Tenskwatawa—meaning "the open door" (a reference to one of Jesus's sayings)—he gained prominence and influence as "the Prophet," alongside Tecumseh. Over the next few years, the brothers assumed fearsome proportions in the minds of many white people as Indians by the hundreds came to live in the Prophet's new town at Greenville, in western Ohio. Not all Indians, however, followed the Prophet's teachings. In 1811, a group of Ottawas informed the secretary of war, "Our ears are closed to those bad birds [i.e., Tecumseh] which sing around us." These Ottawas called Tenskwatawa a "pretender" who was "fraught with bad and foolish advice," for "whosoever listened to the advice of the Prophet or his followers, would be destroyed by the American People."[20]

White Americans developed two dominant strains of thinking about Native Americans. According to one, represented by Thomas Jefferson, Indians could become like white people in morality, religion, habits, and other markers of civilization. White frontier men and women (called "Long Knives" by Indians) often held the other line of thought. Many Long Knives believed Indians were a nuisance best moved out of the way. Wanting the land for themselves, Long Knives regularly stole Indian horses and killed Indians without compunction, though Indians also did their share of killing. Between the somewhat benign attitude of Jeffersonian philosophers and the malignancy of frontier squatters, U.S. policy officially promoted conciliation with native peoples. But U.S. military forces were not willing to punish white people for killing Indians and ultimately intervened on behalf of whites, time after time.

Tenskwatawa preached a new religion—sometimes persecuting Christianized Indians, having them burnt alive—and this lost him and his followers the goodwill of friendly white Christians. For example, neighboring Moravians had recently had some success in converting Delaware Indians, who were themselves flocking to Tenskwatawa's vision. But the Moravians could not stomach Tenskwatawa's anti-Christian rhetoric and behavior. This loss of goodwill made it easier for white Americans, near and far, to think of all Indians as "heathen," unrepentant, and dangerous—hence, unworthy of kindness. These feelings were summed up in piles of letters sent to Congress during the decade after Tenskwatawa's transformation.

An 1809 letter says, "The influence of the Prophet has been great." A year later, Congress received word that "there can be no doubt of the designs of the Prophet and the British agent of Indian affairs, to do us injury." A more obvious stereotyping was provided in an 1811 letter: "Whether the Prophet intends to make war, or not, partial war must continue to be the consequence . . . such is the nature of Indians, that they cannot be collected, and kept together, under such circumstances, without having their minds prepared for war; and, in that situation, it is almost impossible to restrain them from premature acts of hostility." The mere gathering of Indians in one place would, therefore, "be sufficient to justify" an attack on the Prophet's town.[21] Indeed, U.S. frontier officials reasoned, the Indians were doubly dangerous because of their growing alliance with the British, which became fully established just before the War of 1812.

During the years that worried letters like these made their way to Congress, the agents of government, like William Henry Harrison, were meeting with Tecumseh and other Native American leaders to try to reach accommodations. Native unity had its limits, and U.S. officials worked hard to exploit the fissures. In 1810, Harrison and Tecumseh met and exchanged two days' worth of clashing history lessons. The meeting was precipitated by the Treaty of Fort Wayne, arranged for in 1809 by Harrison, who gathered together a few chiefs, got them drunk, and had them sign away lands that belonged to other tribes.

Tecumseh refused Harrison's invitation to meet inside, so they shared the trees' shade and grounds near the governor's mansion at Vincennes (modern-day Fort Knox). Tecumseh was known to be long-winded, well informed, and polite and direct. The surviving copy of his speech was transcribed and translated on the spot by one of Harrison's men. After hearing Harrison, Tecumseh responded, "Brother, I wish you to listen to me well." After this fraternal overture, Tecumseh said that after being treated fairly by the French a long time ago, the British had become the new "Fathers" of the Shawnees, in the 1760s. But the British had acted poorly, with "treachery." Tecumseh said the British "never troubled us for our lands but they have done worse by inducing us to go to war," a reference to the past three decades of conflict, beginning with the Revolution. Tecumseh knew his people's history well.

"You ought to know," Tecumseh continued, "that after we agreed to bury the tomahawk at Greenville [in 1795] we then found new fathers in the Americans who told us they would treat us well, not like the British who gave us but a small piece of pork every day." However, the Americans did not live up to their promises, either; instead, they "killed some of the Shawnees, Winebagoes, Delawares and Miamies" and took more land. Furthermore, Tecumseh accused Harrison of wishing "to prevent the Indians to do as we wish them: to unite and let them consider their land common property of the whole." In all these accusations, Tecumseh was accurate. In fact, in an 1803 letter to Harrison, President Jefferson had explicitly ordered him to make the Indians servile, disunited, and dependent: "to cultivate an affectionate attachment." Tecumseh had figured out, or at least guessed, Jefferson's purpose: "Perhaps it is by direction of the President to make those distinctions. It is a very bad thing and we do not like it."[22]

Harrison began to respond to Tecumseh's accusations and requests for the return of land improperly sold. In the midst of Harrison's reply, Tecumseh became agitated and stood up with his tomahawk; blows were barely avoided. According to historian Alvin M. Josephy, the next day Tecumseh sent an apology and Harrison came to his encampment to talk further, during which time they were seated on a bench. Tecumseh kept sliding toward Harrison, pushing him to the edge. Tecumseh pointed out that this nudging was exactly what was happening to the Indians.[23] Nothing lasting was agreed to, and Tecumseh departed for a further tour of negotiations with other native peoples.

The United States granted none of Tecumseh's requests, and in a message to the Indiana legislature, Harrison asked, "Is one of the fairest portions of the globe to remain in a state of nature, the haunt of a few wretched savages, when it seems destined, by the Creator to give support to a large population, and to be the sea of civilization, of science, and true religion?"[24] This was the man with whom Tecumseh had talked, the man who would become president in 1841, a true believer in white civilization, a slave owner, and a killer of Indians. He was not the first of his kind elected to the White House, nor the last.

In 1808, two years before the meeting with Harrison, Tenskwatawa moved his town into the Indiana backcountry, on the Tippecanoe River, directly south of Lake Michigan. Relations with neighboring whites had become strained, and so many followers had flooded the encampment at Greenville that Tenskwatawa could not feed them all, even with help from a nearby Shaker community. The new location was dubbed Prophetstown. For two years, Tenskwatawa's reputation had risen and fallen. During times of famine, people tended to believe less in his divine sanction. When he could demonstrate power—as in his accurate prediction of an eclipse, which he had learned from traveling astronomers—Tenskwatawa's authority grew. However, as historian David Edmunds pointed out, the 1809 Treaty of Fort Wayne took credibility away from Tenskwatawa; he could not prevent the thievery of Indian lands.[25] Tenskwatawa's decline marked the full ascendancy of Tecumseh.

The year that everything changed was 1811. Governor Harrison had become convinced that Tecumseh and Tenskwatawa meant to attack the capital, Vincennes, even though both men repeatedly sought to assure him otherwise. Tecumseh knew a war was coming, but he wanted to add southern Indians to his confederacy; he needed time. On his way south in July 1811, Tecumseh stopped to see the governor. The meeting was tense. Soon after Tecumseh departed, Harrison led a mixed army of militia and federal troops slowly north toward Prophetstown, beginning in late September. Along the way, Harrison and the Prophet parleyed, but in the early morning rain of November 7, the Prophet's forces struck at Harrison's encampment, barely a mile away from Prophetstown. Tenskwatawa figured that a preemptive attack would be the best defense.

Two Indians nearly killed Harrison. They had been told he would be riding a white horse, but in the confusion of the attack, Harrison jumped on a subordinate's black horse, so the assassins shot the wrong man. The Battle of Tippecanoe was confusing and short-lived. While both sides suffered heavy losses, the Indians were routed, and then Prophetstown was leveled, destroyed. Tenskwatawa's credibility died on the instant. He had promised his followers that the Master of Life would protect them from American bullets, but no such deity intervened. The great confederacy of the North, as much a product of Tenskwatawa's charisma as of Tecumseh's powerful orations, fell apart in the Wabash Valley and left Canada and the Indians of the Great Lakes a weaker target for American designs.

Although western troubles had helped spark the War of 1812, conflict between whites and Indians did not necessarily lead to alliances among Indians. While the Prophet was losing his town, Tecumseh was in the Carolinas and Georgia, trying to rally the Chickasaws, Choctaws, and Creeks into the confederacy. Only the Creeks were interested. A leading Choctaw named Pushmataha listened politely to Tecumseh's plea for alliance and then responded with a resounding refusal. "The great Shawnee orator," Pushmataha began, "has portrayed in vivid picture the wrongs inflicted on his and other tribes by the ravages of the paleface . . . naturally we sympathize with the misfortunes of his people." Sympathy did not, however, turn into alliance. Pushmataha continued, "Mistake not, [Tecumseh's] language means war. And war with whom, pray. . . . If we take up arms against the Americans we must of necessity meet in deadly combat our daily neighbors and associates in this part of the country near our homes."[26] The Choctaw were not willing to sacrifice local harmony for an ideal of Indian unity. The Shawnees and the Choctaws were not the same, even if lumped together under the word "Indian."

In Tecumseh's speech to the gathered Choctaw, he had said, "The whites are already nearly a match for us all united, and too strong for any one tribe alone to resist . . . they will soon conquer us apart and disunited, and we will be driven away from our native country and scattered as autumnal leaves before the wind."[27] Tecumseh was right, and the leader Pushmataha was short sighted and too trusting. Tecumseh returned to Indiana after the Battle of Tippecanoe and upbraided his brother, the Prophet, for attacking too soon. Many of their confederates had abandoned the cause and Tecumseh had to busy himself stitching back together the tattered remains. Now war was upon them, and they turned even more to the British for supplies of powder and shot.

The British commander in the West was Henry Procter, a cautious man whose temperament did not suit him to the task. Tecumseh wanted a war of offense that would carve out a permanent home for Native American peoples in a portion of the land they had been promised by the United States. Although Procter's strategy briefly fulfilled Tecumseh's wish (as with the taking of Detroit in 1812), Procter was unwilling and unable to sustain a prolonged strike into U.S. soil. At Fort Meigs (southwest of Lake Erie) in April 1813, a combined British and Indian assault failed to take the fort but did lead to the capture of hundreds of Kentucky militia members—many of whom were killed in the running of a gauntlet where Indians lined up in two rows and clubbed Kentuckians forced to sprint along the gap. When Tecumseh arrived on the scene, he stopped his men from killing the rest of the captives. His native allies took what loot they could and dispersed. Neither the Indians nor the Canadian militia had any interest in a long siege. Fort Meigs was saved, and when Lake Erie fell to the United States later in the year, the war in the West was all but over.

Tecumseh asked Procter for ammunition to take the fight south, but Procter declined, saying that it was time for a retreat up the Thames River. Tecumseh gave in and went northeast with the thousand-or-so remaining warriors, women, and children who remained loyal to his banner. William Harrison pursued with nearly 5,000 troops, and because Procter neglected to burn the bridges he crossed, Harrison's more agile force caught the beleaguered British, Canadians, and Indians on October 5, 1813. British forces withered under the American advance. Tecumseh's men were arrayed in the forests along the road. The fighting became hand-to-hand, swords, tomahawks, and knives slashing and stabbing. Somewhere in the melee, Tecumseh dropped to the earth, never to stand again. His brother was there, though not as a combatant. Tenskwatawa never fought.

The name for this war, the War of 1812, makes only so much sense. It lasted through 1814. For Canadians, it was the second time they had been invaded by the United States. For the Indians of the Great Lakes region and of Florida, the war was a land grab, and it was their land that got grabbed. The war represented a culmination of Tecumseh's efforts, a chance to wield Native American energy in unison, to put a stop to 200 years of stolen homes, stolen fields, broken promises. Tecumseh's opportunity fell beneath the weight of many factors: the expanding white population, Native American disunity, the enemy's guns and ammunition, and the Christian belief in divine sanction mingled with a commonplace racism that taught white sons and daughters to despise those with dark skin. The 1814 Treaty of Ghent between Britain and the United States simply returned borders to the status quo ante, what they had been in 1811. But it signaled the last time that the United States and Britain would fight as opponents. Andrew Jackson's victory in New Orleans heralded the call of a new nationalism, and the close of the war secured new portions of the West for U.S. occupation.

The Star-Spangled Banner

In the summer of 1813, before the British burned the White House and before Tecumseh died in Canada, Mary Pickersgill began work sewing an enormous U.S. flag. She apparently often labored until midnight throughout the summer to complete the flag on time, with help from one daughter and at least one slave. For final assembly, she and her helpers spread out its two-foot squares on the floor of a brewery where they could be stitched together—with a final tally of about 350,000 individual stitches.[28] On August 19, the commander of Maryland's Fort McHenry, Major George Armistead, paid Pickersgill $405.90 for the flag, a handsome fee. One year later, less than a month after Dolley Madison fled from Washington, DC, a British fleet sailed into Baltimore's harbor and commenced shelling Fort McHenry, where Pickersgill's 30 by 42-foot flag normally waved. However, the shelling of the fort coincided with a heavy rainstorm, and Pickersgill's flag was kept inside; a smaller "storm flag" flapped over the fort during the battle.[29] The artillery bombardment lasted twenty-five hours, beginning at 6:30 AM on September 13. Bombs and shrapnel wounded twenty-four U.S. soldiers and killed four. But Major Armistead refused to surrender. A British land invasion of the city could not succeed without the British fleet being able to sail past Fort McHenry, and in the face of Armistead's steadfast resolve, the British gave up and sailed away.

During the bombardment, a lawyer, slave owner, and poet named Francis Scott Key had been stuck on a boat in Baltimore harbor, enthralled by the explosions. After the shelling stopped, Scott wrote his impressions of the event as a poem on the back of an envelope, capturing the "dawn's early light" and the "twilight's last gleaming." He also saw Pickersgill's stand-in flag. Within two days, a local newspaper published the poem, and soon other papers all along the coast picked it up. A local Baltimore publisher, Thomas Carr, took Key's suggestion that the poem be set to music (in particular and perhaps ironically, to a British melody). When Carr released the song "The Star-Spangled Banner," it quickly became popular. However, Congress did not make it the national anthem until 1931, nineteen years after one of George Armistead's descendants gave Mary Pickersgill's original Star-Spangled Banner—undamaged during the bombardment of Fort McHenry but damaged over the years by dust, exposure to light, and by handing out pieces of it to dead soldiers' families[30]—as a gift to the Smithsonian, where it resides today.

Notes

1. Donald R. Hickey, *The War of 1812: A Forgotten Conflict* (Urbana: University of Illinois Press, 1990), 42.

2. Charles Francis Adams, *Letters of Mrs. Adams, Wife of John Adams* (Boston: Charles C. Little and James Brown, 1840), 2: 240–242.

3. Holly C. Shulman, ed., *The Dolley Madison Digital Edition,* "Abigail DeHart Mayo to Dolley Payne Todd Madison, 23 February 1804," (Charlottesville: University of Virginia Press, 2004), http://rotunda.upress.virginia.edu/dmde/DPM0069.

4. Sarah Luria, "National Domesticity in the Early Republic: Washington, D.C.," *Common-Place.org* 3, no. 4, July 2003, http://www.common-place.org/vol-03/no-04/washington/).

5. Shulman, ed., *The Dolley Madison Digital Edition,* "George Watterston to Dolley Payne Todd Madison, 28 February 1812," (Charlottesville: University of Virginia Press, 2004), http://rotunda.upress.virginia.edu/dmde/DPM0311.

6. Hickey, *The War of 1812,* 90.

7. Adams, *Letters of Mrs. Adams,* 778.

8. Shulman, ed., *The Dolley Madison Digital Edition,* "Dolley Payne Todd Madison to Phoebe Pemberton Morris, [ca. 17 October 1812]," http://rotunda.upress.virginia.edu/dmde/DPM0363.

9. Shulman, ed., *The Dolley Madison Digital Edition*, "Dolley Payne Todd Madison to Phoebe Pemberton Morris, [ca. 17 October 1812]" http://rotunda.upress. virginia.edu/dmde/DPM0363.

10. Hickey, *The War of 1812*, 98.

11. Shulman, ed., *The Dolley Madison Digital Edition*, "William Lee to Dolley Payne Todd Madison, 20 March 1813," http://rotunda.upress.virginia.edu/dmde/ DPM0377.

12. Shulman, ed., *The Dolley Madison Digital Edition*, "Dolley Payne Todd Madison to John Payne Todd, 6 August 1814," http://rotunda.upress.virginia.edu/ dmde/DPM0463.

13. Shulman, ed., *The Dolley Madison Digital Edition*, "Dolley Payne Todd Madison to Hannah Nicholson Gallatin, [6] August [1814]," http://rotunda.upress. virginia.edu/dmde/DPM0474.

14. Lucia B. Cutts, ed., *Memoirs and Letters of Dolley Madison, Wife of James Madison, President of the United States* (Boston: Houghton, Mifflin, 1886), 109–110.

15. Cutts, ed., *Memoirs and Letters of Dolley Madison*, 111.

16. Oberg, ed., *The Papers of Albert Gallatin, Microfilm Edition*, "DPM to HNG, 14 January 1815" (Wilmington, DE: Scholarly Resources, 1985), Reel 27.

17. Cutts, ed., *Memoirs and Letters of Dolley Madison*, 125–127.

18. Shulman, ed., *The Dolley Madison Digital Edition*, "Dolley Payne Todd Madison to Hannah Nicholson Gallatin, 5 March 1815," http://rotunda.upress.virginia. edu/dmde/DPM0492.

19. Quoted in John Sugden, *Tecumseh: A Life* (New York: Owl Books, 1999), 215. Bob Blaisdell, ed., *Great Speeches by Native Americans* (Mineola, NY: Dover, 2000), 50.

20. American State Papers, Senate, 12th Congress, 1st Session Indian Affairs, "Extract from the Ottawa nation of Indians, delivered to the Secretary of War, by their delegation, on the 5th of October, 1811," vol. 1, 804, http://memory.loc.gov/cgi-bin/ampage?collId=llsp&fileName=007/llsp007.db&Page=804.

21. American State Papers, Senate, 12th Congress, 1st Session Indian Affairs, "Extracts of Letters Addressed to the War Department," vol. 1, 799.

22. "Tecumseh's Speech to Governor Harrison, 20 August 1810," Indiana Historical Society, Digital Image Collections, http://images.indianahistory.org/cdm4/document. php?CISOROOT=/dc007&CISOPTR=19&REC=18.

23. Alvin M. Josephy, *The Patriot Chiefs: A Chronicle of American Indian Resistance* (New York: Penguin, 1993), 150–156.

24. Anthony J. Hall, *The American Empire and the Fourth World* (Montreal, Quebec: McGill Queen's University Press, 2003), 77.

25. David R. Edmunds, *The Shawnee Prophet* (Lincoln: University of Nebraska Press, 1985), 67–93.

26. W.C. Vanderwerth, *Indian Oratory: Famous Speeches by Noted Indian Chieftans* (Norman: University of Oklahoma Press, 1971), 72.

27. Vanderwerth, *Indian Oratory*, 62.

28. Irvin Molotsky, *The Flag, The Poet & The Song: The Story of the Star-Spangled Banner* (New York: Dutton, 2001), 77.

29. Molotsky, *The Flag, The Poet & The Song*, 90.

30. Molotsky, *The Flag, The Poet & The Song*, 138–139.

10

Andrew Jackson and America

General Andrew Jackson *(Three Lions/Getty Images)*

These days, people often use the word "great" as a beefed-up version of "good." In the 1800s, "great" meant something more like big, out of the ordinary, larger than life. Although slender in frame, Andrew Jackson was a great man, striding through American history possessed by an unalterable sense of purpose. By the time he became president in 1829, at the age of sixty-one, no one would have disagreed about his historical stature, his greatness. However, Jackson's contemporaries did not all agree that he was a good man. Should history judge Andrew Jackson, and if so, whose standards of decency and goodness should be applied? In his day, as in ours, people had conflicting notions of what was right and what was wrong. Therefore, in certain of Jackson's actions and in the reactions to him, much can be learned about the moral codes of early nineteenth-century America.

Many presidents have nicknames, often more than one. Ronald Reagan was "the Gipper" (from one of his movie roles). Reagan's supporters called him "the Great Communicator." Richard Nixon was "Tricky Dick," though not to his friends. Dwight Eisenhower's name got shortened to "Ike." Theodore Roosevelt was simply "Teddy," which he liked less than "Rough Rider"—a reference to his glory days in the Spanish-American War of 1898 (the teddy bear was named after Roosevelt). Andrew Jackson had four nicknames that stuck: "Old Hickory," "Sharp Knife," "the Hero of New Orleans," and "King Andrew I." Jackson's nicknames read like an unofficial record of his adult life, chronicling the moments that marked him in the popular imagination.

The Story of Jackson

Born in 1767 during Britain's twilight in America, Andrew Jackson was permanently affected by the Revolution. He grew up a wild boy in the Carolinas, where two brothers died fighting against the British. When he was fourteen, the British took Jackson captive during the first battle of his life. While a prisoner of war, Jackson refused to clean a British officer's shoes. The man struck Jackson on the skull with a sword, leaving a deep, permanent depression in the cranium, the first wound of many—one that tied him to the United States like an anchor of bone. Andrew's mother died after nursing sick soldiers on a prison ship. The vicious backcountry fighting, the loss of his family, and the final American victory burrowed into Jackson's mind, turning him toward the male ideals of his age: honor, ambition, tough masculinity, and a jubilant faith in America's emerging role as the beacon of virtue.

Jackson earned a number of degrees in gambling, fighting, and drinking, but he took only a few years of formal education, customary for boys in the South. After tearing through a decent inheritance, Jackson straightened his back and sought a law career, most frequently obtained in his day by apprenticing to a lawyer, reading the literature, and applying for the bar. He was admitted in 1787, at the age of twenty, having done little in two decades to distinguish himself as anything more than smart. Or, as his recent biographer Sean Wilentz put it, "Jackson came into the world a perfect nobody."[1]

In 1788, Jackson headed farther west, away from his youthful follies and into the life of an attorney for the region that would soon become Tennessee. On his way to Nashville, Jackson argued a case against Waightstill Avery, who belittled Jackson in front of the courtroom. Young and impetuous, Jackson responded with a challenge to duel. The two men squared off but fired their pistols into the air, satisfying their honor and sparing their lives. Although his first nickname was two decades away, Jackson's character and attitude were already evident. He would fight rather than lose face.

Jackson made it to Nashville in October 1788. While boarding in a local home, he met his true love, Rachel Donelson Robards—a married woman. Her marriage to Lewis Robards, already brittle, broke over Jackson's affection for Rachel. In 1791, Lewis Robards filed for divorce, and Rachel and Andrew Jackson got married. They did not realize that the divorce had only been initiated, not finalized, and this technical slipup would come to haunt their marriage and Jackson's political future in all the petty, sensational ways that private lives get inflated for political gain. At critical future moments, opponents would accuse Jackson of being a marriage-wrecker, while Rachel would get characterized as an adulteress and bigamist, since technically she was married to two men until late 1793. Upon learning of the legal error and after the divorce from Lewis Robards was finalized, Andrew Jackson and Rachel Donelson remarried in January 1794. Andrew Jackson's firmest attachments were being formed: to Rachel and to the United States, both of whom he defended with smiting loyalty.

During the next twenty years, Jackson nearly went to debtor's prison for wild land speculations, served briefly as a U.S. congressman and senator, worked as a traveling superior court judge, became a major general of the Tennessee militia, and purchased the family estate—the Hermitage. Each public accomplishment Jackson used to his advantage. As a representative in both houses of Congress, he pushed the rights of states to regulate their own affairs while drawing heavily on the federal government for assistance in fighting Native Americans, making him popular at home. As a judge, Jackson created statewide political networks where he polished his intellectual image even as he reminded everyone that Andrew Jackson would take care of business in the most direct manner possible.

In one famous incident while he was serving as a circuit judge, Jackson ordered a local sheriff to apprehend a man, Russell Bean, who had cut off his own daughter's ears while drunk, but the sheriff and his deputies were too frightened. So Jackson had himself deputized and faced down Bean in the town square. The criminal tamely submitted to the gun-wielding Jackson, claiming that he saw "shoot" in Jackson's eyes.[2] In 1803, while Jackson was still a judge, the state's governor, John Sevier, saw more than "shoot" in Jackson's eyes. Jackson ran against Sevier for the job of governor, and during the campaign Sevier made cutting remarks not only about the political novice Jackson, but apparently about his wife, Rachel, as well. Guns were drawn, bullets fired, and a duel soon followed that ended in cursing, posturing, and a peaceful ride back into town. This high-tempered fiasco faded in the next duel's shadow.

In 1806, Jackson traded hard words with Charles Dickinson, a well-liked man-about-town and reputed crack shot, who had made unflattering remarks about Rachel Jackson as part of a tit-for-tat with Jackson. The original controversy centered on the financial credit and reputation of Dickinson's father-in-law, whom one of Jackson's friends had accused of passing bad notes when trying to pay off a horse-racing debt owed to Jackson. The conflict led to a field in Kentucky. Dickinson shot Jackson in the chest, where the bullet lodged until the end of Jackson's life, causing him lasting pain. Jackson remained calm, took careful aim (twice), and shot Dickinson dead on the spot.[2] The killing made Jackson something of a pariah for months, primarily because Jackson had immediately fired his pistol after it misfired without giving Dickinson the same chance. Jackson had, some people claimed, broken the dueling code and in the process shamed himself. His reputation, however, would be fully revived by the War of 1812, a necessary uplift considering his involvement in the meantime with none other than Aaron Burr.

After killing Alexander Hamilton in 1804, Burr had eventually made his way into Tennessee, where he cooked up a scheme to invade Mexico and other Spanish possessions. Burr stayed for a spell with the Jacksons in 1806, spreading his charm like poison in the ears of those foolish enough to listen. Jackson listened. He heard in Burr's silvery whisperings an opportunity to gain fame and to furnish planters like himself with the rich soils of the southwestern frontier, which still echoed with clashes between settlers and Indians. The scheme would also remove the old-money landowners of New Orleans and Florida from what Jackson considered their infernal meddling in Indian affairs. Burr was found out, as was Jackson's role in the botched invasion scheme. Burr stood trial for treason and was found not guilty, and Jackson managed to convince John Marshall's Supreme Court—without a trial—that he had been innocent of any treason. This second stain on Jackson's image was painted over in patriotic colors half a decade later.

The War of 1812 was greeted in the white West with great huzzahs. Ohioans looked at Canada in the same way that Tennesseans looked at Florida: with

184

desire. Jackson received command of the state militia. Unfortunately, his superior was General James Wilkinson, a spy in the employ of Spain, who looked at Jackson as an upstart. Ordered in 1813 to march a militia army of about 2,500 to Natchez, Jackson ably complied, even though the weather was nasty—only to be instructed upon arrival that his army was not needed. On the way back to Nashville, offering his horses to sick soldiers, Jackson maintained order and earned immortal devotion not only from his men, but also from many in the nation when they learned of his resolution. During the miserable trek, Jackson was dubbed "Old Hickory" in honor of the hardest tree in the region, able to weather any circumstances. The nickname lasted the rest of his days, although it was soon to be matched by an equally flattering one. However, the flattery and circumstances came at the expense of the Creek Indians.

The War of 1812 separated many Indian nations, and this was true for the Creeks more than for any other people. After a large force of Creek fighters killed the adults and children at Fort Mims in August 1813, Jackson showed his prowess. He was recovering from serious wounds inflicted in a gun-and-knife fight he had had only months before with Thomas Hart Benton (later a powerful senator from Missouri) and his nephew, Jesse, in which Jackson had nearly been killed. Reaching into the well of his character, Jackson (his left arm still in a sling) found the energy to lead, much to the chagrin of the Creek warriors known as Red Sticks, the faction intent on stopping white migration on the frontier. Throughout the remainder of the year and into March 1814, Jackson dealt with short-term enlistees, raw recruits, and skillful Creek armies. But at the Battle of Horseshoe Bend the power of the Red Sticks was shattered, 800 to 900 of them killed. This victory enabled Jackson to dictate terms—even to the many hundreds of Creeks who had fought as his allies. He was named a major general in the U.S. Army, and in the Treaty of Fort Jackson in August, thirty-five chiefs signed away millions of acres. Only one of those chiefs was a Red Stick. The rest had been Jackson's allies in the war, allies whom Jackson now betrayed. As biographer Robert Remini noted, "He ended the war by signing a peace treaty with his Indian allies. . . . All the other southern tribes would one day experience the same melancholy fate at the hands of General Andrew Jackson."[3] Jackson took enough land to form Alabama, ended Creek strength in the South, and was given his second nickname: "Sharp Knife."

Jackson's greatest victory, however, came at the Battle of New Orleans, where he became known as the "Hero of New Orleans." In the wake of his triumph and capitalizing on his authority as a major general, Jackson followed through on old grievances and designs: punishing the Spanish and their Indian allies and taking Florida for the United States. From 1816 through 1820, Jackson—as

Sharp Knife—negotiated with Creeks, Cherokees, and Choctaws, arranging for the peaceful transfer of millions of acres in Georgia and Mississippi in return for small cash payments. Jackson clarified his own position—that Indians were not sovereign peoples, but were instead conquered and subject to the whims and laws of the United States. Thousands of Indians moved west of the Mississippi River, though thousands also remained, for a time.

While these peaceful transactions happened under the threat of violence, the piracy of Florida involved physical violence with the Seminoles. For decades, slaves held in the United States had escaped to Florida, living as buffers around cities like St. Augustine, a small Spanish outpost bordering on acquisitive-minded southern slave owners in Georgia. By the late 1700s, fugitive slaves were also intermingling with Seminole bands, who had themselves been harassing settlements in Georgia. These grievances became a pretext for Jackson's invasion of Florida, which he began early in 1818 with about 3,000 men. Burning one Seminole town after another, Jackson's forces scared tiny Spanish garrisons into surrender, and the Seminoles retreated into the scenery. Along the way, Jackson caught and hanged a Scottish adventurer named Alexander Arbuthnot and a British liaison, Robert Ambrister. Arbuthnot had worked for years with the Seminoles, lately trying to convince them to make peace with the United States. Although Arbuthnot's and Ambrister's executions were in some sense a legal consequence of the war, many people saw them as a further expression of Jackson's ruthlessness. This too—like his first, confused marriage to Rachel—plagued him during his bids for the presidency in the 1820s.

Riddled with old wounds and lingering bullets, Andrew Jackson yanked Florida away from the feeble Spanish empire. Although this feat created an international stir and bred opposition in Congress, Jackson's popularity shielded him from any punishment. In 1819, Spain and the United States recognized the inevitable in the Adams-Onis treaty, which ceded Florida to the United States. The United States grew alongside its new favorite son, General Jackson, who served briefly as Florida's governor in 1821—long enough to yearn for his plantation, the Hermitage, as a refuge from the storms of war and politics. Now fifty-four and carrying three nicknames, Jackson retired with his family (including the inevitable slaves) to a life of dinner parties and pipe smoking, and a future more complicated and difficult than any trials he had yet faced.

The Democratic Age

Andrew Jackson's character was, in many ways, America's character. In Jackson's quickness to violence and usurpation of Native American independence, he was typical of the past and present. Although pacifists and cautious minds abounded, a growing nationalism and pride stemmed from the Battle of New Orleans. George Washington had been celebrated for his military leadership and seeming disinterest in political gain. He had taken the presidency without seeming to want it. Washington had been a man unafraid and stout, his feet planted squarely in the dirt, his attitude aloof from partisan bickering. Jackson made himself Washington's successor: a wartime victor and admired champion of southern causes, like the continuation of slavery and the expansion of U.S. territory. Also like Washington, by the mid-1820s Andrew Jackson stood squarely in the middle of partisan, political mayhem, but where Washington had tried to quell the bickering between Thomas Jefferson and Alexander Hamilton, Andrew Jackson openly participated in the factionalism. Politics were becoming openly nasty.

Jackson embraced what was soon to be known as the second party system, an echo of the old split between Jeffersonian Republicans and Hamiltonian Federalists in the 1790s. During the 1830s and 1840s, Jacksonian Democrats and their Whig opponents battled in Congress and in newspapers about the same issues that had been important ever since the Constitutional Convention: what role the federal government should play in the nation; how to manage the economy; what "democracy" should mean and how it should be enacted. Finally, in his loyalty to what he thought of as the will of the people, often called popular sovereignty, Andrew Jackson embodied changes in the American political and social scene. Though he had achieved wealth, status, and political power, common people loved Andrew Jackson for his humble origins and his gruff toughness. Poor residents of the backwoods of the South who had no money to put into a bank, who scratched a living out of the soil with the help of one slave or no slaves—these political customers supported Jackson because he challenged the moneymen and power brokers from the Northeast. Jackson was the first poor people's president, no matter how many thousands of acres he owned or how many slaves he worked. He wore the populist image well.

By the time the election of 1824 arrived, the state representatives of Tennessee had already dragged Jackson out of retirement and made him—once again—a U.S. senator. (Direct election of U.S. senators did not become law until 1913 with the Seventeenth Amendment to the Constitution.) Jackson contended for the presidency, but lost to John Quincy Adams, even though Jackson received more Electoral College and popular votes. Because no one had received more than 50 percent of the Electoral College votes, the choice for president was thrown into the House of Representatives, and after many deals had been made, Adams was chosen president. Henry Clay from Kentucky had placed his congressional support behind Adams. Soon after, President

187

Adams appointed Clay secretary of state. This "corrupt bargain," as Jackson saw it, embittered him and caused him to see the political world as flawed, as no longer truly republican in its loss or subversion of the popular will. The Republican Party had stood alone, ever since the Hartford Convention of 1814 decomposed the remnants of the Federalist Party. (At Hartford, a few Federalists had expressed opposition to the War of 1812, and when news of their meeting was publicized, the nation responded with disgust.) But now, after 1824, Jackson and his supporters started to create a new political association to propagate their ideas and elevate his chances. For the nation as a whole—all peoples considered—this embrace of a party system may have been the most lasting consequence of the Jacksonian Era.

In 1828, thanks to his lasting popularity and the alliances that were struck (namely with the political organizer Martin Van Buren of New York, who became president in 1837), Jackson stepped into the White House. He had won a vast majority of the votes, and ever since, many historians have regarded this election as the beginning of a new kind of American democracy—one that accepted, even sought out, the interest and action of the "common man." While the franchise—the right to vote—had been extended to most white men in America by 1828 (whereas it had been restricted to property owners only a generation before), the evidence for Jackson having risen on the shoulders of average voters is often seen in his inaugural celebration.

Margaret Bayard Smith (one of Dolley Madison's friends and correspondents) knew Washington, DC, society. She was its voice to the nation, a respected author in her own right. In a letter to a friend, Smith described Jackson's inaugural. The day and its proceedings began in solemn silence, interrupted only by the ceremonial firing of cannons and by a "shout that rends the air" lifting from the throats of "thousands and thousands of people, without distinction of rank, collected in an immense mass round the Capitol." The barely audible hush of Jackson's voice as he took the oath of office drifted through the audience. To Smith, it was an "imposing and majestic spectacle." This "sublime" scene soon metamorphosed into democratic pandemonium.

Earlier in the day, Jackson had proceeded to the Capitol building on foot, with the tame crowds girding his path in polite, orderly lines. However, the people—"Country men, farmers, gentlemen, mounted and dismounted, boys, women and children, black and white"—crashed through the barrier separating them from their hero and descended on Jackson once he finished speaking, "eager to shake hands with him." Jackson managed to get onto a horse and gallop off for the White House, followed by a jubilee of "living matter." The raucous mood soon escalated. Margaret Smith lamented, "the *Majesty of the People* had disappeared," to be replaced by "a rabble, a mob, of boys, negros, women, children, scrambling[,] fighting, romping." Jackson escaped into the

White House through a back door only after being saved from a crushing death by a ring of brave friends. Meanwhile, "ladies fainted, men were seen with bloody noses," china was broken, and carpets tromped with mud. The building was saved by dragging casks of liquor into the yard to entice the mad rabble away long enough to lock the doors behind them.

Smith did not count herself as one of the common masses, and she feared what their rise to power might mean: "It was the People's day, and the People's President and the People would rule. God grant that one day or other, the People, do not put down all rule and rulers. I fear, enlightened Freemen as they are . . . that of all tyrants, [the People] are the most ferocious, cruel and despotic."[4] Sometimes the voice of Washington society, Smith was also the voice of the past, worrying about the wisdom of the crowds. Andrew Jackson served as president for the next eight years, and though he excited poor white men from the South and West to vote for him, Jackson by no means intended to rewrite society. If anything, he tried to govern the way he imagined Thomas Jefferson would have wanted, a goal that set Jackson up for some of his greatest struggles.

Presidential Turmoil

A central feature of Jackson's time in office was heated national debates about the proper role of the federal government in banking and money policies. This topic was crucial for two reasons. Jackson's land speculations in the late 1790s had crumbled because of worthless bank notes, leading to his lifelong dislike of banks and bankers, "paper money, and, above all, debt."[5] And then there was 1819, a year of bad banking—a bad year for just about everybody. After years of a surging economy, a depression hit, caused in large part by the Bank of the United States (BUS) restricting the flow of paper money. Ever since the Treaty of Ghent had ended the War of 1812, giddy American optimism had joined hands with capital investment and new technologies. In 1817, Governor DeWitt Clinton of New York initiated construction of the Erie Canal (a man-made water passage linking Lake Erie with the Atlantic Ocean via the Hudson River), finished in 1825. A state government was contributing to internal improvements, part of what Henry Clay of Kentucky termed the "American System." Other states followed New York's lead, and the old, muddy roads of the past gave way to canals, locks, and good opportunities for making money. Now the farmers and ranchers of the upper West could send their goods to market in the cheapest, fastest way possible. What had been largely a barter economy only a generation earlier turned toward money.

However, the federal government was not in the business of printing dollars, so it was up to banks to provide notes of credit, which served as money.

Banks would issue notes redeemable in gold and silver, and these notes would get traded for services and goods (like land). If, however, people demanded more gold from the banks than was in the vaults, the banks would declare a temporary halt on payments, causing panic and a quick depreciation of the notes. In order to prevent undue speculation, the BUS tried to regulate the value of credit notes. In 1819, the BUS called in many notes from other banks, in essence trying to rein in their behavior, but too many redemptions were demanded and the economy collapsed. Although the BUS soon retreated and money flowed once again, these events scared Andrew Jackson in the same way that Alexander Hamilton's money policies had scared Thomas Jefferson. Jackson thought the federal government should not tamper with the financial system of states or independent banks.

Jackson did not want the federal government to interfere in the states' affairs any more than necessary, and he deemed the BUS's influence unjust, without a visible constitutional mandate. In 1832, during the election season, a consortium of congressmen tried to push through a rechartering of the BUS four years before its legal tenure would expire, but Jackson vetoed the bill. Unable to actually kill the BUS before 1836, after the election Jackson had a loyal appointee—Roger B. Taney—remove all federal monies from the bank, effectively shutting it down. Jackson's animosity to the BUS tore the nation's politics further apart, leading to the formation of the Whig Party. The name "Whig" referred to traditional British politics. Typically, it was the Whigs who opposed the king and his ministers in Parliament. The Hero of New Orleans, Old Hickory himself, transmogrified horrifically—in his opponents' eyes—into King Andrew I. His veto of the bank bill (only the tenth presidential veto up to that point) positioned more power in the executive branch, making the president seem like a king. After all, in 1819 the Supreme Court had ruled that the BUS was in fact constitutional, but Jackson saw it as an agent of federal power sucking liberty away from "the humble members of society."[6] Not for the first time, Jackson ignored a Supreme Court ruling.

Two world views, two pictures of the future, clashed over the issue of the bank, just as they had in Hamilton and Jefferson's days in office. Americans have long sought a balance between liberty and power, and governments represent power.[7] Jackson did see some just uses of federal power and believed firmly in the Union. In fact, during his second term in office, he had to face down the rogue state of South Carolina when it tried to nullify a federal law (a tariff that southern planters thought would mostly benefit New England merchants). South Carolinians claimed that states could choose which federal laws to follow. At a dinner party in 1830, Jackson rose and made a toast to the Union: "Our Union: *It must be preserved.*" Wild-eyed John C. Calhoun, the vice president, followed with a toast to states' rights: "The Union: next to our liberty, the most dear."[8] (Without being able to know it, these national leaders were voicing the same arguments that would characterize the Union and Confederate positions thirty years later at the start of the Civil War.) Andrew Jackson had fought his whole life for the United States, and he would be damned before he saw it disintegrate. Calhoun also wanted to see the nation preserved, and according to Sean Wilentz, he saw "nullification as an alternative to disunion."[9] In 1832, therefore, Calhoun declined to run again for vice president and instead got elected to the U.S. Senate from South Carolina so that he could promote nullification. Jackson threatened South Carolina with federal military intervention if it did not relent and obey federal laws.

Other clashes between liberty and power beset Jackson's time in office. The fraternal organization known as the Freemasons, or Masons, had existed in the United States since 1730, and such leading citizens as Benjamin Franklin and George Washington had joined. The Masons' secret handshakes, hidden rituals, and purported agendas were highlighted in a sensational incident in New York in 1826, when William Morgan was apparently murdered. Morgan was a Mason who tried to publish an exposé of the secret society. He got thrown in jail for a minor debt, and then an anonymous person paid his bail. That was the last anyone knew of William Morgan. His supposed killers were never brought to justice, in part, some claimed, because the grand juries that convened were dominated by Masonic judges and lawyers. It seemed Masons had taken over the country. Even Andrew Jackson was one.

A third, short-lived, national political party formed in opposition to the Masons, named, naturally enough, the Anti-Masonic Party. In 1831, at its convention in Baltimore, delegates from around the country nominated their presidential candidate, William Wirt (who had been attorney general under President Monroe). The Anti-Masons were thus the first party to hold a nominating convention to choose their presidential candidate, a process that all other major parties have followed since then, though that was their only success other than scaring a lot of Masons into becoming ex-Masons. In the 1832 election, Wirt did receive 8 percent of the vote, not enough to dethrone Jackson, but enough to make his political advisers notice. The interest in anti-Masonry spoke to a growing sense in the United States that privilege and secret dealing could overturn the virtues of the republic, just as Jackson had feared in regard to both the BUS and the "corrupt" election of 1824.

The common people whose rights Jackson championed, however, were white, not black or red. With the rarest exceptions, nowhere in America did African-Americans or Native Americans live in true equality with European Americans. In 1831, the Virginia state legislature debated whether to abolish slavery. The heated debates focused on a couple of issues. First, was it proper

191

to strip lawful property from owners, and if so, who should repay the owners for the loss of nearly one-half million slaves? Second, it was unthinkable that black and white people could live together in harmony. Perhaps Texas could be taken from Mexico and turned into a free black state. But Virginians knew the border states of Mississippi and Louisiana would never accept that solution. So the legislators approved a clause to reconsider abolition at some unset, future date. It was better, a majority of white Virginians believed, to hold black people in bondage than to share equality.[10] Race hatred and fear ran too high, particularly in 1831, when the slave Nat Turner led a rebellion that killed sixty white people. Rather than freeing slaves, the Virginia legislature passed laws preventing free black people from attending religious services without a white person present. The right to trial by jury was also taken away. At the same time, the white residents of Georgia schemed to take millions of acres from the Cherokees.

Ever a military man, Sharp Knife, as president, was the commander in chief of U.S. military forces. Jackson used this authority over the army to deal with his old adversaries, the Indians of the Southeast. By 1830, about 17,000 Cherokees lived on a reservation in the northwest corner of Georgia. Many had converted to Christianity. Many spoke English, and the Cherokee language now had a written alphabet, which appeared in their newspaper, the *Phoenix*. Cherokee families built wood-frame houses, owned slaves, tilled farmlands. They had adopted the dress, habits, and customs of white America. But gold lay under the Cherokee hills, and the Cherokee soil was rich too.

In the previous twenty years, more than ten treaties had been signed between the United States and the Cherokee nation, amounting successively to a guarantee of Cherokee sovereignty. The State of Georgia, however, had ceded many of its western land claims in return for an unfulfilled federal government promise to buy Cherokee lands within Georgia and to then cede those lands to the state. So Georgia's governor and its citizens resorted to states' rights arguments to clothe both their greed and their claim that the federal government had reneged on its promise. There could be no nation within a state, Georgia's governor argued, which meant that the federal treaties were worth nothing inside state lines: Georgia could hang Cherokee criminals (which it did in direct opposition to a Supreme Court ruling), and Georgia could arrest Christian missionaries for working in Cherokee territory (which it did for more than a year until the missionaries agreed to give up their evangelizing).

Andrew Jackson affected a caring attitude toward the besieged Cherokees. In 1830, Jackson said, "toward the aborigines of the country no one can indulge a more friendly feeling than myself."[11] This loving lie coincided with passage of the Indian Removal Act, which appropriated federal money for pushing the Cherokees west of the Mississippi River, where a few thousand of them had voluntarily traveled during the 1820s. Continuing his sympathetic song, in 1831 Jackson said, "What the native savages become when surrounded by a dense population and by mixing with the whites may be seen in the miserable remnants of a few Eastern tribes, deprived of political and civil rights, forbidden to make contracts, and subjected to guardians, dragging out a wretched existence, without excitement, without hope, and almost without thought."[12] Rather than using his extensive executive authority and leverage to improve these conditions, Jackson looked forward to removal, saying it would work out well for the United States and would be "equally advantageous to the Indians."

Then, in 1833, getting closer to his own real feelings, Jackson admitted that the Cherokees "have neither the intelligence, the industry, the moral habits, nor the desire of improvement which are essential to any favorable change in their condition. Established in the midst of another and a superior race, and without appreciating the causes of their inferiority or seeking to control them, they must necessarily yield to the force of circumstances and ere long disappear."[13] Now that Sharp Knife spoke from the heart, it was time to arrange for a new treaty.

Twice in the 1830s the Supreme Court under John Marshall ruled on issues pertaining to the Cherokees in Georgia. Essentially the Supreme Court upheld the rights of the Cherokees, stating that Georgians could not enter Cherokee territory without permission, though the court reduced Cherokee status to that of a "dependent" nation. Acting less like the president of the federal government and more like an agent of Georgia, Jackson taunted the Supreme Court for its ruling, purportedly saying, "Justice Marshall has made his decision. Now let him enforce it."[14] Jackson would not enforce the Court's ruling. Instead, he helped secure the Treaty of New Echota, signed by twenty Cherokees who were never elected by the Cherokee nation but had fought with Jackson in 1813 against the Creeks. This new treaty gave Georgia and Jackson what they wanted—title to Cherokee lands in Georgia and permission to push the Cherokees westward. Thousands of Cherokees signed a petition to Congress criticizing the Treaty of New Echota as illegitimate, unrepresentative of their feelings, but their pleas fell as stillborn as the Supreme Court's ruling. By a one-vote margin the Senate approved the treaty in 1836.

Critics of Indian removal were both native and white. Elias Boudinot, editor of the *Cherokee Phoenix*, saw the irony in Jackson's notion that taking Cherokees away from their farms, houses, and churches would civilize them. Boudinot asked, "Where have we an example in the whole history of man, of a Nation or tribe, removing in a body, from a land of civil and religious means, to a perfect wilderness, *in order to be civilized?*" Bothered by Cherokees like Major John Ridge who supported removal, Boudinot said, "We are fearful these men are building castles in the air, whose fall will crush those poor Indians who may be so blinded as to make the experiment."[15] Boudinot looked into the future and saw ruin. However, seven years later he signed the Treaty of New Echota, claiming that the Cherokee cause was a lost cause. In 1830, on the floor of the Senate, Theodore Frelinghuysen of New Jersey proclaimed, "I will raise my voice in support of whatever may appear to be [the Cherokees'] just rights."[16] Frelinghuysen was fighting the impending Removal Act on both moral and legalistic grounds. Unlike Jackson, who thought the states should have jurisdiction over Native Americans, Frelinghuysen and Henry Clay thought the federal government had the authority in this matter. When the Cherokee assembly voted against the Treaty of New Echota in 1835, President Jackson jailed the dissenters, enabling the pro-treaty faction to prevail. Jackson used whatever arguments, whatever logic, and whatever tactics necessary to create the conditions for removal.

Andrew Jackson lived to hear about the Trail of Tears, but it was his successor, Martin Van Buren, who presided over the forced removal of the Cherokees into present-day Oklahoma, sending federal troops to ensure compliance. In the spring of 1838, General Winfield Scott delivered an address to the Cherokees, pleading with them to go west peacefully, to cooperate with the assembled troops so his forces would not have to "resort to arms." He declared himself an "old warrior" who had "been present at many a scene of slaughter." "Spare me," Scott said, "the horror of witnessing the destruction of the Cherokees."[17] Although he instructed his troops to be kind, many were state militiamen not trained to obey, and their prejudices got the worst of them. Concentration camps were built, and often at gunpoint whole Cherokee families were dragged from their homes—some during dinner—and confined in the fenced compounds. While 17,000 Cherokees waited in the camps for the westward march, white Georgians ransacked their abandoned homes. A missionary witness saw "furnished houses . . . left prey to plunderers, who, like hungry wolves, follow in the trail of the captors."[18]

Attempting to make the forced move bearable, General Scott sent the first wave of expelled refugees in June, partway by boat. The summer of 1838 turned out to be murderously hot, literally. Insufficient provisions, heat exhaustion, and disease killed hundreds of the Indians, and the survivors suffered body and soul, many arriving in Indian Territory sick and bereft of family who had died on the trail. Scott prevailed on the administration to wait until the autumn, when conditions should have been better, to send the remaining Cherokees west. But winter came early. Thousands more women, children, and men (some traveling with their slaves in tow) set out in September, and their fate was no better than that of the summer migrants. Only this time it was a killing cold that left them to drag bloody feet through the snow. In

194

all, between one-fifth and one-fourth of the 17,000 Cherokees died on the Trail of Tears. By 1842, nearly all the Chickasaws, Choctaws, Creeks, and Seminoles—who, along with the Cherokees, were called the Five Civilized Tribes—had been forced along similar marches to Indian Territory. Georgia used a lottery system to divide the stolen lands among its white citizens.

Only three years after the end of removal, Andrew Jackson died on his plantation, the Hermitage, still thinking of the Indians as a dying race. Certainly, forcing most southern Indians to migrate west of the Mississippi enabled white and black Americans to think of them as a vanishing race, more folklore than reality. Consequently, voters along the eastern seaboard were less troubled by the ongoing colonization and conquest in the West now that Indians seemed destined to disappear. And the developing reservation policy could be seen as a just, fair, even ethical way of keeping Indians safe from the alcohol, disease, and general change brought by settlers. Jackson's notion that removal to out-of-the-way reservations would be "equally advantageous to the Indians" dominated U.S. policy for the next fifty years.

As president, Andrew Jackson did a lot to change the United States. He furthered the interests of the "slave power" by recognizing the independent Republic of Texas in 1836, which opened vast new lands to cotton culture. He promoted the "spoils system" of giving political appointments to loyal supporters. And although he trumpeted the need for a lasting federal union, Jackson supported states' rights as well, continuing a tradition that eventually led to the Civil War. But Old Hickory—true to his name—had outlived his beloved Rachel, which made his most public years his most lonely. Rachel died in 1828, just before his first inaugural, and some of the bitterness Jackson felt during his presidency resulted from Rachel's death. In true Jacksonian form, he blamed his opponents for slandering her good name, claiming that her heart stopped from the anguish of public humiliation. Like the chivalrous knights that southern gentlemen emulated, Jackson found his next damsel in distress before long.

Love and Politics: A Jacksonian Postscript

Peggy Eaton, a tavern-keeper's daughter, was the wife of Secretary of War John Eaton, Jackson's long-time supporter and friend. Peggy O'Neale Eaton had been married previously to a naval officer who apparently committed suicide. Rumor suggested he killed himself because of Peggy's adultery. John Eaton had met Peggy while her husband was at sea, implicating him in the rumors. To Jackson, the affair smacked of the petty attacks against him and Rachel during their marriage. Society women ostracized Peggy, refusing to visit her, invite her to dinners, or return her calling cards. After his own wife's aggravated death, Jackson rose to Peggy Eaton's defense. Believing that Vice President John Calhoun's wife was the ringleader, Jackson blamed them both for the willful shame heaped on Peggy. These social duels bled into politics, leading the ever-faithful Martin Van Buren to suggest a way out. He resigned as secretary of state and the other cabinet members followed suit, allowing Jackson to appoint men more beholden to him. This tactic also took Peggy Eaton out of the equation, effectively ending what became known as the Petticoat Affair, which ruined Jackson and Calhoun's relationship.

These divisions fired the country with a newfound interest in politics; citizens elected either a Democrat or a Whig to the presidency in every election from 1836 through 1856. By the time of Jackson's death, the United States operated as a two-party system at the national level. However, new parties were created, most importantly the Republican Party, which nominated a former farm boy named Abraham Lincoln in 1860.

While Democratic voters tended to come from rural districts, they lived throughout the country. Even though the nation was developing two different regional cultures—North and South—the emerging Democratic and Whig parties cut across these geographical lines, helping to bond the two halves together. However, the acquisition of ever more territory meant that lawmakers and citizens would continue to argue about the proper place of slavery in the expanding nation. One question burned hottest: should new states allow slavery? Before long, this question and its implications for total abolition would gnaw through the fragile cords of national political parties that made a Whig banker from Connecticut vote the same as a Whig merchant in Georgia. Sixteen years after Andrew Jackson was buried next to his beloved Rachel on the grounds of their Tennessee plantation, the gathering storm over slavery broke into the Civil War.

The Republic of Texas

In the study of U.S. history, it is tempting to focus on the eastern seaboard. That is where money and political power were concentrated almost exclusively until the late 1800s. John Jacob Astor—America's first multimillionaire—lived in New York. The first six presidents all lived within 150 miles of the sea. Most state capitals were located in the eastern halves of their states; Albany and Boston hug the eastern edges. But men made money speculating on western lands. Astor made his fortune in the western fur trade, and Andrew Jackson was the first president from a western state. Deals and dealmakers smelled like cigars and whiskey, an east-west fusion of tidewater tobacco and over-the-mountain grain. But the dealmakers had ambitions without borders.

From the perspective of Mexico, Tejas—Texas—lay to the north, not to the west. From the perspective of Kiowa horsemen, Texas lay to the south. The tilt of the United States westward inevitably brought settlers and those already settled into contact and conflict. Cattle ranchers, tobacco planters, and people simply wanting land spied the northern province of Mexico with interest. Mexican authorities eyed them back with anxiety; yet in 1820 Mexican authorities invited Moses Austin, a Missouri banker, and his family to move to Texas along with 300 other families in the hopes they might bring new prosperity to a sparsely populated province. Although he died within the year before the colony could be formed, his son, Stephen F. Austin, took command of the settlers.

These Anglo settlers were supposed to adopt Catholicism and live as legal Mexican citizens. Instead, they became a first wave of slow conquest, washing Anglos, slaves, and free blacks into the rangelands of the roaming vaqueros —Mexican cowboys—and sparsely settled farm families. San Antonio had the only sizable urban population of Tejanos, never more than about 2,000 during the 1820s. Mexico tried to halt further immigration in 1830. Perhaps 30,000 migrants had already come, and Mexico was afraid the United States might annex the territory. President Jackson even offered to buy Tejas for $5 million in 1830, but Mexico turned down the offer. Mexican fears came true in 1845, when Texas joined the Union as the twenty-eighth state. The intervening fifteen years between 1830 and 1845 would witness myth-making battles and the brief twinkle of an independent nation, the Republic of Texas.

Tejano and Anglo cultures mixed in the ways typical of frontier settlements. Mental barriers of national pride and ambition melted as marriages, Mexican foods like tamales, and trade in silver and cattle brought Spanish and English speakers together. At the same time, Anglo attitudes toward the work habits of Tejanos (like their midday siesta), their Catholicism, and some Tejanos' continuing allegiance to Mexico slowly hardened the initially fluid relationships. While many Tejana women dressed in the fashions of Louisiana and Anglo men dressed in styles reminiscent of Mexican cowboys, their growing similarities did nothing to stop cultural hostilities. And after the coming war, Tejanos would become second-class citizens.

In 1832, eleven years after Mexico became independent of Spain, General Antonio Lopez de Santa Anna became Mexico's president. A vain man, Santa Anna seized power and named himself dictator. In 1833, Stephen Austin traveled to Mexico City, seeking redress for settlers' grievances, in particular a recent set of Mexican laws meant to deprive all residents of Tejas of their autonomy. Santa Anna was merging Tejas with the state of Coahuila to the south while simultaneously cutting off further emigrants from the United States. The plan looked like disaster to both Anglos and Tejanos in Tejas. Mexican authorities threw Stephen Austin into jail upon discovering his advocacy for Texas independence. He languished in jail for two years. Meanwhile, a former war veteran who had lived with the Cherokees, Sam Houston, led a few hundred riflemen in the capture of San Antonio, driving out the small Mexican garrison. War had begun. Tejanos and Anglos fought together for independence from Mexico.

With the Mexican garrison gone from San Antonio, nearly 200 frontier fighters, riflemen, slaves, and a few women and children barricaded themselves inside a former Catholic mission, the Alamo. In early 1836, Santa Anna showed up with his army and demanded that the people inside the Alamo surrender unconditionally. Led by the brash and aggressive William Travis, the Americans tried to hold on against Santa Anna's more than 4,000 Mexican soldiers. The attacks lasted for thirteen days, until March 6, 1836, when the Mexican troops finally stormed the Alamo. Only about fifteen women and children and one male slave, who had been seriously injured with a bayonet, survived. The Mexican soldiers stacked up the bodies of the slain defenders and burned them in heaps outside the old mission. Legendary figures like frontiersman Davy Crocket and the knife fighter Jim Bowie were among the fallen. Their sacrifice blossomed into a symbol. Inspired by the Alamo defenders' heroic tragedy, Sam Houston and a small army of 800 captured Santa Anna in April 1836 and forced him to sign a treaty recognizing Texan independence.

Southern states wanted to embrace Texas, but northern states welcomed it as an independent nation. The South wanted more representation in Congress, but the North wanted no more slave votes in the House or Senate. President James K. Polk, however, broke the congressional stalemate over what to do about Texas by making annexation the key fixture of his run for the presidency in 1844. He threatened Britain with war over the Oregon Country in a famous slogan, "Fifty-four forty or fight!"—a reference to latitude lines at the southern boundary of present-day Alaska. Polk settled for the forty-ninth parallel in 1846, the modern boundary in the Pacific Northwest, right after exciting enough popular support to get Congress to ratify the annexation of Texas, a new slave state that maintained the balance between free and slave states. Although war with Britain was avoided, lingering boundary disputes with Mexico soon led to America's next war.

Notes

1. Sean Wilentz, *Andrew Jackson* (New York: Time Books, 2005), 13.

2. Robert V. Remini, *The Life of Andrew Jackson* (New York: Harper Perennial, 2001), 44.

3. Remini, *The Life of Andrew Jackson,* 85.

4. Gaillar Hunt, ed., *Forty Years of Washington Society: Portrayed by the Family Letters of Mrs. Samuel Harrison Smith (Margaret Bayard), from the Collection of Her Grandson, J. Henley Smith* (New York: Charles Scribner's Sons, 1906), 290–296.

5. Wilentz, *Andrew Jackson*, 21.

6. Francis Newton Thorpe, PhD, LLD, ed., *The Statesmanship of Andrew Jackson: As Told in his Writings and Speeches,* "Veto Messsage—Bank of the United States. (July 10, 1832)" (New York: Tandy-Thomas, 1909), 175.

7. A book that artfully examines the balancing act between liberty and power is Harry L. Watson, *Liberty and Power, Update Edition: The Politics of Jacksonian America* (New York: Hill and Wang, 2006).

8. Remini, *The Life of Andrew Jackson*, 196–197.

9. Wilentz, *Andrew Jackson*, 65.

10. Detailed coverage of these debates is provided in Louis P. Masur, *1831: Year of Eclipse* (New York: Hill and Wang, 2002), 48–62.

11. Thorpe, ed., *The Statesmanship of Andrew Jackson,* "Second Annual Message. (December 6, 1830)," 111.

12. Thorpe, ed., *The Statesmanship of Andrew Jackson,* "Third Annual Message. (December 6, 1831)," 148.

13. Thorpe, ed., *The Statesmanship of Andrew Jackson*, "Fifth Annual Message (December 3, 1833)," 301.

14. Wilentz, *Andrew Jackson*, 140.

15. Quoted in Theda Perdue, ed., *Cherokee Editor: The Writings of Elias Boudinot* (Athens: University of Georgia Press, 1996), 95–96.

16. *Cherokee Phoenix and Indians' Advocate*, Wednesday, March 31, 1830 (vol. II, no. 50, page 2, col. 3a–page 3, col. 1b, www.wcu.edu/library/CherokeePhoenix/Vol2/no50/pg2col3a-pg3col1b.htm)

17. Helen Hunt Jackson, *A Century of Dishonor* (New York: Harper, 1881), 282.

18. Stan Hoig, *The Cherokees and Their Chiefs: In the Wake of Empire* (Fayetteville: University of Arkansas Press, 1999), 167.

11

The United States and the Antebellum West

Samuel Clemens (Mark Twain) *(Time Life Pictures/Getty Images)*

Narcissa Whitman: On a Mission to the Oregon Country

Narcissa Prentiss was a Methodist who wanted to evangelize, to spread the good news about Christ. Narcissa grew up in New York State, where God's fires burned hotly during the early 1800s. Where went the Erie Canal, there went towns—soon followed by preachers. Where went preachers, there went revivals. What has become known as the Second Great Awakening trumpeted new theologies across the states, shaking and thundering the hearts of men and women in week-long, sometimes months-long showdowns between repentance and sin.

The sons and daughters of Puritans had largely settled western New York State, and many had let their religion go lax. They had gone far away from their New England roots and had built few churches in the early years of western settlement. The upright morality and intellectual sermons of the Puritan forefathers seemed to have lost their punch. But men like Charles Grandison Finney, the best-known revivalist, caught the Spirit and sent it pounding into communities up and down the coast, notably in towns like Rochester in 1831. In a few months, Finney swelled pews with new congregants by the hundreds. Around the country, similar miracles spread, though not without complications. Old-style denominations, especially traditional Calvinists of the Puritan mold, saw Finney's preaching style as dangerous and vulgar. He reserved "anxious seats" near the pulpit where wayward sinners sat surrounded by a chorus of onlookers goading them into conversion. To Finney's critics, these tactics seemed to create insincere converts, worked-up followers who would soon work out the spirit.

Finney's theology and exegesis frightened social and religious leaders in the same way Jackson's politics had. He seemed likely to democratize the world more than might be good. Finney taught that men and women could work for their salvation, could do good works and earn their way into Heaven. Such radical theories often ignored skin color, seeing all souls as equal before God, an inspiration to abolitionists. Indeed, for many years Charles Finney served as professor and president of Oberlin College in Ohio, a seat of abolitionism. However, if men and women's souls were equal in God's eyes, their bodies were not equal in America.

Narcissa Prentiss felt the urge to preach the gospel, but she was a woman. The American Board of Commissioners for Foreign Missions refused to sponsor her alone as a missionary. What she needed was a husband, so a quick, arranged marriage to Marcus Whitman set her on the road to Oregon in 1836. Marcus was a doctor who in 1835 had traveled as far as present-day Wyoming, where fur traders and trappers, Indian and white, met at the great rendezvous for days of carousing and trade. Famous mountain men like Jim

202

Bridger came through the rendezvous. Bridger himself would later be instrumental in establishing the Oregon Trail. In 1836, however, there was no Oregon Trail for colonists because Oregon was only gradually beginning to register in eastern minds as a place fit for settlement. Narcissa Whitman and another missionary wife, Eliza Spalding, were two of the first white women to cross the Rocky Mountains. They set an example for others to follow. Both sexes could brave the six to nine months it took to follow the trail.

In 1821, Britain's Hudson's Bay Company had established a presence in the Pacific Northwest in order to make money. But Narcissa and Marcus Whitman did not come to make an earthly fortune. They came to convert Indians to Christianity and to "civilize" them with American-style agriculture, the English language, and new clothes, both age-old goals of American Protestants. Catholics had already claimed souls in the Pacific Northwest. According to author Janet Campbell Hale, an "old prophecy had it that 'three black ravens' would come to the people. Three Jesuit missionaries (or Black Robes) did come to the Coeur d'Alene one day, claiming they brought the word of God. The Coeur d'Alene embraced Catholicism and practiced it as an extension of their traditional religion."[1] Not all Native Americans in the region were as receptive to the Word, as the Whitmans would discover soon after the overland journey.

In the spring of 1836, the Whitmans, Eliza and Henry Spalding, and a few other people, including Indian guides, took steamships up the Mississippi and Missouri rivers. After disembarking, they joined with a fur caravan and traveled as people had for hundreds of years: by foot, horseback, and wagon. Writing to her sister, Harriet, and brother, Edward, in June, Narcissa described her version of roughing it. "Tell mother I am a very good housekeeper on the prairie," she wrote.[2] "Our table is the ground, our table-cloth is an India-rubber cloth used when it rains as a cloak; our dishes are made of tin." Narcissa commented on God's presence and providence at nearly every revolution of the wagon wheel. She was no half-hearted convert of the sort Finney's critics worried about. Getting close to Independence, Missouri (the launch point for journeys along the Oregon and the Santa Fe Trail in coming decades), Narcissa wrote, "I count it a privilege to go forth in the name of my Master, cheerfully bearing the toil and privation that we expect to encounter." She matched service to God with deference to her husband.

Narcissa Whitman brought values with her, especially cultural attitudes toward male and female roles in society. A hardy trail woman who could drink cow's milk direct from the teat in a tin cup hanging from the saddle's side, Narcissa also embraced the "cult of domesticity," the prevailing nineteenth-century notion that women's place was in the home. Home was now a wagon, a rubber pad, the open sky, and a horse's steady gait. In reassuring her family that Marcus had turned out to be a good husband, Narcissa revealed how far under his masculine shadow she dwelt. She wrote, "I have such a good place to shelter—under my husband's wings. He is so excellent. I love to confide in his judgment, and act under him. He is just like mother in telling me my failings. He does it in such a way that I like to have him, for it gives me a chance to improve."

While not all women bought into this mind-set, the attitude was typical. Women's magazines, like the popular *Godey's Lady's Book*, printed mid-century editorials promoting an equal chance at education for women. Education, in turn, would help them better perform their assigned duties as mothers and reformers. In 1850, *Godey's* editors suggested, "Physically and morally, God has made woman worthy to be the mother of mankind." Near the end of the bumpy trail, Narcissa got pregnant, giving her a real chance to "mother mankind." After food supplies—like flour for bread—began to run out, Marcus got his own chance to do something new: cook. Like Lewis, Clark, and Sacagawea before them, the Whitmans came to rely on buffalo, which Marcus cooked three times a day, each piece of the animal roasted in a different way: pioneer barbecue.

The overland trails to New Mexico, California, and Oregon were the primary paths for nearly thirty years, until the completion of the first transcontinental railroad in 1869. But these trails are buried under such dense layers of half-truth that it is rare for a Western movie or novel to let us see the real people through the myths. If, for example, the cowboy is the mythic symbol of the American West, the white cowboy sits alone on the fabled horse. Marcus may have charred buffalo meat in twenty novel ways, but the missionaries and the fur caravan the Whitmans traveled with also brought a herd of cattle to Oregon, and the cowboys who drove the cattle all 2,000 miles were Indian guides.

Native Americans and "pioneers" did sometimes fight, but much less often than they cooperated. A few statistics and numbers clarify truth from legend. One historian estimates that, on average, if all the people who died on the trail to Oregon were spaced out evenly, there would be a corpse every eighty yards. According to another estimate, fighting with Indians caused only 4 percent of deaths.[3] Most people died from cholera, dysentery, and other contagious diseases generated by trail conditions, especially the contamination of water.

While common images of plainly clothed farm families traveling in dust-covered wagons make the migrants look poor, almost all pioneer families were middle-class or richer. It cost about $1,000 to stock enough provisions for the trip; the Whitmans spent $3,000 in Independence. Finally, the West's vastness—its stretched skies and plains of native grasses coating the horizon—shrink the travelers and make their numbers seem few. In the late 1830s, not many people headed to Oregon overland. By 1850, however, travelers going back east, "turn-arounds," hid out from the hordes going west by blazing side trails out of sight. Turn-arounds (often soldiers or explorers) knew that westward-moving settlers and tourists (yes, tourists) expected them to have specific knowledge of what lay ahead. Tired of being pestered, turn-arounds often dashed out of view at the sight of a wagon train. Unoccupied campsites could be hard to find, especially those with ample grass for the cattle. This was nineteenth-century–scale rush hour on the Oregon Trail, with 2,500 migrants traveling in 1846 alone—nearly half choosing Oregon over California that year.

In mid-August, the Whitmans reached "Snake Fort" (a.k.a., Fort Boise) in present-day Boise, Idaho. Narcissa lamented that this was only "the third time I have washed since I left home. But hundreds of miles still lay between Fort Boise and the Hudson's Bay Company's Fort Vancouver in Oregon Country. At this point the migrants must have longed to catch sight of the Pacific. Skinny mountain paths barely wide enough for a horse's body and scant supplies of berries and fish would finally give way to better days. Communities were waiting with stocked larders and soap.

On this last trail, shade was hard to find in the desert's naked sun, but Narcissa wrote, "'The Lord is better to us than our fears.' I always find it so." Faith and food carried her the rest of the way, along with Indian swimmers and canoe paddlers who helped the travelers down the Columbia River. The closer to Fort Vancouver she got, the more Narcissa felt that civilization had been planted in the wilderness. Part way along the Columbia, they stopped at the fort at Walla Walla. Famished again, Narcissa enjoyed the fort's potatoes, bread, and butter—a fattening delight. A "young rooster" sat on the window-sill next to her during breakfast, crowing nonstop. Narcissa remarked, "I was pleased with his appearance. You may think me simple for speaking of such a small circumstance. No one knows the feelings occasioned by seeing objects once familiar after a long deprivation." That was the paradox of the mission: choosing to go into the unknown, yet longing for familiar sights, sounds, and tastes. Narcissa meant to change one corner of the world from "savage" (as she put it) to civilized. However, existing societies were not always eager to be altered, and more than once she would have to let go of her cultural expectations, just as she had ejected mementos from home when they burdened the wagon: "Thus we scatter as we go along."

More than 200 miles down the Columbia was Fort Vancouver, essentially a town, which Narcissa called "the New York of the Pacific Ocean." In charge of the entire Columbia District was the chief factor, Dr. John McLoughlin, called the "White Headed Eagle" because of his bleached shock of hair. Married to a "half breed" wife—Narcissa's words—McLoughlin ruled the region with dictatorial powers and a gentle touch. Though technically ordered to discourage U.S. immigration, McLoughlin did what he could to welcome new arrivals, at one point giving Marcus "leather pantaloons" (chaps). In the midst of a hospital, churches, a jail, and a blacksmith's shop, there was also a school. Narcissa found "about fifty-one children" who had "French fathers and Indian mothers," a common frontier arrangement. McLoughlin's marriage to an Indian woman remained typical for about another ten years. In 1846, the United States acquired the Oregon Country from Britain. When state delegates wrote the first constitution, marriage between whites and anyone with one-fourth or more black, Indian, or Hawaiian ancestry was outlawed. Also, Oregon's constitution prevented African-Americans from living in the state. Narcissa found Oregon in its last stage of relative interracial harmony.

Along with evangelizing, the missionaries' role was to prepare the Oregon Country for white immigration, missionary work being preparatory to invasion. Eliza and Henry Spalding chose to stay with the Nez Percés, who had expressed interest in boarding missionaries. A site for the Whitmans' mission complex was chosen and named Waiilatpu, meaning "Place of the Rye Grass." Waiilatpu was situated in Cayuse territory. Narcissa's first comments about evangelizing to the Cayuses indicate the difficulties of a cross-cultural ministry, in this case the language barrier. "Nothing," she wrote, "is more difficult than for me to attempt to convey religious truth in their language, especially when there are so few or no terms expressive of the meaning." It seemed her first successes were with children, perhaps because their brains were more adaptable, yet Narcissa's efforts rarely led to "the heathen around us . . . turning to the Lord."

In 1837, the birth of a daughter, Alice Clarissa, improved Narcissa's mood. "Plump" Alice slept "all night without nursing more than once." The manna of the baby's presence, however, could not entirely sweeten Narcissa's growing distaste for the very people she had traveled more than 2,000 miles to work with. "To be a mother in heathen lands among savages," she lamented to her family, "gives feelings that can be known only to those who are such. . . . If ever we needed your prayers and sympathies, it is at the present time." From increasing contact with white people, the Cayuses were daily getting sick, which did little to inspire confidence in Narcissa's God. A year later, unlike the sickly Indian children, Alice enjoyed "unremitting health." The little girl "saved" Narcissa from "many melancholy hours" she would otherwise have spent alone when Marcus was gone on trips. The Cayuses gave Alice an "Indian name," "Kayuse Ten-ni—accent on the last syllable." By the age of two, Alice spoke fluent Nez Percé (understood by the Cayuses) and English. She sang Christian hymns to the few Indians who attended church services. She was becoming something of a bridge between the two societies.

In late June 1839, however, Narcissa wrote home to say that "my precious child, Alice Clarissa, now [lies] by me a lifeless lump of clay. Yes, of her I loved and watched so tenderly, I am bereaved. My Jesus in love to her and us has taken her to himself." Although Narcissa was convinced that God took the child, another explanation was simply that no one was watching Alice when she wandered into the Walla Walla River and drowned. Narcissa wrote, "We can in no way account for the circumstances connected with it, otherwise than that the Lord meant it should be so." She added, "Take warning, dear sister, by our bereavement that you do not let your dear babe get between your heart and the Saviour." However, a few months later, Narcissa revealed a resurgent belief in free will: "We see now how [Alice's death] might have been prevented, could we have known or anticipated it." Strengthened by a renewed faith in the efficacy of choice, Narcissa stayed on "among the heathen."

The Whitmans had seven years left to them, not only at Waiilatpu, but also on earth. They had some successes: some Cayuses did begin building farmsteads around Waiilatpu, and Narcissa formed a temperance society to get the Cayuses to avoid alcohol. However, few if any Cayuses converted to Methodism. Part of the failure, Narcissa was sure, owed to the interference of Catholic priests in the area. In 1842, word arrived that the American Board of Commissioners for Foreign Missions wanted to close Waiilatpu because of its poor conversion record. Marcus galloped back east to Boston in the autumn, risking the dangers of the winter mountains. He convinced the board to keep the mission open. On his return to Oregon, almost 900 colonists accompanied him, the first large migration of families to the area. About 4,000 more arrived in 1847. Growing aggravations beset the already brittle relationship between the Whitmans and the Cayuses. The Whitmans put mild poisons into mission vegetables to punish the Cayuses for stealing—though to the Cayuses food was communally owned, so stealing it was impossible. White homesteaders were filling the territory. And invisible companions joined incoming settlers on the trail: measles and dysentery. Marcus's medical skills helped most of the migrants recover, but scores of Cayuses died in agony in 1847. Seeing that the white people lived while the red died, the Indians blamed the Whitmans. In late November 1847, a group of aggrieved Cayuses killed the Whitmans and eleven other people.

Historian Carlos Schwantes says that the "Whitman story reveals . . . an inevitable tension between the missionary ideal of saving Indian souls for the heavenly promised land and the day-to-day reality of providing sustenance to white newcomers and even fostering their settlement of the earthly promised land in Oregon."[4] He blames "culture conflict," rather than nefarious intentions on anyone's side. Whoever and whatever was to blame, the Whitmans' murders sparked retaliation and measures of fundamental consequence to the region. Five of the murderers were taken to Oregon City and hanged. Even though most of the Cayuses had not participated in the "Whitman Massacre" (as it became known), a citizen militia fought a punitive war against them, the first of many wars with the Native Americans of Oregon Territory. The timing was not accidental. The Whitmans' deaths and subsequent warfare gave the United States reasons to try to bring order to the area. Only three years later, in 1850, Congress passed the Donation Land Act, which gave 160 acres to any white man who would inhabit and "improve" the land for at least four years; an additional 160 acres went to a wife. Single women, African-Americans, Native Americans, and Hawaiians were excluded from the land offer. The law portioned out nearly 3 million acres, contrary to the terms of an 1846 treaty with Britain that stipulated the United States had to negotiate land deals with Indians rather than simply handing acres out at will.

While religious missions and farmland lured people from the United States westward, something more tempting winked and beckoned: gold. Narcissa and Marcus died one year before the head-spinning discovery of the flecks and nuggets near John Sutter's mill on the American River in present-day Sacramento, California. Having spent the last years of her life raising Oregon Trail orphans and the children of mountain men (like Jim Bridger's daughter who was deposited at Waiilatpu after Alice Clarissa's death), Narcissa had been preparing in 1847 to greet her sister, who planned on moving to the mission. "Jane," Narcissa wrote, "there will be no use in your going home to see ma and pa before you come here—it will make the matter worse with your heart. . . . If you will all come here it will not be long before they will be climbing over the Rocky Mountains to see us. The love of parents for their children is very great."

All That Glitters: The West Through Mark Twain's Eyes

Since the 1500s, no one in the East or South had paid much attention to California, which Spain did not even colonize until 1769—part of its attempt to keep the Anglos from taking too much land while leading the "heathen" Indians toward God's embrace. By the time of Mexico's independence from Spain in 1821, there were only a few thousand Spanish speakers in the whole of Alta California (the part currently above the national border). The Indian population had been gutted by disease. Beginning in 1834, Mexico divided up the original Franciscan missions between ranchers and farmers. With few Indians left alive and almost no Mexican settlers near the Oregon boundary, a few lots went to U.S. expatriates. One was named Johann Sutter, who settled on the banks of the American River, which runs through Sacramento. Sutter became a Mexican citizen and built a multiethnic settlement of some 1,500 souls, many from the United States. The discovery of gold on his property in

January 1848 brought a stampede, clogging California with about 200,000 migrants in four years.

Who came so far to sift river water for dull gold, to blast hillsides with black powder? The whole world came. From as far away as China, Chile, and Germany streamed the gullible, the desperate, and the lucky. One German emigrant, Heinrich Schliemann, came in 1851, stayed for about a year, traded in gold dust, and made enough money to finance his archaeological digs in northwest Turkey, where he uncovered the ancient city of Troy—made famous in Homer's epic, *The Iliad*. Samuel Clemens, better known as Mark Twain, offered history the perfect misrepresentation. Clemens described "an assemblage of two hundred thousand *young* men—not simpering, dainty, kid-gloved weaklings, but stalwart, muscular, dauntless young braves, brimful of push and energy, and royally endowed with every attribute that goes to make up a peerless and magnificent manhood—the very pick and choice of the world's glorious ones."[5] It should be no surprise that Clemens, author of *The Adventures of Huckleberry Finn* and *Tom Sawyer*, provided a boy's-only snapshot. But his image has persisted: history seems to show more six-shooters than shovels in miners' gnarled hands. By 1850 in California, men outnumbered women twelve to one, but more women soon followed. And the original "forty-niners" included doctors, lawyers, and clerks, as well as "dauntless young braves," chisel-faced toughs, and already-experienced miners.

In certain ways, the gold mines tested people's commitment to emerging middle-class values that stressed the importance of family, sobriety, godliness, and moderation. Men left wives and children at home in search of the increasingly important dollar—ironically abandoning family in order to secure the family's fortune.[6] Liquor and swearing abounded, mocking Victorian temperance reforms and the new verbal chastity of America's revived Protestants. Gold represented the obvious opposite to moderation. Yet all that buried wealth offered struggling clerks, poor immigrants, artisans, lawyers, and farmers —nearly anybody—the chance to advance socially and economically.

In 1861, at the start of the Civil War, Clemens set out at the age of twenty-six for Nevada as unpaid assistant to his brother, who had been chosen secretary of Nevada Territory by President Abraham Lincoln. Clemens began the war with Southern sympathies—even becoming a two-week Confederate militia lieutenant—but an excursion to Nevada seemed more appealing than whistling bullets. In his own tongue-in-cheek manner, Clemens recalled not having wanted his brother to be the only one to "have all kinds of adventures, and maybe get hanged or scalped, and have ever such a fine time, and write home and tell us all about it." In 1872, Twain published *Roughing It*, a reminiscence of these western meanderings during which he himself succumbed to "silver fever," growing as "frenzied as the craziest." The road west for Sam Clemens

209

involved a stage coach, tobacco, a pistol with one significant fault—"you could not hit anything with it"—and stop-offs to change horses at sod houses in Kansas and Nebraska: "It was the first time we had ever seen a man's front yard on top of his house." This emancipating expanse of tall tales and long trails was just the place for a born storyteller.

After reading bloated newspaper accounts that claimed, "The intestines of our mountains are gorged with precious ore," Clemens and four companions bolted for Nevada's Humboldt hills. He had already tried out Carson City—a dusty town "fabulously rich in . . . thieves, murderers, desperadoes, ladies, children, lawyers, Christians, Indians, Chinamen, Spaniards, gamblers, sharpers [swindlers], coyotes (pronounced Ki-yo-ties,) poets, preachers, and jackass rabbits."[7] Although he liked to tell stories about depraved drunks, shoeless Pony Express riders, and manly bacon-and-coffee breakfasts, Clemens went prospecting with a sixty-year-old blacksmith and two lawyers, a more representative, middle-class assemblage than he usually depicted. Though he spent months seeking silver and gold, Clemens found nothing he could hold onto other than stories and images that he soon parlayed into a career as a newspaperman in Virginia City, Nevada, near the site of the gigantic Comstock Lode, first uncovered in 1859. Clemens's impoverishing experiences were more typical than not.

A few people made fortunes on digs and investments. An Idaho couple of Midwestern origins—May and Al Hutton—survived violent labor disputes, an exploding train, and an unjust prison sentence before their aptly named Hercules Mine paid off in the millions. Many miners worked for large companies that could afford deep-shaft operations, without finding it necessary to pay their workers well. Most miners, however, followed a path similar to Clemens's: a few months or years poking about in the dirt and then on to other occupations. Amused by himself, Clemens wrote, "I confess, without shame, that I expected to find masses of silver lying all about the ground. I expected to see it glittering in the sun on the mountain summits." The Humboldt Hills taunted him with fool's gold and a few rocks flecked with hints of real gold. Clemens's team of miners soon "judged that a couple of tons of [those rocks] massed together might make a gold dollar, possibly. We were not jubilant." One exodus of settlers, however, found jubilee in the beckoning West.

Just as Narcissa Whitman came west as a missionary, so too others made the long trip for reasons other than gold-laced dreams. A fifteen-year-old New Yorker named Joseph Smith underwent divine visions and visitations beginning in 1820. Smith's claims about golden plates inscribed with the hidden history of Abraham's lost children inspired a splinter denomination, the Church of Jesus Christ of Latter-day Saints—the Mormons. Equally loved and loathed, the Mormons moved from New York to Ohio to Illinois under

Smith's guidance, searching for a safe location and new converts. Settling at Nauvoo (a name taken from Sephardic Hebrew, which loosely translates as "beautiful"), Joseph Smith rose to near-dictatorial power, including presidency of the Mormon Church, election as mayor, suppression of rival Mormon voices, and marriage to more than twenty women (one of whom was fourteen). Polygamy was a tenet of nineteenth-century Mormon theology and a central problem for them, as most Americans saw the practice as un-Christian and hence immoral. The men of a rival Mormon faction accused Smith of seducing their wives and of exercising excessive authority. Smith ordered their printing presses smashed, and tensions escalated. Jailed on charges of unlawfully declaring martial law, Smith was taken from the jail and shot to death by a mob—of whom five were later tried and found not guilty. American sexual mores may have proved less problematic for the Mormons than their financial success (a source of jealousy), which stemmed from their communal economy. While other Americans were busy embracing the new individualistic pursuit of money, Mormons, also known as Saints, tithed one-tenth of their profits to the church and took specific orders from Smith and his successors. They voted in blocs and pooled their resources, making them an effective, unified force wherever they went. For the Saints, the West looked like a safe haven from persecution and governmental interference.

Starting in 1846, thousands of Mormons headed to territory recently acquired in the 1846–1848 war with Mexico. Their primary destination was the Great Salt Lake, which Smith's successor, Brigham Young, intended to make the heart of an autonomous Mormon homeland, Deseret. He thought the hard work of creating a paradise from a desert would do his people good. Initially, Mormon land claims extended throughout the West: all of present-day Nevada and Utah, plus portions of Wyoming, New Mexico, Colorado, and California. Some Mormons went by ocean (a six-month journey) to populate specific locales in California so that a travel corridor could be created between the sea and the Salt Lake valley. But by the mid-1850s, Brigham Young discouraged further California settlement because—as he correctly surmised—it was bound to be a favored destination of other Americans and hence not safe for Mormons, particularly given the area's sinful reputation. Faced with hostility almost everywhere they went, the Saints retreated to their capital, Salt Lake City, in Utah. Contemptuous of what they perceived as the irreligion of other Americans and energized by their own certainties, the industrious Mormon colonists turned a dry terrain into an irrigated plain. Providing for their own needs, they constructed an iron-smelting factory and built their own railroad lines.

Samuel Clemens stopped for a few days in Salt Lake City on his way to Nevada. While Clemens's comments reveal common animosities of the day, he was amused by the Mormons more than he expected to be, and he was very curious. In an America that had rejected the rule of kings and queens, Salt Lake City was "the capital of the only absolute monarchy in America." Brigham Young directed Latter-day Saint affairs with an unadulterated authority that other Americans found out-of-date and unsettling. And now that the Mormons lived in a separate domain, a mystique surrounded them. For Clemens, "there was fascination in surreptitiously staring at every creature we took to be a Mormon. This was fairyland to us, to all intents and purposes a land of enchantment, and goblins, and awful mystery. We felt a curiosity to ask every child how many mothers it had, and if it could tell them apart." Although Joseph Smith had declared polygamy doctrinal and practicable in 1843, not all Mormons approved of or practiced it. Even so, the idea of having many wives was easy to laugh at (the practice of polygamy is still associated with Mormons even though it was officially outlawed by the church in the early 1890s, in part as a prerequisite of Utah being made a state).

Making fun of everybody else was Clemens's specialty, but he could take doses of his own medicine. On his second day in Salt Lake City, he paid a visit to "the king," Brigham Young, who "seemed a quiet, kindly, easy-mannered, dignified, self-possessed old gentleman . . . simply dressed," straw hat and all. Clemens wanted to be noticed, but try as he might to "draw out" Young into conversation, the older man paid Clemens no attention whatsoever. Ignored, Clemens "subsided into an indignant silence" and nursed his sore feelings. Brigham Young apparently knew just what he was doing, as Clemens discovered. "When the audience was ended and we were retiring from the presence," Clemens recalled, "he put his hand on my head, beamed down on me in an admiring way and said to my brother: 'Ah your child, I presume? Boy, or girl?'"

Both in Utah and Nevada, Clemens was the outsider, the newcomer, the dainty dandy, and though he found Mormons and miners alike an odd bunch, he understood that in their eyes he was "a low and inferior sort of creature." After all, men arriving from the East usually stuck out like well-dressed misfits: "Poor thing, they are making fun of his hat; and the cut of his New York coat; and his conscientiousness about his grammar; and his feeble profanity; and his consumingly ludicrous ignorance of ores, shafts, tunnels, and other things which he never saw before, and never felt enough interest in to read about." Clemens came to identify with the rough manners and easy living of the mining districts, finding charm in the indifference for middle-class sensibility. All the same, boredom and empty pockets overcame quaint sympathies, so leaving Nevada was no problem for Clemens, as he made clear in a letter home to his mother and sister: "Some people are malicious enough to think that if the devil were set at liberty and told to confine himself to Nevada Territory, that he would come here and look sadly around, awhile, and then get homesick and go back to hell again."[8]

Samuel Clemens became Mark Twain in February 1863. "Mark twain" was a phrase used on riverboats (to mark a safe depth), which Clemens had piloted on the Mississippi before the Civil War. The new name held connotations appropriate for a witty man both of the people and above the people. At once he became blue-collar common and literary, elevating river jargon into prose. Most of the California that Twain saw was little different from the scattered mining towns and camps of Nevada, with one exception: San Francisco. With a good port and access to the hinterland interior, San Francisco thrived while other trading towns generally withered after the nearby gold or silver ran out. From a settlement of shrubs, trees, and maybe 800 people in early 1848, the population grew to 25,000 within one year. Twain remembered, "San Francisco was Paradise to me. I lived at the best hotel, exhibited my clothes in the most conspicuous places, infested the opera . . . I attended private parties in sumptuous evening dress, simpered and aired my graces like a born beau." San Francisco's proximity to the bonanza in Sacramento, its harbor, and its easy climate induced the masses to stay. Twain himself lingered in California until 1866, when he caught a ship bound for Hawaii where other stories waited for him.

The Mexican-American War and California

The Anglo inundation of Alta California coincided neatly with a war against Mexico that began in 1846. After Texas became a state in 1845, a border dispute ensued, with Mexico claiming the Nueces River as its northern edge, rather than the Rio Grande (farther to the south), a difference of 130 miles. Both nations had troops in the area, and in April 1846, Mexican troops clashed with the U.S. Army. Some U.S. soldiers died, and President James Polk claimed that Mexico "has shed blood upon the American soil," a shaky claim given the contested location of the border. A declaration of war followed, and the outnumbered U.S. military defeated one Mexican army after another, finally invading Mexico City in 1848 and forcing the Mexicans to surrender.

Expansive land concessions were part of the peace treaty of Guadalupe Hidalgo. The United States took California and most of the rest of the modern Southwest. California had been easily occupied during the war, and it became a state in 1850, a free state. However, while its citizens voted against slavery, they also stripped Mexicans, Indians, and blacks of most civil liberties. As historian Walter Nugent points out, "Nonwhites . . . were ghettoized early. The several thousand blacks in California in 1852 were all free, some operating businesses, churches, and a newspaper. But they were excluded from juries, voting, homesteading, and intermarrying."[9]

To some Americans, the Mexican War was an unethical land grab. Henry David Thoreau was the most outstanding opponent. More famous in history for his 1854 book, *Walden,* he became well known in his time for acting out and speaking out against the war. In 1849, he published "Civil Disobedience," a clear-headed call to resist injustice, in particular slavery, bad laws, and ill-begotten invasions. Thoreau said, "When a sixth of the population of a nation which has undertaken to be the refuge of liberty are slaves, and a whole country is unjustly overrun and conquered by a foreign army, and subjected to military law, I think that it is not too soon for honest men to rebel and revolutionize. What makes this duty the more urgent is the fact that the country so overrun is not our own, but ours is the invading army." Refusing to resist with words alone, three years earlier, in 1846, Thoreau had refused to pay his taxes, an act of civil disobedience that got him thrown into jail for an evening. He might have stayed longer, but a friend—acting against Thoreau's wishes—paid the taxes. Seeing his imprisonment as part of a larger pattern of governmental abuse, Thoreau described the incident in "Civil Disobedience" and commented, "The State never intentionally confronts a man's sense, intellectual or moral, but only his body, his senses. It is not armed with superior wit or honesty, but with superior physical strength. I was not born to be forced."[10] Regardless of Thoreau's activism, the United States, following the dictates of its own "Manifest Destiny" (a term coined by newspaperman John O'Sullivan in 1845), forced Mexicans and Indians to surrender half the continent in under ten years.

Mark Twain bounced, dug, and scribbled across America, frivolous in his gaiety, reveling in the memories of his failures and all the strange characters he met along the way. History treats the gold rush era as a murderous, crazy time, and indeed it was. The Zorro legend, for example, grew from a real-life horse thief named Joaquin Murieta, who robbed Mexican and Anglo alike. Murieta's exploits earned him notoriety, yet he was by no means exceptional. Had Twain heard any, he would probably have spun out a few Murieta yarns for his eager eastern audience.

The history of California in the national setting involves other, larger perspectives. Historians look at the seizure of California as a seed of the Civil War. Its entrance into the Union enflamed existing fears in the South that Congress would soon entertain an imbalance of free to slave states. The continuing role of the West in the escalating sectional tensions between North and South did not escape the attention of contemporary Americans. Henry David Thoreau realized that slavery and the West would tear America apart. He wrote, "This people must cease to hold slaves, and to make war on Mexico, though it cost them their existence as a people."[11]

The West: An Environmental Perspective

As of 2004, Washington State had the fifteenth largest population in the country and the twelfth fastest growing—a population that increasingly damages ecosystems. As late as 1852, Washington was neither a state nor a territory, but rather part of the sprawling blob known as Oregon Territory, which incorporated all of present Oregon, Washington, Idaho, and some of Montana. While about 60,000 people lived in the newly created Washington Territory in 1853, New York City alone already had more than 500,000. Locally, Washington's tiny population was dwarfed further by the grandeur of trees, mountains, and rivers. The Columbia River—which spills more water into the Pacific Ocean than all the other rivers in Washington, Oregon, and California combined—now forms most of the boundary between Oregon and Washington. In the Whitmans' time, the Columbia cut through the imposing Cascade Mountains and offered the only quick means of travel between east and west in a part of the country where coastal rain forests lay within 200 miles of barren desert. Dense-packed Douglas firs rose in 300-foot needled spires along the coast. In the mid-1800s, up to 20 million salmon ran the Columbia annually, and up to 11 million made it past the current site of the Bonneville Dam—built during the 1930s. Now fewer than 150,000 make it that far, and most of the decline results from the 250-plus dams on the Columbia and its tributaries, along with intensive logging that removes river shade and sends eroded soil into the river. Heavy reliance in the Pacific Northwest on hydroelectric power generation means fewer toxins pumped into the air compared to states that rely on coal- and carbon-fueled generation, yet damming rivers also has consequences. Historian John Findlay points out that "by the late 1980s, eighteen different (locally distinct) stocks of salmon were extinct on smaller rivers and tributaries of the Columbia."[12]

Gliding through the rivers and waters of the Puget Sound during the mid-nineteenth century were Salishan-speaking peoples. From the Skagit language in the north to the Wenatchee in the east, there were more than twenty-six separate languages springing from the Salish language base. These people's cultures were as diverse as their languages. The Nootkas lived on an island off the coast of present-day British Columbia in Canada. They had three homes, one for the summer, one for fishing, and another for the winter. The Nootkas built elaborate stages for theater performances and used sea kelp as piping to transmit voices for ventriloquism.[13] The abundance of sea otters, salmon, rain, and vegetation gave them a life of relative ease compared to that of the Shoshones and Paiutes of the interior high desert plains, who during most months endured a hard existence of hand-to-mouth foraging with little luxury. Environments shaped cultures.

215

For centuries the Spanish Empire had claimed theoretical ownership of all this territory, but its ships rarely ventured so far north. Russia also held flimsy claims, but in 1818 the United States and Britain agreed to a legal joint owner-ship—regardless of the thousands of Native Americans living there. Britain first sent Captain James Cook to the northwest coast in the 1770s, during the American Revolution. Cook and his crew visited with the Nootkas, from whom they acquired sea otter pelts. Although he was killed in Hawaii, Cook's men made it to China and exchanged the pelts for a small fortune. Soon ships and adventurers began to ply the waters of the Pacific Northwest coast, searching for new inlets and sources of treasure. For two decades, travelers brought diseases like smallpox and measles with them, and apocalyptic ruin ensued. Native populations died by up to 95 percent, clearing whole ecosystems of people so that traders, missionaries, and other seekers found an environment easier to control and settle. Still, this decimation took place gradually over decades, so Indians were by no means absent when George Vancouver and Peter Puget arrived in 1792 to explore the area for Britain. These royal explor-ers had fought for Britain in the American Revolution, and in territory that would one day become part of the United States they left their names dotting the landscape in what now seems like a parting salute. Puget Sound, the city of Vancouver in Washington, and Mount Rainier are all named after them and their British friends. Western civilization tends to claim land through a twin process. Trees and animals are euphemized into "natural resources." These resources—now linguistically devoid of life—are extracted for use in "grow-ing" economies (a reversal of the life metaphor that makes trees inanimate and the economy animate). Language is used to colonize. Replacing Native American place names and using European names in their stead begins and completes the colonization; however, many rivers and towns in the area still bear original names: the Skagit and Stilliguamish rivers, the cities of Yakima and Wenatchee.

Throughout the 1830s there were more British citizens than U.S. citizens in the Pacific Northwest because of the presence of the Hudson's Bay Company (HBC). HBC policy was strictly economic, though not mercenary. After the Crown gave them exclusive rights over an area stretching from Alaska to the northern edge of California, HBC officials established rules for fair trade and declared that any activities useful to trade would be considered part of the trade, which led them to treat Native Americans with more respect than was typical of U.S. frontier settlements. The HBC built Fort Vancouver on the Columbia in 1824 and soon had elaborate gardens, herds of cattle and sheep, and other endeavors that allowed it to be self-sufficient. To discourage the U.S. presence in the region, HBC officials followed such deadly policies as turning the Snake River basin into a "fur desert" by trapping and killing all the beaver in the zone so that U.S. trappers would find nothing of value. However, during the mid-1820s, storied mountain men like Jedediah Smith traveled through the region and found the beaver bountiful. Tales of plenty reached back east and stoked interest in exploration and settlement. Both British and U.S. citizens saw the land and its life as commodities and resources. Trees, otters, beaver, deer, and minerals were God's gifts to humankind, meant for harvesting and use. Native Americans could either participate in this economy of man's dominion over nature or be dismissed to oblivion. Some native peoples willingly participated in this new economy, changing along with the trade that enveloped them.

After the United States took the Oregon Country in 1846, government officials arrived. Part of their responsibility was making treaties with Native Americans. The process never went smoothly. In Oregon, the lead U.S. negotiator, Anson Dart, tried to offer better deals than the Senate was willing to ratify (for instance, placing nineteen reservations on the west side of the Cascade Mountains, while the Senate and most local whites wanted all Indians to live on the east side, away from fertile land lusted after by farmers and ranchers). Wherever gold was discovered, miners would flock by the thousands, crossing illegally onto Indian reservations. In the 1860s and 1870s, gold miners invaded the lands of the Nez Percés. The U.S. Army briefly tried to stop the rush of miners, but soon gave up the attempt and ended by pushing the Nez Percés onto ever-smaller plots of land. This treatment induced a war with many Nez Percés, led by Chief Joseph, whose small party of women, children, and warriors fought and fled almost all the way to safety in Canada in 1877. The army caught up with Joseph's shrunken band and attacked in the morning, shooting low into tents, intentionally killing babies, children, and women. Joseph's surrendering words continue to echo: "From where the sun now stands I will fight no more forever."[14] U.S. citizens, the army, and Congress repeatedly broke the original treaty made with the Nez Percés in 1855 at Walla Walla. That was typical, almost formulaic: U.S. expansion gripped the continent more tightly than any opposing force.

The nineteenth-century process of treaty breaking was occasionally reversed in the twentieth century. In 1854 in Washington Territory, Governor Isaac Stevens signed the Treaty of Medicine Creek (ratified by the Senate), which stipulated that nineteen separate treaty tribes would permanently retain rights to half the yield of salmon and steelhead in the region. Keeping those rights has been its own battle. During one 1970 incident, nearly 200 police stormed a native fishing site on the Puyallup River. Using teargas and clubs, the police and game wardens attacked and arrested sixty people. Although harassed, beaten, and jailed during the 1960s and early 1970s for trying to fish—for trying to enact their rights—Native Americans in Washington State earned a victory in 1974 when Judge William Boldt honored the 1854 treaty. The Supreme Court upheld this decision in 1979.

Where tens of thousands of Native Americans once lived, there are now more than 6 million people in Washington State (approximately 100,000 of whom are Native American). In 2005, Congressman Jim McDermott summed up the impact of human activities on salmon populations in the region: "Salmon runs are now at 1–3% of the levels they were when Lewis and Clark journeyed through the area."[15] As modern fishing techniques, swelling populations, and the consequences of industry eradicate salmon, government and various advocacy groups work to find solutions to human-generated problems.

Historically, the needs of the many have regularly been weighed against the needs of the few. In the United States, as the edge of settlement moved westward and colonization and disease shifted the numerical balance, Native Americans became the few and European-Americans the many. In the 1940s and 1950s, the Wyam Indians of Oregon, who had a one-hundred-year-old treaty to fish at Celilo Falls on the Columbia, refused to sell their stake in the river's take. A court extinguished those rights. The government declared eminent domain and the Dalles Dam was constructed—finished in 1957. As the dam blocked up the river, Celilo Falls was drowned, so fishing became impossible. The dam had been built to provide electric energy for the increasing population in the greater Portland area. Chief Tommy Kuni Thompson of the Wyams died at the age of 104, two years after the Dalles Dam was built. In Thompson's pocket sat the original treaty his uncle had signed in 1855, promising the Wyams a share of the Columbia's leaping salmon at the site of Celilo Falls. Now that salmon runs have been reduced by up to 99 percent, the fish have become the few, evicted from their rushing eddies, disinherited along with the Wyams.

A central dilemma presents itself throughout these interlocked histories of environmental change. How can society responsibly match its own needs for land, "resources," and electricity with the very real needs of other forms of life—like trees and salmon—upon whom we depend not only for our identities, but for our lives?

Notes

1. Janet Campbell Hale, *Bloodlines: Odyssey of a Native Daughter* (Tucson: University of Arizona Press, 1993), 173.

2. All excerpts from Narcissa Whitman's letters were taken from Narcissa Prentiss Whitman, *The Letters of Narcissa Whitman, 1836–1847* (Fairfield, WA: Ye Galleon, 1988).

3. Carlos Schwantes, *The Pacific Northwest: An Interpretive History* (Lincoln: University of Nebraska Press, 1996), 103.

4. Schwantes, *The Pacific Northwest*, 90.

5. Unless otherwise noted, all Twain quotes are from Mark Twain, *Roughing It* (New York: Harper & Brothers, 1913).

6. For a much fuller examination of how the gold fields tested and shaped middle-class values, see Brian Roberts, *American Alchemy: The California Gold Rush and Middle-Class Culture* (Chapel Hill: University of North Carolina Press, 2000).

7. Albert Bigelow Paine, ed., *Mark Twain's Letters, Volume 1, 1853–1866*, "Part of a letter to Mrs. Jane Clemens, in St. Louis, (Date not given, but Sept., or Oct., 1861)" (New York: Harper & Brothers, 1917), 54.

8. Paine, ed., *Mark Twain's Letters*, 67.

9. Walter Nugent, *Into the West: The Story of Its People* (New York: Vintage, 1999).

10. Henry David Thoreau, *Miscellanies*, "Civil Disobedience" (New York: Houghton, Mifflin, 1893), 131–170.

11. Thoreau, *Miscellanies*, 138.

12. John Findlay, "Lesson Twenty-seven: Extinction in Ecotopia: Environment and Identity in the Late-20th-Century Pacific Northwest," HSTAA432, History of Washington State and the Pacific Northwest, www.washington.edu/uwired/outreach/cspn/Website/Course%20Index/Lessons/27/27.html.

13. Schwantes, *The Pacific Northwest*, 30.

14. Bob Blaisdell, ed., *Great Speeches by Native Americans* (Mineola, NY: Dover, 2000), 148.

15. Rep. Jim McDermott, "Salmon Planning Act Deserves Serious Consideration," House Resources Committee Field Hearing, June 6, 2005, Clarkston, Washington, www.house.gov/mcdermott/sp050606.shtml.

12

Nineteenth-Century Slavery

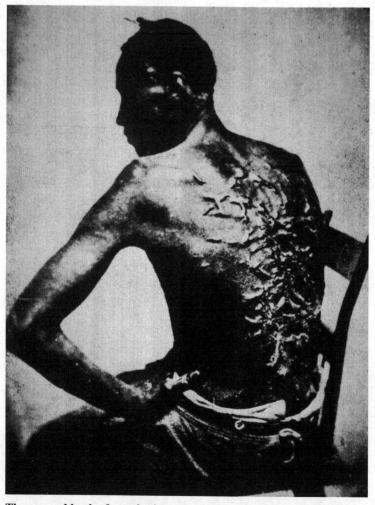

The scarred back of a male slave. *(American School/Getty Images)*

Perspectives

Certain images present themselves at the mention of antebellum slavery: tree-lined promenades leading to white-columned mansions sweltering in the cotton lands of the South; raised scars crisscrossing a brown back; artists' drawings of slave ships, floating bunk-bed prisons where humans were packed like coffins; mad eyes of a leering white man, whip in one hand, looming over a frightened black woman whose own eyes hold no hope at all. Read the narratives of former slaves, and you will know why we see these things. They happened.

Slavery was complex. The study of this subject requires us to seek out the complexities. Many aspects of antebellum slave society are disturbing; some may be surprising. Some free southern black people owned slaves. Some former slaves spoke of owners they liked. Some white people spoke kindly of black people and yet bought them and sold them all the same. Cruelty and abuse were a constant threat and sometimes a common occurrence. Masters raped many slave women. Slaves had no say over where they would live, what tasks they would perform, or how long family members might remain in the vicinity. Yet, in the midst of a villainous system, the men and women who were held as slaves managed to persevere. Slaves did not passively accept their hard fate; instead, they found ways of resisting the complete control many masters wanted to exert. It is important to uncover more of this history than the torments alone, important to understand how African-American slaves eked out a space for marriages, for learning, for religion, for friendships, and for hope. Those are also parts of the history of slavery.

Today's popular sentiment cries out and condemns every slaveholder as evil. How did white people maintain a belief in the positive value of slavery? When we examine different practices and beliefs from the antebellum South, for example, we begin to ponder what portion of human behavior results from culture, from the way people are raised. An abolitionist from Massachusetts might have been owned slaves if he had been born into a slave-owning family in Georgia. Racism may have sprung from some innate tendency to fear and loathe people who are different, or southern whites may have inherited and then bequeathed their slave-holding ideology in a generational cycle, bigotry perpetuated by circumstance.

The "peculiar institution" (a common euphemism for "slavery" as early as the 1830s) held everyone in its thrall. It took energy to rise before dawn and cut sugarcane or pick cotton. It also took energy to police captive workers, to keep them from running away, to teach them select biblical precepts but prevent them from learning to read. Slavery captured slave and master and bound their fates together.

Would you have owned slaves if you had lived in Virginia in 1850? Would you have tried to escape if you had been a slave?

Harriet Jacobs: *Incidents in the Life of a Slave Girl*

In 1820, the slave population stood at about 1.5 million. By 1860, there were 4 million slaves. White owners encouraged slaves to have as many children as possible, even while many owners imperiled slave families by selling the children when profit could be had. From a southern perspective, family was the South. However, for the adult black slaves who were treated like shifty children by their owners, escape to the North shimmered like a mirage. Many slaves faced a choice at least once in their lives between freedom and family.

Harriet Jacobs was born a slave in 1813 in North Carolina. She eventually escaped from slavery and made it to the North. Although free African-Americans could choose to leave their homes, the vast majority of free blacks stayed right where they were, dual testaments to the nature of home and to the strength of family bonds. Jacobs's grandmother, Molly Horniblow, was freed late in life, when she was about fifty, and set up a small but comfortable home in a small North Carolina town, Edenton. Since both of Harriet's parents had died early in her life, she turned to her grandmother time and again for love and help. Horniblow had the respect of whites and blacks in town because of her Christian faith, a life of diligent work and service to local whites, and the delicious jams and preserves she made for sale in Edenton. Not even Dr. James Norcom, the man who owned and tormented Jacobs, wanted to cross Molly Horniblow because she could have brought shame on him, a severe blow in a culture where a good reputation, based on status and moral image, meant everything.

Harriet Jacobs's life revolved around a few common themes: sexual harassment; the attempts of slave women to exert power in a system where overt power was vested in the hands of the master class; the healing, yet sometimes stifling, love of family; and the perseverance of spirit.

In her 1861 autobiography, *Incidents in the Life of a Slave Girl*,[1] Harriet Jacobs tells readers she did not know she was a slave until the age of six, a common awakening in a world where slave children and free often played together for the first years of their lives. For the next nine years, although aware of her status, she was spared many of the worst elements of slave life. She did not work in cotton or sugarcane fields, nor was she whipped, hit, or in general made to exert herself more than what a free laborer would have deemed acceptable. By the time she reached fifteen, however, her owner, Dr. Norcom, wanted to claim Jacobs as a sexual partner. She says, "He tried his utmost to corrupt the pure principles my grandmother had instilled."

Norcom's attempts to coerce her into unwanted sex were unsuccessful, but that did not prevent him from pushing Jacobs into extremes of depression, anxiety, and fear by an unrelenting campaign against her self-defense and better sense. The one reason Norcom did not rape her outright, as far as Jacobs could figure, was his own fear of the censure and stigma her grandmother could cause him in the community at large. People in Edenton already suspected him of having impregnated a number of his other young slave women, an assumption Jacobs says was founded in dismal truth. What is more, he tried to keep his sexual abuse of his slaves out of his wife's knowledge, for that was one of the great indignities white southern wives faced and loathed. White men who failed to live up to their own gallant Christian ideals frequently turned the myth of marriage that glorified southern life into a sham.

Harriet Jacobs plotted a final way of escaping Norcom's advances. She and a local white lawyer, Samuel Sawyer, had a child together, named Joseph. Jacobs knew this pregnancy would stymie Norcom's plans, for he had told Jacobs that he was having a cabin built nearby where he would house her away from prying and protective eyes, a place where he could do what he wanted. When Norcom learned of her pregnancy, she says, "He sprang upon me like a wolf, and grabbed my arm as if he would have broken it."

Over the span of a few years, Harriet Jacobs had another child with Samuel, a girl, Louisa. Norcom's wife had discovered her husband's libidinous behavior, which aroused a devilish malice, rather than sympathy, toward Jacobs. There were fewer and fewer safe places or people left in Jacobs's life. The doctor struck her often and raged against her. He viewed her as uncooperative property, as someone who should do anything he demanded, and for the most part the law was at his back, at least insofar as the law got enforced. Many southern states had laws against murdering slaves, for instance, but since black people could not testify in court against white people, the majority of homicides simply could not be prosecuted.

When Jacobs announced to Norcom that she was pregnant the second time, "he was exasperated beyond measure. He rushed from the house, and returned with a pair of shears. I had a fine head of hair; and he often railed about my pride of arranging it nicely. He cut every hair close to my head, storming and swearing all the time. I replied to some of his abuse, and he struck me. Some months before he had pitched me down stairs in a fit of passion." Harriet Jacobs worried about her daughter's future: her "heart was heavier than it had ever been before. Slavery is terrible for men; but it is far more terrible for women." She now had to fear that her daughter would one day be in a similar, nearly defenseless situation.

Neither Jacobs's children, nor her refusals to have sex with him caused the doctor to abstain from pursuing her. When Jacobs turned away from his every grasp, he fixed on a final offer, one part blatant manipulation, and one part punishment. He told Jacobs she would either live with him in the country or else be moved to his elder son's plantation, where she would be "broken." To keep intact what dignity she felt was still hers, she chose the son's plantation, and there she was sent in a rickety cart. Her children stayed behind at her grandmother's, although they were legally the property of Dr. Norcom, who continued to use them as leverage against an noncompliant Jacobs.

Neither Norcom nor his son wanted to keep Joseph and Louisa once they got older because the two children required food and had developed a strong dislike for the whole Norcom family. Norcom finally accepted an offer made by the children's father, Samuel Sawyer, to buy them and thereby free them, and Samuel in turn let them live on at their great-grandmother's. Remembering the moment when she heard this news, Harriet wrote, "I had my season of joy and thanksgiving. It was the first time since my childhood that I had experienced any real happiness, . . . Whatever slavery might do to me, it could not shackle my children. . . . It is always better to trust than to doubt."

During this emancipation of her children, Harriet Jacobs had escaped from the plantation and gone into hiding in a variety of locations. Then the strangest and most grueling twist of all happened. When she had to move to a new hiding place, the few people with knowledge of Jacobs's location and circumstances could devise only one spot for her in the vicinity (where she wanted to stay to be near her children). A tiny dwelling was made in her grandmother's attic, and there she lived for seven years, unable to do much more than roll from side to side. In Jacobs' words:

> A small shed had been added to my grandmother's house years ago. Some boards were laid across the joists at the top, and between these boards and the roof was a very small garret, never occupied by any thing but rats and mice. . . . The garret was only nine feet long and seven wide. The highest part was three feet high. . . . There was no admission for either light or air. . . . The air was stifling, the darkness total. A bed had been spread on the floor. I could sleep quite comfortably on one side; but the slope was so sudden that I could not turn on the other without hitting the roof. The rats and mice ran over my bed. . . . But I was not comfortless. I heard the voices of my children.

Harriet did not live out her days in this "attic dungeon." In 1842 she escaped to the North, where her children lived with her in freedom. During those years, Harriet Jacobs befriended many noted antislavery advocates, in particular Frederick Douglass, himself a former slave. During the Civil War, Jacobs went back to the South to provide comfort and education to African-Americans whose status hovered between slave and free. In the aftermath of the Civil War, when white people used violence and terror to reestablish authority over African-Americans, Jacobs returned to the North, where she died in 1897.

People in Harriet's day did not always believe her story as told in her autobiography (as the sexual elements of the memoir aggravated Victorian sentiments), calling it fiction used to stir up abolitionist sentiments. But recent historians have researched its accuracy and proven its essential truth.[2] What can be learned from her experiences?

In the minds of slaveholders, slaves equaled money, yet Molly Horniblow offered to buy Jacobs a number of times and was always refused. In fact, Dr. Norcom traveled three different times to New York trying to find Jacobs, twice during the years she spent in the attic and once afterward, and on each of those trips he spent literally hundreds of dollars—altogether more than he could have earned selling Jacobs even at the best of times. What did Harriet Jacobs really represent to Norcom beyond her economic value? What did she represent to other people?

Even though a master could effectively kill a slave and get away with it, even though white men could rape black slave women with impunity, even though a slave could be whipped for picking cotton too slowly, *did* white people have total control over the slave population, and maybe over all black people living in the South? How does Harriet Jacobs's life as a slave offer perspective on this question of control?

Here is Jacobs's answer: "My master had power and law on his side; I had a determined will. There is might in each."

Rebecca Felton: The Mind of a White Southerner

Women owned slaves, and Rebecca Latimer Felton was one of those women. In her eighties when she wrote *Country Life in Georgia in the Days of My Youth*,[3] Felton spoke of slaves with degrees of civility and perhaps warmth, and her words reveal the extent to which owners believed that slaves were childlike members of an extended family. After graduating from college in 1852, Felton helped run a plantation in Georgia, which meant she delegated work and orders to the people living and working in and around her home. She summarized her own life by saying, "I married shortly after I was eighteen, and my entire life was soon absorbed in home service and home making and the care of my babies and the duties that fell upon women of my class and kind in caring for a considerable number of slaves and in keeping up with the requirements of a plantation home in the country." From her perspective, slaves were merely one part of a busy, responsible life, no more unusual than horses or hired help. To a plantation mistress, slavery simply was.

During the middle decades of the nineteenth century, white southerners, responding to the growing storm of abolitionist attacks, concocted theories about black people's inherent inferiority as a way to justify slavery as a positive good. One part of this theorizing involved thinking of black people as passive and lazy. Early in her memoirs, Felton wrote, "The Red Indians of North America refused to become the white man's slave, while Africa made no resistance. . . . The African in the slave-holding states did not rise up in defense of democracy or human freedom when the Federal armies of the North had overrun and subjugated the slave owning Southern Confederacy." She saw African-Americans as unresisting participants in their own plight.

The life of a Georgia plantation mistress consisted of hard work, many duties to oversee, and intermittent loneliness. Felton recalled, "large families were the rule, visiting was constant, and in times of festivity or bereavement, there were crowds of willing helpers to laugh with the happy or weep with the suffering ones." However, when not visiting or celebrating, many white women on plantations were more frequently alone than were the African-American slaves picking cotton and growing vegetables for the "family," which was how planters referred to all the residents, free and unfree, on their premises. Fifty percent of African-Americans lived on plantations with at least twenty slaves. Though these slaves had little else, they at least had communal living and bonds of family and friendship. Rebecca Felton had what slaves did not—her freedom. While she was theoretically free to do as she pleased, her life was intertwined with the lives of her slaves, her freedom being in direct disproportion to their servitude.

Most of Felton's comments about the black people who lived with her downplay the devastating aspects of slavery, another hallmark of most slave owners' thinking. As Felton described going to church, "It was a great time with children, negro nurses and dogs. There was always a spring of good water close about. The mothers provided biscuit and teacakes for their hungry tribes." Black women did more than set tables in the big house and cook the food. They literally raised little children. At a party in her youth, Rebecca's black "Mammy" caught her and a friend underneath a table gobbling food the way "one pig helps another." Her Mammy promptly took her home and reported the unseemly incident to Rebecca's mother. She recalled, "I ate under a table, out of a scrap bucket, with all the indignation that Mammy was capable of expressing by words and looks and gestures. . . . So far as I know nobody but Mammy ever suffered stifling mortification about it." Whether her "Mammy" cared as much as Rebecca imagined, the black woman's welfare depended on teaching the white child behaviors and ways of carrying herself befitting the gentry—another strange twist in the history of slavery. Slave women taught free daughters how to behave in a polite society to which African-Americans were not welcomed other than as servants.

Felton knew that slavery was economics, that white people measured wealth by counting slaves, and she argued that the Civil War resulted from a secession designed to accomplish one goal—the continuance of slavery. However, she found it surprising that southerners were unable to see the impossibility of maintaining the institution of slavery in a world where most other countries were setting everyone free. Britain had outlawed slavery throughout its empire in 1833. The czar of Russia freed millions of serfs in 1863. The slaves of Haiti had cast off the yoke of their French masters in the 1790s. "I am amazed," she said, "at the lack of foresight in a business way. Every nation that was civilized had abandoned domestic slavery except Brazil, when our people were apparently confident that it was a permanent thing, commanded by the Bible and ordained of God." While she found her countrymen's thinking limited, she offers a specific explanation for the central wrong of slavery: miscegenation—procreation between white and black people.

Perhaps 10 percent of children born to slaves were of part white and part black ancestry (called "mulattoes"). Many of them were sold away from the sight of their black mothers and white fathers for two primary reasons. First, these children continued to be property. Second, and arguably more important, mulatto children were a reminder to plantation masters and their wives of marital indiscretion, of infidelity. Felton's thinking indicates a belief in the sanctity of racially homogeneous marriages and families, a philosophy that underpinned the idealism of white southerners, if not the practice of white men, particularly when they did not treat all their offspring as kin. Rebecca Felton put it this way: "There were violations of the moral law that made mulattoes as common as blackberries. In this one particular, slavery doomed itself. When white men were willing to put their own offspring in the kitchen and corn field and allowed them to be sold into bondage as slaves and degraded them as another man's slave, the retribution of wrath was hanging over this country and the South paid penance in four years of bloody war."

Felton's comments on slavery and the Civil War suggest at least a latter-day admission that holding people as slaves was wrong on its own terms. "I am now," she commented as an old woman, "too near to the border land of eternity to withhold my matured conscientious and honest opinion. If there had been no slaves there would have been no war. To fight for the perpetuation of domestic slavery was a mistake. The time had come in the United States to wipe out this evil." Her "matured" opinion about slavery labeled it "evil," but that was her analytical mind speaking. When she was merely relating events and stories, she mentioned slaves in simple, factual terms—often endearing and fond. These attitudes were not mutually exclusive: she may have felt tender and loving and yet continued to hold slaves in bondage according to the custom of her world. "Once," Felton recalled, "I was 'candle-holder'

228

at a big negro wedding at Grandmother's home. The girl was a housemaid but the groom lived several miles away and came to his wife's home every Saturday night to stay until Monday morning daylight... I was very fond of the bride-to-be [a slave]." The Felton family's endearing feelings toward the engaged slaves did not exclude administration of what she called a "matrimonial catechism." Felton's grandfather interviewed the slave-groom, asking him, "'Will you act the dog and beat my good darky when you get mad with her?'" The groom "gladly answered 'no.'"

In her final summation of slavery, Rebecca Felton said, "The crime that made slavery a curse, lies in the fact that unbridled lust placed the children of bad white men in slave pens, on auction blocks, and no regard was shown to parentage or parental responsibility in such matters . . . women were afraid to make public outcry." As a plantation mistress, she felt a responsibility to her family, one part "white" and "the other colored," at the same time she felt a loyalty to the Confederacy, which denied 4 million African-American slaves the legal right to have families of their own. After all, owners could keep together or break apart slave families at will. As Harriet Jacobs's memoir highlights, one of a slave mother's greatest fears was separation from her children. And Rebecca Felton pointed out that Southern custom would have "outlawed the most consecrated preacher known to that era of our history if he had dared to say that a slave woman had divine right to own her own liberty or direct the lives of her own children."

Nat Turner and Slave Resistance

Nat Turner was not a large man, standing no taller than five foot eight and weighing about 160 pounds. The midnight light of August 21, 1831, would have illuminated the physical marks of slavery upon his body. Turner had knock-knees, a distorted wrist, and scars on his face. The typical slave diet of corn and bacon may have provided enough calories but certainly not enough nutrition. Whippings, brandings, and sunup to sundown labor bent hands and cracked feet. Slender Nat Turner, a thirty-one-year-old preacher and field hand who had sowed the fields and reaped the harvests of southern Virginia for at least twenty years, took a hatchet to the head of his owner and led nearly seventy other African-American men on a murderous circuit of neighboring houses for more than a day, trying to live up to the divine calling he had felt for more than a year to lead his people to freedom.

This brief uprising of the downtrodden illustrated the reserves of discontent and agitation harbored by most (if not all) of the slave men and women in the antebellum South. Turner's rebellion, which sparked a series of brutal responses and legislative measures by the white people of Virginia, also demonstrated the overall strength of the slave system, both in its means of control and in the desire shown by a majority of whites to maintain slavery.

Whereas the black slaves of Haiti had liberated themselves in a bloody struggle against their colonial French masters in the 1790s and the slaves of South American empires sometimes banded together by the thousands to fight back against their oppressors, North American slave women and men rarely resisted physically beyond the level of the individual. Many explanations have been suggested to explain the relatively small number of uprisings. Slaves did not want to endanger nearby family members. The average farmstead had only a small numbers of slaves. And Southern whites made society-wide efforts to monitor and police their slaves' activities. Escaping for a few days into the woods or the swamp was common, as were feigning illness, working slowly when possible, breaking tools, and upon occasion truly escaping. These tactics of subverting the authority and power of white owners were endemic throughout the antebellum South, but they do not explain how every once in a while revolts were planned and (less frequently) carried out.

It is hard to determine if the revolt led by Nat Turner was an aberration, an unusual occurrence, or just a better-publicized, slightly more successful version of what many slaves did. There were many little-known, rarely mentioned instances of slaves joining together to fight back, insurrections that happened nearly everywhere slavery existed. In 1800, a slave named Gabriel (sometimes called Gabriel Prosser) organized a slave revolt that whites discovered and suppressed, leading to Gabriel's death and that of a handful of others. In 1811, a Louisiana uprising led by Charles Deslondes involved more slaves than Turner's (400 compared to 60). In 1822, Denmark Vesey, a freeman living in Charleston, South Carolina, was discovered as the leader of a planned insurrection. Each of these rebellions incited fear in local whites, yet they stirred fewer long-term fears . . . but why? The answers may lie in geography, given Virginia's historically prominent role in the country. Slave revolts in the early 1800s seemed to end before they began, until Nat Turner's.

In Southampton County, Virginia, where Turner lived, the economy was thriving; there were more black people than white, a common feature of life throughout many of the established agricultural regions of the South. White people were afraid. Slave states had statutes on the books that allowed masters to mete out punishments as they saw fit. South Carolina allowed white people to strike a free black person, but the theoretically free African-American was not allowed to respond even in self-defense. That was the ironic world that Nat Turner lived in, a place in time where empowered white people feared oppressed slaves and free blacks alike.

Nat Turner turned to the Bible to find his inspiration, the same book used by many slave owners and white southern preachers to justify holding people in chains. Although reading was practically and legally prohibited for slaves during most of the nineteenth century, some still managed to learn; Turner claimed to have picked up his skill in reading spontaneously. Turner certainly knew the scriptures—well enough, some claimed, that he could quote the whole text, word for word. He favored a few short passages. In his *Confessions*—a statement given to a local attorney after his capture in October 1831—Turner said a "particular passage" from the Bible had "struck" him.[4] In the midst of prayer, he heard a voice say, "Seek ye the kingdom of Heaven and all things shall be added unto you." He claimed the voice was the same Spirit that had spoken "to the prophets in former days." For Nat Turner, the message reinforced a sense of divine calling. Over the next years, he saw visions that emphasized what he believed God wanted of him. "I discovered," he recalled, "drops of blood on the corn as though it were dew from heaven . . . and I then found on the leaves in the woods hieroglyphic characters." About these portents, he said, "it was plain to me that the Saviour was about to lay down the yoke he had borne for the sins of men, and the great day of judgment was at hand." Nat Turner believed he would be judged according to his acts, and so he acted.

Turner and the other conspirators agreed on July 4 as the date of their planned uprising, but it had to be passed over because Turner got sick. He waited for a sign from heaven, which came in the guise of an eclipse. On August 21, over pork, cider, and brandy (although Turner abstained from alcohol), he and a few men met in the woods near Turner's plantation. At about two o'clock in the morning, as he explained in his *Confessions*:

> Hark got a ladder and set it against the chimney, on which I ascended, and hoisting a window, entered and came down stairs, unbarred the door, and removed the guns from their places. It was then observed that I must spill the first blood. On which, armed with a hatchet, and accompanied by Will, I entered my master's chamber, it being dark, I could not give a death blow, the hatchet glanced from his head, he sprang from the bed and called his wife, it was his last word, Will laid him dead, with a blow of his axe, and Mrs. Travis shared the same fate, as she lay in bed.

For a day and a half, Turner and about sixty other self-emancipated slaves tramped through the roads and fields of the surrounding countryside, killing every white person they could find except one impoverished white family and a plantation household where it was likely Turner's wife, Cherry, lived. The vengeful marauders took horses, guns, and machetes, but in the end their weapons were no match for the swift might of local militias and federal troops, altogether numbering perhaps 3,000, who converged on the scene.

Turner and his band killed nearly sixty white people, but between Turner's followers who were killed in melees with troops, Turner's followers who were later tried and hanged, and other black people in the area upon whom white vigilantes wreaked injustice out of fear and hatred, perhaps 200 black people died as a consequence of the rebellion. The white response was instantaneous, and once again the lack of a tradition of combined resistance worked against African-American fighters in the antebellum South. There was no general slave uprising or collusion or banding together. The vast majority of neighboring black people did not swing their hoes or knives in defiance of the bonds that held them.

For nearly two months Nat Turner hid on the very boundaries of his former master's plantation, coming out at night to reconnoiter the area for news and water. Eventually, one Benjamin Phipps, armed with a shotgun, apprehended Turner in the same cotton lands of his youth, labor, and short-lived resistance. A court sentenced Turner to be hanged until dead. He died on November 11, 1831.

Although Nat Turner meant to free his fellow bondsmen and women, slavery became more entrenched, not less. Turner's insurrection may have backfired by spurring white southerners to defend their way of life, to further tighten the restrictions on black people's behavior. After the revolt, for instance, the process of manumission (freeing slaves) was made illegal in South Carolina. No new free black people were allowed to move into Virginia, and neither free nor enslaved African-Americans were allowed to meet for prayer or religious services without someone white in attendance. None of these laws was strictly enforced, especially after the passage of some years, but they indicated the efforts that whites made to maintain slavery in the face of resistance.

Most slaves resisted their owners' authority in myriad subtle ways. Many also ran away—intending to go only for a short while, a few ran away for good, and probably a smaller number physically lashed out at an owner or overseer. Nat Turner and his band of fighters were, thus, both within and outside the patterns of slave resistance, escaping only through death but willing to face that eventuality all the same.

Solomon Northup: Slave Migrations and the West

Slavery was not a monolithic experience. A slave's life involved as many nuances and individual peculiarities as free life. Slaves had marriages, sometimes separate-if-meager incomes (which some were allowed to pursue on Sundays, their "day off"), specialized skills (carpentry, shoe making, preaching, etc.), dances, unique medical practices, churches to attend, and more besides. Not every second was spent in torment, although many were. Solomon Northup, who was born a free man in New York State in July 1808, was kidnapped and sold into slavery at the age of thirty-three. His memoir, *Twelve Years a Slave*, depicts the variety of experiences in a slave's life and forced a contemporary northern reader to imagine that any white person raised in a southern slave society would probably find the institution acceptable.[5]

Solomon Northup grew up with all the possibilities his status offered and few of the restrictions he would have faced as a free black man in the South. In 1829 he married Anne Hampton. They had children and soon moved to Saratoga Springs, New York, where they worked at a number of jobs within communities where they felt accepted and highly regarded. Solomon was gifted on the violin, a skill he turned into cash when occasion called for a reel or a jig. He recalled, "In the winter season I had numerous calls to play on the violin. Wherever the young people assembled to dance, I was almost invariably there. Throughout the surrounding villages my fiddle was notorious." Perhaps it would have been better had it not been notorious. In 1841, two white men invited him to accompany them to Washington, DC, under the pretense of their wanting him to play his fiddle at certain events throughout the country, for which they promised to compensate him well. In Washington, within "the shadow" of the Capitol, his employers drugged Northup and sold him illegally to a trader, William Burch, who maintained a legal holding compound for human chattels. Burch transported Northup out of freedom and into the hellish depths of Louisiana slavery, where he remained for twelve years, without anyone else the wiser, other than the scoundrels who had tricked him.

Between 1619 and 1808, perhaps 600,000 African people sailed to North America on the Middle Passage, the journey straight from Africa. In 1808, Congress ended the Atlantic slave trade. A greater and lesser-known migration began at the close of the Revolutionary War and lasted until the Civil War. During these seventy years, slave owners and traders forced approximately 1 million African-Americans into an exodus from northern and seaboard states to the west and southwest.

In colonial times the lands from Virginia south into Georgia were used to grow tobacco, rice, and indigo, and to some extent for animal husbandry and staple crops. Tobacco agriculture wore out the nutrients in the soil and left rich earth barren. Rice took longer to mature than tobacco, so its profit hinged on a long wait unsatisfying to people who borrowed heavily and wanted a quick turnaround on their investments. Cotton had also been grown, but picking the seeds out of the fibers was so labor-intensive as to make the crop very little profitable. Then, in 1793, Eli Whitney invented the cotton gin, which could separate seeds from cotton at previously unimaginable rates, approximately ten times faster than by hand. Cotton transformed the South (and the North).

Now slaves could stop picking out seeds and be put to work planting them and harvesting the rewards. What wealth was at hand and how much new land could be put into cultivation were determined only by the time it took to occupy acreage, clear it of trees, and drain away the swampy waters. Tennessee, Mississippi, Louisiana, and Texas beckoned to aspiring and established planters alike. The climate was right, and the fortunes of the South would once more be rich.

Solomon Northup spent a couple of weeks in William Burch's slave pen in DC. There Burch beat Northup into submission with a wooden paddle and a cat-o'-nine-tails for declaring his status as a freeman. "It seemed," Northup recalled, "that the lacerated flesh was stripped from my bones at every stroke." After breaking Northup's will to resist, Burch shipped Northup by paddleboat and then steamship to New Orleans, heart of the Deep South slave trade. On the journey there he heard stories that were commonplace during these decades. Eliza, a young mother of two, had been sold by the daughter of her deceased former lover and owner (who had been planning to free her). Eliza's fate involved the loss of both children to different buyers and shipment into cotton and sugarcane country, where she died the slow death of bereavement. Richard, also a former freeman beaten brutally by a gang of ruffians and sold illegally into slavery, died of smallpox aboard the ship, but not before passing the disease on to others, including Northup.

Upon arrival in New Orleans, Northup was informed of his new name: Platt—forwarded without Northup's knowledge to the management of the slave pen in New Orleans. A slave's name, in many ways, defined his or her identity. The surname typically came from the first owner, and the first name usually came from a large stock pool of slave names, which were intended to emphasize the separateness of African-Americans and to further confine them inside a nomenclature of powerlessness. Whites commonly used "nigger" as a name. "Platt," though not associated with an owner's last name, was meant to strip Solomon Northup of his previous identity, a name used like a mask.

After recovering from smallpox, which left him permanently scarred, Northup was purchased by a planter named William Ford, the first and nearly only good fortune to befall him in his twelve years of captivity. Just as every person held as a slave was different, so was each master. Northup's years of servitude were largely characterized by the personalities of the men who owned him. In Northup's words:

> In many northern minds, perhaps, the idea of a man holding his brother man in servitude, and the traffic in human flesh, may seem altogether incompatible with their conceptions of a moral or religious life. From descriptions of such men as Burch . . . they are led to despise and execrate the whole class

of slaveholders indiscriminately. But I was some time [Ford's] slave . . . and it is but simple justice to him when I say, in my opinion, there never was a more kind, noble, candid, Christian man than William Ford. The influences and associations that had always surrounded him blinded him to the inherent wrong at the bottom of the system of Slavery. He never doubted the moral right of one man holding another in subjection. . . . Nevertheless, he was a model master, walking uprightly, according to the light of his understanding, and fortunate was the slave who came to his possession. Were all men such as he, Slavery would be deprived of more than half its bitterness.

William Ford put "Platt" to work on his Red River plantation in the southwestern portion of Louisiana, not far from Texas, in swamp-covered, forested terrain. This was cotton country, which meant hard labor for most slaves, especially so because planters had discovered how the season for corn growing dovetailed with cotton's—a system that kept slaves working year round. For a while Northup found his way out of field labor because of the carpentry skills he had developed in New York working on the Champlain Canal. He suggested, devised, and built a system of rafts to transport the lumber milled at Ford's operation on one of the bayous, a secondary business venture. Part of Northup's focus came, he said, "from a desire to please my master," a feeling he was soon to lose when Ford, who had earlier undersigned a brother's debt, was forced to sell off some property to pay his brother's creditors. Solomon Northup was part of that property, and he was transferred to the mean hands of William Tibeats, a drunk and vicious carpenter who more than once attempted to murder Northup out of nothing more than unprovoked anger. "I was doomed to endure," Northup recounted, "such bitter trials as the poor slave only knows, and to lead no more the comparatively happy life which I had led in the 'great Pine Woods,'" the region surrounding Ford's plantation.

Northup's tenure with Tibeats lasted no more than a few months, during which time Northup proved himself the better carpenter of the two: "I was his faithful slave, and earned him large wages every day, and yet I went to my cabin nightly, loaded with abuse and stinging epithets." Verbal abuse turned to physical assault, and on a day that Tibeats sought to whip Northup for someone else's mistake, Northup the slave beat his master rather than suffer a whipping he in no way had earned. "I was guilty of no wrong whatever," Northup wrote, "and deserved commendation rather than punishment." The ensuing events spoke to many things. Tibeats gathered neighboring overseers and returned to the sight of his humiliation in order to hang Northup. But because the two carpenters had been working on Ford's plantation, his overseer intervened on Northup's behalf, claiming that not only was Tibeats a "scoundrel" but that he could not kill Northup because Ford still held a mortgage of $400 on Northup and because the law forbade the wanton killing of slaves, a law that relied on the intervention of well-intentioned white people for enforcement.

With a few brief exceptions, the next ten years of Solomon Northup's life were spent as the slave of Edwin Epps, a man whose temperament and conscience lay somewhere between Ford's and Tibeats's. Consequently, Northup spent most of his time as a typical plantation slave. He toiled in the cotton fields and was sometimes hired out to local sugarcane farmers for harvest season along with other slow cotton pickers like himself. He slept on a dirt floor with only one blanket for warmth, ate corn meal and bacon, and generally had little time to himself. The two mitigating factors in this life were his skill with the violin and his creativity with tools. The first got him sent around to neighboring plantations to play at festivals, a sideline that kept some coins in Northup's pockets. And his carpentry enabled him to do odd jobs around the plantation and to build fishing weirs to trap bayou fish, a necessity if slaves were to have enough protein in their diets. Most slaves had fewer options than Northup because they had not been raised to think independently, to read, to write, or to show initiative. Northup managed to employ all those skills while maintaining a feigned but believable deference to Edwin Epps, a feat that allowed Northup a hint of independence—enough so that he managed to strike up a friendship with a traveling white laborer named Samuel Bass. Bass came from Canada and agreed to mail a letter for Northup, a letter that spelled out his whereabouts and secured him his freedom after making it all the way to the governor of New York.

Deliverance came in the first days of January 1853. A representative from New York arrived along with the sheriff to release the man known throughout the bayou as Platt. In Northup's words:

> Emotion choked all utterance, and I was silent. . . . I walked out into the yard, and was entering the kitchen door, when something struck me in the back. Aunt Phebe, emerging from the back door of the great house with a pan of potatoes, had thrown one of them with unnecessary violence, thereby giving me to understand that she wished to speak to me a moment confidentially. Running up to me, she whispered in my ear with great earnestness.
>
> "Lor a'mity, Platt! wha d'ye think? Dem two men come after ye. Heard 'em tell mass you free—got wife and tree children back thar whar you come from. Goin' wid em? Fool if you don't—wish I could go."

Solomon Northup returned home after a stop in Washington, DC, where he undertook fruitless proceedings in court to prosecute William Burch, the owner of the first slave pen Northup was kept in. Pleading ignorance of Northup's status as a free man, Burch claimed he had lost the sales records, a plea the court accepted.

Once back in his home state, Solomon Northup embraced his wife and children and had this to say in his own conclusion:

> My narrative is at an end. I have no comments to make upon the subject of Slavery. Those who read this book may form their own opinions of the "peculiar institution." What it may be in other States, I do not profess to know; what it is in the region of Red River, is truly and faithfully delineated in these pages. There is no fiction, no exaggeration. If I have failed in anything, it has been in presenting to the reader too prominently the bright side of the picture. I doubt not . . . that hundreds of free citizens have been kidnapped and sold into slavery, and are at this moment wearing out their lives on plantations in Texas and Louisiana. But I forbear. Chastened and subdued in spirit by the sufferings I have bore, and thankful to that good Being through whose mercy I had been restored to happiness and liberty, I hope henceforward to lead an upright though lowly life, and rest at last in the church yard where my father sleeps.

"The Love of Freedom"

Slavery as a system was in flux. Cotton, for instance, had not been much of a cash crop until after Eli Whitney's innovative cotton gin of 1793. Because of the continuing improvements that various mechanics made to gins, an ever-expanding volume of cotton could be processed yearly throughout the South. The gin breathed new energy into slavery, led to the exodus of owners and their slaves to the west, increased the value and production of cotton to the point that the total annual export of cotton was worth more than all other national exports combined.[5] Some of these changes were measured in the span of an individual life.

The chances that a slave family in the northern South would remain together decreased over time as slaves were sold to the south and west. Legislatures tightened laws restricting slaves from getting an education, meeting together in groups (even to pray or study the Bible), and being freed. While some slaves did gain permanent freedom in the North through their own efforts and the help of people like Harriet Tubman (who transported friends and relatives along the Underground Railroad), many more hoped to either buy their own freedom or be manumitted by a master, which often happened in a will. However, after Nat Turner's bloody uprising, many states began to make it harder (if not legally impossible) to free slaves under any circumstances. Southern whites were becoming convinced that the presence of free black people increased the odds of slave rebelliousness and agitation.

Slavery was entrenched, but its roots went deeper the farther south a person traveled. Some of the northern states of the South had sizable free African-American populations. In 1810, for example, about 10 percent of the black people in Virginia were free. And by 1860, Delaware's slave population made up less than 2 percent of the total number of residents. In Mississippi, however, by 1860, "free blacks constituted only 0.2 percent of the population," and throughout the entire Deep South, by 1860, "only 1.5 percent of blacks . . . were free."[6] Through the 1820s and 1830s, some slaves still lived in the North, with more than 3,500 throughout the North (mainly in New Jersey) as late as 1830. The North's economy benefited from the slave system, primarily by using its cotton to make textiles. In general, however, the labor needs of the North were less suited to slavery because the growing season was too short for farmers to keep slaves working year round. Northern slaves were concentrated in cities where labor needs were plentiful. Northern slavery was brutal in its own right, but there simply were not the same economic, social, or historical attachments to slavery that were to be found in the South. So it is not surprising that New Jersey, which passed the last of the northern states' emancipation laws, set a schedule in 1804 for freeing male slaves when they reached the age of twenty-five and female slaves at twenty-one. However, even with the gradual emancipation law in place, slavery persisted in New Jersey until 1846.

There were almost 4 million slaves in the South in 1860 on the eve of the Civil War. There is no good evidence to suggest that slavery would have been voluntarily given up in the Deep South any time soon; indeed, in the decades that followed the Civil War, many southern whites reestablished labor and social systems that closely resembled slavery. Whether living as a craftsman in Charleston, a sugarcane cutter in Louisiana, a wet nurse in Georgia for a mistress with four children, or as one of two slaves on a small cotton farm in Virginia, African-American slaves had to fight for their dignity, their pride, and the chance that a day might come when there would be no more shackles, or forced moves away from family members, or cold nights spent on dirt floors with nothing to fill the belly but rancid pork and cornmeal biscuits.

About the despair that filled the days of slaves, Solomon Northup said, "I knew not now whither to look for deliverance. Hopes sprang up in my heart only to be crushed and blighted. The summer of my life was passing away." Slaves shared a passionate longing for freedom and liberty: "ninety-nine out of every hundred [slaves] . . . cherish in their bosoms the love of freedom, as passionately as" the whites who wrongly believed that slaves were treated well. Millions of people died, in Northup's words, "toiling . . . never destined to breathe, as I now do, the blessed air of liberty, nor to shake off the heavy shackles that enthrall them, until they shall lie down forever in the dust."[7]

Notes

1. All quotes pertaining to Harriet Jacobs, unless otherwise noted, were taken with permission from Harriet Jacobs, *Incidents in the Life of a Slave Girl: Written by Herself*, University of North Carolina at Chapel Hill, http://docsouth.unc.edu/fpn/jacobs/jacobs.html. This work is the property of the University of North Carolina at Chapel Hill. It may be used freely by individuals for research, teaching and personal use as long as this statement of availability is included in the text. Permission to quote from each of the UNC works listed in this book was granted by Mike Millner, Information and Communications Specialist, Library Digitization Services, Wilson Library, CB#39902.

2. See Jean Fagan Yellin, *Harriet Jacobs: A Life* (New York: Basic, 2003); and Deborah M. Garfield and Rafia Zafar, *Harriet Jacobs and Incidents in the Life of a Slave Girl* (New York: Cambridge University Press, 1996).

3. For all quotes pertaining to Rebecca Latimer Felton's life, unless otherwise noted, were taken with permission from Rebecca Latimer Felton, *Country Life in Georgia in the Days of My Youth*, University of North Carolina at Chapel Hill, http://docsouth.unc.edu/fpn/felton/felton.html. This work is the property of the University of North Carolina at Chapel Hill. It may be used freely by individuals for research, teaching and personal use as long as this statement of availability is included in the text.

4. All quotes pertaining to Nat Turner's insurrection were taken with permission from, *The Confessions of Nat Turner, the Leader of the Late Insurrection in Southhampton, VA*, University of North Carolina at Chapel Hill, http://docsouth.unc.edu/neh/turner/turner.html. This work is the property of the University of North Carolina at Chapel Hill. It may be used freely by individuals for research, teaching and personal use as long as this statement of availability is included in the text.

5. Andrew K. Frank, *The Routledge Historical Atlas of the American South* (New York: Routledge, 1999), 42.

6. Peter Kolchin, "Slavery and the American Revolution," in Rick Halpern and Enrico Dal Lago, eds., *Slavery and Emancipation* (Malden, MA: Blackwell, 2002), 112.

7. All quotes pertaining to Solomon Northup's experiences were taken with permission from Solomon Northup, *Twelve Years a Slave*, University of North Carolina at Chapel Hill, http://docsouth.unc.edu/fpn/northup/northup.html. This work is the property of the University of North Carolina at Chapel Hill. It may be used freely by individuals for research, teaching and personal use as long as this statement of availability is included in the text.

13

The Coming of the Civil War

Sojourner Truth *(Hulton Archive/Getty Images)*

A Slow-Building Fire

When it started, the Civil War was not fought to end slavery. But without slavery, the Civil War never would have been fought. In 1861, under the pretense of defending their individual rights, eleven Southern states seceded from the United States and formed the Confederate States of America. President Abraham Lincoln's remaining Union went to war against these breakaway rebels in order to keep the nation together, not to end slavery. For the Confederates, the war was a second American Revolution fought in the name of liberty and independence. To Southerners, slavery *was* the South, as an 1836 letter by John C. Calhoun (the former vice president) makes clear: "[Abolition] strikes directly and fatally, not only at our prosperity, but our existence, as a people."[1] White Southerners' liberty rested on slavery and the culture that came with it: a way of life; a skin-color social hierarchy; leisure for a few white people rich enough to own more than a handful of slaves; a thriving cotton economy; the chivalric myth of noble patriarchs, swooning ladies in hooped gowns, gracious manners, and a happy, servile black underclass. The South was also protecting its honor, maybe more than anything else. For the thirty years prior to 1861, increasing numbers of Northerners criticized slave owners and slave culture, often in the most insulting terms. With their way of life under attack, most Southerners responded by defending slavery and all that came with it as natural and good. When Lincoln's Republican Party came to power in 1860, dedicated as it was to stopping the expansion of slavery, the South declared independence, and the Civil War began.

Why did history go this way? Were there no compromises that could be made to keep slavery safe in the South and safely out of the North? Must a society have sufficient cultural commonalities to have the kinds of trust and honesty that foster civil debate and produce laws that feel just? If so, does the coming of the Civil War teach us how to identify the kinds of significant differences that can lead to disunion?

The Constitution itself was a kind of compromise, one that allowed the South to keep its slaves. By 1820, cotton had become the South's paramount crop. As the reign of "King Cotton" spread out into Alabama, Tennessee, Mississippi, and Texas, the numbers of slaves and slave owners increased. Prices for slaves rose, and the whole affair became much more profitable. Until about 1830, the North contented itself with abolishing the Atlantic slave trade (in 1808), freeing its own slaves, and getting on with the massive changes that Yankees and mid-Atlantic Northerners seemed to embrace: building canals and railroads, inventing things, and adopting an investment-capital, wage-based economy. The economies of North and South were interlocked. The North depended on cotton from the South. There seemed reason to believe that this mutually beneficial relationship could be maintained indefinitely. Money tempts people to do many things, but it did not keep the North and South in a harmonious orbit forever.

Continual aggravations scratched at the consciences of Northern men and women from the 1790s onward. Their responses scratched back at the honor and fears of many in the South. The Northwest Ordinance of 1787 prevented slavery from extending into any new, northern territories or states. But the Constitution provided for the return of runaway property, for the continuation of the international slave trade, and for slaves counting as three-fifths of a person for representation in Congress. The Fugitive Slave Act in 1793 forced the North to help the South retrieve runaway slaves. That legal obligation felt wrong to the small but growing ranks of Quakers and their allies who had become outspoken in their opposition to slavery on basic moral terms. The Louisiana Purchase of 1803 opened vast lands to settlement and created a lingering question: could slavery expand into the Louisiana Purchase? The question became critical in 1818–1819 when Missouri tried to enter the Union as a slave state. The issue was temporarily resolved in 1820 when Maine gained admittance as a free state and Missouri as a slave state. A line was also extended westward through the remainder of the Louisiana Purchase territory: above the latitude of 36°30' no slave states would be allowed. These measures maintained the balance so that North and South held equal numbers of votes in the Senate—such that with equal numbers of free and slave states, North and South would have equal numbers of senators. But the ballyhooed Missouri Compromise stirred up as many tempers as it calmed. Thomas Jefferson referred to this crisis as a "firebell in the night," alerting the nation to a mounting problem of such proportions that further cataclysms would surely follow. Jefferson was "filled with terror," he told a friend. With the Missouri Compromise, the issue of slavery was "hushed, indeed . . . for the moment," but Jefferson believed this to be at best a "reprieve, not the final sentence." In fact, the passions elicited by the debate over Missouri struck Jefferson like the death "knell of the Union."[2]

Because the United States was expanding, it had to deal time after time with this question of whether slavery would also be allowed to expand. Had there been no new territory available, maybe North and South could have settled into their own ways, ignoring each other's differences. The Louisiana Purchase, the lands gained in the Mexican War, the smaller Gadsden Purchase in 1853 (which added more land in the Southwest), and the acquisition of Oregon were like dry tinder thrown onto a smoldering heap. Northerners were outraged at the immorality of slavery; Southerners were outraged at hypocritical Northerners who denounced slavery while still making money from the slave trade and slave-grown cotton. Northerners feared that black people would be allowed to move into the West where racist Northern whites did not want them either as neighbors or as competition for jobs; Southerners feared that Northerners would not let slave culture spread.

Until the 1850s, most members of Congress devoted themselves to keeping the nation calm and together. Compromise followed compromise. Some citizens, however, who could follow their own impulses without regard for getting reelected, came up with a solution that avoided the whole issue of the spread of slavery in the United States. In 1816, the American Colonization Society was organized, its goal to raise money for sending "the Free People of Colour" "back" to Africa, where of course next to none of them had been born. This exodus of freed, unwanted American-Africans founded the nation of Liberia, with its capital, Monrovia, named after President James Monroe. Until colonial Liberia declared independence in 1847, about 10,000 African-Americans were sent under this scheme, a tiny number in comparison to the nearly 2 million slaves kept in Southern bondage by 1820. Colonization could not work because there was not enough money, ships, or consensus to transport 2 million people to Africa from the United States. The plan, however, had been acceptable to people in the North and South. It recognized that slavery was not right, but its goal entailed the separation of the races, which appealed to a majority of white Americans. One speaker at the Colonization Society's eleventh annual meeting claimed that the work being done was "the greatest deed that humanity ever performed."[3] Colonization was, at its base, inherently racist. It was not meant to teach white people that black men and women were their equals. Colonization could get whites to act in a new way (freeing their slaves and sending them far away), but it did not aim to change how whites felt or what they believed (that white was better than black).

North and South Go Their Separate Ways

In the two decades before the Civil War, trains, the telegraph, droves of immigrants, factories, and growing cities wrenched society out of its agrarian idyll. Although most of the population continued to live in tiny towns and on farms throughout the whole of the 1800s, the balance was shifting to an urban order, especially in the North. The personal relationships of village life scattered into the anonymity of new faces crowded together in the taverns, outdoor markets, and streets of New York and Philadelphia, Boston and Providence.

Sports had long been a pastime, but like so much else, competitions had been local. Strands of wool woven around cork had served as a ball for local boys who played "base ball" with few rules in weedy fields or empty city lots. But by the late 1850s, teams from different cities competed in front of large crowds trucked in on local railroad lines. Even more wondrously, news of the games zipped along a different kind of line—telegraph wires. By 1853 there were 23,000 miles of wire transmitting messages using Samuel Morse's code, first tapped out commercially between Washington, DC, and Baltimore in 1844. Men gathered in alehouses and cheered their champions on to glory with each click and clack of the telegraph. Agreed-upon rules for boxing and baseball circulated in the 1820s and were codified during the 1850s, allowing the matches to be nationalized. In fact, the intercity rivalries provided a start for what became the National League, established in 1876. Only seven years before that, the Cincinnati Red Stockings became the first professional team—the first to pay all the players a salary. Rules and salaries for professional men were becoming the hallmarks of urban living, even for grown men who used a stick to hit a ball and run in semicircles on a grassy field. Victorian-era reformers and managers used rules to tame what they considered the dangerous immorality and rude barbarity of the "lower sorts," like the Irish habit of "grogging," or drinking on the job. Daytime nips on the bottle no longer seemed conducive to productivity in the ordered, controlled factory environments rising in the North.

From 1845 to 1855, more than 1 million Irish left the potato blight and famine and emigrated to America. A few headed inland, but most stayed near the coast—working on railroads and canals and disturbing many native-born Americans who shivered at the thought of so many Catholics flooding their Protestant paradise. Many Irish had been sympathetic to the cause of America's black people while still at home in Ireland. England had treated the Irish as an underclass for 300 years, so the Irish could sympathize with the plight of another oppressed group. Once in the United States, however, Irishmen in the South were given the most dangerous jobs because slave owners had more invested in the skin of a slave than in the day wages of "Irish niggers," as they were sometimes called. And Irishmen and African-Americans competed for jobs as teamsters and dockworkers in the North. The Irish began to accentuate their own whiteness by degrading black people. As the Irish acculturated, many adopted the prevailing racist attitudes and beliefs of the country they had moved to.[4]

Politics kept the Union together and drove it apart. The Whig and Democratic parties were national, each having voters in the North and South, preventing the two halves from naturally drifting apart. Although the Whigs represented a more typically northern agenda—high taxes on incoming foreign items, government money for roads and canals—there were Southerners with the same interests. The Democratic Party tended to favor states' rights, in particular leaving the regulation of slavery up to each individual state. The Irish became a major political constituency that the Jacksonian Democrats and the Whigs courted. The Whigs sided more often than not with anti-immigration nativists, like the short-lived Know-Nothing Party of the 1850s, which tried to pass laws preventing immigrants (especially the Irish Catholics) from achieving citizenship for up to twenty years after landing. This pushed many Irish to embrace the Democrats instead, the party that also represented the pro-slavery argument. In cities like New York, Democratic Party functionaries greeted bewildered Irish immigrants when they arrived and offered jobs and housing in return for political support. A lasting political link between Southern Democrats and Northern Democrats who sympathized with the South was strengthened through this inclusion of the Irish into their party. This gravitation of interests was called the "slave power" by scared contemporaries, and the slave power invigorated itself with fresh votes in the shape of the Democrats as long as that party remained national in scope.

The cultures of the North and South had been different for 200 years, and time amplified those differences. Wage labor spread in the North beginning in the first decades of the 1800s, as small factories in Waltham, Lowell, and other towns dotted the rivers of Massachusetts. For the first time in American history, women left the home *not* to get married, serve as a maid, or live with a relative, but to work outside of the "domestic sphere." By itself this heralded a major shift in notions about a proper society. Could these women's virtue be shielded from vice and corruption? The South did not often ask itself such questions about its white women because most Southern white women lived with few advantages other than their skin color. Work habits were oriented to age-old rhythms of child rearing and farm work. Only about 5 percent of all Southern white women lived on large plantations. They lived the myth: personal servants, tutoring in the classics, lessons in music and etiquette. The South did have its major cities—Savannah, Charleston, and New Orleans—but overall the South was an agrarian, rural place.

As the 1800s progressed, the North's population outpaced the South's, leading to a gradual Northern domination of the House of Representatives. Although the three-fifths clause in the Constitution had given the South an advantage for decades in the number of representatives sent to Washington, DC, enabling Jefferson to win the presidency in 1800 and Missouri to enter the Union as a slave state, population expansion in the North made up the difference by the 1830s. Southerners worried that a Northern-dominated, Whig Congress might legislate against slavery, and their fears were stoked by a loose coalition of abolitionists, dedicated to removing the stain of slavery from the United States.

In fact, the first woman in the United States to directly address a state legislature was Angelina Grimké, who in 1838 riveted the packed Massachusetts legislature with her thoughts on the errors of slavery. Locals crammed the hall so full that it seemed the balcony might collapse. Grimké remembered thinking that by breaking out of the domestic sphere and speaking publicly on the dreaded slave question, "We Abolition Women are turning the world upside down."[5] A month later, at Pennsylvania Hall in Philadelphia, an enraged crowd made so much hubbub the speakers could barely be heard. Grimké calmly announced, "As a southerner I feel that it is my duty to stand up here tonight and bear testimony against slavery. I have seen it . . . I know that it has horrors that can never be described." As rocks crashed through the windows of the brand-new building, she continued speaking, undisturbed as the "mobocratic spirit" escalated. "What is a mob?" she asked. "What would the breaking of every window be? What would the leveling of this hall be? Any evidence that we are wrong, or that slavery is a good and wholesome institution?"[6] Grimké's lecturing for the American Anti-Slavery Society worked like a lightning rod for public opinion. Southerners and Democrats vilified her as a disturber of the peace and a perverter of women's delicate modesty. Yet she was an artful speaker. In 1838 Grimké married Theodore Weld, a prominent abolitionist in his own right, and thereby demonstrated that a strong public woman could also be a wife. She removed herself from the public eye but continued to advocate in writing for the sake of slaves.

Abolitionists like Angelina Grimké targeted the South, gradually driving a deep wedge between the slave states and the free. The national political parties could hold the nation together only so long as each party represented people from both sides. Abolitionists inspired new agendas and hence new political parties—like the Free-Soil Party and the Republicans—that imbibed some of the spirit of the abolitionists: opposition to slavery.

Abolitionists in Society: William Lloyd Garrison

It may be easier to change what people do than to change what they believe. A history of opposition to slavery stretched back to colonial days, but the movement gained new energy in the 1830s when a cadre of social visionaries began to make a noticeable difference in American culture and society: the abolitionists—those men and women who lectured, wrote, preached, and suffered, trying to convince the nation to end slavery immediately. People like William Lloyd Garrison, Angelina and Sarah Grimké, Frederick Douglass, John Brown, Harriet Beecher Stowe, and Sojourner Truth dedicated themselves to forcing the issue into the public consciousness. Their efforts contributed significantly to causing the Civil War and hence to ending slavery. They did not, however, find a way to cure racism. In fact, many people opposed to the "peculiar institution" disliked slavery and black people at the same time. Many people opposed to the "peculiar institution" did not like abolitionists, either.

247

Many social reform crusades sprouted in early nineteenth-century America. Preachers had fertilized the soil. Abolition was only one kind of reform, and at first an unsavory one that drew more hostility than praise. The first well-known abolitionist was William Lloyd Garrison, a poor dreamer who believed it was God's will that whites, blacks, men, and women should share the earth as equals. Garrison changed the language of emancipation in the nation by hurling insults and demands at the South, demanding immediate freedom for all chattel slaves. To most people, North and South, Garrison was dangerous, unhinged, an anarchistic revolutionary bent on sacrificing peace, order, and prosperity for an ideal few believed in.

Other types of social crusaders inspired more widespread support. Fired by ministers like Charles Finney and his exhortations to battle sin with good deeds, temperance workers set out to replace wine with water. Some wealthy patrons of preacher-inspired philanthropy, like the New York merchant brothers Lewis and Arthur Tappan, funded both abolitionists and temperance workers. The Tappan brothers fell under the spell of Charles Finney and spent generously, funding religious colleges where Finney's disciples could be trained to spread the gospel and improve American society. Gradual emancipation—the slow and methodical freeing of slaves over a long period of time—received general support throughout the United States (even in the South up until the 1830s).

In 1831, at the age of twenty-six, William Lloyd Garrison published the first issue of his own newspaper, *The Liberator*, dedicated entirely to abolition. He had recently moved to Boston after having been jailed in Baltimore, Maryland, for making libelous remarks in an antislavery newspaper. Garrison was a convinced Baptist, steeped in the reform-minded theology of his era. He had little money, but he did find patrons for his cause, in particular Lewis and Arthur Tappan, who underwrote his newspaper schemes with cash. In the 1820s, Garrison had joined the American Colonization Society (ACS), but in 1829, he exhibited more purely abolitionist intentions at an ACS meeting in Boston, where he lectured his fellow members on their misguided approach. A minute into his speech, Garrison argued, "a very large proportion of our colored population were born on our soil, and are therefore entitled to all the privileges of American citizens. This is their country by birth, not by adoption." It was time, he insisted, to turn the society's Christian charity toward home, toward "our own degraded countrymen." Members of the ACS included James Monroe, Francis Scott Key, and Andrew Jackson, living patriotic icons. Garrison had grown tired of their tinny trumpet blowing on Independence Day: "I am sick of our unmeaning declamation in praise of liberty and equality; of our hypocritical cant about the unalienable rights of man."[7] Early solutions to America's racial problems focused on getting black people to leave the country permanently. Slave owners feared retribution from emancipated African-Americans, and most white people in the South thought of black people as inferior, unfit for civilization. Many Northern whites did not want to compete with black people for jobs, and plain race hatred ran deep in both North and South. Garrison annoyed them all, intentionally.

By 1831, Garrison broke from the ACS and advocated for complete, immediate emancipation of all slaves: the very definition of abolition. In the first issue of *The Liberator*, Garrison explained his new principles and goals. He would work out of New England, not because it might be safer than the South or more receptive to his message, but quite the opposite. In New England, Garrison said, he "found contempt more bitter, opposition more active, detraction more relentless, prejudice more stubborn, and apathy more frozen, than among slave owners themselves."[8] Racism and discrimination flourished in the North where white citizens could pride themselves on not actually owning slaves. However, whites rarely treated African-Americans with respect or equality.

In 1831 in Canterbury, Connecticut, a young Quaker teacher named Prudence Crandall opened an elite school for wealthy children, all of them white. Before long, Sarah Harris—an African-American woman—asked for admittance. Knowing the risk she was taking, Crandall accepted Harris into the school. This open interracial mixing brought the folk of Canterbury to the school building, where they poisoned the well with feces, smashed the windows, threw chicken heads at the students, and one night entered the building and destroyed everything to be found downstairs, while terrified girls huddled upstairs. Doctors and pharmacists refused to offer their services when needed, and the state legislature soon passed a law making it illegal to teach out-of-state black children, whom Crandall had invited and admitted to the school after neighboring whites withdrew their children. Prudence Crandall was arrested and bailed out of jail only after being put into the same cell a murderer had recently vacated. These were the conditions that Garrison also faced when he took up the torch of his new cause.[9]

On one antislavery tour of New England in 1835, a thousand-man mob descended on the balding, bespectacled Garrison at a meeting of the Boston Female Antislavery Society. At the urging of Boston's mayor, Garrison sneaked out a back window, but the mob spotted him. The only way to save the abolitionist leader was to throw him in jail for the night. The crowd certainly had tar and feathers in mind, if not the hangman's noose. By 1838, Garrison had made himself into a fringe element by declaring that American churches and the government were both guilty of supporting slavery. In his own colorful wording, he charged "the compact which exists between the North and the South is a covenant with death and an agreement with hell—involving both parties in atrocious criminality."[10] In 1854, he publicly burned a copy of the Constitution. While most people thought him crazed, Garrison could not be ignored and neither could the cause of African-American freedom.

The Liberator never had a big subscription list, no more than 1,400 by 1834, most of the subscribers African-American—indicative of the spotty support Garrison gained in white circles. The newpaper's delivery was semilegally stopped throughout the South by the postmaster of the United States. Southerners fatuously blamed Nat Turner's 1831 rebellion on Garrison's editorials, although not a single subscription was held in Virginia. Abolition as a cause and as a means to emancipating black people was not popular anywhere at first. As late as 1851 the *New York Times* referred to the "craziness of Garrison."[11] Slaves were property, worth literally billions of dollars, and Americans saw property as the basis for liberty. By demolishing slavery in an instant, Garrison would also throw away property and liberty—so his detractors argued. To traditionalists, he seemed likely to overturn every precious scrap of decency in the nation: property, liberty, the social divides between white and black, and the purity of women by allowing them to speak and lecture to mixed-sex audiences.

As one slave owner from Georgia wrote in a letter that Garrison then published, "With the utmost astonishment and indignation, sir, I have read one of the late numbers of this most slanderous and villanous publication." The man thought Garrison was "absolutely destitute of every patriotic principle . . . to disseminate doctrines and principles so entirely at variance with the peace, happiness and prosperity, nay the very existence of the Republic." This indignant Georgian, signing off as "A Slaveholder," decided that since Garrison evidently had thought these policies out clearly, his "motives, then, must be unholy, illegal, unjustifiable . . . to destroy the peace and harmony of the country."[12]

That a southern slaveholder deemed Garrison "unholy" was no surprise. It did not take long, however, before the emerging abolition movement in the North split and grew into hundreds of different chapters and organizations. The splitting often reflected the need for more localized efforts than the American Anti-Slavery Society, founded in 1833 and centered in New York, could provide or direct. The appearance of new organizations owed something to Garrison's extreme advocacy of an immediate end to slavery and his inclusion of women in the movement. And as women and blacks began to take prominent roles in the abolition movement, some northern whites became uncomfortable, not wanting to associate publicly or professionally with African-Americans. In the long campaign by which legal slavery was slowly checked in the United States, African-Americans were active participants, not meek, browbeaten stereotypes waiting for help from empowered white friends. The same can be said for women. Prudence Crandall did not hang back in the shadows, and neither did Angelina and Sarah Grimké.

The Grimké Sisters and the Seneca Falls Convention

The Grimké sisters were from South Carolina, daughters of slave-holding privilege, but they wanted none of it. When only four years old, Sarah witnessed one of the family slaves being whipped. Later that day she tried to catch a boat to the North, where she would never have to see such scenes again. In the 1820s, both sisters stepped out of one culture and into another when they moved to Philadelphia, where they soon became prominent abolitionists. The Grimké women abhorred the Southern social system because it had become dominated by an allegiance to white supremacy. While Southern whites prided themselves on a chivalrous myth, all the cotton blossoms in Dixie could not hide the truth: black people suffered at the discretion of white masters, regardless of the homey phrases most slave owners used to describe their white-and-black "families." William Lloyd Garrison had the credibility of an outraged Christian. The Grimkés had the credibility of Southerners who knew firsthand what they were talking about.

In 1835, the American Anti-Slavery Society flooded the South with pamphlets that denounced slavery. It also flooded Congress with petitions containing hundreds of thousands of signatures, most of them collected by abolitionist women going door-to-door. (In response, a Louisiana "vigilance committee" posted a $50,000 reward for the capture—dead or alive—of Arthur Tappan, president of the American Anti-Slavery Society.[13]) The following year, in direct reaction to anti-slavery sentiments and petitions that reached all the way to Congress, the South's political leaders forced through Congress a gag rule, which lasted until 1844, forbidding the reading of any petition pertaining to abolition. Through a coalition of Southern and Northern Jacksonian Democrats, Congress itself was suppressing the U.S. citizen's constitutional right to petition Congress.

Recognizing, therefore, the futility of appealing to Congress, in 1836 Sarah Grimké wrote "An Epistle to the Clergy of the Southern States." Addressing the South's moral leaders in their own language, through biblical interpretation, she wrote, "under the Jewish dispensation . . . 'he that stealeth a man and selleth him or if he be found in his hand, he shall surely be put to death.'" With a biblical injunction against slavery established, she pointed out the divine retribution that was sure to follow a continued flouting of God's law: "If [God's] law were carried into effect now . . . would he not instantly commission his most tremendous thunderbolts to strike from existence those who are thus trampling upon his laws, thus defacing his image?"[14] Such Christian

251

arguments, however, proved ineffective. For example, the Southern Baptist Convention first met in 1845 to assert its commitment to slavery.

While fighting for the rights of African-Americans, abolitionist women often battled for their own rights as well. A World Anti-Slavery Convention was held in England in 1840. A number of American reformers attended, including Elizabeth Cady Stanton and Lucretia Mott, who met on the trip. Hypocrisy hit them in the face. While there to support the rights of black people, male attendees prevented women from serving as delegates to the convention. Garrison, arriving late, refused his seat as a show of solidarity with the women, who sat segregated, behind a curtain. Mott reported that one male delegate "thought Women constitutionally unfit for public or business meetings."[15] Returning to the States, Stanton and Mott worked out a plan to hold a woman's rights convention, which took place at Seneca Falls, New York, in 1848. More women than men attended, and Stanton not only insisted that "all men and women are created equal," but furthermore demanded that women should be given the vote. Stanton's call for female suffrage was even more ludicrous to her contemporaries (including other women) than Garrison's suggestion that white and black were equal.

In the "Declaration of Sentiments," published as a pamphlet, Mott and Stanton declared, "the history of mankind is a history of repeated injuries and usurpations on the part of man toward woman, having in direct object the establishment of an absolute tyranny over her." They went on to say, "He has compelled her to submit to laws, in the formation of which she had no voice. . . . He has withheld from her rights which are given to the most ignorant and degraded men—both natives and foreigners."[16] Most men were no more pleased to read these statements than were slave owners pleased to read Garrison's tirades. One feather-ruffled newspaper, the *Oneida Whig*, blurted out in response, "Was there ever such a dreadful revolt?" Written, one would assume, by a man, the startled *Whig* article continued: "The [Seneca Falls Convention] is the most shocking and unnatural incident ever recorded in the history of womanity [*sic*]. If our ladies will insist on voting and legislating, where, gentlemen, will be our dinners and our elbows? where our domestic firesides and the holes in our stockings?"[17] Social incredulity and shock were often enough to keep mid–nineteenth-century feminists from getting very far. The women of 1848 knew this. Elizabeth Cady Stanton and Lucretia Mott wrote, "in entering upon the great work before us, we anticipate no small amount of misconception, misrepresentation, and ridicule."[18]

Frederick Douglass and Sojourner Truth

The Garrisons and Grimkés of America served their purpose with the advantage of light skin giving them access to most venues in the North. Black abo-

252

litionists like Frederick Douglass and Sojourner Truth were living proof in the North that slaves were real people who suffered and that African-Americans contained the same moral, intellectual, and general human potential as people of any other "race."

Frederick Douglass was born probably in 1818 in Maryland. He spent his first six years in a one-room cabin under the care of his grandmother, also a slave. His grandmother lived more or less autonomously, raising her owner's slave children a few miles away from his main plantation mansion. Douglass's grandmother walked him to the plantation when he was six and left him there. For the next fourteen years, Douglass toiled over mule teams, suffered the insults of tongue and lash, and worked in Baltimore as a caulker for a ship builder, nearly losing his life to a group of jealous ship carpenters who disliked his presence among them as an apprentice "damned nigger" caulker. He convinced one of the two brothers who owned him to allow him to live independently in return for whatever money he could earn. Then Douglass set himself free by dressing in sailor's clothes and using another black man's free papers to escape to Philadelphia. He soon went to New York, where he met Garrison and other leading abolitionists. With a handsome face and a fine mind, Frederick Douglass was well suited to his task—working in public for the abolition of slavery.

Douglass published two autobiographies prior to the Civil War, edited his own newspaper, the *North Star*, and toured the country speaking and lecturing. In 1852, he spoke in his hometown at the Rochester Ladies' Anti-Slavery Society meeting. Douglass reminded his audience, as he always did in both print and speech, "the distance between this platform and the slave plantation, from which I escaped, is considerable." He explained that for millions of Americans, July 4 was not a day of celebration. "I am not," he said, "included within the pale of this glorious anniversary! Your high independence only reveals the immeasurable distance between us. The blessings in which you, this day, rejoice, are not enjoyed in common." It was no surprise, then, that his voice might tremble and quake. "Oppression," he said, "makes a wise man mad." Echoing the words of Angelina Grimké and William Garrison before him, Douglass blasted away at the church for its role in maintaining slavery: "the church of this country is not only indifferent to the wrongs of the slave, it actually takes sides with the oppressors. It has made itself the bulwark of American slavery, and the shield of American slave-hunters." The women in his audience may have read Amelia Bloomer's newspaper, *The Lily*, published in nearby Seneca Falls, and even considered wearing the new skirt-pants she advocated, but almost all would have been revolutionaries only up to a point. Douglass could not shy away from the truth, however, so he risked losing his audience in the hope he could teach them something essential. He pointed to "scattered" religious exceptions, like the abolitionist minister Henry

Ward Beecher. Otherwise, the "existence of slavery in this country brands your republicanism as a sham, your humanity as a base pretence, and your Christianity as a lie." Since the church had betrayed blacks for generations, Douglass believed the best hope for abolition resided in the Constitution because it contained "principles and purposes, entirely hostile to the existence of slavery."[19] In each critique—first of practiced religion and then of the Constitution—Douglass indicted what was wrong but left his listeners with a sense of purpose. Hope remained. A few preachers advocated abolition as a Godly cause, and the word "slavery" was nowhere in the Constitution, even though it was implied in a few key roundabout phrases.

Douglass and William Lloyd Garrison parted ways during the 1840s—partly due to Garrison's condemnation of the Constitution "dripping as it is with blood." Garrison called it a pro-slavery document and thought that either it should be rewritten or the Northern states should secede from the Union. (When the Southern states actually seceded in 1860–1861, Garrison wanted to let them go. He figured that slaves could then escape to a free nation, from which they could not be extradited. He also thought that international pressure would force the Confederacy to end slavery.) Garrison wanted no part of politics and no part of violence. However, Douglass endorsed violence in the cause of abolition and in 1851 proposed that politics was a necessary arena for abolitionists. Douglass himself did not kill for freedom, but he did take physical action by administering the regional Underground Railroad and by risking his life every time he traveled. Some days when Douglass arrived at his newspaper office, fugitive slaves were sitting on the steps waiting for him to help them escape to nearby Canada.

Though Douglass escaped punishment, other abolitionists had been mobbed and killed already. On November 7, 1837, thirty-five-year-old Elijah Lovejoy died while trying to defend his fourth printing press from a mob—three had already been demolished. As the editor for the *Alton Observer*, he had come out in direct opposition to slavery, an unwelcome development in Alton, Illinois, where many citizens either supported slavery, disliked black people, or at least wanted to keep radical politics out of their domain. Now, under poor cover of night along an Illinois bank of the Mississippi River, Lovejoy and some friends moved the printing press into a warehouse, barely getting it away from stone-throwing, torch-wielding pro-slavery men. A mob fired rifles through the windows, and then a boy climbed a ladder, blazing torch in hand, intending to burn the warehouse down. Lovejoy sneaked outside and toppled the ladder. Once again the ladder went up. Once again Lovejoy sneaked outside, but this time he was shot five times and died moments later. The printing press was shattered and scattered into the river. Lovejoy's murder and martyrdom aroused great passion in the abolition movement, inspiring abolitionists to declaim the right to freedom of the press, even while Southern legislatures sent memos to their Northern counterparts requesting that all writings likely to stir up slave discontent be banned.

Nineteenth-century Americans generally regarded women as the protectors of virtue, the moral instructors of the next generation. This status gave female abolitionists a good chance to stir an audience's sympathy. Whose heart stays cold when told by a woman that she had to give breast milk to other people's babies before her own children could suckle? Whose heart stays cold when told by a woman that her children were torn from her? Isabella—born a slave rich in color in 1799—changed her name to Sojourner Truth in 1843, a testament to the two things she did best: travel and truth-tell. Truth became famous after a series of newspaper articles depicted her assertive testimony in front of a mixed-sex audience in 1851 at the Women's Rights Convention in Akron, Ohio, where she told of having thirteen children "and seen 'em mos' all sold off to slavery, and when I cried out with my mother's grief, none but Jesus heard me!"[20]

As the leader of the convention, Frances Dana Gage, described the uproar twelve years later: "The leaders of the movement trembled upon seeing a tall, gaunt black woman in a gray dress and white turban, surmounted with an uncouth sunbonnet, march deliberately into the church, walk with the air of a queen up the aisle, and take her seat upon the pulpit steps. A buzz of disapprobation was heard all over the house . . . 'An abolition affair!' 'Woman's rights and niggers!' . . . 'Go it, darkey!'"[21]

The next day, as captured in a newspaper article, six-foot-tall Sojourner Truth strode again to the front of the audience and declaimed, "I am a woman's rights. I have as much muscle as any man, and can do as much work as any man. I have plowed and reaped and husked and chopped and mowed, and can any man do more than that?" She added, "why children, if you have woman's rights, give it to her and you will feel better." Truth knew rightly enough that men clung to tradition and feared the world changing in front of them: "But man is in a tight place. The poor slave is on him, woman is coming on him, he is surely between a hawk and a buzzard."[22] Twelve years later, Frances Gage explained just how well Sojourner Truth could do her work. "I have never in my life seen," Gage reminisced, "anything like the magical influence that subdued the mobbish spirit of the day, and turned the sneers and jeers of an excited crowd into notes of respect and admiration."[23] This kind of "magical influence" was precisely what Southerners aimed to stop.

The Southern Response to Abolition

Methods of suppressing abolitionists involved three tactical responses—verbal, legal, and physical. Such methods coincided with a vigorous attempt by

Southerners to expand the borders of slavery into the West above the latitude line of 36°30' set by the Missouri Compromise of 1820. The more vocal and numerous the abolitionists became, the more defensive Southerners became. After all, abolitionists were attacking the foundations of Southern social beliefs. Slavery had long been thought questionable, but now slaveholders themselves were being denounced as immoral wretches. So slaveholders responded by defending slavery as a positive good. The most famous defender of all was George Fitzhugh. In *Sociology for the South*, Fitzhugh claimed, "the Negro" was "but a grown up child, and must be governed as a child." The method of governance was, obviously, slavery. According to Fitzhugh, this benevolent parenting of blacks had, in fact, done wonders. "The negro slaves of the South," Fitzhugh claimed, "are the happiest, and, in some sense, the freest people in the world."[24] Fitzhugh's tap dance did not convince his abolitionist foes to lay down their pens, smash their presses, and buy fields full of slaves. No one in the South really expected such results, but between suppression of abolitionist literature and the dissemination of perspectives like Fitzhugh's, white Southern society further embraced its culture. While the South's apologists painted slavery in rosy pastels, its politicians used their leverage during the 1850s to strengthen existing national slave laws.

California entered the Union in 1850 as part of a package of laws commonly known as the Compromise of 1850. The able old negotiator, Henry Clay of Kentucky, orchestrated the deal—his parting act. He had already patched together the Missouri Compromise thirty years earlier. As part of the Compromise of 1850, Northern congressmen, now influenced by twenty years of abolitionist lectures and leaflets, stopped the slave trade in Washington, DC, but acquiesced to the theoretical expansion of slavery into New Mexico and Utah—both of which had proslavery constitutions but no more than a few slaves. Along with other rewards, Southerners got a fresh Fugitive Slave Act, one of the most divisive laws ever passed in the United States. It allowed slave owners to hire bounty hunters to travel into Northern states to retrieve runaways. Furthermore, in any contested case, the presiding commissioner—empowered with the authority of a judge—would receive five dollars for deciding in favor of the accused runaway and ten dollars for deciding in favor of the bounty hunter. In other words, commissioners would make twice as much to send a black woman back into bondage as to keep her free. The new law provided a tempting inducement for slave catchers to kidnap free African-Americans as well as catch runaway slaves. The Fugitive Slave Act seemed preliminary to slave owners imposing slavery in free territory. The North's fear of an unleashed "slave power" heightened in 1854 when Senator Stephen Douglas of Illinois succeeded in demolishing the Missouri Compromise of 1820. According to his Kansas-Nebraska Act, the territories of Kansas and Nebraska would be separated, and their citizens would decide whether or not to legalize slavery, a principle known as "popular sovereignty." The specter of slavery crept north, and in a few sensationalized cases, blacks were torn from their homes and shipped "down the river" in chains.

The best-known case of a former slave being dragged back to the South occurred right after passage of the Kansas-Nebraska Act. After escaping from Virginia, Anthony Burns was working in a clothing store in Boston. Walking home from work on May 24, 1854, he was arrested and taken to prison, pending his hearing before a commissioner. The town of Boston and surrounding communities rallied to Burns, filling the street with thousands of protesters demanding his release. Leading citizens in Boston offered to pay Burns's owner $1,200—more than Burns's market value as a slave—but the federal government prevented the transaction because President Franklin Pierce wanted to show his Southern supporters that he would uphold a federal law. Troops took Burns to a ship and sent him back to Virginia. Although Northern friends later purchased his freedom, Anthony Burns's forced return to slavery by the federal government itself provided abolitionists with a poignant example of slavery's insidious reach. States throughout the North passed personal liberty laws that gummed up the process for bounty hunters and fugitive slave commissioners. The Northern states were fighting back against a federal law in a contest divided along clean, sectional lines: North versus South. Henry David Thoreau, who nearly a decade earlier had advocated nonviolent resistance against the Mexican War, now argued for violent resistance against a government that so nakedly supported slavery. In his journal, he wrote that the Burns trial was really "the trial of Massachusetts. Every moment that she hesitates to set this man free, she is convicted." Furthermore, Thoreau railed that rather than silently acceding to the federal government's manhandling of Anthony Burns, he would "touch a match to blow up earth and hell together. As I love my life," Thoreau concluded, "I would side with the Light and let the Dark Earth roll from under me, calling my mother and my brother to follow me."[25]

When Garrison first published the *Liberator* in 1831, abolitionists could be counted on fingers and toes. Their ranks had swelled into the hundreds of thousands by the 1850s. This popularity resulted from effective organizing, an uplifting cause, and persuasive spokespeople. There had always been more people in favor of slow emancipation than outright abolition. However, the two interests found a political meeting point in 1848 with the creation of the short-lived Free-Soil Party, which lasted from 1848 to 1852. Though unable to elect its candidate—former president Martin Van Buren—the Free-Soil Party brought together people who disliked slavery purely and simply with those who feared its spread into the Northwest on socioeconomic grounds. Where went slavery, there went more black people and more competition for labor and wages. The Free-Soil Party's complete opposition to the expansion of slavery attracted voters from the Democratic Party and set the conditions for a remaking of the political map with the creation of the Republican Party in 1854. The Republicans fielded western explorer John C. Frémont for president in 1856, followed only four years later by Abraham Lincoln. Abolitionists, gradual emancipationists, and now many Republicans accused the federal government of supporting slavery, and that is just what the federal government seemed to be doing.

In 1857, the Supreme Court made a crucial ruling in *Dred Scott v. Sanford.* Dred Scott was a slave who had been taken north into Illinois, a free state, and then into the free territory of Wisconsin. After his owner died, Scott appealed for freedom on the basis that a person simply could not be a slave after prolonged habitation in a free state or territory. The Supreme Court asked, "Can a negro, whose ancestors were imported into this country, and sold as slaves, become a member of the political community formed and brought into existence by the Constitution of the United States, and as such become entitled to all the rights, and privileges, and immunities, guarantied by that instrument to the citizen?" The Court, ruling seven to two, answered no. The majority opinion was that "we think [Negroes] are not [citizens], and that they are not included, and were not intended to be included, under the word 'citizens' in the Constitution."[26] In effect, slavery could go into Northern territories by virtue of the Constitution itself, regardless of any congressional agreements to the contrary. The slave power was having its way.

The *Dred Scott* decision made the Republican Party viable. Its central platform was that slavery must be prevented from moving into the territories. *Dred Scott* repudiated the widely held Northern "free soil, free labor" sentiment and sent Democratic voters into the Republican camp. The war of words intensified. No one became a better advocate for Republican theory than Abraham Lincoln. This rail-thin, log-cabin lawyer from Illinois joined the Republican Party in 1856, after having served a brief spell in the U.S. House of Representatives. In 1858, Lincoln ran for a U.S. Senate seat against the Democrat Stephen Douglas, the "Little Giant," a portly political lion. The two men toured Illinois in a series of debates, and although the relatively unknown Lincoln lost the election to Douglas, Lincoln placed his name into national ledgers and newspapers. Most memorably, Lincoln said, "'A house divided against itself cannot stand.' I believe this government cannot endure, permanently half slave and half free ... It will become all one thing, or all the other."[27]

Since 1831, much more ink than blood had been spilled in the quest to find an answer to the slavery dilemma. John Brown did his utmost to alter the ink-blood balance. A New England abolitionist who threw his body where other activists threw only their opinions, Brown and five sons moved to Kansas in 1855, part of the Northern effort to overwhelm the territory with enough free-soil voters that slavery would be ruled out of the state constitution by ballots. But proslavery ruffians from Missouri leaped the state boundary to harass and intimidate antislavery settlers, voting illegally and burning Lawrence, the seat of the antislavery movement. Brown, his sons, and a few partisans retaliated two days later by killing five proslavery settlers. News of the massacre hit the nation's newspapers, giving Brown fame and notoriety. This was the first of Brown's two acts. The second would be bolder and one of the last sparks to ignite the Civil War.

Abraham Lincoln's and Sojourner Truth's oratories, Garrison's and Douglass's newspaper diatribes, and various congressmen's speeches enflamed the sectional crisis. Harriet Beecher Stowe made a popular-culture appeal to the antislavery feeling in America when she began publishing magazine installments of *Uncle Tom's Cabin*, a stark portrayal of slavery. Stowe had no firsthand experience of slavery, but she had read the literature and listened to lectures by Douglass and other abolitionists. Her imagination fired by their images, Stowe depicted a whip-wielding owner, Simon Legree; an obedient slave, Uncle Tom; and a host of other heart-yanking characters. In the pages of Stowe's novel, white men did whatever they wanted to black women, and the shame burned hot across the nation. The book sold about 300,000 copies in 1852 when it was released as a single volume. President Lincoln reportedly told Harriet Stowe, upon meeting her early in the war, "So you're the little woman who wrote the book that made this great war."[28] Her contribution was surpassed by few people, and John Brown may have been one of the few.

White Southerners feared two things most of all: the federal government's interference with their business and slave insurrections. Nat Turner's 1831 rebellion was the last frightening reminder of what slaves could do when given the opportunity. John Brown's Kansas raids, though led by a wiry white man, sounded the same alarm bells that had rung through the Cotton Kingdom in 1831. Brown eventually left Kansas and traveled through New England, gathering money and able-bodied men for his next adventure: a planned raid on the federal arsenal at Harpers Ferry, Virginia. Brown wanted to grab weapons and draw the area's slaves to his banner. Then he and the emancipated warriors would ride through the hills, helping more slaves to free themselves. Though without money of his own, Brown had reputation and he knew the leading abolitionists, including Frederick Douglass. Brown invited Douglass for a last meeting to convince the ex-slave to join in the attack, but Douglass knew it could lead only to the grave. On October 16, 1859, Brown and eighteen men took the arsenal at Harpers Ferry. The act was both a dismal failure and his greatest success.

No slaves in the area volunteered to join his team (probably because he had failed to let them know he was coming), and within hours Brown and his men were surrounded by militia and federal troops led by a gifted colonel, Robert E. Lee. A few men escaped, two of Brown's sons were killed, and he was wounded and captured. First hated by his captors, Brown soon earned their respect for his convictions, but he set a morbid fear deep in their bones: the North would respect no boundaries in its war on Southern rights. Not unlike Lincoln's previous suggestion that "a house divided against itself cannot stand," Brown made his own prediction. On his way to meet the hangman's noose on December 2, a month after his trial began, he passed along a note to one of his jailers that said he was "certain that the crimes of this guilty land will never be purged away but with blood."[29] Brown's own snapped neck helped make the vision true.

The final step into disunion took only two more things: Abraham Lincoln's election to the presidency by Northern voters only (his name was not on Southern ballots at all), and the decision of South Carolina in December 1860 to secede from the nation, immediately followed by other Deep South states. When we look backward through history, everything seems inevitable since we know it has already happened. But people in the forward flow of time cannot see into the future. No one in 1855, for example, could have said with certainty what would happen after the election of 1860. Almost nobody in the nation knew who Abraham Lincoln was in 1855. But a series of events dating from his birth illuminate why civil war erupted.

Slavery's inclusion in the Constitution in 1787 ensured that slavery would remain a source of controversy. The emancipation of Northern slaves over a fifty-year period further separated the cultures of the North and the South. The drift into Northern wage labor and Southern slave labor was part of other changes: more capital investment in the North, leading to more factories and railroads; more foreign immigration into the North, where there was also an educated and vociferous free black population. As the nation moved westward, the two sections quarreled over whose economy and culture would prevail. That issue, more than any other, created friction and forced Congress to cobble together compromises and laws meant to placate the apparently irreconcilable feelings of North and South. The abolitionists and their more numerous and moderate antislavery allies shoved Northern opinion into such a stance that it became irreconcilable to the South's culture. The abolitionists were moral alchemists, turning a malleable problem into a brittle cause that shattered the nation's unity when Abraham Lincoln got elected. Although Lincoln led the North into war in order to keep the nation together, he was known for his feelings about slavery. "As a nation," Lincoln said, "we began by declaring that 'all men are created equal.' We now practically read it 'all men are created equal, except negroes.'"[30] That was precisely the hierarchy that the Confederate States of America intended to maintain.

Notes

1. John Ashworth, *Slavery, Capitalism, and Politics in the Antebellum Republic* (New York: Cambridge University Press, 1995), 137.

2. Thomas Jefferson to John Holms, October 22, 1820, *The Thomas Jefferson Papers at the Library of Congress*, http://memory.loc.gov/cgi-bin/ampage?collId=m tj1&fileName=mtj1page051.db&recNum=1237.

3. "M. Harrison to the Society," *The Eleventh Annual Report of the American Society for Colonizing the Free People of Colour of the United States* (Georgetown, DC: James C. Dunn, 1828), 16.

4. See Ronald Takaki's discussion in *A Different Mirror: A History of Multicultural America* (Boston: Little, Brown, 1993), 147–151.

5. Gerda Lerner, *The Grimké Sisters from South Carolina: Pioneers for Woman's Rights and Abolition* (Oxford, UK: Oxford University Press, 1967), 9.

6. Charles Wilbanks, ed., *Walking by Faith: The Diary of Angelina Grimké, 1828–1835* (Columbia: University of South Carolina Press, 2003), xi.

7. William Lloyd Garrison, *Selections from the Writings and Speeches of William Lloyd Garrison* (Boston: R.F. Wallcut, 1852), 52–53.

8. Garrison, *Selections,* 62.

9. For a lengthier telling of Prudence Crandall's story, see Gail Collins, *America's Women: Four Hundred Years of Dolls, Drudges, Helpmates, and Heroines* (New York: HarperCollins, 2003), 161–165.

10. Howard W. Caldwell, *A Survey of American History: Source Extracts* "W.L. Garrison in Faneuil Hall, 1843" (Lincoln, NE: J.H. Miller, 1898), 156.

11. *New York Daily Times,* September 18, 1851, 2.

12. George M. Fredrickson, ed., *Great Lives Observed: William Lloyd Garrison* (Englewood Cliffs, NJ: Prentice-Hall, 1968), 102–104.

13. Daniel Wait Howe, *Political History of Secession: To the Beginning of the American Civil War* (New York: G.P. Putnam's Sons, 1914), 66.

14. Mason I. Lowance, ed., *Against Slavery: An Abolitionist Reader* (New York: Penguin, 2000), 203–204.

15. Kathryn Kish Skla, "'Women Who Speak for an Entire Nation': American and British Women Compared at the World Anti-Slavery Convention, London, 1840," *Pacific Historical Review* 59, no. 4 (1990): 453–499.

16. Albert Benedict Wolfe, ed., *Readings In Social Problems* (Boston: Ginn, 1916), 442.

17. David A. Copeland, *The Antebellum Era: Primary Documents on Events from 1820 to 1860* (Westport, CT: Greenwood, 2003), 303.

18. Wolfe ed., *Readings,* 444.

19. Joshua Gottheimer, *Ripples of Hope: Great American Civil Rights Speeches* (New York: Basic Civitas, 2003), 45–49.

20. Mari Jo Buhle and Paul Buhle, eds., *The Concise History of Woman Suffrage* (Urbana: University of Illinois Press, 2005), 104.

21. Buhle and Buhle, eds., *Concise History of Woman Suffrage,* 103.

22. Quoted in Nell Irvin Painter, *Sojourner Truth: A Life, A Symbol* (New York: W.W. Norton, 1996), 125–126.

23. Buhle and Buhle, eds., *Concise History of Woman Suffrage*, 105.

24. Mason I. Lowance, *A House Divided: The Antebellum Slavery Debates in America, 1776–1865* (Princeton, NJ: Princeton University Press, 2003), 127.

25. Henry David Thoreau, *The Writings of Henry David Thoreau* (New York: Houghton, Mifflin, 1906), 12: 314–315.

26. Edward Elliot, *Biographical Story of the Constitution* (New York: G.P. Putnam's Sons, 1910), 362–363.

27. Howard Wilford Bell, ed., *Letters and Addresses of Abraham Lincoln* (New York: H.W. Bell, 1903), 105.

28. Richard D. Heffner, *A Documentary History of the United States, Expanded and Updated Seventh Edition* (New York: New American Library, 2002), 153.

29. F.B. Sanborn, ed., *The Life and Letters of John Brown, Liberator of Kansas, and Martyr of Virginia* (Boston: Roberts Brothers, 1891), 517.

30. Bell, ed., *Letters and Addresses of Abraham Lincoln*, 91.

14

The Civil War

Abraham Lincoln *(Alexander Gardner/Getty Images)*

Strategies and Realities

"Murder" and "war" are legal definitions of similar behavior. Murder is illegal killing. Killing in war is simply state-sanctioned. More than 600,000 soldiers died during the Civil War, more than all the soldiers who have died in all the other wars fought by the United States (including the Revolution). Fewer than half died on the battlefields. Bullets, musket balls, and cannon fire tore their bodies apart. Rifle bullets that penetrated the abdomen or chest cavity often zigzagged through the organs, causing irreparable internal bleeding. About 23,000 Union and Confederate soldiers died at Antietam Creek near Sharpsburg, Virginia, on September 17, 1862. At one juncture, 2,200 died in twenty minutes. (As historian James McPherson pointed out, "More than twice as many Americans were killed or mortally wounded in combat in a single day at Antietam as in the War of 1812, the Mexican War, and the Spanish-American war [of 1898] *combined.*"[1]) More than half of the 600,000 deaths occurred off the battlefield, the result of wounds and disease, mostly caused by unsanitary conditions. Surgeons operated with saws and knives, rarely cleaning them between patients. Antibiotics did not exist, so bacteria and gangrene festered.

To say that this was the world's first large-scale, "modern" war is to say that people had learned to kill each other in greater numbers over wider distances. Revolutionary-era muskets had poor accuracy beyond 100 yards and could be fired only two or three times a minute at best. Most Civil War soldiers used rifles, whose rifled barrels had spiral grooves etched into them, giving better accuracy and range. Repeat-action Spencer rifles could fire seven shots in a row, while Enfield rifled muskets were accurate well past 400 yards. Most soldiers, therefore, had to face the prospect of being pierced with a bullet fired from an unseen gun, and soldiers' diary entries and letters home are suffused with residual battlefield terror. Then again, not all soldiers felt terrified in combat. After the first major battle of the war at Bull Run on July 21, 1861, Confederate soldier Clinton Hatcher wrote, "Besides wanting to stick my bayonette in a Yankee I wish to see if I can feel as cool when marching on the steel as I did while the balls were whistling round me."[2]

Camp and trail life conspired with terror and disease to whittle at men's frayed emotions. Union officers were entitled to at least one trunk of personal belongings that got carried in a wagon. Enlisted men hefted their own stuff, typically at thirty to forty pounds per pack. When in camp and not too ill to indulge, soldiers commonly attended prayer meetings, played cards or dominoes, wrote letters and waited for letters, and drank and smoked. When the war started in 1861, there were only 16,000 men in the regular U.S. Army. Throughout the South and the North, militia calls had been typical, but most militia musters had become excuses for socializing, dancing, and drinking. So it was the job of generals to train their men to function as armies, which meant endless drilling—a method to either cure boredom or induce it, depending on an individual's perspective. Sarah Wakeman sneaked into the army with a little gender switcheroo, calling herself "Lyons Wakeman." On March 29, 1863, she wrote to her father to say, "I like to drill first rate." She was one of perhaps 400 women who concealed their sex well enough to hoist a gun, march in formation, and withstand the carnage of this Brothers and Sisters War. Sarah died of dysentery before the end of hostilities, but her letters home testified to her contentment with the soldier's life: "I don't know how long before i shall have to go into the field of battle. For my part i don't Care. I don't feel afraid to go. I don't believe there are any Rebel's bullet made for me yet. Nor i don't care if there is. I am as independent as a hog on the ice."[3]

When hunger, marching, and sickness followed defeat, morale sank—as was the case for Union soldiers after Fredericksburg in 1862, when desertions reached 200 per day. In June 1863, in the nearly defeated town of Vicksburg along the Mississippi, Confederate soldiers wrote their commanders, "If you can't feed us, you had better surrender."[4] Vicksburg surrendered six days later, on July 4.

Probably nothing could really tame gnawing hunger, pus-filled wounds, phantom memories of missing limbs, or the sight of decapitated friends. Surreal joy did, however, sometimes visit the war's combatants. Two nights before the end of 1862, about 45,000 Union troops faced 36,000 Confederates outside Murfreesboro, Tennessee, at a place called Stones River. The weather had been miserable, and as usual rocks and mud served as padding for bedrolls. To soothe themselves, military bands on both banks of the river played favored songs while the soldiers sang along. One man, Sam Seay, later remembered the music from the bands drifting through the winter air far off into the distance. The Confederates offered up a patriotic rendition of "Dixie," the Confederate anthem: "In Dixie Land I'll take my stand / to live and die in Dixie." The shivering men in blue chorused back with "Yankee Doodle," an old ditty from the Revolution open to new verses and impromptu updates. Suddenly, on one side or the other, someone took up the tune "Home Sweet Home." Strains of "Yankee Doodle" and "Dixie" trailed away, and soon a cross-river, eighty-thousand-man, Confederate-Union harmony filled the cold night air. Later, in wonderment, Seay recalled how "as if by common consent, all other [songs] ceased, and the bands of both armies as far as the ear could reach, joined in the refrain. Who knows how many hearts were bold next day by reason of that air?"[5] The next day, fully one-third of all those bold hearts stopped beating, were wounded, or went missing: about 25,000 casualties.

In its larger dimensions—of strategy, tactics, and objectives—the Civil War lasted for four years and stretched from the eastern seaboard to a little west of the Mississippi River. At the onset, both sides had clear objectives. The South wanted total independence, the opportunity to establish its own laws and carry on its traditions. The North wanted to prevent the South from leaving the Union. The eradication of slavery became a Union goal as of January 1, 1863, when President Abraham Lincoln's Emancipation Proclamation went into effect. The Proclamation was more a statement of intention than reality. Technically, it freed only a few slaves, those living in Union-occupied territory throughout the Confederacy (in places like the sea islands off the coast of South Carolina). Other than that, the Emancipation Proclamation *stated* that all slaves in the Confederacy were free, but it did not touch slavery in Maryland, Delaware, Kentucky, or Missouri, which had remained in the Union. So long as the South remained unconquered, the Proclamation meant nothing to the slaves other than as a promise and a whisper. Those who heard of it sometimes took to their heels and escaped to a Union Army camp, just as many had been doing since the shooting started in April 1861. The Emancipation Proclamation, ineffectual as it was at first, altered the meaning of the war by making it into a moral crusade. The nations of Europe, already unlikely to recognize Confederate independence, became totally unwilling, given their own recent swing to the abolitionist camp. The Union Army was now one of conquest, reabsorption, and liberation. The Proclamation also cleared a path for the Thirteenth Amendment to the Constitution, which ended slavery on December 6, 1865, though it barely even made its way through Congress.

Confederate strategy relied on a few approaches. Most simply, the Confederates wanted to fight a defensive war, for which the Southern populace was well suited. Traditions of horsemanship, marksmanship, and militarism pervaded Southern culture. Johnny Reb could ride, shoot, and fight through a known terrain with a friendly populace. Plus, a majority of Southern whites felt the cause was worth a sacrifice. The Confederacy desperately needed munitions and ships from Europe, and obtaining recognition of Confederate independence was also a primary goal. British guns and ships were delivered, but not one nation ever stepped forward to call the Confederacy a sovereign nation. The South applied cotton leverage in the first year of the war by instituting a voluntary quarantine on exports, hoping to force British textile laborers to demand recognition of the Confederacy in order to get the cotton needed for business and jobs. The strategy never worked. The British had a surplus of cotton, and they soon turned to Egypt and India to grow more. In the end, the Confederacy had to rely on itself: on its black slaves to continue laboring in fields and factories; on its white men to fight; on its white women to support the men by running homes, farms, and some plantations. The Confederates hoped that the North would lose its taste for death and let the South go its own way. That was what defensive war meant at first: wearing down the Union will to throw sons at bullets. But by late 1864, defensive war meant trying to save farms and houses from complete destruction as Union general William Tecumseh Sherman took his 55,000 Union troops on a punitive march from Atlanta to the sea.

Union strategy also went through an evolution as Northern politicians and generals adapted to changing circumstances. By April 1861, seven Southern states had already seceded. They demanded that the United States remove all its military personnel from the remaining fortifications of Dixie. In South Carolina, one symbolic stronghold jutted out of Charleston's harbor: the unfinished stone hulk of Fort Sumter. Lincoln took office in March and decided to force the rebel states into the status of aggressors. Rather than ordering the few dozen troops at Sumter to evacuate, and rather than steaming a squadron of Union gunboats into the harbor, Lincoln merely tried to have the fort resupplied. This the South would not allow, and Confederate troops fired the first shots of the war on April 12, playing into Lincoln's hands with cannon balls. Now he could order troops to respond to violence in kind, to quell an insurrection, a domestic disturbance. The shelling of Fort Sumter was a diplomatic and political coup for Lincoln, giving him cause and justification for retaliation.

Battles were fought on three fronts: on the water, in the East, and in the West. The Union Navy remained superior in numbers, training, and armaments throughout the war, creating a perforated blockade of Confederate shipping and allowing the Union to occupy coastal areas with relative ease early in the conflict. The land war in the East centered almost exclusively in Virginia from 1861 until 1864. Richmond, Virginia, became the Confederate capital, a taunting neighbor to Washington, DC, 100 miles away. Lincoln wanted to capture Richmond and its leaders (including the Confederate president, Jefferson Davis), but was unsuccessful until the closing days of the war in April 1865. Confederate General Robert E. Lee's Army of Northern Virginia matched every saber thrust, cavalry charge, and hesitant tactic thrown at it by the larger Union armies for almost three years. One indecisive Union general after another disappointed Lincoln in the East. From the egomaniacal George McClellan (who called Lincoln an "idiot" and "the Original Gorilla") to the equally hesitant and unprepared George Meade (who took command of Union troops three days before the near-apocalyptic Battle of Gettysburg in July 1863), not one Union general in the East ordered all available troops into a big battle for three straight years. Victory required boldness, daring, and maybe even a pinch of insanity, but Lincoln's eastern commanders suffered from caution and hesitancy.

As poetic justice would have it, the region that sparked the war became the region that decided the war. The expansion of the nation into the West had inflamed sectional grievances for decades, and until 1864 the Union's major offensive land victories all came in the West. The unexpected successes of two brilliant men kept Union hopes alive and alleviated Lincoln's frustrated need for competent generals. Ulysses S. Grant was a once-upon-a-time military officer, former heavy drinker, and lousy businessman. One of Grant's recent biographers describes him as "an ordinary-looking man . . . five feet eight inches tall and weighing 135 pounds, somewhat stooped and with a short brown beard, a quiet man who smoked a pipe." Grant "had never wanted a military career."[6] He was, in a word, unexpected. William Tecumseh Sherman, also a West Point graduate, had recently done well . . . as a banker. Sherman got regularly and inaccurately labeled as a certifiable, mood-swinging lunatic (his moods did swing wide, but the only lunacy was opposing him in war). Grant and Sherman directed one victory after another, rising through the ranks based on outstanding ability. Grant eventually became Sherman's superior and friend, and they were both willing to commit their whole force to a battle when needed. After the war, Sherman looked back on their relationship, half smiling, half serious: "General Grant is a great general. I know him well. He stood by me when I was crazy and I stood by him when he was drunk; and now, sir, we stand by each other always."[7] Grant's tactics and superior forces defeated Robert E. Lee's dwindling army. Sherman's forces burned and sacked the South into submission.

Union strategy involved preventing the Confederacy from achieving recognition of its supposed independence, capturing Richmond, and squeezing the rebel states from all directions (in what got mockingly labeled the Anaconda Plan), all the while trying to reintegrate the Confederate states loyally back into the nation. These objectives required tact and a kind of sacrificial devotion that depended on military victories and belief. Grant and Sherman's armies provided the victories, which instilled belief that the South could be tamed. Northern antiwar Democrats, dubbed "Copperheads" because they seemed to poison the war effort, lost their hiss with each Confederate defeat. Soldiers, in particular, tended to vote for Lincoln and to despise Copperheads. Sarah Wakeman, the cross-dressing Union volunteer from New York, told her father, "I would like to see some of them Copperheads Come down here and get killed. It would do me good to see it done."[8] White Northerners fought for the cause of reunification, for the bounty money offered to enlistees, for adventure, or simply because they got drafted—which became a serious problem in the summer of 1863 (culminating in five days of anti-war, anti-draft rioting in New York City) as the war dragged on and voluntary enlistments barely dribbled in.

But African-Americans needed to believe that the war would offer them something more than they had been getting in America—ideally, equality.

Many white people had conflicted feelings about black people, wanting them to have freedom from slavery but not equality. Other white people were simply racist. In August 1864, a vein-popping citizen wrote to Lincoln, "Equal Rights & Justice to all white men in the United States forever—White men is in Class number one & black men is in Class number two & must be governed by white men forever." By that point, Lincoln and Congress had ordered the creation of all-black regiments: black men with guns, one of the two things white men feared most (the other was black men with white women). An Ohio man preparing to enlist said, "I don't think enough of the Nigger to go and fight for them. I would rather fight them."[9] The Emancipation Proclamation opened the door to black men serving in the ranks at the same time it turned the war into a social revolution. The Proclamation amplified existing hostile feelings but also gave Americans an opportunity to rise to the occasion. Black soldiers' distinguished service in battle forced white troops who had long thought African-Americans incapable of fighting to recognize them as not only capable but patriotic. The comments of an Illinois soldier, Charles W. Wills, suggest this gradual transformation:

> I never thought I would, but I am getting strongly in favor of arming them, and am becoming so [color] blind that I can't see why they will not make soldiers. A year ago last January I didn't like to hear anything of emancipation. Last fall, accepted confiscation of rebels' Negroes quietly. In January took to emancipation readily, and now believe in arming the Negroes. The only objection I have to it is a matter of pride. I almost begin to think of applying for a position in a [Negro] regiment myself.[10]

Approximately 180,000 black men served in 166 all-black regiments during the war, although only about 100 blacks ever made it into the commissioned officer corps. Still, these were advances in such a racist era, and with every impressive move black soldiers made, they gained white allies—at least in the North. Union strategy gradually incorporated freedom as a goal for African-Americans, and African-Americans became the agents of their own liberation.

A war to end the nation was also a war to save the nation. What follow are vignettes of major participants who shaped the war and of a few minor participants who slogged through the mud of history deposited ingloriously at their feet by a conflicted, divided country.

Abraham Lincoln: Part 1

Who was this lanky giant occupying the White House, the man whose good friend, Joshua Speed, said, "I never saw so gloomy and melancholy a face in my life"?[11] Abraham Lincoln had done many things: farming in Illinois, stopping to read books at the end of some furrows so the horse could take a break; running a law practice and sharing a bed with Joshua Speed (yes, a bed, not just the room, a commonplace arrangement for men); serving one term as a congressman from Illinois; marrying Mary Todd, whose family initially disapproved of the match because Abraham seemed unlikely to amount to much. A burden seemed to exist in Lincoln, visible in his sunken cheeks, like a premonition of the future.

Though he was a serious man, Lincoln liked a joke as well as any and could tell them better than most. He was well known for risking danger during years when many people would have liked to see him dead. A writer for *Harper's* magazine recalled passing the White House on a summer morning and seeing "the President standing at the gateway, looking anxiously down the street." The reporter said hello, and Lincoln replied, "Good-morning, good-morning! I am looking for a news-boy; when you get to that corner I wish you would start one up this way."[12] Lincoln's friends chided him for being so careless since assassinations had already been plotted against him. Lincoln had only one answer for their worries: "If they kill me, the next man will be just as bad for them." Notoriously scatterbrained, Lincoln mused that he was like the "old Englishman who was so absent-minded that when he went to bed he put his clothes carefully into the bed and threw himself over the back of the chair."[13]

His humor also surfaced on the campaign trail. While stumping for president in 1859, Lincoln stood before a crowd in Cincinnati, Ohio. Halfway through a long speech, Lincoln took a breath and said, "I am in some doubt whether to introduce another topic upon which I could talk awhile." The crowd was with him, crying out "Go on" and "Give us it." So Lincoln continued: "It is this then: Douglas's popular sovereignty, as a principle, is simply this: If one man chooses to make a slave of another man, neither that other man or anybody else has a right to object."[14] The crowd broke out into cheers and laughter.

Lincoln's public jokes were meant to make a point, and here he got to the heart of the Republican Party platform: if through Stephen Douglas's "popular sovereignty" new states could choose whether or not to have slavery, then they could choose any fool thing they wanted. The joke sat on a razor's edge of truth. In Lincoln's opinion, slavery had gone on too long and corrupted men's thinking. In a private letter written in 1859, Lincoln said, "he who would be no slave must consent to have no slave. Those who deny freedom to others deserve it not for themselves."[15] Not many slave owners would have agreed with him.

As late as 1862, congressmen from the four Union slave states refused to consider any emancipation legislation whatsoever, a stance that nudged Lincoln toward independent action: the Emancipation Proclamation. If Congress could not see that slavery had caused the war and therefore needed to be ended by the war, Lincoln had come to understand this—often at the prodding of men like Frederick Douglass, who visited Lincoln in the White House more than once and received warm welcomes. In 1864, Lincoln ushered Douglass into the executive house to find out what the graying abolitionist and former slave thought about the Proclamation. Lincoln said to Douglass, "There is no man in the country whose opinion I value more than yours."[16]

During his 1860 campaign for the presidency, Lincoln had done what he could to straddle two lines: the Republican stricture that slavery must not expand, and the Southern fear that a Northern president would interfere with slavery where it already existed. When Lincoln was sworn in as president on March 4, 1861, he explained one more time that the federal government should not tamper with a state's own business: "I have no purpose, directly or indirectly, to interfere with the institution of slavery in the States where it exists. I believe I have no lawful right to do so, and I have no inclination to do so." Seven states had already seceded and four more would do so within a few months. Lincoln could be patient with regard to emancipation, but he would not wait a day to keep the nation together. Early in the war, he explained why the Union had to be maintained: "The central idea pervading this struggle is the necessity . . . of proving that popular government is not an absurdity. We must settle this question now, whether in a free government the minority have the right to break up the government whenever they choose."[17] The United States had afforded him, a poor boy, "an unfettered start, and a fair chance in the race of life." That was the promise of free labor and free soil, and if states could secede, America would become unable "to elevate the condition of men" as it crashed toward anarchy.[18]

Congress happened not to be in session when the shelling of Fort Sumter started in April 1861. This president of principles had a choice to make: would he call Congress back to draft wartime laws, or would he issue presidential edicts? Lincoln chose to run the war without Congress until July, relying only on his cabinet and advisers. This was unprecedented. He immediately called for army volunteers. In certain rebellious, unruly cities and districts, Lincoln revoked the writ of habeas corpus (which permits an arrested citizen to have the charges revealed in court in order to determine whether the charges are lawful). Lincoln also declared a blockade of the southern coastline, which could have been construed as a declaration of war by itself, a power reserved specifically for Congress. These momentous decisions, which arguably stripped people of their civil liberties, rested on the same principles Lincoln had been articulating for four years, which he had eloquently summarized at the end of his first inaugural address in words directed toward the rebels:

"You can have no conflict, without being yourselves the aggressors. You have no oath registered in heaven to destroy the government, while I shall have the most solemn one to 'preserve, protect and defend' it." Lincoln was willing to sacrifice life and liberty, in the short run, he told Congress in 1862, for the long-term maintenance of a government he believed offered the "last best, hope of earth." In some of the prettiest words a president has ever used, Lincoln hoped that the "mystic chords of memory, stretching from every battle-field and patriot grave to every living heart and hearthstone all over this broad land, will yet swell the chorus of the Union when again touched, as surely they will be, by the better angels of our nature."[19] It was not angels, however, who descended on the war's first battlefield at Manassas Junction near the little creek known as Bull Run.

Rose O'Neale Greenhow: Confederate Spy

Troops from both sides had been massing between Richmond and Washington since the end of May 1861. On a July morning in his headquarters near Manassas Junction, General Pierre G.T. Beauregard—a New Orleans Creole who had led the capture of Fort Sumter only months before—received a secret message from Washington, DC. Sixteen-year-old Bettie Duvall handed over a scrap of paper informing Beauregard, now the commander of Confederate forces, that Lincoln's army would attack on the sixteenth, within the week. Bettie had openly made her way past federal forces and into this stronghold of secessionist strength under orders from her ringleader, "Wild Rose" O'Neale Greenhow, a favorite of Washington society and a Confederate spy. The scrap of paper bore her initials, "ROG."[20]

Rose Greenhow smoothed her elegant way through capital society. She was the aunt of Stephen A. Douglas (Lincoln's senatorial opponent in 1858), and she dined for a time with William H. Seward, Lincoln's secretary of state. The height of her influence came with the presidency of James Buchanan, who left the White House as Lincoln entered it. She was no Republican, to be sure. A daughter of the northern South, Greenhow had been raised by her aunt, who maintained a boardinghouse for congressmen. Raised in power, she cultivated her own. As the old saying goes, you can take a lady out of the South, but you cannot take the South out of a lady. As the secession crisis sped into disunion, Rose Greenhow chose what felt naturally like her side: the Confederacy. Spies, hidden agendas, and plots spiderwebbed the nation. In March 1861, President Lincoln himself had to travel incognito into the capital under the protection of private detectives to avoid being assassinated by a band of secessionists. Washington City bristled with the bayonets of recruits marching to the tune of "Yankee Doodle." Many civilians fled for points farther north, fearing the imminent combat that everyone knew to expect. Wild Rose stayed put, nursing a dying daughter, Gertrude, and scheming treason, regardless of the letters she received from her other children who begged her not to associate with secessionists. As Greenhow's recent biographer, Ann Blackman, notes, "But for the company . . . of Little Rose, now eight years old, she was alone, a Southern widow in a Northern town."[21]

In the greater DC area, there were more than 50,000 Union troops, with more arriving daily. The main corps of 35,000 was led by General Irvin Mc-Dowell. Many of the ablest U.S. Army officers had resigned their commissions to fight for the Confederacy—like the aristocratic Robert E. Lee, who had captured John Brown only two years earlier. Even so, an overwhelming population, industrial capacity, and Yankee optimism convinced most Northerners that secession would be short-lived. The *New York Times* commented on July 21 that McDowell's force "was not an army, in the strict sense of the word, and a military man might have smiled at an order of march having the artillery in front and the cavalry in the rear. It was a gathering of armed men, making up their deficiency in tactics and discipline by the moral bond which unite them in a common cause." This troop "presented a very fine spectacle," so fine that congressmen, senators, their wives, and assorted other picnickers trailed along, hoping to catch a good view of the whipping that McDowell was expected to administer to the rebels.[22] Victory was assumed.

On the morning of July 16, Rose Greenhow sent nine words to General Beauregard: "Order issued for McDowell to march upon Manassas tonight."[23] Sure enough, McDowell got his troops under way that evening, heading southwest toward the Manassas Gap Railroad and, thanks to Greenhow, a better-prepared Confederate force. In the nearby Shenandoah Valley, the aging Union general Robert Patterson was under orders to contain the 12,000 infantry of Brigadier General Joseph E. Johnston and the cavalry of Colonel Jeb Stuart. When Beauregard read Greenhow's coded letter, he sent roundabout word to Johnston to sneak around Patterson's containment force. This was done with a nimble, diversionary strike by Stuart's cavalry: Patterson got distracted, and Johnston got out by train. Rose Greenhow's spying had made the difference.

After a running series of skirmishes along the way, the armies smashed into each other under a melting sun on the afternoon of July 21, 1861. Fighting with what a *Times* correspondent called "terrible tenacity," the Union troops killed their way across Bull Run creek. In the midst of "hot and steady" battle, it seemed secession would drown in shallow water.[24] Then generals Johnston and Thomas "Stonewall" Jackson rallied their troops. (Jackson's nickname came from the way he seemed to stand like a stonewall against which the waves of blue and bullets would crash.) The last of Johnston's 12,000 troops arrived in the middle of the melee, at about four o'clock, when they could add a fresh surge to the Confederate counterattack. What could have been a Confederate rout turned into a disordered Union retreat. Irvin McDowell, who had never commanded in combat, did his schoolbook best, but he was outwitted, both before the battle and during.

On their way back to the federal capital, Union soldiers dropped their backpacks, rifles, even handcuffs. McDowell telegraphed to headquarters to say that "the men having thrown away their haversacks in the battle and left them behind, they are without food; have eaten nothing since breakfast. We are without artillery ammunition. The larger part of the men are a confused mob, entirely demoralized."[25] Seized cannons, powder, and shot padded the Confederate victory, making one truth inescapable: the South now had a fighting chance. A *New York Times* reporter captured the somber mood in Washington. Lines of wagons "continually" arrived, "bringing in the dead and wounded," and soldiers told their stories to "greedy listeners." As far as the *Times* reporter was concerned, "the feeling is awfully distressing. . . . The greatest alarm exists throughout the city."[26] Thanks to the distance separating Manassas Junction and Washington, Union defenses were secured, however, and the capital was in no real danger. Besides, the Confederate soldiers were tired, had used up most of their shot, and reeled at the sight of the carnage. A Virginia rifleman put it this way: "today I went to the battle feild to help bury the dead the Awfulls scene I evir witnessed In my life hundreds of dead & wounded on the field yet the yankees sent in a flag of truce and got some of their wounded."[27]

Working from notes he took at the time, Walt Whitman, the poet who first captured America's spirit in words, reflected on the way that Abraham Lincoln took the defeat of the First Battle of Bull Run. "He endured," Whitman wrote, "that hour, that day, bitterer than gall—indeed a crucifixion day—that it did not conquer him—that he unflinchingly stemm'd it, and resolv'd to lift himself and the Union out of it." While Lincoln absorbed the news and replaced McDowell with the handsome George McClellan, the streets teemed with citizens and soldiers. In Whitman's words, "amid the deep excitement, crowds and motion, and desperate eagerness, it seems strange to see many, very many, of the soldiers sleeping—in the midst of all, sleeping sound. They drop down anywhere, on the steps of houses, up close by the basements or fences, on the sidewalk, aside on some vacant lot, and deeply sleep."[28]

Rose Greenhow had been in New York on the day of the fight, but she returned immediately to the capital. She visited Congress, where she spoke to several Republicans, for whom she had only disdain. "Several crowded round me," she remembered, "and I could not help saying that, if they had not '*good blood*,' they had certainly '*good bottom*,' for they ran remarkably well."[29] Greenhow's scorn did nothing to conceal her operations within the city. Regular informants visited her home. Her circle had grown wide enough to draw attention.

A man named Allan Pinkerton, head of a famous detective agency bearing his name, was put in charge of creating a "secret service" to figure out what the Confederate forces were up to and how many of them there were (which he botched by exaggerating their numbers). Pinkerton was also set to spying on the spy: he was to play spider to Greenhow's fly on the wall. And he caught her, fairly easily. One night, through the double pane of rain and glass, Pinkerton watched Rose Greenhow confer in her house with a Union Army captain who was showing her a map. Soon thereafter, on August 23, Pinkerton had her confined to house arrest. In January 1862, she and her young daughter were transferred to a jail, locally termed "Greenhow Prison," in honor of its most illustrious guest. Only months later, Lincoln, rather than having her executed, deported her to the grateful hands of Jefferson Davis, president of the Confederacy. Greenhow died two years later on a return trip from Europe, where she had worked as a Confederate diplomat, dealing in her persuasive skills of tongue and mind. In the midst of trying to break through the Union blockade around Wilmington, North Carolina, she drowned trying to make it to shore in a rowboat, a Union ship giving chase in rough waters, her body weighed down with gold earned from the sale of her memoirs.

First Bull Run set the mark for a corrosive stalemate in the East that lasted more than two years. The North won some defensive battles, as at Gettysburg, Pennsylvania, in 1863, when Robert E. Lee made a valiant, but failed effort to punish the Union on home territory and to make the anguish of war so visible that Northerners would let the South go free. At Gettysburg, North and South were punished, but the South more so. The strength of Lee's army was shattered, his ability to make offensive war bled away into the fields, hills, and cemeteries outside a small town where his soldiers had gone to requisition much-needed shoes. Still, none of Lincoln's eastern commanders could win a truly decisive victory (entailing the utter destruction of Lee's Army of Northern Virginia) until Grant was put in command in 1864. Up to that point, western victories provided what buoyancy there was in the Republican plan to force the South back into the nation.

Mathew Brady and War Photography

How did people in the Deep South or the high North know what was going on in the shooting zones of Virginia, Maryland, Pennsylvania, and Tennessee? They read plenty of newspaper accounts, which brought events from the corpse to the editor's desk to the breakfast table much more quickly than had been possible prior to telegraph technology. But an ambitious man named Mathew Brady did more than any other single individual to get the world to *see* the Civil War. Brady was a photographer.

Born in 1823, he opened a portrait studio in New York City in the 1840s and made himself relatively famous taking images of the truly famous and wealthy. Photography as both a chemical process and an art transformed rapidly during Brady's lifetime, from the early process known as daguerreotype to the speedier method involving treated paper and glass plate negatives—a system better suited to mobility. Just before the Civil War, Brady moved to Washington, DC, and opened his National Photographic Art Gallery, ideally situated for both his talents and the coming storm. Ideal, at least, for everyone else: Brady became the most celebrated photographer of his generation, but he died penniless.

First Bull Run was Brady's first attempt to capture the light and shadows of battle, but he ended up running away from the Confederate advance along with everyone else attached to the Union Army. Looking like a charming scientist in his long, linen duster, Brady got lost in the woods and took three days to find his way back the twenty-fives miles to Washington—armed, for what good it would have done him, with a sword borrowed from the Fire Zouaves, a regiment of former firefighters who suffered terrible losses during the battle. However, it was at Antietam, Maryland, that Brady made his mark.

The battle at Antietam took place in 1862. It was Robert E. Lee's first attempt to invade the North. He wanted Maryland because it was full of secessionists. Lee wanted to surround the Union capital and force Lincoln to either capitulate or flee. Instead, the armies savaged each other in some of the most gruesome murder of the war. Mathew Brady had, by that point, employed a number of other photographers to aid him. Together they took many more pictures than he did. In the aftermath of the slaughter—about 23,000 men killed in twelve hours—Brady took the stark, black-and-white images and hung them at his New York studio for all to see. There were the Confederate dead in a dry ditch, scorched earth all around, with the remnants of trees like matchsticks in the background. In another lifeless scene, the dead lay abandoned by a fence, empty cart tracks running toward the horizon past empty bodies, one man fallen away from his comrades, more forlorn than the rest. Elsewhere on Brady's studio walls were incongruous photographs of Lincoln and McClellan sitting under the white canopy of McClellan's tent—the president with knees nearly touching the table bottom and eyes gazing out of the frame; the general looking at his commander, expectant. Words were not needed, only eyes and enough daylight to see how people died and killed. War suddenly seemed less distant. As the *New York Times* described the scene in Brady's studio on October 20, 1862,

Mr. Brady has done something to bring home to us the terrible reality and earnestness of war. If he has not brought bodies and laid them in our door-yards and along the streets, he has done something very like it . . . there is a terrible fascination about it that draws one near these pictures, and makes him loth to leave them. You will see hushed, reverend groups standing around these weird copies of carnage, bending down to look in the pale faces of the dead, chained by the strange spell that dwells in dead men's eyes.[30]

Mr. Brady died in a charity ward of a New York City hospital in 1896. Congress had given him $25,000 for his prints in 1875, but that was too late to cover the debts he had made taking the pictures, printing them, and publishing them during the war. Only two years earlier, in 1873, he had filed for bankruptcy. His labors benefited the nation as a kind of sacrifice; the same could be said for the dead at Antietam, whose accidental poses in death he immortalized.

Emma LeConte and William Tecumseh Sherman: The Coming of the End Through Southern Eyes

Columbia, South Carolina, February 15, 1865, nighttime: "Nearer and nearer, clearer and more distinctly sound the cannon—Oh, it is heart-sickening to listen to it! . . . Just now as I stood on the piazza listening, the reports sounded so frightfully loud and near that I could not help shuddering at each one."[31] The Yankees had arrived, General Sherman's murdering, plundering, burning dogs of war. They had been making their way painstakingly eastward across the heart of Dixie into the state where it all began, South Carolina. Columbia was the capital, and it had to be brought to heel. Sherman had Grant's and Lincoln's approval to destroy the South's will to fight, indeed to cause enough horror that the memory would prevent any thoughts of secession for generations to come. Hard-shelled Emma LeConte, a true Confederate patriot, trembled in her room, though she felt there was "something exciting—sublime—in a can-nonade." Emma was sixteen. Her father worked as a scientist for the Confed-eracy, and he was well connected, frequently traveling throughout the South inspecting deposits of potassium nitrate for use in medicines and munitions. With Sherman certain to enter the city, Emma's father left, though he had only been home a few days. Just before his departure, Emma wrote, "My great fear now is for father—Oh, if he were only gone—were only safe!" Emma, her mother, and extended family remained behind, hoping their own safety was not at risk. Would Sherman and his Yankee troops add to their reputations as pigs by trashing the city and molesting its fair residents?

Emma well knew the story of the Confederacy's fall from grace. By June

1862 it had seemed the noble South could both protect itself and carry the war to the enemy—General Lee had defeated the army of that great bumbler, George McClellan, at the Battles of the Seven Days. Only months before that, in April, the barbarians Grant and Sherman had nearly lost all (including their lives) at the church-field battle of Shiloh, hundreds of miles west in Tennessee, where Sherman's hand was torn up by grapeshot and Grant was almost decapitated by a cannon ball. Grant had camped with his back to the river, having erected no defensive earthworks at all, and Sherman was some miles away. The hero of Manassas, Pierre Beauregard, and other flowers of Southern manhood attacked early on a Saturday morning, relentlessly pushing back the Yankee invaders, driving them into ditches, slaughtering them under peach trees. But Grant received 20,000 fresh recruits during the night, enough to claim the field on Sunday. Although Beauregard had retreated, the war of Northern aggression now had a price in bodies attached to it high enough to make mothers and politicians pause.

To Southerners like Emma LeConte, it had seemed that that infidel Lincoln was poised to tumble; his fall seemed certain. Before the misfortune of Gettysburg in July 1863, Northern armies in the East had received wearying, humiliating wounds at Fredericksburg in December 1862 and at Chancellorsville in May 1863. But a month after Lee's army limped home from the gore of Gettysburg, Lincoln's number one henchman and lackey, the drunkard Grant, managed a daring but sickening victory over the hilltop fortress-city of Vicksburg on the Mississippi, the last best hope for the Confederacy to hold onto the river. Whoever controlled the river controlled the West, and Grant's cannons pounded Vicksburg into submission, stealing the water for Union commerce and armies. Grant took command of all Union forces and transferred to the District of Columbia area, where he and Lee spurred their exhausted, often dispirited men into one conflagration after another: the Battle of the Wilderness, May 1864 (30,000 combined casualties); the Battle of Cold Harbor, June 1864 (16,000 combined casualties); the siege of Petersburg, begun in June 1864. The Southern wherewithal to withstand Union armies slowly disintegrated.

By February 1865, Emma's home city, Columbia, was occupied. She was concerned not with far-off rumors or certainties, but suddenly with the here and now. The previous September, Sherman's raiders took Atlanta, and since then they had marched relentlessly to the sea, freeing slaves, eating crops, burning crops, tearing up train tracks, killing. At one o'clock in the afternoon on February 17, clouds of smoke drifted by, and Emma looked out to see "that hateful symbol of despotism," the United States flag, being raised over the State House. Worrying that her safe haven in a house located on the South Carolina College campus—recently requisitioned for use as a hospital—would be sacked, Emma relaxed when she learned that "Sherman . . . promised not to disturb private property."

Her "thankful" feelings turned to "misery and agony" during the night. Throughout the long evening, Emma watched the city go up in flames. "Imagine night turned into noonday," she wrote, "a copper colored sky across which swept columns of black, rolling smoke glistening with sparks and flying embers." While Emma stared transfixed at the burning of a third of the city, General Sherman was in the streets, actually trying to stop the fires. He sent teams of men out in bucket brigades to douse the flames, and he ordered that no more fires be set; but the wind was against him, and bolls of cotton floated through the streets, catching ablaze, setting new fires along with other dancing sparks and embers. Many of Sherman's men got drunk, carousing and sprinkling turpentine before dropping matches, as Emma put it, "in the presence of helpless women and children." Toward morning the wind subsided, and the fires were contained, but not before the real lasting damage was done: creating the Southern sense that this was Sherman's intentional doing. "Strange as it may seem," wrote Emma after the night of fires, "we were actually idiotic enough to believe Sherman would keep his word! A *Yankee*—and *Sherman!*"

A week of "desolation" and "monotony" passed. Emma toured portions of the city. The Court House that had lately flown the Yankee flag was rubble. African-Americans streamed in from the countryside looking for food. Sherman posted a guard to protect the hospital, so Emma's home was spared. Her father returned to great rejoicing, and Emma felt happy enough to write more, though all she could find were pencils, the ink all gone. To the north, the siege of Petersburg continued, a protracted trench war with many battles (and at least 70,000 casualties by April). Petersburg and Lee's starved, dwindling army were all that stood between 100,000 Union soldiers and the capture of Richmond. The only other sizable Confederate force was General Joseph E. Johnston's, which Sherman had been pursuing for months. Incredibly, the Confederates fought on: food mostly gone, shoes mostly gone. Emma said it best: "As far as I can see, the people are [not] demoralized and [are] more determined than ever." But Richmond was captured on April 2. Jefferson Davis and the government clattered by train farther south, wanting to raise new armies, wanting to carry on. But Robert E. Lee, although knowing his men's resolve and unshaken will, nonetheless realized by the morning of April 9, 1865, that to fight any longer was futile. Lee's commitment was to an ideal, not to a lost cause. He met his former West Point classmate Ulysses S. Grant to sue for terms of surrender in a house in the tiny town of Appomattox Court House. Lee's attire was crisp, sharp. Grant's clothes were tattered, the coat that of an enlisted man. But the terms of surrender were not humiliating. In fact, they were generous: the Southerners could take home their horses and mules to use for the summer planting and harvest. Grant meant not to punish, but to heal, making peace with grace, just as Lincoln urged in his Second Inaugural Address: "with malice toward none; with charity toward all."

Neither loss in war nor human nature easily lent itself to charity, and though Robert E. Lee regarded Grant with kindness after Appomattox, many in the North and the South looked across the Mason-Dixon line and wished for evil to fall.

Abraham Lincoln: Part 2

Lincoln survived the war, as a man and as a president. In March he was sworn in for the start of his second term. By April 14, Lincoln expected to hear news that Johnston's army in North Carolina had surrendered to Sherman, placing the rebellion into history. On that foggy April night, Mr. and Mrs. Lincoln departed in a coach for Ford's Theater. An irresponsible policeman and two friends, Major Henry Rathbone and Miss Clara Harris, accompanied them. The audience cheered for Lincoln when he entered the theater and the band played a tune in his honor. The four friends made their way to a box overlooking the stage, and Lincoln settled into a rocking chair to enjoy the performance, laugh a little, and distract himself from the diplomacy and politics of "reconstruction" that lay ahead. The fighting was over, but the war was not—how would all the contradicting desires and interests of the citizens be met? Could Southern society be altered to preserve dignity and honor while simultaneously ensuring some kind of equality for the 4 million black people who had no one to count on other than themselves and the vocal minority of "radical Republicans" in the North?

Lincoln never got a chance to answer these questions. Shortly after nine, a popular and dashing actor named John Wilkes Booth opened the door to Lincoln's box and shot the president squarely in the back of the head with a derringer pistol. Mary Todd Lincoln was holding her husband's hand as he slumped forward. She screamed as John Booth slashed at Major Rathbone's cheek and jumped out into the air and onto the stage—where he broke his shinbone and called out a Latin phrase, "*Sic semper tyrannis!*" ("Thus always to tyrants!"), before limping out to his waiting horse. Lincoln was still breathing, but his breath did not last long. At 7:22 AM on April 15, he was pronounced dead.

What did Emma LeConte have to say when she heard the news? "Hurrah! Old Abe Lincoln has been assassinated! It may be abstractly wrong to be so jubilant, but I just can't help it." This was the reaction John Wilkes Booth had hoped for throughout the South. The North, however, lamented and felt vengeful.

More than 1 million men had been gored and wounded in the four years of the war, and another 600,000-plus had died. Sherman's march through the South had been effective in forcing the Confederacy to concede, but he had sown bitterness. The freeing of slaves and the need to integrate them into society caused at least as much anguish. Racists who had lost a war were not going to turn charitably to women and men they regarded as inferior and suddenly vote with them, dine with them, and work with them on an equal footing. Did Lincoln's assassination make the coming reconstruction of the nation worse? He had already experimented with his style of reconstruction in the western states of the Confederacy, like Tennessee. Military men governed, including Sherman after Shiloh. Though not everyone had been happy with the result, the process was working in these test cases as well as could be expected, perhaps. Now it would be up to Congress, President Andrew Johnson (a man whose heart was Southern), and a few military leaders to forge a new nation on the ashes of victory and loss.

Notes

1. James McPherson, *Battle Cry of Freedom: The Civil War Era* (New York: Oxford University Press, 2003), 544.
2. "Clinton Hatcher to Mary Anna Sibert, July 27, 1861," The Valley of the Shadow: Two Communities in the American Civil War, Virginia Center for Digital History, University of Virginia, http://jefferson.village.virginia.edu/vshadow2/.
3. Lauren Cook Burgess, ed., *An Uncommon Soldier: The Civil War Letters of Sarah Rosetta Wakeman, alias Pvt. Lyons Wakeman* (New York: Oxford University Press, 1995), 42.
4. McPherson, *Battle Cry of Freedom*, 636.
5. Sam Seay, "The Union Approach," National Park Service, Stones River National Battlefield, www.nps.gov/stri/historyculture/unionapproach.htm.
6. Charles Bracelen Flood, *Grant and Sherman: The Friendship That Won the Civil War* (New York: Harper Perennial, 2006), 9.
7. John G. Barrett, *Sherman's March Through the Carolinas* (Chapel Hill: University of North Carolina Press, 1956), 25.
8. Burgess, *Uncommon Soldier*, 37.
9. Randall M. Miller and John W. Zophy, "Unwelcome Allies: Billy Yank and the Black Soldier," *Phylon* 39, no. 3 (1978): 234.
10. Charles Wright Wills, *Army Life of an Illinois Soldier* (New Wilmington, PA: Globe Printing, 1906), 183–184.
11. Stephen B. Oates, *Abraham Lincoln: The Man Behind the Myths* (New York: Harper Perennial, 1984), 42.
12. Francis Bicknell Carpenter, *The Inner Life of Abraham Lincoln: Six Months at the White House* (New York: Hurd and Houghton, 1872), 63.
13. Oates, *Abraham Lincoln*, 49.
14. William Dean Howells and John Lord Hayes, eds., *Lives and Speeches of Abraham Lincoln and Hannibal Hamlin* (New York: W.A. Townsend, 1860), 143.
15. Howard Wilford Bell, ed., *Letters and Addresses of Abraham Lincoln* (New York: H.W. Bell, 1903), 142.

16. Oates, *Abraham Lincoln*, 119.

17. Stephen B. Oates, *The Whirlwind of War: Voices of the Storm, 1861–1865* (New York: HarperCollins, 1998), 36.

18. Bell, ed., *Letters and Addresses of Abraham Lincoln*, "First Message to Congress, July 4, 1861," 203.

19. Bell, ed., *Letters and Addresses*, "First Inaugural Address," 199.

20. Ann Blackman, *Wild Rose: Rose O'Neale Greenhow, Civil War Spy* (New York: Random, 2005), 6.

21. Blackman, *Wild Rose*, 37.

22. *New York Times*, "The Advance of the Army—A Grand Spectacle—Probable Duration of the War" (New York: July 21, 1861), 5.

23. Blackman, *Wild Rose*, 40.

24. *New York Times*, "The Greatest Battle Ever Fought on This Continent" (New York: July 22, 1861), 1.

25. John Alexander Logan, *The Great Conspiracy* (New York: A.R. Hart, 1886), 3: 338.

26. *New York Times*, "Retreat of Gen. McDowell's Command from Manassas" (New York: July 23, 1861), 1.

27. Diary of Michael Reid Hanger, Augusta County, Virginia, 1861, The Valley of the Shadow: Two Communities in the American Civil War, Virginia Center for Digital History, University of Virginia, http://jefferson.village.virginia.edu/vshadow2/.

28. Walt Whitman, *Two Rivulets: Including Democratic Vistas, Centennial Songs, and Passage to India* (Camden, NJ: 1876), 61–62.

29. Blackman, *Wild Rose*, 48.

30. *New York Times*, "Brady's Photographs: Pictures of the Dead at Antietam," October 20, 1862, 5.

31. All quotes from Emma LeConte can be found in Emma LeConte, *Diary, 1864–1865*, Documenting the American South, or, The Southern Experience in 19th-century America. This work is the property of the University of North Carolina at Chapel Hill. It may be used freely by individuals for research, teaching, and personal use as long as this statement of availability is included in the text. http://docsouth.unc.edu/fpn/leconteemma/leconte.html.

15

After the Civil War

Mary Ames and Emily Bliss *(Used with permission of Documenting the American South, The University of North Carolina at Chapel Hill Libraries.)*

The Difficulties of Reconstruction

In the two decades after 1865, the recently reunited United States had to figure out how to be one nation again at the same time that the challenges of Southern society took center stage. What would freedom mean for African-Americans? Who would rule in the Southern states? Would it be the old coalitions of plantation owners, the same ones who had supported the Confederacy? Could traitors get pardons and become politicians and leaders of the nation they had recently abandoned?

From the vantage of 1865, no one could foresee the South's future. Few white Southerners wanted a social revolution, while all African-Americans did. Presidents and congressmen had to navigate against the racket of competing voices calling out for mutually exclusive demands. In January 1865, General William Tecumseh Sherman issued Field Order 15, giving land to the freed people on the South Carolinian sea islands—awakening hopes for forty acres and a mule. The land allocations were subdivided into forty-acre parcels and the army also distributed worn-out mules. Freed families streamed to the islands and planted vegetables and rice. The land had been owned by white people who had deserted it early in the war, but the freed people argued that 200 years of hard labor had certainly earned them a right to some acreage. Within the year, President Andrew Johnson returned the lands to the former owners, overruling Sherman's efforts and appeasing Southern whites.

Following Lincoln's assassination, Andrew Johnson stumbled through three years as president, facing impeachment along the way for his opposition to Congress's efforts to reform the South through constitutional amendments and civil rights laws. Johnson vetoed more than one law designed to secure civil rights for blacks. In the House of Representatives, a Radical Republican named Thaddeus Stevens, looking very dour and stern in his photographs, led the charge against Johnson's interference with progressive racial policies in the conquered South. In the 1866 congressional elections, Republicans took enough seats to override presidential vetoes. Stevens's brief popularity, however, could not overcome the blunders of fellow Republicans or the durability of white supremacy in the South.

Ulysses S. Grant became president in 1868 and miraculously lasted through two terms that included one scandal after another and a nation-shaking depression in 1873. The depression partly resulted from the Crédit Mobilier scandal: various congressmen and other public officials had been siphoning off millions of dollars in public monies originally intended for a transcontinental railroad. But Grant had entered the White House with volcanic popularity. People liked his small-town simplicity. Besides, Grant had won the war. He was a hero who rarely let the attention go to his head. Grant enjoyed racing his carriage through the streets of the capital, and when he got stopped by a police officer for speeding, Grant insisted on being given the ticket and allowing his carriage to be impounded. But Reconstruction ate holes in his presidency.

In 1868, Grant ran under the slogan "Let Us Have Peace." The sentiment could not overcome the civil war still raging in the South between African-Americans bent on gaining civil rights and ex-Confederates bent on maintaining supremacy. The most notorious group of domestic terrorists, the Ku Klux Klan (KKK), used every bloody means possible to keep African-Americans from voting. They lynched; they shot; they burned crosses and threatened. The white-hooded Klansmen were terrorists, and only one force could stop them—federal troops. Congress passed a law, the Force Act, enabling Grant, in 1871, to rush troops into the South where they arrested and imprisoned hundreds of Klansmen. White Southerners simply took off the white sheets and kept resisting Reconstruction. Radical Republicans like Thaddeus Stevens in the House and Charles Sumner in the Senate tried to do right by the freed African-Americans, but a reluctant, tired North and an intransigent white South prevented any long-lasting, structural changes to Southern society.

South Carolina briefly enjoyed a state assembly with more black representatives than white. Mississippi elected a black U.S. senator, and African-Americans filled ballot boxes with votes for Republican candidates throughout the late 1860s and 1870s. Ultimately, however, Southern whites reestablished political and economic control. Reinvigorated white racists "redeemed" the South by passing a host of unsavory laws called black codes, which permitted sheriffs, for example, to forcibly place the children of African-Americans into "apprenticeships" on neighboring plantations. Also, African-Americans left slavery with no money and no land. With freedmen too poor to buy their own property, sharecropping resulted, a system in which landlords made sure to keep their tenant farmers in a cycle of debt that prevented them from easily leaving. African-American sharecroppers continued to till land owned by their former slave masters. Slavery had ended but slave conditions continued.

In 1877, Rutherford B. Hayes took over the presidency. Hayes was not popular in the South, but an election debacle in 1876 earned him the necessary Southern electoral votes. Three Southern states, including Florida, had had their ballots challenged. The responsibility of choosing the president fell to a congressional committee, which picked Hayes. Although Hayes was a Union veteran and a Republican, his ascension to the presidency signaled the end of federal Reconstruction in the South. Hayes had no political capital to continue Reconstruction. After sixteen years of strife, most people in the North wanted to get on with their lives and stop hearing about all the problems in the South: Ku Klux Klan violence, voting fraud, disgruntled whites anxious over the loss of their property and workers. The freedmen had lost their allies. Not surprisingly, Northern whites allowed their Southern counterparts to resume lording it over Southern society.

Back in 1862, when the Civil War was still in an early phase, William Tecumseh Sherman had written to a Southern acquaintance, Thomas Hunton, with whom Sherman had attended West Point. Miffed at Hunton's choice to fight for the Confederacy, Sherman conceded, "We are Enemies, still private friends."[1] If Sherman could be "still private friends" with a traitor and a rebel, was it any wonder that a nation ruled mainly by white supremacists would return the South to the hands of its old masters when the experiment in Reconstruction seemed too tiring, too dangerous, and too little possible?

Reconstruction: Black and White

Freedom is choice. Slavery is the lack of choice. When slavery was banned throughout the United States with the passage of the Thirteenth Amendment, freed men and women made the most of their new circumstances. Some traveled across the states, looking for children, spouses, parents, and other family members who had been sold away. Some bought land or took the land of their former owners and kept on planting the same crops, herding the same cattle, but on their own terms, on their own time. Most white Southerners could not abide all this change, all this black freedom.

In 1865, a young former Confederate named Edwin McCaleb captured the exasperation and outrage that fellow whites felt. "We can never," he exclaimed, "regard the Negro our equal either intellectually or socially." McCaleb thought that if the South could have a "system of gradual emancipation and colonization our people would universally rejoice and be glad to get rid of slavery." Instead, he predicted that "this sudden system of Emancipation, this spasmodic transformation of the ignorant Negro from a peaceful laborer who has been accustomed to have all needs [provided] to a self reliant citizen will paralyze the productive resources of the South." While McCaleb railed against the loss of unpaid workers and the ensuing "famine" he expected, a deeper fear underlay his complaints: interracial mixing. McCaleb was certain that the federal government intended to encourage "miscegenation." In that case, "if such a detestable dogma becomes a law we shall soon have a race of mulattoes as fickle and foolish as the Mongrel population of Mexico never content with their present condition."[2] Racism and economic concerns mixed in McCaleb's mind into a desire to keep African-Americans subordinate and submissive. The Civil War had ended slavery, but left the slaverholder's mind intact.

Southern whites like McCaleb saw few options, all involving intimidation, coercion, and a resistance to the Reconstruction policies being legislated by Congress. Abraham Lincoln had wanted to let the rebel states back into the

Union without fuss or vengeance. Lincoln imagined forgiveness. His successor, Andrew Johnson, imagined one thing but did another. Johnson was from Tennessee, a Confederate stronghold. A member of the Democratic Party, he had been chosen as Lincoln's running mate solely because the Republicans wanted to boost their support in the 1864 presidential race: Johnson could secure votes for Lincoln that Lincoln could not get by himself. Had anyone known Lincoln was going to be assassinated, greasy-haired Andrew Johnson would never have been chosen for vice president. As a Southerner and former slave owner, Johnson's sympathies lay with the South, even though he detested the richest planters, whom he blamed for having caused the Civil War in the first place. By autumn 1865, half a year into his three-year presidency, he had shifted from promising to punish the South to essentially pardoning every former Confederate officer and legislator who begged or groveled enough. Under Johnson, it seemed, the South would not be reconstructed—it would be returned to the past. With Andrew Johnson in the president's seat, Southern racists had only to sit back and wait.

As always, if African-Americans wanted something, they largely had to go about getting it for themselves. Granted, the federal government helped somewhat. In 1865 the Freedmen's Bureau was established, headed by General Oliver O. Howard, described by historian W.E.B. DuBois as "an honest man, with too much faith in human nature." Howard tried his best to provide opportunities and fairness for freed people while simultaneously doing what President Johnson demanded. Congress and the freedmen tugged Howard one way; the president pulled Howard the other way. The Freedmen's Bureau sent teachers (mostly women) into the South, built schools for African-Americans, adjudicated labor disputes between white landowners and black workers, and tried to enforce the provisions of the Fourteenth and Fifteenth Amendments to the Constitution, which provided basic civil rights, including voting rights, to all citizens, regardless of skin color. Although the Freedmen's Bureau came under some criticism for doing as much to force black people back onto plantations as it did to get them wage contracts, the agency was as true a friend to the freed people as it could be, given the state of affairs in the nation in 1865. Here was what Howard and the Freedmen's Bureau workers faced, in DuBois's words: "A curious mess he looked upon: little despotisms, communistic experiments, slavery, peonage, business speculations, organized charity, unorganized almsgiving,—all reeling on under the guise of helping the freedmen, and all enshrined in the smoke and blood of the war and the cursing and silence of angry men."[3] With only 900 officials assigned to deal with labor disputes, court cases, and reform throughout eleven Southern estates, the Freedmen's Bureau was hamstrung from its start.

What the Freedmen's Bureau could not do for African-Americans, many did for themselves. In August 1865, a Cincinnati newspaper printed a letter from a freedman to his former master. It was time for a white man to listen to a black man. Jourdon Anderson was a father, a husband, a laborer, and a former slave from Big Spring, Tennessee. Apparently, his former owner—Colonel Anderson—had sent a letter to Jourdon Anderson requesting that he and his family return to work at the Big Spring plantation, only this time they would be paid. Jourdon Anderson had other ideas. However, assuming his former owner was willing to pay the equivalent of a lifetime's worth of back wages, Anderson was willing to let bygones be bygones. In a conciliatory, friendly voice, Jourdon Anderson teased and toyed with Colonel Anderson. "I suppose," Jourdon began, that any would-be readers "never heard about your going to Colonel Martin's to kill the Union soldier that was left by his company in their stable"—not exactly the kind of revelation a Southern man would want broadcast in 1865. Jourdon Anderson showed himself forgiving in the face of Colonel Anderson's obvious lack of grace: "although you shot at me twice before I left you, I did not want to hear of your being hurt, and am glad you are still living." Readers must have guffawed at the scenario: a gunslinging, homicidal plantation owner inviting a former slave to return to the plantation, "promising to do better for [Jourdon] than anybody else" could. Jourdon informed the colonel, "I have often felt uneasy about you." And no wonder.

Getting down to business, Jourdon Anderson wanted to know exactly what wages the colonel proposed to pay. Life in Ohio was better, much better, than it had been in Tennessee. The children were going to school, Jourdon got paid twenty-five dollars a month, and overall the whole family felt "kindly treated." If only Colonel Anderson could be more specific about the wages, Jourdon could "decide whether it would be to my advantage to move back again." That was the crux of the issue: choice. Jourdon was free and doing well, but at least in the mock-serious world of the letter, he would consider a return to the plantation if the price were right. Therefore, Jourdon thought a display of the colonel's sincerity, "justice and friendship" might establish the proper basis for a new relationship. A few simple calculations added up to the total amount due. "I served you faithfully for thirty-two years, and Mandy [Jourdon's wife] twenty years. At twenty-five dollars a month for me, and two dollars a week for Mandy, our earnings would amount to eleven thousand six hundred and eighty dollars." One can imagine Colonel Anderson's eyes bulging at the number. Pretending that the colonel would be disposed to see the justice of the request, Jourdon wrote, "Please send the money by Adams's Express, in care of V. Winters, Esq., Dayton, Ohio." Finally, unwilling to continue the charade any longer, unwilling to let the colonel or readers of the newspaper think that forgiveness could be found in back wages or any other form of apology or restitution, Jourdon Anderson concluded the letter:

Here I draw my wages every Saturday night; but in Tennessee there was never any pay-day for negroes any more than for the horses and cows. Surely there will be a day of reckoning for those who defraud the laborer of his hire.

In answering this letter, please state if there would be any safety for my Milly and Jane, who are now grown up, and both good-looking girls. You know how it was with poor Matilda and Catherine. I would rather stay here and starve—and die, if it come to that—than have my girls brought to shame by the violence and wickedness of their young masters. You will also please state if there has been any schools opened for the colored children in your neighborhood. The great desire of my life now is to give my children an education, and have them form virtuous habits.

Say howdy to George Carter, and thank him for taking the pistol from you when you were shooting at me.

From your old servant, Jourdon Anderson[4]

It is no great stretch to imagine that Colonel Anderson decided not to pay the eleven thousand dollars in back wages. It is no great stretch to imagine that Jourdon Anderson and his family remained in Ohio.

The freedom to choose a way of life that Jourdon Anderson touted in his letter was not consistently enjoyed by African-Americans throughout the United States in the wake of the Civil War. Before the war, only four states had given black people the right to vote. Public facilities in the North had been segregated, and although free in theory, Northern black people were not free to go to most colleges or to manage businesses owned by whites. The war gave reformers an edge, however. After fighting for emancipation, how could Northern whites continue with such obvious bigotry? Within a decade, voting rights were extended to black people throughout the North, and restaurants, theaters, and hospitals were gradually integrated. As Jourdon Anderson's letter makes plain, education was seen as the golden key to opportunity.

The Civil War had accelerated two related trends: people moving to cities, and people working for wages. Factories expanded production during the war to feed and equip the soldiers. Commerce and trade increased, and the new jobs were mainly urban. In America's cities, then, an education could make the difference between poverty and wealth. Farmers benefited from schooling but had never needed books or university professors to teach them how to plant and harvest. Doctors, lawyers, professors, teachers, engineers, bankers, and other wage workers either needed or at least benefited from a college degree. Many Southern blacks wanted to get off the plantation, away from the oversight and authority of their former owners. Education could elevate them while laws and federal agencies could do little more than ensure poverty pay and debt.

Guns and armies set black people free. Now the ABCs could give them a new life.

Mary Ames: A New England Woman in Dixie

Mary Ames and her friend Emily Bliss arrived on Edisto Island, South Carolina, in May 1865 to open a school for some of the 10,000 African-Americans living there, former slaves who were hungry for education. The two New England women had been sent south by a Boston agency working in tandem with the newly created Freedmen's Bureau. The Freedmen's Bureau provided contacts and helped with housing and food, but the teachers who ended up going into rural districts, like Ames and Bliss, had to fend for themselves, which meant relying on the people they had come to teach. New England had not been ravaged by the war, other than having lost thousands of its sons in the fighting. For New Englanders who remained at home, crops grew, breezes blew, and houses stood unscathed. In the South it was different. Although some regions escaped any serious fighting, much of the land and its buildings were scarred from four years of war. The inhabitants had suffered, but they had also grown used to their circumstances. Northerners coming south to help were shocked on arrival.

Traveling from the North was wearying and difficult. When the two women arrived in Charleston, Emily Bliss, "weary, discouraged, and homesick, threw herself sobbing into" the arms of Mr. James Redpath, head of the Freedmen's Bureau in Charleston.[5] It became apparent to Mary Ames that her traveling companion was barely suited to the task ahead. Mr. Redpath "wished us to remain in the city and teach in the public schools, and was quite disturbed and disappointed that we objected," Mary Ames jotted into her diary. "We felt that we were not fitted for regular teaching. We were then offered a position on one of the islands where several thousand negroes were sent after Sherman's march. That suited us, and we were ordered to leave in two days." Edisto Island, their destination, had become a microcosm of the Reconstruction experiment. At the onset of the war, the U.S. Navy had seized the island. The plantation owners fled, leaving rich farmlands and houses for their slaves, who naturally set about farming and living as freely as any had ever hoped for. Fighting on the island had devastated many of the buildings, but society was still possible. By 1865, this environment had less of the racial strife and weariness that plagued Charleston, and it was assumed to be an easier posting for two fragile Yankee women.

Mary Ames and Emily Bliss were at the vanguard of a revolutionary effort to plant primary schools and universities throughout the South, what the historian W.E.B. DuBois called "the crusade of the New England schoolma'am."[6] Within a few years, there were more than 3,000 teachers working with the freed people, and by 1869, more than half of those teachers were black, some from the North, many also from the South. The challenges were overwhelming: lack of supplies, books, and facilities; hostility from local whites; malnourished students; heat and sickness. Yet black people wanted to learn, were hungry for knowledge, famished by generations of illiteracy. This thirst for words, ideas, knowledge, and possibilities overcame the disadvantages of poverty. Freed people demanded literacy. And it was not just children who went to these new schools. Adults attended too, working all day in the fields as they had always done, but taking night classes sometimes twice a week. Some schools, like Tuskegee Institute, were designed to teach manual labor skills in agriculture and the building trades. Later, at the turn of the twentieth century, black American leaders debated and feuded over which type of education—liberal arts or trades—made better sense for black people in a wider United States society that was still not accepting of black equality. But in 1865, when Ames and Bliss arrived on Edisto Island, teachers and students alike were overwhelmed with getting down the basics: the alphabet, spelling, calm classroom behavior.

Mary Ames's time on Edisto Island—slightly more than one year—is the story of teaching under unusual circumstances, friendship between black and white, and the central importance of education. It is also the story of rattlesnakes in the bedroom, mosquitoes, sandy beaches, humid days that reduced the New England schoolma'ams to listless lumps, and nights spent without sleep reading cherished letters from home. What did the people of Edisto Island want after their chalky blackboard lessons? They wanted land, family, and salvation. Ames captured the rapture of her pupils' yearning in one of their invocations: "When Gabriel blow his horn for Massa Jesus would he please blow a little louder?" African-Americans wanted what anyone wanted—the better things in life, the good things: plenty of food, some time off, the spirit of joy, a paying job, and freedom.

When Ames disembarked at Edisto Island on May 10, 1865, it seemed to her "like fairy land—everything so fresh and green—the air so soft . . . the live-oaks in the background, with their hanging moss, had a very picturesque effect." Fairyland got hot fast. The next day, the two newcomers

reached what must have once been a pretty avenue, now rather forlorn. Driving in, we found negro cabins on either side, and a large house at the end. The inhabitants of the cabins came flocking out to welcome us with howdys, and offers of service to the missis. The former owner of the plantation was Dr. Whaley, the possessor of a hundred slaves, many of whom were now returned and living in the cabins. He deserted the place four years before, and the house had a desolate appearance—the windows gone, and shutters hanging by one hinge. Our trunks, box, and chairs were placed on the piazza and the army wagon was driven away. We looked at each other; our hearts were full, and if we could have seen any honorable way to escape and go home we certainly should have gone.

Instead they chose two rooms in the mansion, which were littered with debris. "Uncle Jack and Aunt Phoebe," who lived in adjoining cabins, cleaned the rooms with moss, there being no brooms on the premises. After a dinner of crackers, tea, and blackberries, Bliss and Ames headed upstairs to bed. On the stairs, they "were met by an angry old woman, who said we had taken possession of her quarters, and must pay her for them. We were frightened, and explained that we were sent by the United States Government, and must be respected accordingly. She went away, but soon began to throw stones and pieces of crockery into our open windows." Alarmed, Ames "got out the hammer we had brought in our box and kept it in my hand all night, ready to beat out the brains of any one attacking us." And that is how her teaching career began—under attack from an old woman wielding crockery shards, in a dirty room, surrounded by people desperate for what the new teachers had to offer.

The next morning, Mary Ames unfurled a U.S. flag. The "negroes" gathered around it, appreciating what it heralded. A husband and wife, Jim and Sarah, along with their six children, offered to stay with Ames and Bliss in the house, making them feel safe. Sarah and Jim had followed Sherman's army as he marched away from Charleston, Sarah carrying a two-year-old baby in her arms for more than 100 miles, the other children staying in front of her where she could keep her eyes on them. After another dinner of crackers and tea, the teachers went to visit their new neighbors. "Their faces shone when we told them why we had come. They all seemed decent and sensible creatures." Although the Army commissary four miles away supplied food for the freed people, the general plan was for blacks to feed themselves as soon as possible. Ames explained that "Sherman's plan is to have the negroes take care of themselves; they have planted corn, beans, and cotton, and are to repay the Government when their crops are gathered. This seems to be understood by all."

During 1865, the Freedmen's Bureau and the army distributed literally millions of meals throughout a South whose crops had been ravaged by Sherman's army. Sherman's troops had also destroyed railroads and bridges in their efforts to cripple the Southern will to fight. Now that the war was over, the infrastructure needed to transport food was gone: railroad ties bent and twisted, draft animals eaten or emaciated. And former slaves were not willing to work fourteen hours a day or seven days a week. Black women had long wanted to live the way wealthy white women did—at home, taking care of the children, which meant that fully one-half of the black workforce vanished from the fields. One-fifth of Southern white men had died during the war. Everywhere there was the absence of standing, healthy bodies. Even though the U.S. government now had to feed the defeated South, American culture did not encourage handouts. In particular, white people had long thought that black people were lazy and shiftless, a useful stereotype that allowed slaveholders to justify their practice of forcing slaves to work. But why would African-Americans have wanted to work hard for someone else when the only pay was fatty pork, maggot-ridden corn meal, and abuse? White people failed to see that their own prejudice and discrimination had pushed black slaves to resist slavery by doing what they could to labor slowly.

W.E.B. DuBois called this the "problem of work," the fundamental historical problem being that slavery was an economic system best suited to medieval feudalism, not to a cash-based, modern industrial economy.[7] In DuBois's opinion, black people needed to be trained to work as modern laborers, responding to the incentive of good pay for hard work. But most white Southerners preferred to get the former slaves back onto the plantations to labor for next to nothing or for nothing at all. So white people said that black people would not get handouts for long. Newspaper cartoons depicted black people lounging around, eating and lollygagging. From 1865 to 1867, during the period of "presidential Reconstruction" under Andrew Johnson, former Confederate politicians and officers took over Southern state legislatures and passed laws designed to keep African-Americans servile. All the while, government meals went to starving black *and* white people. In some military districts, white people took more meals than black people did, but this fact was generally ignored in favor of the racial stereotype of the shiftless "nigger" wanting something for nothing. Mary Ames quickly saw through the false notions and lies. She saw just how hard black people were willing to sweat for the lives they wanted.

Less than a mile from their new plantation home, Mary Ames and Emily Bliss found a church. "The frame," Ames wrote, "of the organ remains, the windows are gone, doors off their hinges, and pews mutilated, but we decided that it would serve our purpose well as a school-house." The following Monday, May 15, the school opened with "fifteen scholars, nine boys, and six girls. Some were decently clad, others filthy and nearly naked. One or two knew their letters. None could read." The next day twenty-eight students showed up. One of them, a boy named John, was "nearly naked, and so filthy" that Ames sent him off to bathe in a creek. The tide came in and pulled John out to sea, where he drowned. Ames felt grieved and guilty: "it was a terrible shock to us, and I felt partly responsible." Nevertheless, she faced her main responsibility. Within days there were "sixty scholars" packed into the rickety church, many of them "rather unruly." Ames recognized that "poor Emily is not adapted to deal with rough boys. I am obliged to go to her aid and, stamping my feet and shouting my commands, bring them to order." Some things, apparently, never change.

The two teachers also devised other tactics to control their classes. One day a man came into the school and sat down in a back pew; "the boys thought we had engaged him to whip them if they misbehaved. We have found out that the boys are afraid of their fathers, who are 'Great on licking,' so we shall threaten to report them if they are unruly." Another tactic was less threatening: "Emily is a good singer, and when the school is too much for us, we start singing, and that calms them down." Yet the shenanigans and difficulties continued; on one June day of "intolerable" heat, Ames had "one hundred and one scholars—too many—cannot keep order with so many. I am well worn out before noon with shouting and stamping, for I am obliged to help Emily when she gets into difficulty." Their best tactic became simple adaptation to the new environment. Ames got to know and like her "scholars," and they in turn came to like her: "We stayed after school closed with three unruly boys, . . . who confessed that they liked to tease us; but they were ashamed and promised to do better in the future."

Less than a week into the semester "a woman came with a prayer-book, asking to be taught to read it." Ames told the woman "we would teach her willingly, but it would be some time before she could read that. She was satisfied, and as she was leaving, put her hand under her apron and brought out two eggs—one she put in Emily's lap, the other in mine." Trading eggs for education, the woman was probably offering everything she could spare. Bliss and Ames promised a twice-weekly evening class for the older people who had to work in the fields during the days. Ames wrote, "We had our first evening school for men and women on our piazza. It was well attended, all sitting on the floor and steps. One woman, who was much bent with rheumatism, and seemed very old, said she was 'Mighty anxious to know something.'" Though conditions continued haphazard—"Jim has put up our stove; the pipe being too short for the chimney, he has put it out a window"—those were heady, ebullient times: "Nearly the whole school escorted us home to-day," Ames noted. Afterward, teachers and students sat on the piazza sewing and mending clothes.

When the weather grew too hot to walk to the church, they held class at the mansion. In fact, the students were becoming so eager to learn that they demanded lessons all the time—even on a Sunday. "No churchgoing—too warm," Mary wrote. "We seated ourselves on the piazza to write letters. Soon a crowd of children were around us, all wanting books, and before we knew it we were teaching school." One bright student was not content with getting an education for himself: "George is patient and promising. We are surprised at the ease with which he acquires the sound of words. He teaches his father after leaving us."

Although challenges and difficulties remained, progress was being made.

One day "several children came and demanded clothing as a right. A girl brought back a dress, saying it was 'scant.' She wanted a fuller skirt and a hoop-skirt." Fashionable nineteenth-century women's clothes tended to be restricting and uncomfortable: corsets to bind the midriff and make the waist look slender; hooped skirts that billowed out around the ankles and made walking tricky. Nevertheless, these young girls wanted what was best, not just what was available. A sense of entitlement and a sense that clothing was a "right" were hopeful signs. The former slaves of Edisto Island were imagining a better future. And their teachers understood how much this possibility meant. One day, "a woman who brought some cucumbers said she would make any sacrifice to serve us, who were doing so much to teach her children, who knew nothing but how to handle a hoe."

In the evenings, the children sang songs, and Ames and Bliss told stories like "Red Riding Hood," which the students had never heard. Mary Ames laughed into her diary that "they particularly delight in singing 'Hang Jeff Davis to a sour apple tree.'" At the end of June, Ames and Bliss relocated to the island's coast. The windward weather was cool and temperate. Another abandoned mansion sat waiting for them, and for the rest of the summer they held smaller classes on the coast, delighting in letters from home and visits from Jim, Sarah, and their children—the family who had roomed with them at the first house. But October became the month of shattered dreams, the month that General Howard of the Freedmen's Bureau personally visited the island to tell everyone about President Johnson's latest decree. The mansions, plantations, and farms were being returned to the white owners, who had fled four years earlier. As Ames described the scene, "At first the people could not understand, but as the meaning struck them, that they must give up their little homes and gardens, and work again for others, there was a general murmur of dissatisfaction." Two of the largest plantation owners had accompanied General Howard, and Mary witnessed these men and their former slaves saying "How dy" to each other. One black man said that "he had lived all his life with a basket over his head, and now that it had been taken off and air and sunlight had come to him, he could not consent to have the basket over him again. It was a hard day for them." The African-Americans of Edisto petitioned President Johnson to reconsider the severity of giving all the land back to the white people, leaving the black families with nothing. The petition had no effect.

At other places in the South some lands were made available to African-Americans, but often the land was not arable or the black farmers were given no seeds or tools to work it. The old property rights arguments were made to justify returning land and power to white people. By 1877, the Democratic Party regained a majority of seats in Southern legislatures. Democrats got elected to governors' seats, and the Republican effort to reconstruct Southern society failed. In a couple of key Supreme Court cases, the Fourteenth and Fifteenth Amendments to the Constitution were rendered mute and ineffective. The Court ruled that the Fourteenth Amendment could be used to prosecute state governments that limited civil rights, but that the amendment did not justify prosecuting *individuals* who hindered civil rights. This ruling opened the proverbial door to vigilante injustice. When Congress and the courts were not rolling back victories and rights, local terrorist organizations were doing the evil work. The Ku Klux Klan, founded by former Confederate officers as a sort of fraternal organization, soon morphed into a secretive brigade of scared white people who feared losing their racial privileges and prerogatives. From their fear came hatred, and from their hatred came ugliness and violence. Hundreds of black people were killed by hooded Klansmen, and many more were threatened enough to either keep them from voting or get them to vote for Democratic candidates. The Grant administration passed laws to prevent Klan activities, but the laws did not work, could not work. After the war a U.S. Army of more than 1 million men in 1865 was almost instantly reduced to 38,000, most of whom were stationed in the West where new wars were being fought against Native Americans. Laws that could not be enforced were meaningless. In most places, education was all that was left.

Mary Ames and Emily Bliss stayed on Edisto Island until the end of the summer of 1866. They lived in three different mansions and taught hundreds (probably thousands) of students, young and old. They shared wagon rides with skeletal horses, beef cooked to such exhaustion that it tasted like "queer bacon," the shouts and ecstasy songs of prayer meetings, and the final sorrows of the African-American populace who were being sold short one more time in the United States. Ames knew that "the white people of Edisto [had] indeed suffered, but now their homes are to be given back to them. The island negroes and those brought here by our bewildered, blundering Government have had, and will have, harder days than their masters. Among those that we have known, however painful their experience, and whether accustomed formerly to easy routine as house-servants or to rougher field service, not one among them would choose ease with servitude rather than suffering with freedom." As some of the black people left the island in the wake of General Howard's visit and as other black people began signing sharecropping contracts, Mary Ames and Emily Bliss packed up their belongings and said good-bye to their "negro friends."

W.E.B. DuBois and the "Problem of the Color Line"

Looking back over his shoulder forty years after emancipation, in 1903 W.E.B. DuBois wrote *The Souls of Black Folk*, a book about race, history, and soul. DuBois was the first African-American to earn a PhD at Harvard. In 1909, he helped found the National Association for the Advancement of Colored People, the NAACP. Dr. DuBois fought eloquently and forcefully for African-Americans to be fully accepted into society. In those thirty-some years between emancipation and the turn of the century, he witnessed the calamity of a shattered experiment, the quick erosion of black civil liberties. In *The Souls of Black Folk*, he captured the disorientation and optimism that enveloped the first "New England schoolma'ams" as they entered the unreconstructed South:

> Behind the mists of ruin and rapine waved the calico dresses of women who dared, and after the hoarse mouthings of the field guns rang the rhythm of the alphabet. Rich and poor they were, serious and curious. Bereaved now of a father, now of a brother, now of more than these, they came seeking a life work in planting New England schoolhouses among the white and black of the South. They did their work well. In that first year they taught one hundred thousand souls, and more.[8]

Mary Ames did what she could for more than a year often admitting in her diary that going home would have been far preferable to the snakes and heat of South Carolina. Eventually she did go home, a choice available to her. But her scholars stayed behind, trapped into a cycle of poverty and debt established by history, tradition, and the unwillingness (or inability) of Southern whites to change.

DuBois prophesied that the problem of the twentieth century would be the "problem of the color-line."[9] However, as industrial capitalism increasingly dominated the economy, the landscape, the politics, and the social relations of the United States, the problem of the twentieth century also came to involve the poverty line, the class line. White did continue to lord it over black in most cases, but as the twentieth century neared, a vast gulf grew between the few white families that owned most of the nation and the rest of the country who were struggling to make do.

Notes

1. Amy Murrell Taylor, *The Divided Family in Civil War America* (Chapel Hill: University of North Carolina Press, 2006), 81.

2. Edwin H. McCaleb, "To T.P. Chandler, Esq.," Gilder Lehrman Institute of American History, www.gilderlehrman.org/search/display_results.php?id=GLC01594.

3. W.E.B. DuBois, *The Souls of Black Folk* (Chicago: A.C. McClurg, 1903), 22–23.

4. Lydia Maria Child, *The Freedmen's Book* (Boston: Ticknor and Fields, 1865), 265–267.

5. All quotations from Ames's diary can be found in Mary Ames, *From a New England Woman's Diary in Dixie in 1865* (Springfield, MA: 1906), Documenting the American South, University of North Carolina, http://docsouth.unc.edu/church/ames/menu.html.

6. DuBois, *Souls of Black Folk*, 25.

7. W.E.B. DuBois, "The Problem of Work," *AME Church Review* 19 (October 1903).

8. DuBois, *Souls of Black Folk*, 25.

9. DuBois, *Souls of Black Folk*, 40.

About the Author

Jason Ripper lives with his wife, Diane, and their two children in Bellingham, Washington, a gentrified redoubt of 1960s America. He strives to make history more interesting for the general reader, and currently teaches history courses at Everett Community College.